Our Musical Heritage

THE PRENTICE-HALL MUSIC SERIES

Our Musical Heritage

A SHORT HISTORY OF MUSIC

SECOND EDITION

by Curt Sachs

NEW YORK • PRENTICE-HALL, INC. • 1955

Printed in the United States of America

"Narrative history has the merit of telling what happened. But the reflective mind wishes also to know *how* things happen and *why* things happen."

—JAMES WESTFALL THOMPSON
A History of Historical Writing

PREFACE TO THE SECOND EDITION

IN PREPARING this new edition — improved (it is hoped) and enlarged in its chapters on music since 1800 — the author enjoyed, as always, the untiring help of his friends in the Music Division of the New York Public Library, but above all the indefatigable collaboration of his wife. He also profited greatly from the amicable criticism of experienced teachers. He has conscientiously tried to satisfy all of them, which, not for the first time in history, has proved to be impossible. What to do, for example, when half of the critics ask for more biography, and the other half, for no biographic material at all? Or when some clamor for less advanced treatment and other for more advanced discussion? Or when some find laudatory words for sections that others deem unnecessary? In order not to lose his identity, the author requests the readers to accept the book as it now reappears and to bypass sections or study them according to individual needs and interests. A book cannot suit everybody's taste and requirements unless there is absolute uniformity among readers, and this is not even desirable.

The letters with which we indicate the notes of our musical system are given in italicized capitals without any additional symbol — as *C D E* — when they do not belong to a particular octave. Otherwise, mere capitals indicate the octave from the lowest *C* of the 'cello upwards; small letters, the octave from the lowest *c* of the viola upwards; one-lined *c'* is the colloquially so-called middle *C*; two-lined *c''*, the one above; and so on.

The dates of individual works occasionally differ from those in other books and in our own first edition. Of the five kinds of dates — beginning, completion, performance, publication, copyright — I have tried to give the date of completion wherever possible.

From the PREFACE TO THE FIRST EDITION

TO WRITE a new history of music, after so many other histories of music, is an audacious enterprise — justified only if the new history differs essentially from all its predecessors. . . .

In the first place, [this work] gives fairly equal space to all the phases of musical development, whether or not they belong to the pitifully restricted repertoire of our concert and home music. It does not carelessly skip the earlier stages on the ground that the average music lover does not know the music — for such an argument would wrong the very meaning of history. Even the most elementary history should impart to its students a notion of the limited scope of the time in which we live and a sense of the vast horizons that a knowledge of the past unrolls. Even the most elementary history should make its readers aware that the world of today and of ourselves is only a link in the endless chain of ages, each of which has tried to create a supreme expression of its mind and its trend, of its faith and its will. And even the most elementary history should be free from the outworn, naive concept that such a chain represents a development from stages immature, preparatory, and therefore negligible, to unprecedented climaxes.

In the second place, this book avoids the somewhat cheap, misleading, and primitive method of focusing the reader's attention on the names of composers and other personalities, and tries rather to give him an idea of the essential trends of thought and style. To this end, care has been taken to restrict the number of names and the biographical details as much as possible. . . .

To quote from Christopher Simpson, author of *The Division-Violist* of 1659: *How far I have acquitted my self herein, must be referred to the Book it self; which hath now put on the confidence to appear in Publick.*   CURT SACHS

BIBLIOGRAPHY

A VERY LIMITED LIST of books has been added to each chapter. These lists are not meant to be complete: many works are unavailable in college and local libraries or at booksellers'; and, alas, our very modest reading knowledge of foreign languages would anyway be a serious handicap in a field in which the great majority of contributions have been made in languages other than English. Therefore, the short bibliographical appendices, concentrating on books of recent date and, so far as possible, in the English language, are intended to give only a first help to those who want to go into details that the present book must leave untouched.

The following, equally limited list contains the books of a general character which have no place in the sectional bibliographies: musical encyclopedias and dictionaries, histories, and a historical anthology.

Grove's Dictionary of Music and Musicians, 5th edition, 9 volumes, London, 1955.
Thompson, Oscar, *International Cyclopedia of Music and Musicians*, New York, 1939; 5th edition, 1949.
Apel, Willi, *Harvard Dictionary of Music*, Cambridge, Mass., 1944.
Baker's *Biographical Dictionary of Musicians*, 4th edition, New York, 1940, supplement to 1949.
Cobbet, Walter W., *Cyclopedic Survey of Chamber Music*, 2 volumes, Oxford, 1929/30.
Loewenberg, Alfred, *Annals of Opera 1597–1940*, Cambridge, 1943.
Sachs, Curt, *Reallexikon der Musikinstrumente*, Berlin, 1913.
Láng, Paul Henry, *Music in Western Civilization*, New York, 1941.
The Norton History of Music, planned in 6 volumes, of which 5 have been published so far: I by Curt Sachs, II and III by Gustave Reese, IV by Manfred Bukofzer, VI by Alfred Einstein.
The New Oxford History of Music, planned in 11 volumes, in process of publication since 1954.
Strunk, Oliver, *Source Readings in Music History*, New York, 1950.

Davison, Archibald T., and Willi Apel, *Historical Anthology of Music*, Cambridge, Mass., 1946/1950.
Parrish, Carl, and John Ohl, *Masterpieces of Music before 1750*, New York, 1951.

The column, "Listening," at the end of each of the earlier chapters in the first edition has been dropped. Since recordings both of older and of recent music have incredibly gained in quantity, and partly in quality, and are gaining from day to day, a number of guides and critical manuals in this field have been published and are in easy reach.

CONTENTS

NOTE: Plates I through XVI appear
Following page 112.

1

THE PRIMITIVES

MYTHOLOGY is wrong. Music is not the merciful gift of benevolent gods or heroes. Wrong is the banal desire to see all slow, imperceptible germination emerge ready-made from the head of a single inventor; music is not the clever exploit of some ingenious man. And wrong, so far, are all the many theories presented on a more or less scientific basis—the theories that man has imitated the warbling of birds, that he wanted to please the opposite sex, that his singing derived from drawn-out signaling shouts, that he arrived at music via some coördinated, rhythmical teamwork, and other speculative hypotheses. Were they true, some of the most primitive survivors of early mankind would have preserved a warbling style of song, or love songs, or signal-like melodies, or rhythmical teamwork with rhythmical worksongs. But such songs are conspicuously absent.

To call living primitives to the witness stand will at first sight bewilder those who are not familiar with modern methods of settling questions of origin. They probably would prefer the more substantial, indeed irrefutable, proofs of prehistorians, who excavate the tombs and dwelling places of races bygone. But not even the earliest civilizations that have left their traces in the depths of the earth are old enough to reveal the secret of the origins of music. Moreover, the digging spade yields little in the field of music: the songs of Stone Age men have faded away, and their instruments were probably, in the majority of cases, made of wood or cane and other materials too perishable to resist decomposition in ten thousand or a hundred thousand years of interment.

Thus, the prehistory of music is after all referred to the anthropological method: to look for primeval tribes which, having retreated to far-away isles, secluded valleys, or inaccessible jungles, have in

1

their growth been arrested on the level of Stone Age civilizations in practically unadulterated condition.

This method is not without dangers. Are we sure indeed that their condition has been unadulterated after eons amidst an ever-changing world? Nobody could ignore so pregnant a question, and, yet, a scholar with a solid anthropological background can easily elude the pitfalls of rash conclusions.

This, then, is the inevitable fact: whoever wants to know the origins and early rise of music must read them from fossil remains in primitive life of today.

The branch of learning in charge of collecting and reading these fossil remains is none too adequately called Comparative Musicology or, better, Ethno-musicology. Astride between anthropology and the history of music, its students are concerned with the phonographic recording, the analysis, and the interpretation of primitive music in all its forms.

PRIMITIVE are the half-civilized tribes all over the world, and 'primitive' to a certain extent also are a great many peasants, fishermen, and cattlemen in Europe and white America. Not primitive, on the contrary, are the upper strata of the oriental high civilizations, in the Near and the Middle East, in India and the East and Southeast of Asia. Outlining primitive against non-primitive music, and thus achieving an actual, strict definition of primitive music, is just as difficult—if not altogether impossible—as a definition of any action of man that reflects his spiritual rather than his practical world. An attempt to characterize the music of the primitive would probably stress the total lack of theoretical system or even of basic laws, not to speak of notation, and would dwell on its social, collective, and more or less unindividual nature, which has allowed a tenacious tradition to be all-important from age to age. Maybe the characterization would also emphasize the largely magical function of primitive music, which has hindered it from being an art in its own right, meant to amuse or to edify. But anybody really familiar with the musical life of the primitives would more than hesitate to include these traits in a binding definition.

THE NON-AESTHETIC NATURE of primitive music is particularly obvious in the field of its instruments (*cf.* the illustrations in Sachs, *The History of Musical Instruments*, pages 27-48).

The number and variety of instruments in the primitive world are amazing. All suitable raw materials that nature offers are eagerly taken and turned into some sound-producing implement: bone into whistles and bull-roarers; reed into stampers, trumpets, and flutes; nuts and calabashes into rattles; shells and hollow branches into trumpets; trees into gigantic slit-drums; pits in the earth or logs of trees and pieces of animal skin into drums. At an early stage of civilization, mankind learns how to produce a sound by striking, slapping, pounding, shaking, scraping, rubbing, blowing. All this is done immeasurable eons before the invention of pottery and metal founding.

But in every part of the world, in north and south and east and west, the instruments thus won serve magical rather than musical aims. Admirably well as early men and women know how to make and to handle their instruments with skill and imagination, they care little for aesthetic issues. The instruments, in all their properties, are meaningful, not attractive or beautiful. Their significant sounds, as soft or strong or muffled or shrill; their outer shapes, as round or pointed; their colors, as lifeless white or bloody red; their very motion, as striking, stamping, scraping, or rubbing—they all entangle the early instruments in an intricate maze of pre-musical, magical connotations, far from aesthetic pleasure. Both as objects and as sound-emitters, the instruments stand for the mystic realms of the sun and the moon, for the all-creative male and female principles, for fertility, rain, and wind; and they act as the strongest charms at man's disposal when he performs the vital rites of magic to protect his health and existence.

They had a long, long way to travel before they grew from terrifying, magical charms into musical instruments for pastime and pleasure —from screaming bone whistles into soft, melodious fingerhole flutes, or from roaring megaphones into noble, solemn trumpets. Musical in the proper sense of the word, despite all magical connotations, are only the rhythmical instruments which answer the innate urge of man for regular, audible motion: rattles, stampers, or drums. And musical they are indeed: nothing could be more fascinating than to watch a Negro drummer or marimba player, to hear the inexhaustible richness of his rhythmical patterns and to observe the incomparable skill with which he strikes his instrument.

Stringed instruments, on the other hand, have been arrested in their most primeval state all over the world. For a primitive man has little reason to develop a class of instrument whose future lies in melody. To him, melodic expression is the realm of the singers, and he does not think of allowing his instruments to trespass and poach on vocal grounds.

Of these two opposite grounds, the vocal field possesses by far the older rights. Tribes in the lowest stratum of culture do sing, but have no instruments.

Music BEGAN WITH SINGING. The singer, impelled to give an orderly shape to the sound of his voice, found two different, opposite ways of expression. One has led to a style in which a simple, monotonous singsong conveys the text as an unassuming vehicle only and allows the words to be the sole focus of attention: it is *logogenic*, or word-born (without being recitative or speechlike). The other style, much less interested in words, consists in fierce discharges of excess force, irritation, and tension: it is *pathogenic*, or passion-born.

The earliest logogenic melodies—in Patagonia, Ceylon, and elsewhere—alternate between a mere two notes at any distance from each other. The distance varies with the races and tribes; it is here a short wholetone, here some size of third, and exceptionally even a fourth. But it is constant within the same piece and usually also within all tunes of a tribe.

In a long evolution, whose stages we easily trace, the original range of logogenic music has grown. Another and still another note has crystallized around the nucleus of two; in earlier stages only timidly at the beginning or the end of a tune and not in the middle, where tradition prevails and stubbornly resists innovations, but in later stages with greater assurance and consistency. Nevertheless, even in riper, elaborate styles the original nucleus of two can very often be clearly distinguished.

In the pathogenic style, on the contrary, the voice leaps noisily up to the top and staggers to the bottom in wild and rumbling cataracts of shouts and wails, in which, in the process of growing organization, some definite intervals, as octaves, fifths and fourths, or even thirds, become accented footholds.

A merger of the two elementary styles begins when the logogenic singsong reaches or even exceeds the range of a fourth and there resistlessly succumbs to the inherent urge of this interval to descend rather than to mount. Quite often, the result is a form of singing in which the melodic line, beyond the meek subservience to the words in the logogenic style and beyond the unbridled emotion of the pathogenic style, takes the lead in its own right and becomes *melogenic*.

It deserves attention that in all these styles the size of the standard step—for instance, the wholetone, the minor, or the major third—depends upon the motor type of the singer. Tribes that dance in wider strides and leaps seem as a rule to sing in thirds or fourths rather than in seconds, and the women of a tribe sing very often in considerably narrower steps than do the men, just as their dancing steps and gestures are shorter.

Dr. Heinz Werner's research with phonograph recordings of the babble songs of European children three and four years old shows the amazing fact that the children's singing style is very close to the earliest singsong of two, three, and four notes in primitive cultures. In this case, too, in the current of evolution, the trend becomes descending once the range of a fourth has been reached.

Over and over again, alas, our children repeat the tiny pattern of their melody, and so do the primitives. Dramatic development towards a melodic climax or embodiment of the small in larger patterns are not yet considered, either in the world of the child or in that of the primitive.

Still, in the endless repetition of a monotonous phrase, which in the form of the Catholic supplication or litany has survived in the modern world, the primitives have found two ways into a higher organization.

One of these two ways is the regular alternation between two answering half-choruses (*antiphony*) or between a leader and an answering chorus (*response*)—a way of vitalizing tedious repetition, dear ever since to singers in the East and in the West.

The other way into higher organization has affected the individual phrase itself, and that on a remarkably low level of civilization. Two consecutive *phrases* unite to form a *period*, in which, as in a modern song, the first of the phrases ends in suspense on a less important note, while the second, similar phrase ends on the principal note and thus concludes the period. Technically speaking, a very early stratum of humanity created the all-important form known as question and answer, as antecedent and consequent, as half and full cadence, or, in the colorful language of the Middle Ages, as the *overt* and the *clos*.

POLYPHONY is hardly essential in the world of the primitives, though it exists both in the modest sense of using coincident notes and in a more presumptuous meaning.

When a group of people happen to sing the same melodic line without imposing on the performers the kind of rigid discipline characteristic of modern music, the result is a chance progress, as of people who join in a leisurely walk without falling in step or caring for any strict coördination of their movements. Such pseudo-unison is called *heterophony*, from the Greek word *héteros*, 'different.'

It also happens that several singers perform the same melody but at different pitches, so that two (or more) parallel lines, instead of one single line, are heard. Such parallels exist in many intervals, from the natural, entirely unconscious octaves in which the sexes or the ages sing together, through the semiconscious fifths and fourths, down to conscious, artful, and western-like thirds, and even to trenchant seconds.

There are also sustained *pedal* notes, or *drones*, above or below the melody, as the primeval ancestors of modern organpoints. Lastly, a few tribes around the equator have developed actual canon singing as a consequence of impatient overlapping when groups in antiphonal or responsorial singing do not wait until their turn has come but enter before the leading voice has finished. Indeed, the natives of Flores sing in the strictest canon above a double drone of tonic and fifth, like that of a bagpipe.

Thus the primitives or—what amounts to the same—prehistoric races planted the seeds from which all higher music sprang in the East and the West.

Once more: that which separates primitive from higher music is the repetitiveness within the individual piece, without development to any climax and, in general, its essential dependence on tradition and the total lack of any intellectual approach, be it a script or a system in even the most rudimentary form.

READING

Curt Sachs, *The Rise of Music in the Ancient World, East and West,* New York, 1943: Section One. Curt Sachs, *The History of Musical Instruments,* New York, 1940: First Part. Curt Sachs, *World History of the Dance,* New York, 1937: Part One. Curt Sachs, *The Commonwealth of Art,* New York, 1946: Chapter One. Curt Sachs, *Rhythm and Tempo,* New York, 1953.

The monographic literature describing primitive music is too vast to enter such a short reading list, and all available special bibliographies are no longer up-to-date, in view of the rapidly increasing contributions in this field.

2

THE ORIENT

ORIENTAL MUSIC, extending all the way from Morocco —and even parts of Spain—to the Malay Archipelago and spanning five thousand years from the remotest antiquity to the present day, has despite its differences in space and time, a common stock of features sharply distinct from those of primitive music and also from those of western and northern music in the Later Ages.

The end of the first chapter hinted at the systematic, almost scientific approach in the higher civilizations of the East, at least in the hands of an upper class of musicians. This restriction points also to another important fact: the music of the high oriental cultures relies on professional musicians. The common, collective music of the tribe has become a separate *folk music*.

The contrast is particularly manifest in the musical scenes of the Old Testament. In the nomadic times of the second millennium B.C., all the women sing and drum and dance on festive occasions, and to hear the soothing melodies of a lyre even King Saul must send for the shepherd David; but in the sedentary times of the first millennium B.C., the Temple of Jerusalem has its thoroughly organized and trained professional choir and orchestra of Levites with an annexed conservatory where 288 students are taught in 24 classes.

Within the musical profession, oriental lands have different classes or castes with different backgrounds, duties, and rights. They often are so strictly separated from each other that they sing and play in different styles and have the privilege of certain instruments and even of certain tunings.

What distinguishes oriental music more than anything else is its surprising stability, tenacity, and inertia. Oriental music has on the whole been stationary; it has changed only at a rate which seems negligible when measured against the amazing speed of western developments in the last one thousand years from parallel *órgana* down to Beethoven and the styles of Schoenberg and Stravinsky.

Chinese music has still many traits of the 'classical' age, that is, of times two thousand years ago; and the principal instruments of China's national music—chimes of bells or stones and the longish zithers, neckless instruments with silken strings—are mentioned as early as the times around 1000 B.C. Despite decay, despite the age-old influx of Mongolian, Indian, and other musical idioms of the West, with all their oboes and cymbals, lutes and fiddles, the ancient pentatonic scales (see below) have tenaciously held their ground while Europe was consistently evolving from stages much earlier than the conception of gamuts to diatonic, chromatic, and twelve-tone scales; and the typically Chinese set of twelve non-tempered and ever uncertain, confusing semitones, or *lüs*, which a more than doubtful legend ascribes to the third millennium B.C., has yielded little of its unfortunate tyranny.

India is in a similar position. In all the fourteen or more centuries gone by since Bhárata wrote his bulky Sanskrit treatise on the arts of the theater, including the music of his time, the country has faithfully kept her complicated system of *śrutis*, or microtones, as the component parts of her tones and semitones; she has kept her *grāmas*, or basal scales, and all the intricacies of *rāgas* and *tālas*, or patterns of melody and of rhythm. No matter how many instruments—lutes and fiddles, oboes and drums—reached the country through the Indus valley in the northwest in the centuries after Bhárata, they never were able to change the age-old spirit of Indian music.

Near Eastern music—Arabian, Persian, and Turkish—still adheres to the practice and theory of the tenth century and uses essentially the same instruments that the earliest illuminations of Muhammedan books depict: the long-necked fiddle, the pear-shaped lute, the trapezoidal zither, the simple vertical flute without a mouthpiece, and the frame drum with its jingles. Nor has its noisy outdoor music changed, with its double-clarinets, oboes, trumpets, and kettledrums.

THE PREPONDERANTLY VOCAL character of all oriental music is another of these immutable factors. True, there has been purely instrumental music, but essentially to accompany dances. The whole Old Testament has just two evidences of music without dance or voice: when young David plucks the lyre to ease King Saul's depression (I Samuel 16:23); and the other one, when Saul meets "a company of prophets coming down from the high place with a harp, and a tabret, and a pipe, and a lyre, before them" (I Samuel 10:5). Neither in the Middle East nor in India did music without singers ever gain any importance comparable to that which instrumental music has reached in the West since the Baroque—not to speak of its preponderance in the eighteenth and nineteenth centuries. Only in the Far East— in China, Korea, Japan, and the Malay Archipelago—did instrumental music attain a certain independence. There have been chamber ensembles and orchestras in the central and western parts of the Orient, to be sure. But whether we look at the bands that the court painters of ancient Egypt depicted on the walls of royal tombs, or at the huge orchestras of more than a thousand pieces that the annalists of Chinese emperors describe, or at the band from ancient Elam or Persia on a famous relief in the British Museum, there are always singers who join the instruments in a common performance.

With the prevalence of singing, melody proper is the only essential element of music. True, simultaneous sounds have by no means been foreign to oriental music. Drones or pedal notes, the accidental consonances and dissonances resulting from a wilfully inexact unison (*heterophony*), and even the casual accompaniment of outstanding notes by some octave, fifth, or fourth are frequent. But nowhere do they interfere with melody, nowhere do they become a real polyphony, counterpoint, or harmony. This is the reason why melody, which in the West relies on harmony so much that it often condescends to serve merely as a connecting line from chord to chord, has in the East developed to a refinement unknown in the white continents.

Most oriental melodies are organized in the framework of a falling fourth, which has been discussed in the previous chapter. Descending by steps or jumps, they come to a landing on the lower fourth and thus assume the form of a *tetrachord*, or group of notes within the interval of the fourth as the skeleton (*tetra* means 'four'). Inside the fourth, the steps are often vague and changing even within the same melody.

Any melodic continuation beyond the fourth tends again to a setting in another similar tetrachord, which connects with the first one either by *conjunction* or by *disjunction*. Conjunct tetrachords share the bounding note and result in a *heptad*, or group of seven, as the next higher organization. Disjunct tetrachords, on the contrary, follow a tone apart and therefore result in an *octave*, or set of eight.

Notwithstanding minor deviations, most scales are either diatonic or else pentatonic.

Conjunct:

Disjunct:

While we colloquially use the word scale for the raw material of any melody, careful terminology would call a quality like pentatonic or diatonic, not a scale, but rather a *genus*, or *gender*: a gender denotes the sizes of steps within a melody but not their particular sequence. The sequence in which these steps appear, tone–tone–semitone or tone–semitone–tone, constitutes a mode. "A mode"—to quote from the author's *Rise of Music in the Ancient World* (page 67)—"is brought about by selecting one note of the endless set as a starter or tonic. All modes of a genus, though following the same sequence of notes, differ in the tonal relations within the octave, since their tonics differ: each mode implies a structure and tension of its own."

The diatonic, or heptatonic, gender—called after Greek *dia*, 'throughout,' and *hepta*, 'seven'—has seven steps in the octave, similar to the sequence of white keys on our pianos, five of which are whole-tones, and two, semitones. This leaves two wholetones and one semitone to each tetrachord.

As a remarkable variety, the scale which, more than any other scale, sounds oriental and is a favorite in the Near East and India as well as in those western scores which try to convey the local color of the Orient, has, within the tetrachord, an augmented wholetone between two semitones as G A♭B C — which we westerners know from our so-called harmonic minor scales.

The pentatonic gender, on the contrary, has only five steps in the octave, Greek *pente* denoting 'five.' In most cases, three of these five steps are wholetones, and two, minor thirds, in an *anhemitonic*, or halftoneless, sequence, like that of the black keys on our pianos. In a few countries, however, such as in ancient Greece and in modern

Japan, pentatonic scales are incongruously (though beautifully) composed of semitones and major thirds, as:

E CB|B GF# (descending conjunct)
E CB|A FE (descending disjunct)

The term pentatonic is correct even when the melody does not reach the range of an octave (so that there are, properly speaking, less than five steps). The alternation of either wholetones and minor thirds, on the one hand, and of semitones and major thirds, on the other hand, justifies the name whatever the span of the melody may be.

T RANSCRIPTION AND CENTS. The steps of oriental music are often not only vague and changing but in principle so different from those of our own 'well-tempered' octaves of twelve exactly equalized semitones that transcriptions into western staff notation with its strictly set-off lines and spaces necessarily distort the specific character and flavor of oriental music and, for that matter, of primitive music, too. This shortcoming has been a much resented handicap in all our efforts to render exotic music in a readable form. So far, there is, despite a number of recent suggestions, not one adequate script in existence.

A scholarly approach, however, cannot acquiesce in ignoring the characteristic and highly important differences between oriental and western steps and must be able to convey an idea of their sizes even if this cannot be done in the way of notation.

Previous scholars described a step between two notes by the ratio of their two frequency numbers: when a step connects a note of 481 vibrations per second and another one of 441 vibrations, their ratio is 481:441. This designation is correct, but not exactly elucidating. What we need and want to know is: how far is it from the first to the second note? Or, to express it scientifically, we are not interested in intervals, but rather in distances.

The problem amounts to transforming division into subtraction, quotients into differences. This can be done by a simple logarithmic operation.

The most widely used logarithmic method of finding musical steps or distances is the System of Cents that Alexander J. Ellis published in London in 1884. The following are its most important features:

(*1*) The well-tempered (piano) octave is the measuring frame work. Each of its twelve equal semitones is subdivided into 100 cents, or hundredths:

100 cents:	semitone	700 cents:	fifth
200 cents:	tone	800 cents:	minor sixth
300 cents:	minor third	900 cents:	major sixth
400 cents:	major third	1000 cents:	minor seventh
500 cents:	fourth	1100 cents:	major seventh
600 cents:	augmented fourth	1200 cents:	octave

The non-tempered, perfect fifth would measure 702, and the perfect fourth, 498 cents.

(*2*) The logarithm of a cent is .00025, since it derives from the twelfth part of an octave, which in itself has the ratio 2:1. As a shortcut, the following table of cents and logarithms may be welcome:

Cents	Log.	Cents	Log.	Cents	Log.
100	.025	10	.0025	1	.00025
200	.050	20	.0050	2	.00050
300	.075	30	.0075	3	.00075
400	.100	40	.0100	4	.00100
500	.125	50	.0125	5	.00125
600	.151	60	.0151	6	.00151
700	.176	70	.0176	7	.00176
800	.201	80	.0201	8	.00201
900	.226	90	.0226	9	.00226
1000	.251				
1100	.276				
1200	.301				

(*3*) To find the cents equivalent to a certain ratio, the easiest way is to reach for a table of logarithms: (a) look up the logarithms of each number; (b) subtract them; (c) compare the difference with the shortcut table, computing the hundreds, tens, and units, and you have the desired cents.

If there is no table of logarithms at hand, you avail yourself of the auxiliary number 3477 (which is easy to memorize, since the total of its digits is $7 + 7 + 7$); then you multiply the difference of the two vibration numbers by 3477, and divide this product by their sum. The ratio 481:441 gives:

$$481 - 441 = 40$$
$$40 \times 3477 = 139{,}080$$
$$481 + 441 = 922$$
$$139{,}080 \div 922 = 151$$

This result is a good example of the superiority of the cent system. The ratio 481:441 does not convey any clear picture of the distance between the two notes in question. But the number 151, cent equivalent of this ratio, shows impressively that the distance is midway between 100 and 200 cents and therefore between a minor and a major second: it is a three-quarter-tone.

With the aid of this practical method, it is easy to win a clear and graphic picture of all the scales occurring in oriental music.

B EFORE EXPLAINING the scales of the Orient, it should be made clear that exactness in the intonation of steps or individual notes has little interest for singers but is of paramount interest to people who are at a loss as to how to tune or even to build their instruments.

Among the innumerable scales devised between Morocco and East Asia, two have played a particularly decisive and often confusing role, even in the history of western music down to the present time. Musicians have called them, with a certain optimism, 'natural,' 'just,' or even 'pure.'

The obviously older of these two 'natural' scales—quite wrongly called 'Pythagorean' after the none too certain role of Pythagoras in developing it—relies on man's innate awareness of perfect fifths and fourths—a perfectness and satisfaction that probably is caused by the very simple ratios between the frequency numbers of tones a fifth or a fourth apart, 3:2 and 4:3 (*cf.* Appendix). Wherever instruments have *open* strings (not subject to stopping; harps and lyres, for example) the only natural way of tuning is to start from a certain string (say *C*) and tune another string to its upper perfect fifth (*G*), then revert to *D*, a fourth down, and go up to *A* by another fifth, and again revert to *E*, a fourth down, and so on. The opposite way, descending by fifths and going up by fourths, is just as good. In either form, we call this way of construction the *cyclic* or, colloquially, the *up-and-down* method. It yields both perfect fifths and perfect fourths. But it never leads to a perfect octave. It is easy to see that any progress in fifths means multiplying the ratio 3:2 by itself; and no power of 3 can ever coincide with a power of 2, which the octave 2:1 requires. The nearest note to an octave which the progress in fifths can provide is a *B*♯, which is 24 cents, or an eighth of a tone, too high. This critical difference of 24 cents is known as the *Pythagorean comma* (which must not be confused with the Didymean comma to be mentioned later).

The second and later of the *natural* methods relies on the proper division of a string and therefore is a *divisive* method. Sumer, Babylonia, and the adjacent countries were the first to have lutes, or stringed instruments with necks, on which the melody was produced, not by passing from string to string, as on harps and lyres, but by pressing down (stopping) and thus shortening one string at different places. In doing this, the players—or rather the *scholars* who observed them—found that the three 'perfect' intervals, the octave, the fifth, and the fourth, appeared when the strings were stopped in one-half, one-third, and one-fourth of their length. Indeed, an excellent major third was found in one-fifth, and an equally satisfactory minor third in one-sixth.

Still, thirds as well as seconds were different in the two methods. In the cyclic method, every wholetone (as the difference of a fifth, 3:2, and a fourth, 4:3) measures 9:8, or 204 cents. Consequently, the major third, being the sum of two wholetones, measures two times 9:8, or 81:64. In the divisive system, on the other hand, the major third, being stopped on one-fifth of the string, measures only 5:4, or 80:64. The difference 81:80 is called the *Didymean comma* after the Greek theoretician Didymos. It is equivalent to 22 cents, or about a ninth of a tone.

Having a major third of a slightly lesser size, the divisive system cannot have two wholetones of 9:8, or 204 cents. The second one is a little smaller, for subtracting the first tone of 9:8 from a third of 5:4 yields a tone of only 40:36, or 10:9, which corresponds to 182 cents.

Moreover, the semitone, being the difference between an unchanged fourth and a lesser (major) third, must necessarily be larger in the divisive than in the cyclic system. A simple arithmetic operation shows that it is 16:15, or 112 cents, as against 256:243, or 90 cents.

Graphically:

	CYCLIC		DIVISIVE	
C–D	9:8	204 c.	9:8	204 c.
D–E	9:8	204 c.	10:9	182 c.
E–F	256:243	90 c.	16:15	112 c.
		498 c.		498 c.

The irreconcilable divergence between the two methods harassed the music of the West no less than that of the East, until the equal temperament, or division of the octave into twelve equal semitones, at last did away in the eighteenth century with the dubious so-called 'natural' intervals.

Temperament, or tuning compromise, in some form, however, is neither a western nor a modern achievement. It exists everywhere and in every time, now as a spontaneous, now as a wilful alteration of nature.

Wilful alterations are particularly striking in Southeast Asia and the western Muhammedan world.

In Southeast Asia, we find interesting and often fascinating changes in pentatonic genders. The two leading genders of Java and Bali— *salendro*, or *slendro*, and *pelog*—have almost lost their original character. *Salendro* once had minor thirds and wholetones, but so much have the thirds been shortened and the tones enlarged that they are virtually equalized and form an awkward set of five even steps, each of which measures around 240 cents, or six-fifths of a tone. The other gender, *pelog*, originally had major thirds and semitones, like the Japanese scale, which are not entirely lost but have been disfigured. The change seems, in either case, to be due to the neglect of finer shades, and a golden mean allows playing in different modes on the same instrument without additional gongs or slabs (in the same way that the E on a western keyboard, tuned down by a quartertone, would allow playing all pieces in both C major and minor). Such subterfuge is perfectly possible: the messages of the ear are decoded in our brains, and psychological interpretation often gets the better of physical facts—witness the *salendro* pieces, which all seem to be built of thirds and wholetones, although any experiment proves that there are none.

The 'neutral' third between the major and the minor third, to which the parenthesis in the last paragraph alludes, has indeed been realized in Siam. Obviously for the same purpose of a master-key arrangement for all possible modes with the least amount of notes, the scale is divided into seven equal steps which measure seven-eighths of a normal tone. Each two of them provide a neutral third of about 343 cents—that is, a major third less the two wanting eighths, or a quartertone—and the player can easily play in any of his pentatonic modes by skipping notes wherever he needs his thirds.

The music of the nearer Orient boasts of its three-quartertones.

Their reason for being was obviously that the players, forced to perform according to the divisive method and faced with two neighboring wholetones difficult to keep differentiated, tended to exaggerate the difference and thus assimilated the size of the minor wholetone so much to the size of the semitone that—once more in order to avoid too tiny a dissimilarity—they equalized the minor wholetone and the semitone to form a three-quartertone each. The result in cents is 204 + 147 + 147 = 498 cents.

Although the three-quartertone scale is actually a scale, there have never existed those intricate "scales" of seventeen or even twenty-two steps per octave that superficial knowledge has hung upon the Arabs and the Hindus. And since they have never existed, they cannot be claimed as godfathers to modern western quartertone music.

Actually, these so-called "scales" constitute the raw material out of which quite ordinary seven-tone scales are formed for use in melody. The famous alleged seventeen-tone scale of the Arabs reads:

SSs	SSs	SSs	SSs	SSs	SS

where capital S stands for a semitone of 90 cents, and lower-case s for the tiny supplement, or *comma*, of 24 cents that two semitones need to form a major wholetone. In western terms, this set allows for building, say, a major scale by organizing, without disarranging, the seventeen steps in this way:

SSs	SSs	S	SsS	SsS	SsS	S
204	204	90	204	204	204	90

that is, in tone, tone, semitone, tone, tone, tone, semitone. Or else we could build our ascending minor scale, again by organizing, without disarranging, the elements as:

SSs	S	SsS	SsS	SsS	SsS	S
204	90	204	204	204	204	90

that is, in tone, semitone, and four subsequent tones, plus a final semitone.

In a similar way, the Arabs build their own modal scales: the seventeen elements allow the two semitones to stand wherever they are required. And the same is true of the alleged twenty-two tone or *śruti* scale of the Hindus, which is more complicated only because it takes care of the divisive principle with its two sizes of wholetones.

In modern western music the scale as such is directly connected with the melody, one being the dead abstraction, and one, the live realization, but the Orient separates the two by an intermediate concept, the pattern.

THE PATTERNS. To the freedom of western music, which allows, and even expects, a composer to create melodies of a fully individual character, the Orient opposes a strict, compulsory law, which forces composers to keep within two dozen or a score of traditional patterns, called *rāgas* (sing. *rāga*) in India and *maqamāt* (sing. *maqām*) in Arabian countries. Such a pattern—as, say, *rāst* in Persia, *mālkos* in India, or *nawā* in the western Orient—is characterized not only by its scale but also by its particular tempo, general curve, emotional atmosphere, and even melodic turns. The composer's freedom is limited to the few traits which do not interfere with the immutable qualities of the pattern.

Those readers familiar with the three orders of Greek architecture will easily understand what such restriction means. The Hellenic builder was bound to the general plan of the temple and also to the proportions of the columns and to the particular forms of the architraves, friezes, and cornices that either the Doric, or the Ionic, or the Corinthian order provides. But he did not copy; all the Doric, Ionic, and Corinthian temples, uniform at first sight, have individual traits.

In the music of the Orient, the melodic pattern is so vital that it is preconceived in lyrical poetry even before the words are composed: Arabian and Persian poets publish their poems in bunches under the headings of the patterns which should be used in composition—at the beginning the *rāst* poems, then the *mahur* or the *kardan* poems. In a similar way, some fifty of the Hebrew Psalms have individual headings to indicate which pattern should be followed, such as *shoshanim*, or *idutun*, or *mahalat*.

Conforming to melody patterns is intimately related with the strange procedure of 'putting together' one's melodies—in the truest sense of the word *com-ponere*—out of a limited stock of ready-made, characteristic melodicles, or turns.

This mosaic composition is best known from the ancient and modern cantillation of the Jewish liturgy. The cantor sings the Five Books of Moses all through the year in an easily flowing melodic train, which actually is the skilful, expressive combination of a score of given melodic turns, an everchanging nosegay from a modest, though beautiful, flower bed.

This kind of composing has not been abandoned in the later West. It has left its traces in the Gregorian chant, in the Lutheran chorale, the Calvin psalter, the art of the *Meistersinger*, and the folksong of all countries. Indeed, Wagner's principle of piecing together an unending melody out of *leitmotives*, particularly in the *Ring des Nibelungen*, is technically, though not spiritually, the principle of ancient Jewish cantillation.

R HYTHM, too, has been typified in India and the Muhammedan Orient.

When a Hindu or an Arab speaks of rhythm, he hardly thinks of equal beats in a western sense, with stresses on every fourth or fifth or seventh beat. Oriental rhythm is not qualitative, a question of stresses, strong and weak. It is quantitative, a question of duration, of long and short.

To give an example: a dactylic meter would, in western qualitative conception, be strong-weak-weak, in triple time; it would, in eastern quantitative conception, be long-short-short, in duple time.

Such quantitative rhythm, particularly in India, is organized in standard patterns, many of which are complicated and, from our view-point, hard to grasp: say, a seven-unit pattern of three *plus* two *plus* two, a ten-unit pattern of seven *plus* one *plus* two, or a fourteen-unit pattern of five *plus* five *plus* two *plus* two. Ceaselessly repeated all through a piece, these patterns are often emphasized on one or two hand-beaten drums with delicate shades of pitch and timbre. So important is the rhythmical pattern of a piece that it often forms a part of its title. As we in the West would say, sonata in *F* major, the Hindu would say, *rāga* such and such, *tāla* (rhythmic pattern) such and such.

N OTATION, one of the characteristic features of high civiliza-tions, exists in the East in various forms, although it is on the whole much less important than western notation.

(1) *Ecphonetic* or *group* notation is a script in which some symbol
—a figure, a letter, a hook, or any other sign—denotes a whole characteristic group or formula of notes, a *melodicle*, as the present author
has called it. Examples are the tropes, or *ta'amim*, which go with every
syllable of the Old Testament, also the Byzantine, Ethiopian, and
Indian *veda* notations, and, most probably, the secret script of
Babylonian priests.

(2) *Neumatic* or *cheironomic*, that is 'gesture,' notation depicts
the strides of the melody in individual signs—up, down, up-up, down-
down, up-down, down-up, and so on—without indicating their pitches
or width. The best examples are the early medieval neumes of Europe,
which the fourth chapter will discuss. Kindred systems exist in the
ancient Orient.

(3) *Pitch* notation, on the contrary, provides an individual sign—
usually a letter—for each degree of the scale, without indicating steps
as such. The majority of Indian and Far Eastern notations are of this
kind.

(4) *Tablatures*, or fingering scripts, independent from absolute
pitches, denote the strings to be plucked and the fingers that have to
do the work. They are used in the Far East by players of the long-
zithers.

Staff notation, developed in Europe around A.D. 1000, does not exist
in the Orient except as a recent importation from the West.

The oriental world is also far from having any adequate notation
of time-values (for which the musicians of Europe themselves had to
fight a thousand years and which they eventually achieved only under
the pressure of their unoriental polyphony). Rhythmical signs exist
in parts of the East, but they are in a rudimentary stage and have no
real importance.

THE INSTRUMENTS of the Orient show their most peculiar
features when compared to the instruments that we use ourselves.

The first, most striking difference is the lack of keyboards, which
would indeed be meaningless in a monophonic civilization. Where
they have been imported from the West in recent times, they are
misused against their nature. The Arabs play in empty octaves on
the piano, and the Hindus, in single, sustained notes on the harmonium.

The second difference that strikes the eye is the rudimentary state in which the brass and woodwinds have been left. Horns and trumpets, never used in oriental art music, are "natural," without any keys or slides or valves. And the numberless families of flutes and reed-pipes have open holes. And rightly so; for while the modern West insists on just intonation within a rigid equal temperament, the East expects a flexibility, which in Japanese flute blowing is carried as far as driving up almost every individual note.

For a similar reason, stringed instruments are often left without frets, so that the finger can freely glide along the fingerboard. This is particularly significant in the case of the lute—above all, the short-necked lute—which is unfretted in its native western Orient but, when accepted in Europe during the Middle Ages, was at once provided with frets. Whenever oriental instruments have frets, they are easily shifted, such as the tied-on metal frets of the Indian *vina* (illustration in the author's *History of Musical Instruments*, page 225) or the loosely set bridges on the *koto* of Japan. Indeed, in both the latter instruments and in numerous others, the strings are thin enough and sufficiently high above the fingerboard to be conveniently driven up in pitch by an increase of pressure.

Bowed instruments are immeasurably inferior in make and play to the violins of the West. Plucked instruments, on the other hand, attain a delicacy that in the world of the white man only a few exceptional players achieve.

The Orient holds absolute superiority in the realm of drums and *idiophones*. This scholarly name implies that the instruments sound (*phon-*) by their own (*idio-*) nature without needing a special tension, like drum-heads or strings; and the class includes a dizzying mass of wooden, bamboo, stone, glass, porcelain, and metal implements, to be pounded, shaken, rubbed, or struck. The West has borrowed several of them under the popular misnomer percussion, such as church bells, gongs and cymbals, xylophones and metallophones (illustrations in *The History of Musical Instruments*, page 192), and, quite lately, the small rectangular redwood block with two lateral slits that the Chinese use in their temples.

Drum playing with the bare hands has, particularly in India and the western Orient, reached a perfection in technique, variety of timbre, and intricacy of rhythm that America and Europe with their cruder stick-beaten drums have not been able to imitate.

MAGIC CONNOTATIONS.

Rhythmic and melodic patterns, genders and modes, scales and individual tones, and the very instruments have, in the Orient, more than aesthetic qualities. They are a decisive power in the delicate relationship of man and the forces of nature which, friendly or hostile, determine his fate. They are magic.

Sound has indeed the strongest magic quality of all that man can produce. A visible, touchable object may act on nature and destiny by the force of its peculiar matter or color, but these connotations must be *known*. The power of sound, on the contrary, is felt, as irritation, terror, peace. The magical role of music has, as a consequence, always been important in the beliefs of oriental nations. We read in the Bible that the Hebrews smashed the walls of Jericho with the sound of seven rams' horns; and in Greek mythology, the other way round, that Kadmos, the founder of Thebes, built the walls of the town with the tones of Amphion's lyre. Chinese and Hindu tales are full of episodes where singers make spring and summer, fall and winter, fire and water with their melodies. Ancient Mexican slaves went to their death while scraping bones and whistling their bone flutes to secure a life to come. And the Jewish highpriest wore bells and jingles on his garment when he passed the threshold of the Holy of Holies "that he not die."

As a consequence of such beliefs, music is not only connected with religion and its rites but also with cosmology, that is, with the meaningful interrelation of all the various aspects under which the universe presents itself, be they cardinal points, seasons, colors, matters, or natural phenomena.

In China, for instance, the drum is, through its skins, related with the cardinal point north, the season winter, and the element water. The pan-pipes, through bamboo, are identified with east and spring and mountain. The zither, through the silk of its strings, is joined to south and summer and fire; the bell, through its metal, belongs to west and autumn and dampness.

In a similar way, each of the twelve semitones of the Chinese musical system belongs to a certain hour of the day and to one month of the year, so that, as a curious consequence, the sacred hymns are sung in twelve different keys during the year, rising by a semitone from month to month. Again, the normal five notes of the Chinese scale stand for (1) north, the planet Mercury, wood, and the color black; (2) east, Jupiter, water, and violet; (3) center, Saturn, earth, and yellow; (4) west, Venus, metal, and white; (5) south, Mars, fire, and red.

In India, too, the various patterns or *rāgas* are related to the colors, days of the week, elements, heavens, planets, seasons, signs of the zodiac, voices of birds, man's ages, human complexions, sexes, temperaments, and what not; and the *rāgas* are all assigned to certain periods of the day and must not, even at the present time, be played at improper hours. Correspondingly, one Arabian *maqām*, or melody pattern, belongs to the sign of the Ram in the zodiac and to sunrise, and it heals the eyes; another belongs to the Twins and the time of nine o'clock and is supposed to cure palpitation of the heart and dementia; a third one is connected with the Fishes, morning, and headache; a fourth, with the Bull and colds; a fifth, with the Lion and colic; a sixth with Capricorn and heart diseases.

But very little has survived of these connotations in the consciousness of the modern listener. Oriental music has almost entirely passed from the magical or half-magical stage to the aesthetic stage, in which all music—religious tunes excepted—is meant to please, and nothing else.

The kind of pleasure that it conveys may be a stronger delight than the one that western music inspires in the average listener. And on the whole, an essentially greater part of eastern music seems to soothe the mind and give it peace.

READING

Curt Sachs, *The Rise of Music in the Ancient World, East and West*, New York, 1943, Sections II, III, IV, VI. Curt Sachs, *The History of Musical Instruments*, New York, 1940, Second Part. Curt Sachs, *World History of the Dance*, New York, 1937, Chapter 4. Curt Sachs, *The Commonwealth of Art*, New York, 1946, Chapter One 2. Curt Sachs, *Rhythm and Tempo*, New York, 1953.

Here, too, the numberless monographs on the musical systems between the North of Africa and the East and Southeast of Asia must be left to intenser studies. The reader might look into the literature quoted in the author's *Rise of Music*.

3

GREECE AND ROME

THE MAGIC MIGHT of music was a leading belief of the Greeks no less than of the Eastern world. They gave it an incomparable allegory in the beautiful myth of the Thracian Orpheus, who with his singing overthrew the laws of nature, tamed the wild beasts, and rescued his wife Euridice from the realm of the dead.

In actual life, the musico-magic ideas of Hellas concentrated largely on healing of the body as well as the soul. The choral paeans in honor of Apollo were originally medicine songs with the traits of primitive shamanistic rites. As late an author as the grammarian Athenaios, who lived around 200 A.D., assured his readers earnestly that "persons subjected to *sciatica* would always be free from its attacks if one played the pipes in the Phrygian *harmonia* over the parts affected"; and Aristotle, more convincingly and even in agreement with modern healing methods, related that persons in religious frenzy or otherwise insanely overwrought could be brought back to themselves again by carefully chosen melodies.

Such beliefs explain why in the ninth century, as the Greeks report, the Cretan composer Thaletas appeared at the side of Lykurgos, the lawgiver of Sparta, and why in a time of unrest, around 650 B.C., the Delphic oracle advised the Spartans to appoint the musician Terpander, that his melodies might pacify the city. The good and the evil, order and chaos depended on music.

It was a logical climax that in the fourth century B.C. the greatest philosopher Plato recommended—as Confucius had done a hundred years before him in China—that the ideal State be erected upon the foundation of music and that any change in the traditional ways of music be resisted lest such deviation lead to a fatal change in the State as well.

This was by no means the fantastic, utopian concept of a single philosopher. In the same spirit of serious anxiety, the conservative Spartans were alarmed when, around 400 B.C., the then "modern" musician Timotheos of Miletos performed with four additional strings on his lyre, and the court ordered them to be snipped off.

But the scientific mind of the later Greeks was not satisfied with mere tradition, belief, and experience. It needed a well-established system, a theory of the psycho-physiological effects of music on the State and on man, or, as they put it, a theory of the *ethos* of music.

This system they based on the age-old cosmology of the Orient.

In the complicated eastern concept of the world, certain patterns of melodies, or even single notes, were connected with certain planets and hence with the ethical qualities that the planets were supposed to impart to man: Jupiter, majesty; Mars, virility; Venus, effeminacy; Mercury, shiftiness; Saturn, sadness.

At least in later periods after the Golden Age, Greece knew these connotations but understood them in a purely ethical rather than in a magical sense: she dropped the planets as causes and established a direct psycho-physiological link between music and character. Thus, Aristotle could say in *Politics*: "The musical modes differ from one another, and those who hear them are differently affected by each. Some of them depress, as the so-called Mixolydian, others enfeeble the mind, as the 'relaxed' ones, others, again, produce a settled, moderate mood, which appears to be the peculiar effect of the Dorian, while the Phrygian inspires enthusiasm." But there was little consistency. Other writers called the Dorian virile and bellicose; the Hypodorian, majestic and stable; the Mixolydian, pathetic and plaintive; the Phrygian, agitated and Bacchic; the Hypophrygian, active; the Lydian, mournful; the Hypolydian, dissolute and voluptuous.

What were these mysterious Dorian, Phrygian, Lydian, Mixolydian? The general assumption has been that character and mood belonged to the various modal scales thus named—scales that differed in the arrangement of their whole tones and semitones exactly as our Church modes and our minor and major do. This cannot be true, or at least it cannot be the whole truth. Modal scales, that is, the lifeless arrangements of tones and semitones, have little to offer in the way of *ethos*. They are but dead abstractions of the only thing that can impress the soul— melody, with all its significant turns and expression. There must have been an intimate, indelible connection between the scale of a certain name and all the melodies that followed it. In other words, the existence of *ethos* suggests that Greece, like the Near and Middle East, must have known what the Hindus call *rāga* and the Arabs *maqām*, the homogeneousness, in structure, mood, and character, of all the melodies belonging to a certain scale. Greece must have had melodic patterns. This train of thought would, at least partly, solve the fascinating, age-old problem of the Grecian *ethos*.

IT WAS PARTICULARLY on account of *ethos*, of the character-forming qualities of melodic patterns, that music, including pipe- and lyre-playing, was considered one of the most important branches of learning, often had precedence over grammar and arithmetic in school, and was, in Arcadia for example, compulsory up to the age of thirty.

Music resounded all over the country and its colonies. But comparatively little of it was professional. The oldest professional was the blind Homeric bard, a poet, singer, and lyre-player in one, who entertained the guests at the banquets of the great with the epical deeds of their ancestors. This honored, unassuming bard developed gradually into an arrogant, spoiled virtuoso who, in royal attire and with an impressive retinue, participated in the national contests, toured from city to city, and gave recitals in overcrowded arenas.

Music belonged to the drama too. The actors sang in what probably amounted to recitatives and *ariosi*, and the chorus, marching up in a semicircle in front of the stage and commenting on the action and fate of the heroes, performed in those responding antiphonies of a strophe, a similar antistrophe, and a different epode, which foreshadowed the so-called bar-form AAB of the *troubadours, Minnesinger,* and *Meistersinger.* Music was indispensable in the many solemn processions to temples and sacred woods at home (plate I) and to the national shrines in Delphi or Olympia, where the townships tried to outdo each other in the number, size, and quality of their choirs. Music embellished the home. Every man was expected to sing at banquets and to accompany himself on the lyre, and the ladies in their rooms amused themselves with singing and playing the lyre, while their oriental slave girls would strum the eastern harp.

THE GREEKS stressed vocal music at the cost of instrumental music in all these activities, and not only because they belonged to antiquity and to the eastern Mediterranean. As a basically classical-minded nation, they expected from their arts a distinctness and un-equivocal character that only words could convey to music. Hence Plato, the arch-classicist, haughtily asked what, after all, a melody and a rhythm could mean unless there was a text. Which was exactly the famous question of the French: *Sonate, que me veux-tu?* (Sonata, what do you want of me?) Instrumental music meant so little that the instruments—lyres and pipes—were left in an astonishingly primitive stage. Not until postclassical times, after the Golden Age of Perikles, were the instruments improved and was an independent instrumental art encouraged. This sequence is in keeping with the general laws of evolution: instrumental music with its vaguer meaning has come to the fore in all postclassical phases.

Since harmony did not exist and counterpoint was accessory, Greek music was essentially melody and rhythm; that is, an orderly succession of notes and time-values. Either one of these depended on the laws of poetry. Poetic meters, anapaests and dactyls, iambs and trochees, were so exactly rendered that composers hardly ever cared to write the symbols that notation provided for rhythm, and the sequence of notes paid attention to the natural inflection of the Greek language, rising on an acute accent and, with less consistency, rising or falling on a grave or a circumflex.

However, it is important to know that, of necessity, all our descriptions of Grecian melodies imply a certain oversimplification. Music, almost exclusively focused on singing, had none of the clear-cut tempered scales that instrumental music wants and foments. Actually, the theorists, sandwiched between the need of the scientists for logical rule and the freedom of intonation that the singers demanded, followed two opposite trains of thought: The school of Aristóxenos (fourth century B.C.) left the supreme judgment to the ear, while the school of Ptolemaios (second century A.D.) submitted to the rule of simple mathematical ratios.

As a consequence, the Greeks had officially no less than eight different sizes of thirds, seven wholetones, thirteen semitones, and nine quartertones or, better, microtones. Unofficially, every singer or player did as he deemed best. Moreover, Greek musicians felt free, in linking two tetrachords to form a heptad or an octave, to shade either one in a different way. Such confusing plenty of theoretical shades was not meant to be sophistication, it was an attempt to avert chaos and anarchy by legalizing the principal current trends.

The role of musical theory was indeed preëminent. Philosophers, scientists, mathematicians, and historians made their contributions. Music itself and the psychology and physiology of sound perception were frequent themes of scholarly search and reasoning. And so was acoustics, the physical aspect of music. Vibrations were discovered to be the cause of sound, and there is little doubt that the discoverer was Lasos of Hermione, who was Pindar's teacher around 500 B.C. A hundred years later, Archytas of Tarentum found that hearing even implied two kinds of vibrations: stationary waves within the instruments and the throat, and progressive, spheric waves in the surrounding air to convey them to the ears. And the fourth century B.C. established a complete (though not fully preserved) theory of rhythm and melody under the leadership of Aristotle's disciple, Aristóxenos of Tarentum.

This theory has been the weightiest heritage left by ancient music. The melodies of Greece have faded away, but all the musical treatises of the Islamic Orient—Arabian, Persian, Turkish—are based on the system of Greece. And so are the musical treatises of the western Middle Ages. The medieval theory of interval ratios with the string-dividing monochord as the measuring device, the eight Byzantine *echoi*, the eight western Church modes, the neumes, and the letters of the alphabet as the names of notes—all these and many other concepts were taken from the Greeks. It was Hellenic antiquity and hardly anything but Hellenic antiquity that allowed the learned monks of medieval Europe to lay the theoretical fundaments of western music.

R ELICS. Only eleven pieces, or fragments of pieces, of Greek music have been preserved, either on stone or on papyrus. Those in best condition are:

Two hymns addressed to Apollo, from the middle of the second century B.C., engraved in stone on the treasury of the Athenians at Delphi.

A short *skolion*, or drinking song, on the inconstancy of life, composed by a certain Seíkilos (Sicilian) in the second or first century B.C., engraved on a tomb stele at Tralles in Asia Minor.

Three solemn hymns by Mesomedes, to Helios, to Nemesis, to the Muse, from the second century A.D.

Pindar's first Pythian ode, however, though printed by preference in many handbooks, is today considered a forgery.

It is remarkable that among eleven pieces only one is instrumental. And the few measures of which it consists seem to be an etude for the lyre rather than an actual composition.

From these eleven relics and from the scattered evidences of theory, we piece together the elements of Greek composition.

M ELODY, GENDERS, MODES. The unit of Greek melody was the tetrachord, which has been described in detail on page 10. As in the Orient, the Greeks connected two tetrachords by conjunction to form a heptad, or by disjunction to form an octave. With the growing conception of the octave as a normal span, the older heptads were often supplemented by an additional tone above or below, the *proslambanómenos*.

The inner organization of the tetrachord decided the gender and mode.

A *gender* provided the sizes of steps within the tetrachord, notwithstanding their sequence. There was:

(1) A *diatonic*, or *heptatonic*, gender of two tones and one semitone (as in our modern system).

(2) A *pentatonic* gender of a minor third and a tone, which later was split into two semitones and thus produced the so-called *chromatic* gender.

(3) A *pentatonic* gender of a major third and a semitone, called the *enharmonic* gender (which must not be mistaken for the entirely different modern conception of the same name). The semitone of this gender was later split into two microtones (not exactly quartertones).

The following graph will give an idea of these three genders:

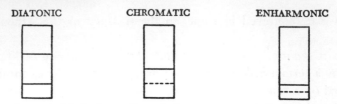

The *modes* provided the order of these steps, particularly in the diatonic gender. The Dorian tetrachord had the semitone at the bottom, the Phrygian in the middle between the two tones, and the Lydian on top.

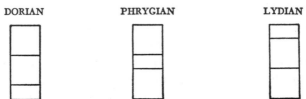

There is little doubt that the enharmonic gender, which had its closest relatives in Japan, India, and Egypt, was the earliest in Greece. It became diatonic and Dorian when, at a time unknown, it accepted a filling note within its major third—exactly as the similar Japanese scale developed to the diatonic *zoku-gaku*. In an analogous way, the chromatic gender seems to have begotten the diatonic Lydian and Phrygian modes.

The actual number of Grecian scales is not exhausted with the enumeration of the three genders and the three tetrachords. To judge from the little that we know, they must have been a confusing group; some were tense and others relaxed, some disjunct and others conjunct, some pure and others mixed, some plagal (with the fifth on top) and others authentic (with the fourth on top), some denoted structures and others keys, which would follow each other now in a diatonic sequence (that is, a tone or a semitone apart), now at a distance of three-quarter tones—just to mention a few of the endless possibilities.

At last, in postclassical times, the Greek musicians radically simplified, clipped, and normalized such luxuriant growth. Ignoring subtle differences in the structure of modes, they squeezed seven of them into a unifying framework, which they called the Perfect System and first described in the fourth century B.C. Its diagram is on the following page.

To understand and interpret the Perfect System, a few essential facts must be realized.

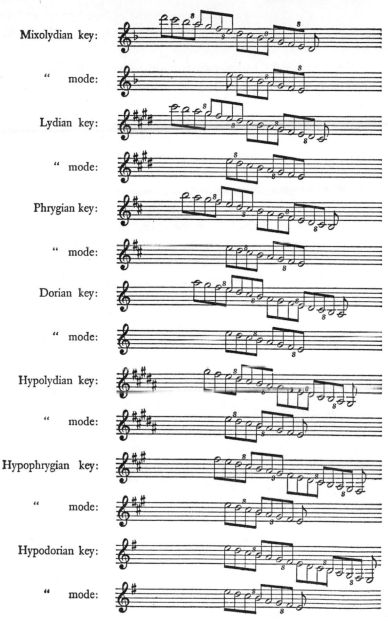

Mixolydian key:

"   mode:

Lydian key:

"   mode:

Phrygian key:

"   mode:

Dorian key:

"   mode:

Hypolydian key:

"   mode:

Hypophrygian key:

"   mode:

Hypodorian key:

"   mode:

s indicates the semitone

(1) Greek melodies and Greek instruments rarely exceeded the range of one octave.

(2) The modes had to show within this central octave and could

do so only by the sharping or flatting of some of its seven notes (as we moderns would change the *C* major key into *C* minor by flatting *E*, *A*, and *B*).

(3)   But the Greeks had names for only seven notes in the octave (like our current *do-re-mi* solmisation). They had no means to indicate any sharps or flats.

(4)   As a consequence, the Greeks could not avoid doing what we ourselves are forced to do in our "movable *do*" solmisation: shift the *do-re-mi-fa* series up or down as a whole so that, whatever the absolute pitch might be, the group *mi–fa* would always fall on a semitone, be it *f#–g*, *c#–d*, or *g#–a*.

(5)   The shift of *mi–fa*, in our solmisation, implies a (tacit) shift of *do*, *re*, and the other degrees of the scale. In other words, whoever transfers *mi–fa* from *e–f* to *f#–g* cannot avoid calling *d* his new *do*, and *e*, his new *re*. In doing so, any mode that he establishes with the help of *mi–fa* appears as a section cut out of a transposed major scale.

(6)   If you replace the modern series *do re mi fa sol la ti* by the seven Greek names (but in descending order) *nētē paranētē trítē paramésē mésē lichanós parhypátē hypátē*, which the following graph represents as *n pn t pm m l ph h*, each Grecian mode must evidently appear as a Dorian standard scale (page 31). Key and mode are two aspects of the same phenomenon.

The reader who so far has followed our complicated explanation will readily understand the seemingly cryptic difference between the two conceptions *thesis* and *dýnamis*, which has caused much headache to generations of scholars. A note, says the Greek, can be *mésē* by *thesis*, and *lichanós* by *dýnamis*. What does this mean? Once more, our

```
Mixolyd-
   ian:    A   G    FE   D    C    Bb A    g    f e
           n   pn   t  pm m         l  ph h
Lydian:    G#    F#   E   D#  C#  B   A G#  f#  e
           n     pn   t  pm  m   l   ph h
Phrygian:  F#   E    D C#   B    A   G F#  e
           n    pn   t  pm m     l   ph h
Dorian:         E    D  C B     A   G   F E
                n    pn t pm   m    l  ph h
Hypolydian:      e D#  C#  B   A#  G#  F#  E D#
                 n  pn  t  pm m   l   ph h
Hypophrygian:    e   d  C#  B    A G#  F#  E   D C#
                 n   pn    t pm  m  l  ph h
Hypodorian:      e   d   c B    A   G F#  E   D   C B
                 n   pn    t pm m   l  ph m l  ph h
```

n — nete	m — mese
pn — paranete	l — lichanós
t — trite	ph — parhypate
pm — paramese	h — hypate

modern solmisation will help to comprehend this double name and meaning. In C major, C is *do* and D is *re*. But in all the other keys, the notes have two names according to whether you apply the 'fixed *do*' or the 'movable *do*' solmisation. In D major, G is *sol* in the 'fixed *do*' system but *fa* in the 'movable *do*' system. The Greeks would have said: G is *sol* by *thesis*, and *fa* by *dýnamis*. Indeed, the Dorian scale would behave like our C major: its notes stand like fixed stars around the immutable *mésē* or solar center of the musical space. The notes of all the other scales obey a twofold orientation. In Phrygian, for instance. *A* is *mésē* by *thesis*, that is, by its immutable station in space, but it is *lichanós* by *dýnamis*, or by its relative, functional position within its scale.

P OLYPHONY. The question of whether or not the music of Greece had any element beyond a mere melodic line has been the topic of hotter arguments than the temperate atmosphere of scholarly research would seem to admit. There were, of course, no fugues in Greece, nor was there harmony in the sense of four-part setting with sixth and seventh chords on a figured bass. Not these nor other naive conceptions of western Europe two thousand and more years after the bloom of Hellenic music must lead our deductions, but rather the much closer conceptions of the ancient eastern world (of which the pugnacious pro and contra authors had no knowledge).

Although there was never part-singing in Greece except in the natural parallel octaves imposed by the natural ranges of boys' and women's voices, we can today not doubt that instrumental accompaniment availed itself of several forms of independence.

(1)   Octaves, fifths, and fourths were considered consonant; thirds and seconds, sixths and sevenths, dissonant.

(2)   The existence of parallel fifths or fourths cannot be proved, but is quite possible.

(3)   It can be proved, however, that the Greeks, both in early and late times, preferred two-part setting to unaccompanied melodies. A certain author, probably of the first century A.D. and wrongly called Longinus, even states that melodies were "usually" sweetened by fifths and fourths.

(4)   Two passages five hundred years apart, in Plato and in Athenaios, hint at an actual two-part counterpoint, of which, to be sure, we do not know the rules. Plato mentions inadequate music teachers who, playing with pupils only twelve years old, would "answer closer by wider steps, lower by higher notes, and faster by slower notes"; and Athenaios admonishes two pipers to keep their voice parts clear apart without confusing the listener.

R HYTHM. The Greeks had mainly a metrical, quantitative rhythm, in music as well as in poetry. It showed in the contrast of long and short, not of strong and weak. A dactyl, for example, was not thought of as strong-weak-weak but as long-short-short, and an iamb as short-long. A verse foot, or single metrical pattern, had two beats, an *arsis* ('lifting') or upbeat and a *thesis* ('setting down') or downbeat, whether it consisted of two, three, or five time-units. *Arsis* and *thesis* were of equal length in an anapaest, with the two shorts on one beat and the long on a second beat. *Arsis* and *thesis* were of unequal length in an iamb, with the short on one beat and the long on a second beat. In every case, the short, in our transliteration represented by an eighthnote, is the indivisible *chronos prōtos* or 'first time,' that is, time-unit.

The principal meters were:

pyrrhic	♫	spondee	♩ ♩
iamb	♪♩	trochee	♩ ♪
anapaest	♫♩	dactyl	♩ ♫
		paión or cretic	♩. ♩

These simple meters could easily be combined to form some larger pattern. The combination of two different meters was called a dipody; of three, a tripody; of four, a tetrapody. One tetrapody, described as a processional rhythm, was:

$$♪♩ \quad ♫♪♩ \quad ♩ \quad ♪$$

or iamb-pyrrhic-iamb-trochee. The second movement of Beethoven's Seventh Symphony gives an idea of dactyl-spondee dipodies; its consistent metrical pattern is long-short-short-long-long.

I NSTRUMENTS. The Greeks, like the Etruscans and the Romans, used two main types of instruments: lyres and pipes.

The lyres were of several forms, all of which had, instead of a neck, the characteristic yoke of two diverging arms with, on top, a crossbar from which the strings stretched down between the two arms and along the front of the box. The two ground forms were distinguished as the *kithara* and the *lyra*. (Keep the specific Greek term *lyra* and the generic English term *lyre* apart!) The *kíthara*, a professional's instrument, was solidly, sumptuously joined and held upright before the left side of the player's chest (plate I). The *lyra*, on the contrary, an instrument of beginners and mere amateurs, was loosely assembled from a few rods and a skin-covered tortoise shell and appears always in an inclined position (illustration in the author's *History of Musical Instruments*, page 128).

The Homeric lyres, the *phorminx* and the *kítharis*, seem to have had only three or four strings (on which the ancient enharmonic melodies could be easily played), but the classical *kíthara* and *lyra* had, as a rule, five or seven strings; indeed the former of the two was given, in later times, nine and even eleven strings.

For solo performances, the *kíthara* could be played with the bare fingers of the two hands, like a harp. But singing was accompanied, on either instrument, in a very peculiar manner, which, incidentally, has been preserved to this day in far-away Nubia, on the Upper Nile. From the rear, the outstretched fingers of the left hand deadened all the strings but one at a time, while the right hand, armed with a heavy *plektron*, or plucker, scratched across the bunch of strings all at once and thus produced the only note not deadened by the left hand.

Harps (to be held on the lap) were rare and seem to have been played chiefly by oriental slave girls.

Most pipes of antiquity—called *aulós* (plur. *auloí*) in Greek and *tibia* (plur. *tibiae*) in Latin— were exciting oboes, not, as a careless translation implies, mild and soothing flutes. They were invariably made in pairs. The player had both reeds in his mouth and held and fingered, one hand to each, the two slender tubes, which diverged like an upside-down letter V (plate I). As far as we can see, one tube played the melody, and the other, a sustained pedal note; that is, they acted as the chanter and the drone of what amounted to a Scotch bagpipe. The comparison is completed by the tight-fitting bandage around the cheeks of the piper, which shows that the Greeks, like oriental pipers, used the inflated mouth as a windbag to feed the two pipes independently of respiration and to hold the tone indefinitely.

We do not know exactly how the pipes coöperated with the voices. From a number of passages in contemporary writings, however, we can safely conclude that they accompanied in: (1) preludes, interludes, and postludes; (2) occasional consonances, as octaves, fifths, and fourths, though not in thirds; (3) free counterpoint, maybe of the heterophonic kind.

Flutes, in the actual meaning of the word, were rare and unimportant. A transverse flute in modern form was known at least in Etruria in the second century B.C., but so far, we find it depicted on only one relief. The panpipes or *syrinx*—a raftlike bundle of one-note flutes so often claimed as a characteristic instrument of the Greeks—was merely a shepherd's instrument and apparently a late one.

Percussion took little part in orthodox music. Circular frame drums, cymbals, and clappers (plate I) were on the whole confined to rites and dances of oriental descent, such as the ecstatic worship of the seasonal god Dionysos and the mystic cults of the Earth.

NOTATION. The Greeks had two notations of a peculiar, indeed, unparalleled kind. One of them was called the Vocal Notation and consisted of the letters of the alphabet in descending order (the first letters belonging to the highest notes) and was later expanded upward beyond *alpha* and downward beyond *omega* by additional symbols. However, instead of following the scale—*alpha* for the first, *beta* for the second, *gamma* for the third note—the symbols were grouped in triads, each consecutive three belonging to one string of the lyre: *alpha beta gamma | delta epsilon zeta |* and so on (diagrams in the author's *Rise of Music*, pages 304, 305). All the third letters, such as *gamma* and *zeta*, denoted one of the open strings of the lyre; the second ones, as *beta* and *epsilon*, indicated the same strings stopped near their upper ends by the index finger to sharp the original notes (usually by a semitone); and the first ones, as *alpha* and *delta*, once more the same strings stopped by the middle finger, which had to be used whenever the index was already busy.

The older Instrumental Notation followed the same triadic principle. But the scale ran upwards (as do all instrumental scales). The letters were taken from an archaic, Semitic alphabet, and they were distributed in sequence, so that all of them denoted open strings, while their flatted, prone position prescribed the stopping index, and their reversed position, the stopping middle finger.

Both the Greek notations, thus, were 'tablatures,' or fingering scripts, not pitch notations. This seems illogical in the case of a vocal script, since the voice had apparently nothing to do with strings and fingering. Actually, the singer was expected to accompany himself on the lyre, and his notation was correctly the singer's instrumental notation.

Although the Greeks had an open-string symbol for each of the seven notes of the octave, they never used all of them at a time. Instead, they would represent, say, the semitone *E–F* as *E–E#*, and the semitone *B–C* as *B–B#*. This awkward spelling proves that the lyre had only five, not seven, strings per octave and that any additional strings did not make it heptatonic but continued the pentatonic series above and below. The lyre was a pentatonic instrument without semitonal distances, and the player had to stop the missing notes of his heptatonic melodies on the lower string: *C* on the *B*, and *F* on the *E* string.

Why then the open-string symbols for *C* and *F*? Because the lyre had three different (pentatonic) tunings, selected according to the tonalities in which it had to perform: (1) *e g a b d'*, or (2) *e g a c' d'*, or (3) *f g a c' d'*, two of which required a *C*, and one an *F* string.

A HISTORY OF MUSIC in Greece cannot be written unless additional material is found. But certain facts allow us to sketch a picture of changes, which show that there was no quiescence in taste, ideas, and forms of expression, and also that the musical changes, as far as we know them, coincided with similar changes in the other arts.

We may confidently neglect the general statements of various writers from all the periods of antiquity who glorify the noble simplicity and dignity of the music of yore without exactly telling us what olden times they had in mind. There are a few better reports. We hear that the seventh century B.C., with Terpander and Archilochos in the lead, complicated both the meters in melody and the accompaniment on the lyre. In 596 B.C., at a time when vase painters were turning to a realistic, narrative style, the piper Sakadas won a brilliant victory in the Pythian games with an amazing piece of program music, which represented, on a single pair of pipes, Apollo's fight with the dragon. And the ecstatic dithyrambs in honor of the god Dionysos, wild-grown and unruly, were in the sixth century tamed, accepted in recognized music, and even imposed on Athenian contests.

Of the Golden Age in the times of Perikles, we know hardly more than that from Aischylos to Euripides, from the first to the second half of the fifth century B.C., the meters of choral songs in tragedy became increasingly complicated.

But towards the end of the Periklean time, late in the fifth century, an open revolution broke out. In one of his comedies, which were mainly satires of up-to-date matters and current events, the Attic poet Pherekrates (fl. c. 430 B.C.) had Music enter the stage in rags as a downtrodden woman and whimper that once she had been respected, but that the modern composers, ignorant of the dignity of old and the beauty of melody, had badly dishonored and abused her.

The leaders of the maligned new school were two non-European Greeks, Phrynis of Mytilene and his disciple Timotheos, "the redhead" of Miletos. Alas, no relics convey an idea of these personalities and their revolutionary style.

We are more fortunate concerning the time around 150 B.C., when the fine arts tried to revert to archaic styles. Two preserved musical pieces of some extent, the Delphian hymns to Apollo, illustrate the musical contribution to this reactionary archaism in their half-forgotten enharmonic heptads in the older style with major thirds and uncleft semitones and an apparently outmoded five-beat meter.

The ending phase of Hellenic music shortly before and during A.D. is almost entirely unknown. But it seems that in Greece—as apparently everywhere—the original plenitude of modes was more and more reduced, in number and importance; that the diatonic gender was given exclusive rights, except when wilful archaism revived the ancient enharmonic gender; and that a purely instrumental music was allowed, more than before, to come to the van.

This also seems to be true of the music of Rome. As early as in times B.C., the Romans expressly accepted Hellenic music—the *ritus Graecus*—and founded a Society of Greek Singers. But above all, they accepted the theoretical system of Greece and its later developments. They have also been commended for the introduction of various military trumpets and horns, the *cornu*, the *lituus*, and the *tuba*.

But this can hardly be the whole truth. The Roman Empire, as a supranational organism, is not thinkable without a continuous influx and exchange of foreign musical styles from western and northern Europe, from Asia, and from Africa. Archaic trends in the older layers of today's Italian folksong hint at an Italian, non-Greek heritage, be it Etruscan or otherwise, and the chant of the Catholic Church, grown in Roman times on Italian soil, must hold Italian elements. We do not know the ancient musical language of Italy. But we must not allow the Greek terminology in which the Roman theorists explained the music they heard to deceive us. The idea that the incomparably gifted peoples of Italy availed themselves of the decaying music of Greece for five hundred years without any positive contribution of their own seems absurd.

READING

(*Unfortunately, this list is limited to the author's books.*) *The Rise of Music in the Ancient World*, New York, 1943. *World History of the Dance*, New York, 1937. *The Commonwealth of Art*, New York, 1946. *The History of Musical Instruments*, New York, 1940. *Rhythm and Tempo*, New York, 1953.

4

THE EARLY MIDDLE AGES

UP TO A.D. 1000

A VITAL JEWISH HERITAGE in early Christian music has become so evident in the past few decades that the scholarly world is inclined to see the principal sources of Catholic music in the cantillation of the Synagogue.

The first three facts to capture the attention are: that the earliest Christian congregations developed within the Synagogue; that they kept the Jewish cantor as their *psalmista*; and that the early liturgy of the Christians, which also took over the thrice Holy, *Kadosh Kadosh Kadosh*, as the *Sanctus Sanctus Sanctus*, and the Benediction or Graces, *Baruh atā Adonaj*, as the *Gratias agimus tibi*, *Domine*, lived mainly on Jewish psalms. To this day, the so-called psalm tones of the Church, that is, the melodic formulas on which the psalms are chanted, have the closest parallels in the liturgy of oriental Jews.

The late Abraham Z. Idelsohn was even able to show that a good number of Catholic melodies still exist in the liturgy of those oriental Jews who had lost contact with the Palestinian homeland after the Babylonian Exile (597 B.C.) and, living in pagan (later Muhammedan) surroundings, were never in touch with Christian communities. These melodies must have lived in Israel before the destruction of the Temple.

Another traceable source of Christian melody was Hellenic music. Of its relics, one from Oxyrhynchos in Egypt, written on papyrus in the third century A.D., is in itself a Christian hymn. Of the other ten melodies, no less than three are claimed to have been converted into Catholic tunes: the delightful *Skolion* of Seíkilos into the Palm Sunday antiphon *Hosanna filio David*; the Hymn to the Sun by Mesomedes into an *Alleluia* jubilus; and the Hymn to Nemesis, also by Mesomedes, into a *Kyrie rex genitor*.

41

But this claim is misleading. The very fact that no less than three out of ten preserved melodies show a close relationship to later Christian melodies is against all laws of probability. Such coincidence could be acceptable only if Greece—which after all boasted of the eastern origin of her music—also had the oriental concept of those melodic patterns that the Hindus call *rāgas* and the Arabs, *maqamāt* (*cf.* page 18). This would mean that there was not just one individual Skolion, composed by Seíkilos, or one Hymn to the Sun, composed by Mesomedes, but many similar melodies, in which the personal contribution of the composer was limited to minor details without affecting the general line of the pattern.

Actually, no modern music historian admits a decisive influence of Greek on Christian music.

However, it cannot be doubted that important contributions came from Greece as much as from other non-Jewish countries. Even in the earliest time of Christendom, the apostolic mission among the pagans must necessarily have opened the Jewish-born liturgy to gentile influences; the newly converted heathen, in Egypt, Palestine, Syria, Asia Minor, Greece, and Italy, must at least have provided their national manners of singing, if not actual melodies of their own.

This must have been the case particularly in the improvisations, which were a recognized privilege granted to the cantors and also to certain laymen who had the gift of praising God in sudden inspiration. God-possessed improvisations, to be sure, could not create a new and Christian musical style; they were adaptations of melody patterns from their native environment. Whoever has witnessed such outbursts in the Holy Week at Seville in our own days must realize that the rapt *saettas*, which then spring up in the streets before the sacred images, are truly Andalusian and nothing else.

The absorption of so many different national styles in one homogeneous Catholic style was only possible because the countries around the eastern Mediterranean had musical idioms that, in all their diversity, were comparatively close to each other. True, we do not know much of the tunes once sung all over that enormous area. But in return, we have one testimony that rarely deceives—the instruments. There are the significant double-oboes, in use from Persia to Egypt and Rome. And there is, as the second common instrument of that province, the lyre, which the Nubians on the upper Nile still play in the curious fashion of the Greeks some thousand years ago. Of vocal music, we know one fact of particular significance for early Christian music: antiphonal singing in two responding choruses was practised all the way between Mesopotamia and Libya on the African coast.

Of paramount interest, from this viewpoint, is the report of the Greek historian Herodotos in the fifth century B.C. that "the Egyptians have, with other curious pieces, a certain melody, which is also sung in Phoenicia, Cyprus, and elsewhere, but differently named in each of these countries. It is quite similar to the tune that the Greeks have known under the name of Linos. I wonder whence they got the Linos song, as I wonder about so many things in Egypt. For it seems to me that it has been in use from the oldest times."

The common musical language of the eastern Mediterranean widens the soil from which the early Christian song could draw its sap. Growth and final unification, however, can hardly be thought of without the specifically Roman, Italian dialect of this common language.

ALL ANCIENT CHRISTIAN MUSIC was vocal. "We need one instrument: the peaceful word of adoration, not harps or drums or pipes or trumpets," said St. Clement of Alexandria around 200 A.D.

This peaceful word of adoration has been performed by officiating priests, by professional solo singers or *cantores*, by the choir or *schola*, and by the congregation. Women, originally admitted, were excluded from the choirs in A.D. 578, except, of course, in convents.

All liturgical singing of the Catholic Church has been known under the names of *chant*, *chorale*, and *plainsong*, whatever its form or style.

Two basic types appear from the very beginning: *accentus* and *concentus*. The former term denotes the monotonous psalmody of the priest; *concentus*, on the contrary, is the freer melody of the choir and the soloists. Both can be 'direct,' that is, all choir or all solo, or else 'antiphonal' or 'responsorial.' In the (true) antiphony, two half-choruses alternate; in the responses, an answering chorus—usually the congregation—interrupts the priest or the soloist. However, the so-called *antiphon* in the liturgy has greatly lost the antiphonal, alternating character and is direct.

The musical liturgy of the Catholic Church consists of Masses and Offices.

The Mass, as the central ceremony, is the celebration of the eucharist, that is, the Sacrament of the Body and the Blood of Christ. Its words took centuries to develop, and its music, a thousand years. Since it was still incomplete in the tenth century, it will be described in the following chapter.

Offices, or Canonical Hours, are held eight times a day under the names of (1) Matins, (2) Lauds, (3) Prime, (4) Terce, (5) Sext, (6) None, (7) Vespers, and (8) Complin(e).

Three main forms to be sung in the Offices are psalmody, Magnificat, and hymns.

A complete psalm is preceded by a choral antiphon. The psalm itself is recited by the priest according to one of the eight 'psalm-tones,' which, complying with one of the eight Church modes each (*cf.* below), provide for every double-verse of the text a similar melody: an ascending initial, a middle, a descending final formula of a few notes each, and between them only one monotonous, ever-repeated note, the *tenor* or *tuba*. When the priest has recited all the verses of a psalm, the chorus repeats the antiphon. In the interest of coherence, the end of the psalm is expected to prepare the re-entry of the choral part. To this end, most of the eight psalm-tones have a number of exchangeable concluding formulas or *differentiae*. The prayer books omit the psalm of the priest and print the framing antiphon only once. But they add the appropriate *differentia* with the baffling text *euouae*. This cryptic symbol is taken from the last words of the Minor Confession of Faith, *Gloria patri et filio . . . sEcUlOrUm AmEn*, which concludes every psalm in the Catholic liturgy (plate V).

The Magníficat, one of the so-called canticles, is Mary's praise of God when she learns that Jesus will be born from her womb: *Magníficat ánima méa Dóminum*—My soul doth magnify the Lord, and my spirit hath rejoiced in God my Savior (St. Luke 1:46–55). It is sung at Vespers in a psalmodic style by alternating choruses in true antiphony.

Hymns in praise of God are, on the contrary, freely invented, not taken from the Scriptures. They also differ in the strictness of their rhythms and easily caught up tunes. Most follow the simple, popular pattern of four trochees or iambs, such as *Crúx fidélis ínter ómnes* or *Deús creátor ómniúm*. They are, and probably always were, sung in strong—weak, not in long—short, patterns. One of the greatest hymns, the *Te Deum laudamus* (Thee, God, we praise), or shortly *Te Deum*, has generally been attributed to Saint Ambrose (333–397), bishop of

Milan, but was not composed by him. The fact is true, however, that the Church is indebted to him for introducing the oriental hymn to the liturgy as an entirely novel feature.

Although the hymns have been kept, that part of the *Ambrosian Chant* which takes its texts from the Scriptures has survived only in the cathedral of Milan. Everywhere else, its florid, exuberant cantillation has yielded to the less oriental *Gregorian Chant*, called for Saint Gregory I, the Great, Pope of Rome from 590 to 604. Gregory is no longer credited with composing melodies himself, but he certainly was the energetic organizer and world-wide unifier of the liturgical melodies.

If the Gregorian version was able to conquer its rival versions, the Ambrosian chant in Milan, the Gallican in France, and the Mozarabic in Spain, it was unable to keep its own tradition. This loss was hardly due to a nascent polyphony, which demanded mutual adaptation of the concurring voice parts and hence some sacrifices of their identity. It rather occurred under the influence of totally different rhythmical concepts outside the chant. As early as the eleventh century, the distinction of syllables long and short had become uncertain in the liturgy and was abandoned more and more, since even notation was too vague for keeping such a distinction alive.

NOTATION in the early Middle Ages was, from the ninth century on, preponderantly 'neumatic' (from Greek *neuma*, 'nod'). It depicted, in characteristic dots and dashes, hooks and flourishes, the essential melodic steps and combinations of steps that formed a melody, as:

punctum	single note
virga	single note
pes or *podatus*	up
scándicus	up-up
clivis	down
clímacus	down-down
tórculus	up-down
porrectus	down-up
scándicus flexus	up-up-down
porrectus flexus	down-up-down
tórculus resupinus	up-down-up
pes sub punctis	up-down-down, etc.

There also were neumes to indicate *tremolo* and other manners of singing (e.g., *quilisma*). Plate II shows neumes above the syllables in a gradual (cf. p. 59) of the twelfth century.

The weak point of the neumatic script was its inability to mark individual pitches or time values. A *scándicus* would indicate that two upward steps were required, but would not say on what note the singer had to start, how large the steps should be, and how long the three individual notes were. The neumes, therefore, were useless except for vocal music, in which the pitches were regulated by tradition while the rhythm was oratorical, without meter or time.

However, the tempo and even the intensity were for a time denoted in the so-called Romanian letters, allegedly of the eighth century, with, for example, *b* standing for *bene* or much, *c* for *celériter* or quickly, *e* for *expectare* or hesitate, *f* for *frangore* or fortissimo.

Later, in the tenth century, the south of Europe began to space the neumes, that is, to place them in the modern way at different heights according to their pitches. Indeed, the end of the century prepared the way for the later staff by introducing one single red reference line for *f*, which left the other notes at some undetermined distance above or below.

While the distances from note to note thus became increasingly certain in later manuscripts, the time values—long and short—were left as doubtful as ever. As a consequence, the rhythm of Gregorian melodies is still an open question and has been the object of bitter controversy. The victorious interpretation, today compulsory in all churches, is the one of the Benedictines in the French monastery of Solesmes. It gives in principle the value of one eighth note to every single symbol, but allows the voice to dwell on accented syllables and to stretch the final notes of a phrase or 'distinction,' right before the vertical dash or *divisio* that serves as a caesura.

CHURCH MODES. The Gregorian Chant or plainsong, derived from oriental and Mediterranean melodies, is inevitably based on their characteristic modal principle. Every melody is expected to comply with a certain form of the octave—a Church or ecclesiastical mode—which differs from all the other Church modes in the arrangement of the five tones and the two semitones. In the first mode, conveniently represented as the (white-key) octave on *D*, the semitone (*E–F*) occurs in the second place; in the third mode, represented as the octave on *E*, the same semitone occurs in the first place. A clarifying diagram will show how this works.

Four of the eight Church modes, the odd-numbered first, third, fifth, and seventh, are called *authentic*; the other four, the even-numbered second, fourth, sixth, and eighth, are called *plagal*. Authentic, like modern, octaves stand on the lowest note or *finalis* and hinge on the fifth or *confinalis* (only the third mode has its confinal on the sixth, in order to avoid the *B*, whose pitch—♭ or ♮—was uncertain. The four plagal modes have the opposite structure: they are a fourth lower than the corresponding authentic modes but hang from the final, which is common to both groups. Each plagal mode, however, has a confinal of its own, independent of the confinal of the corresponding authentic mode (*cf*. diagram).

All Church modes are thought of and represented as white-key scales without sharps or flats. Still, two cases of a special nature ask for a flatted *B*.

One of them occurs in the first mode, on *D*, where for reasons of natural singing any *B* leading down to *A* must be flatted. The old Latin rule reads:

> *Una nota super la*
> *Semper est canendum fa.*

Which in English might be:

> Single notes on top of *la*
> Always must be sung as *fa.*

The syllable *fa*, as the following section will show, forms a semitone with its lower neighbor wherever it stands.

The other case occurs in the fifth mode, on *F*, where again the *B* is left natural when it leads upwards, but is flatted when it leads downwards.

The notes, and therewith the ranges, of the Church melodies are purely relative, not representing absolute pitches. In the first place, the homophonic, one-voice character of the chant makes any definite pitch unnecessary; in the second place, the different tessituras of priests, of cantors and choruses, of boys and men and nuns make any definite pitch impossible; and in the third place, the conception of absolute pitch was unknown in the Middle Ages. The Dominican Jerome of Moravia (thirteenth century) expressly wanted everybody to sing at a medium pitch, since getting too low meant ululation and getting too high meant screaming. Besides, even before A.D. 1000, the liturgy asked for a pitch higher on certain occasions than on others.

There is a final point to discuss. From the tenth century onward, some scholarly monks compared the Church modes to the modes of the ancient Greeks and gave them the following names, which, though little used in the Church, are to this day alive in the language of counterpoint students:

First:	Dorian	Second:	Hypodorian
Third:	Phrygian	Fourth:	Hypophrygian
Fifth:	Lydian	Sixth:	Hypolydian
Seventh:	Mixolydian	Eighth:	Hypomixolydian

Unfortunately, the labels were misplaced. The first mode, on *D*, is related to Phrygian, not to Dorian; and the third mode, the other way around, to Dorian, not to Phrygian. The medieval monks were well aware that Hypodorian had had the lowest and Mixolydian the highest place in the system. But they did not understand that the Grecian scales had been higher or lower only *qua* transpositions of the standard scales, such transposition showing merely within the untransposed central octave as a mode (*cf.* page 31). They misunderstood it so much the more as they themselves had neither sharps nor the conception of key. Owing to this misinterpretation, they shifted their scales *and* changed their modal arrangement.

T ROPES AND SEQUENCES. Where the sacred texts depart from the grandeur of Biblical texts and liturgical formulas to establish a personal tie between the divine and man, the singer abandons the unemotional atmosphere of the plainsong and seeks a way out into the freedom of inspired, subjective melody. Although the priests, anxious to protect the suprapersonal character of the service, have always restrained the autonomy of religious poets and singers, they gave way— both in the Christian and in the Jewish liturgy—in one episode of the cult. The cantor, intoning the *Alleluia* (from Hebrew *hallelujáh*, praise ye the Lord) was allowed to effuse his exaltation in free, enthusiastic melodies and to enrapture priest and congregation in his godly *Jubilus*.

This free coloratura style has often been called 'neumatic.' The word should be correctly spelled *pneumatic*. It has nothing to do with *neuma*, 'sign,' but derives from *pneuma*, 'breath.'

The flowing alleluias that the early Gregorian chant had taken from the Jewish liturgy proved to be a precious but onerous heirloom. Products of a mature oriental art, the endless coloraturas on the one concluding vowel -*a* were entirely foreign to the voices, technique, and taste of Western and Central Europe.

As a consequence, the monks in Gallic and Germanic lands began to tamper with the traditional melodies in order to make them subservient to the domestic principle of syllabic singing—one syllable for each note. The first variation was to invent additional texts on which to sing the endless chains of notes. But this was only the beginning. Within a short time, the Gregorian alleluia melodies yielded to sharply outlined, rhythmical tunes of western cast, which were, on festive occasions, performed by powerful choirs of boys and men and often in solemn antiphony.

These pieces were called by an older name for the Jubilus: *sequentia*. Its usual written abbreviation *pro sã*, which means that the following passage should be sung in place of the Jubilus (*pro sequentia*), is said to be responsible for the second name of the sequence: *prosa*. But this etymology is rather unsatisfactory.

The earliest sequences of which we know belong to the ninth century and appear to have had their home in French monasteries. From there, they were carried to the great Benedictine abbeys on and near the Lake of Constance, St. Gall and the Reichenau. Particularly, one of the outstanding men of St. Gall, Brother Notker the Stammerer (*c*. 830–912), has been credited with composing sequences. But none of those connected with his name can actually be traced to him, and he himself claims only to have had a hand in writing texts.

The form of the sequence seems to stem from the Celtic *lay*, with which it shared the main principle of composition: that every two consecutive lines of the text follow the same melody, *AA BB CC DD*, and so on. This would be only natural. The French monasteries in which the sequence originated stood on ancient Celtic ground, the abbeys on the Lake of Constance had been founded by Irish monks, and the oldest known musician of St. Gall, Moengal or Marcellus (*c*. 860), had come from Ireland like Saint Gall himself. The Celtic theory does not contradict the opinion of the late Dr. Peter Wagner that the sequence was related to the form of Byzantine hymns. For the Irish monks were the chief apostles in the West of Byzantine lore and tradition.

Hundreds of sequences were written and sung in the centuries after A.D. 1000, but the Council of Trent (1545–1563) intervened with what seemed to the clergy to be an abuse and allowed only four to be sung:

Dies irae (Day of wrath), composed in the thirteenth century, in the Mass for the Dead.
Lauda Sion Salvatorem (Praise, O Zion, the Savior), on *Corpus Christi*.
Veni Sancte Spiritus (Come Holy Ghost), on Pentecost.
Victimae paschalis laudes (Praise of the Easter victim), on Easter.

The year 1727 restored a fifth sequence, the *Stabat Mater dolorosa* (The dolorous mother stood), today ascribed in Saint Bonaventura (1221–1274) rather than to Jacopone da Todi, on Friday before Palm Sunday and on the third Sunday in September.

While the Council was lenient in the case of the sequences, it did away strictly with the tropes.

Tropes had the same principle as the sequence: syllabic texts were invented to carry ticklish melismatic passages. In several episodes of the liturgy, the text was so short that the melody, in way of compensation, distended every syllable in an elaborate melisma or coloratura. This antisyllabic attitude, again, presented often insurmountable difficulties to northern singers. As a consequence, they tried to make the melisma syllabic by the introduction of filling words. Good examples are the various appropriate expletives, such as *ineffabilis et interminabilis, immense et omnipotens,* that they added to the opening section of the Mass with its mere six syllables, *Kyrie eleison.*

Some of these tropes overpassed the goal, grew to considerable length and importance, and disrupted both the liturgical text and its melody. They became one of the most dangerous loopholes through which the trends and strains of secular music invaded the strict cantillation of Gregory. Indeed, as early a man as Notker's contemporary, Tuotilo of St. Gall, is reported to have accompanied the tropes—lo and behold—on a stringed instrument.

But there also were tropes which, more or less independent of the regular words and melodies of the liturgy, sprang from the urge to make a new contribution to the inherited stock.

Some of these latter tropes, written for Christmas or Easter in the form of question and answer assigned to different singers, led to the liturgical drama and eventually to the oratorio. At Winchester Cathedral, for instance, the Easter trope *Quem quaéritis* (Whom are you seeking?) was, in the tenth century, actually staged: "While the third lesson is being chanted, let one of four brethren approach the sepulchre and sit there quietly with a palm in his hand. While the third respond is chanted, let three brethren follow and let them, stepping delicately as those who seek something, approach the sepulchre. These things are done in imitation of the angel sitting in the monument and the women with spices coming to anoint the body of Jesus. When he who sits beholds the three approach him, let him begin in a dulcet voice of medium pitch to sing *Quem quaeritis.* And when he has sung it to the end, let the three reply in unison *Ihesu Nazarenum . . .*" (Extracted from E. K. Chambers' translation of the original Latin text in his *Mediaeval Stage.* The whole passage is reprinted in Gustave Reese, *Music in the Middle Ages,* page 194 f.)

These liturgical dramas came to a peak much later in the Passion plays, when on four days of Easter week the tragic end of Christ was acted according to each of the Evangelists, one priest with a lower voice representing Jesus, another one, with a medium voice, the narrator, and a third, with a higher voice, the Jews. The three singers performed in plain cantillation without any accompaniment. Therefore, this kind of Passion is called "chorale" or *plainsong Passion*, in contradistinction to the *polyphonic Passion* of the Later Ages.

Byzantine chant. A few words must be said on the liturgical singing in Byzantium, the eastern part of the Mediterranean, which Emperor Constantin the Great had united as an East Roman Empire in A.D. 330 with Constantinople (today Istambul) as the capital. The significance of this singing is that Byzantine music is the common ancestor of all the musical liturgies of the Orthodox East-European Churches—Russian, Serbian, Bulgarian, Rumanian, and Greek.

Less than forty years after the foundation of Constantinople, the Council of Laodicea (A.D. 367) prohibited the participation both of instruments and of congregations in the liturgy. Orthodox music has been purely vocal.

Chiefly modeled on Jewish patterns, the chant of the Eastern Church was similar to the cantillation of the Western Church and, in a related way, found its melodic organization in *echoi* (sing. *echos*), which, however, were melody patterns like the Arabian *maqamāt* rather than merely modal scales. But its texts were Greek, independent of psalms or other scriptural poems, and shaped in metrical forms like hymns.

The types in which the chant appeared were first, in the fourth and fifth centuries, *troparia* (sing. *troparion*), or insets between the recitation of psalms, and, in the seventh century, *kontákia* (sing. *kontákion*), or lengthy odes consisting of a short proem and from twenty to thirty stanzas with refrains. In the eighth century, both the *troparia* and the *kontákia* were abandoned in favor of the so-called *kanon*, or cycle of nine hymns, with the same melody (*heirmós*) repeated in each of the stanzas.

Our knowledge of the oldest orthodox music, however, is limited. The Byzantine neumatic notation of the first millennium is undecipherable, and the next of kin of the Byzantine chant—the Armenian, Coptic, Ethiopian, and Syrian cantillations of that time—have left no notations at all.

Whatever their similarities and whatever their differences were, they have one negative fact in common: they never developed into polyphony. The art of heaping and weaving several voice parts was a typically western achievement.

THE ONLY POLYPHONIC FORM in early medieval times was the *diaphony* or 'singing apart,' oftener called the *órganum* (a name to be accented on the first syllable). It was first described in the ninth century (though *not* by the monk Hucbald), but seems to have existed a long time before in folk music, in which art it survives to this day in Iceland. Indeed, there is a strong possibility that it was used in the Church itself, at least in the seventh century. A group of liturgical singers then had the title of *paraphonistae*, the term *paraphonia* denoting a fifth or fourth consonance.

Órgana were performed by soloists in alternation with the plainsong cantillation of the chorus.

There were two forms, one strict, one free. In either one, an evenly and very slowly progressing liturgical melody, the *vox principalis*, was accompanied below by a *vox organalis*. Later terminology called the *principalis* a *tenor*, or sustained, part, or else a *cantus firmus*, that is, a fixed melody taken from the Gregorian chant to serve as the musical and spiritual backbone of a polyphonic composition.

In the stricter *órganum*, the *organalis* accompanied in solemn fifth or fourth parallels—*paraphoniae*—from the beginning to the end. On festive occasions, the larger cathedrals and abbeys would enrich this simple parallel by doubling either voice, the lower one at the octave above, and the higher one at the octave below, with the result of a triple parallel in piled-up octaves, fifths, and fourths.

The freer *órganum* started in unison. After the first note, the accompanying organal voice marked time by repeating the initial note until the principal voice was a fourth away. From then on, it followed in parallel fourths until, at the end, the two voices reconverged to unison.

In either form of *órganum*, the notes of the two voices coincided strictly. They stood note against note or, in Latin terminology, *punctus contra punctum* (whence our word *counterpoint*, although the note-against-note form is today only one of its subdivisions or species).

The origin of the name *órganum* is an open question. A connection with the organ has been considered, with the idea that this instrument might have played the organal voice, but recent scholars reject this suggestion as unfounded. However, this rejection should be revised in face of the decisive fact that the medieval organ played in octave and fifth parallels exclusively.

The medieval organ was indeed what modern terminology calls a mixture. The operation of each individual key, or slider, as we should rather say, was answered, not by one pipe, but by two or a whole rank or compound of pipes. Such a compound consisted of the note requested, its octave, double, triple, and maybe quadruple octave, and of fifths between several of them. The famous organ of A.D. 980 in the monastery at Winchester, England, had ten such pipes to each slider, and later medieval organs, up to twenty. No stop existed to disconnect, say, the double octaves or the triple octaves. All larger organs played in multiple parallels of fifths and octaves throughout. Small wonder that contemporaries compared their sound to the roar of thunder.

How tenacious this principle was appears from the fact that in Italy such stopless mixture organs were still built as late as the middle of the fifteenth century.

THE STRUGGLE FOR ORDER. Europe had joined the evolution of music as a primitive country, without notation, without a system of any kind, without regulation. Everybody, juggler, bard, or peasant, fiddled and sang to his heart's content, and it did not matter whether he took the whole- and semitones a trifle larger or smaller. He probably did not even know what whole- and semitones were. But when people began to sing in counterpoint, when organs, chimes, and harps had to be tuned, tradition and personal taste were no longer sufficient. As the latest of the great civilizations, the West had to do what the Orient had done millenniums before: proceed to a lawful system of steps and intervals, of con- and dissonances.

In such an attempt, the musical ear could hardly be accepted as a reliable guide and still less as an unbiased judge. Medieval man trusted authority, not his senses. Here too, as everywhere else, he effaced himself behind the authority of the ancients, Greeks and Romans. But alas, the Greeks had had no less than eight quite different sizes of thirds and twenty different seconds. Which were the 'correct' ones?

In eight or nine hundred years, the question was asked again and again and never answered for good and all. The scholars reckoned and reasoned, quoted and speculated, and still no final solution was found.

At least, a few kinds of instruments with fairly preservable pitches were built, to help in establishing standards and to facilitate the training of musicians.

The first of these instruments was the *monochord*, described in the musical bible of the Middle Ages, the five books *De Musica*, in which Theodorich's unfortunate chancellor Boethius had, around A.D. 500, given a last *résumé* of the ancient theory of music. The monochord had a long and narrow sound box with a single string under which a movable bridge could be shifted along a graduated scale, thus allowing the tester to read immediately the mathematical ratio for each position of the stopping bridge (*cf.* plate XV in the author's *History of Musical Instruments* on p. 256).

A second instrument was the bell chime, called, in the plural form, *cýmbala*, a set of tuned bells on a horizontal bar, to be struck with one or two hammers. A third instrument was the organ.

However, the naïve formulas of medieval bell founders betray all the desperate uncertainty in the struggle for scales and intervals. As late as the twelfth century, one of them recommended choosing an arbitrary weight of metal to start with and just calling it *C*, to add an eighth of this weight for *D*, and eighth of the new weight for *E*, and so on—without realizing that the weight alone was not the only agent involved. And in a similar, insufficient way, the organ builders determined the lengths of their pipes from the ratios of the intervals desired, but failed to take the equally important diameters into account. Thus, even the instruments were doubtful helps, and the situation would have been hopeless had not the human musical mind, as a rule, emended and adjusted the questionable message received by the ear. For music is after all a case of psychology, not of physics—of mental interpretation, not of the imperfect sounding mediums.

A long, long road was still ahead.

Secular music, which probably found its way into the liturgy via sequence and trope, has of necessity a more than modest place in this survey: contemporary sources, written by clerics for clerics, did not condescend to mention it; and folk music itself, depending on oral tradition, seldom availed itself of notation. All conclusions must be drawn from indirect evidences—from a few songs of the time preserved in later notation, from the popular music of jugglers and minstrels from ages after A.D. 1000, and from the folksongs of today, with their amazing tenacity.

All these evidences bear witness to one fact: the non-Mediterranean secular music of Europe did not follow the tetrachordal and modal style of the Church (except in cases of wilful imitation). Instead, it organized its tunes in thirds: their framework consisted of one third, or of two, three, four, and even, as in today's folksongs of Iceland and Scandinavia, of five thirds heaped above one another. Such chains complement each two consecutive thirds to form a fifth. Therefore, the thirds are major and minor in regular alternation.

The resulting chains were not scales, but loose organizations, pieced together out of single elements without any thought given to higher units beyond the fifth. The decisive change forward came from the organizing power of the octave, of which, as the evidence shows, the northerners became increasingly aware. For we find tertial chains in which the third of the thirds, a seventh away from the groundtone (as C–E, E–G, G–B), was sung but was at once pulled up to make an octave. Wherever this happened, the third-fifth-octave skeleton of later western music was established. Where the major third was in evidence, as in the chain F–A–C, the major mode was the necessary outcome. A chain with the minor third in evidence, as D–F–A, led to the minor mode.

Harmony, too, is, at least partially, an outgrowth of the tertial chains. Whenever a musical style demands accompanying notes, it prefers them at intervals similar to those that it favors as melodic steps. In other words, the intervals used in coincidence agree with the intervals used in succession. Thus, the tertial melody of the western past begot our triadic harmony.

The characteristic alternation between the tonic and the dominant chord in our harmony is, in a similar way, prepared by the alternation of such triads as successive steps in the medieval chains of thirds, as C–E–G and G–B–D.

READING

Gustave Reese, *Music in the Middle Ages*, New York, 1940: Sections 3–9. Curt Sachs, *The History of Musical Instruments*, New York, 1940: Chapter 14. Curt Sachs, *The Rise of Music in the Ancient World*, New York, 1943: Section Seven. Curt Sachs, *World History of the Dance*, New York, 1937: pages 248 ff. Curt Sachs, *The Commonwealth of Art*, New York, 1946: Chapter 3. Curt Sachs, *Rhythm and Tempo*, New York, 1953. Egon Wellesz, *A History of Byzantine Music*, Oxford, 1949.

5

THE ROMANESQUE PERIOD

A.D. 1000–1150

THE MASS, the central ceremony of the Catholic Church, was completed in the eleventh century by the addition of the *Gloria* and the *Credo* sections. Since then, it has followed this plan: While the priest betakes himself to the altar, the singers begin the *antiphona ad introitum* or simply Introit (entry). This is sung by one singer on weekdays and minor feasts, by two singers on Sundays and other feasts, and, where possible, by four singers at solemn occasions. An asterisk in the prayer books marks where the chorus takes over.

The Mass itself has five principal sections, called after their initial words *Kyrie, Gloria, Credo, Sanctus,* and *Agnus.* The first section, a prayer for mercy, consists of nine invocations in Greek, the language of the Eastern Church: three *Kyrie eleison* (Lord, have mercy upon us), three *Christe eleison* (Christ, have mercy upon us), and again three *Kyrie eleison.*

Thereupon the priest intones the *Gloria in excelsis Deo* (Glory be to God on high), and the choir continues *Et in terra pax homínibus bonae voluntatis* (And peace on earth to men of good will). The Gloria is followed by an *Epistle* from the Apostles and a *Lesson* from the Gospels.

The third main section opens with the priest's intonation of the confession of faith, *Credo in unum Deum* (I believe in one God), and is taken up by the chorus on the following words *Patrem omnipotentem* (The omnipotent Father). It includes the sections *Et incarnatus est* (And was incarnated) and *Crucifixus* (Crucified), which are often independent movements in polyphonic settings of the Mass.

The *Offertory* and, as a prayer of thanks, the *Preface* are heard while the holy wafer is being prepared. The Preface leads without a break into the *Sanctus Sanctus Sanctus* (Holy, Holy, Holy) with the *Osanna*, or *Hosanna in excelsis*, and the *Benedictus qui venit in nómine Dómini* (Blessed be he who cometh in the name of the Lord); and the threefold *Agnus Dei qui tollis peccata mundi* (Lamb of God who beareth the sins of the world) concludes the Mass, but has the *Communion* as an epilogue after the partaking of the wafer.

At last, the priest dismisses the congregation by chanting the words *Ite missa est* with the choral response *Deo gratias* (Go, [the congregation] is dismissed. Thanks to God). It is from the word *missa* that the Mass has its name.

The plan just outlined shows the Ordinary or skeleton of the Mass for almost all occasions where a Mass is said or sung. For each of its sections, the liturgy provides a selection of melodies; in other words, there is not just one Kyrie or one Gloria melody, but quite an impressive number of them.

Right here, the student should realize that the later polyphonic 'concert' Masses, such as Bach's B minor Mass or Beethoven's *Missa solemnis*, are not suitable for liturgical use because (1) they are too long, (2) they repeat the words of the text, and (3) they give to the chorus and orchestra the incipits of the Gloria and of the Credo— *Gloria in excelsis Deo* and *Credo in unum Deum*—which the liturgy assigns to the intoning priest before the chorus takes over with *Et in terra pax* and *Patrem omnipotentem*.

The so-called Proper of the Mass, as against the Ordinary, provides, for every day and for every special occasion, exchangeable parts either to be added to the Ordinary or else to replace unsuitable parts of the Ordinary. The Introit at the beginning of the Mass, for instance, is exchangeable; but the two principal variable sections are inserted between Lesson and Epistle. One is the responsorial and highly florid *Gradual*, and the other, the *Alleluia*, a dithyrambic praise of God with an extended *jubilus* coloratura on the ending vowel *a*. Where the occasion is too mournful to admit an *alleluia*, a *tract* in the second or eighth mode (on *A* or *D*) is sung in direct psalmody without choral responses.

The best known of these mournful Masses—and one particularly important for music students in view of later polyphonic compositions, by Mozart, Berlioz, Verdi and many others—is the *Missa pro defunctis* or Mass for the Dead, which must be sung at every funeral service (*cf.* page 61). Its Introit is a prayer for eternal rest, *Requiem aeternam dona eis* (whence the short-name of the Mass: *Requiem*). The *Gloria* as well as the *Credo* are omitted, and the *Alleluia* is replaced by the sequence of the Last Judgment, *Dies irae, dies illa* / *Solvet saeclum in favilla* (Doomsday, day of terror / Grinds to dust the world of error). The first page of the Mass for the Dead in the official Roman version is reproduced on page 61.

Of the many liturgical books that the Catholic Church has printed for laymen and priests:

> The Kyrial contains the Ordinary of the Mass.
> The Missal and the Gradual (plate II) contain both the
>   Ordinary and the Proper of the Mass.
> The Breviary and the Antiphonal contain the Offices.
> The Responsorial contains the liturgy for Matins.
> The Vesperal is for Vespers.
> The Processional is for processions.
> The Pontifical is used for bishops' functions.

The *Liber Usualis*, a more recent, comprehensive book of the Catholic Church, is the most important for the music student, combining the Gradual and the Antiphonal, Masses and Offices.

B EFORE the eleventh century had reached its middle, three outstanding clerics presented the musical liturgy with a few pieces so full of beauty, ecstasy, and power that the Church has kept them to this day.

The most remarkable among these masters was Heriman the Cripple, or, latinized, Hermannus Contractus (1013–1054) of the monastery Reichenau on the Lake of Constance. Giving the most sublime expression to the newly sprung-up worship of the Virgin, he created the three antiphons known as *B.M.V.*, or *Beatae Mariae Virginis*, namely:

> *Alma redemptoris mater.*
> *Ave praeclara maris stella.*
> *Salve regina misericordiae.*

or, metrically in English:

Missa pro Defunctis.

Intr. VI.

R EQUI- EM * ae-tér- nam do-na e- is Dómi-

ne:. et lux perpé-tu- a lú- ce- at   e-   is. *Ps.* Te de-

cet hymnus De- us in Si- on, et ti-bi reddé-tur vo-tum in Je-rú-

sa-lem: * exáudi o-ra-ti- ó-nem me- am, ad te omnis ca-ro

vé-ni- et.   Ré-qui- em.

VI.

K Y- RI- E * e-   lé- i-son. *iij.* Chri-ste   e-   lé- i-son. *iij.*

Ký- ri- e e-   lé- i-son. *ij.* Ký-ri- e,   * e-   lé- i·son.

Intr. stands for *Introitus*; VI denotes the sixth Church mode or Hypolydian, with C–F–C as the skeleton and F as the final.

The clef makes the fourth line c. The syllable *re* has a *sálicus*; the syllable
qui, a *punctum*; the syllable *em* a *punctum*. The following asterisk marks
the entry of the chorus. *Ae* has a *sálicus*; the syllable *ter*, a compound of a
clivis and a *porrectus*; the syllable *nam*, a *clivis*. The following vertical dash
marks a "minor" division; the through dash after *Dómine*, a "major" division.
Ps. marks the beginning of a psalm verse to be sung by soloists. The note-like
signs at the ends of the staff lines are *custodes*, or "directs," which warn the
singers of the first note on the following staff.

The flat at the beginning of the *Kyrie* indicates flatting the subsequent B.
It is not a key signature. The symbols *ij* and *iij* denote one and two *repetitions*.

> Queenly mother of the Savior.
> Hail, brightest star upon the ocean.
> Homage to thee, oh queen of compassion.

Throughout the later centuries, numberless polyphonic compositions based on these melodies have proved the timeless grandeur of Heriman's work.

The second of these great composers was Bruno, Count of Egisheim in Alsace—thereafter (1048–1054) Pope Saint Leo IX—who created an ecstatic far-flung *Gloria in excelsis Deo*, which the Church has listed as the *Gloria I* (in the eighth, Hypomixolydian, mode) among the *Cantus ad libitum*. The reader finds it in the American edition of the *Liber Usualis* on page 81.

The third composer, creator of the granitic, hymn-like Easter sequence *Victimae paschalis laudes*, is supposed to be the Burgundian Wipo (d. c. 1048), chaplain to the German Emperor Henry III.

Still, these three great names and their work have been overshadowed by the contributions to theory, of the same age, by Guido of Arezzo.

SOLMISATION. Guido of Arezzo, who lived from about 995 to 1050, was a Benedictine monk of outstanding merits. Although he cannot claim the total of all the musical inventions that later centuries lavishly ascribed to him, he composed an influential book on music, the *Micrólogus de disciplína artis músicae*, perfected the staff notation on its way from neumes to plainsong script, and introduced the old oriental solmisation.

Solmisation was a method of singing any melody of the Church on only six syllables—*ut re mi fa sol la*—the two syllables *sol* and *mi* providing the name. The point was that the syllables stood for the notes of the melody according, not to their pitches or absolute position in musical space, but to their relative position. In this, Guido's solmisation was similar to the modern 'movable do' method: the step *mi–fa* invariably denoted a semitone. A singer who memorized some tune with the appropriate syllables could hardly ever be mistaken: the step *mi–fa* was always a semitone, while all the other steps were major seconds.

There was one disconcerting difficulty, though. When a melody exceeded the range of six notes, the set of six syllables was obviously insufficient. It was even misleading when the note *B* had to be flatted —for instance, in the frequent turn *A–Bb–A*, which, according to the very nature and meaning of solmisation, required the syllables *mi–fa* on *A–Bb* just as the preceding part of the melody had needed them on *E–F*.

In order to introduce this second *mi–fa*, the singer held other similar sets of syllables in readiness and 'mutated' from one to another set according to the requirements of his melodies.

Mutation, or melodic modulation, required a kind of marshalling yard where melodies could be shifted from track to track. Such a yard was found in an ingenious system of three overlapping hexachords, or (diatonic) sets of six notes, all similar in structure but different in pitch. Following the major mode, they were sung on the syllables *ut re mi fa sol la*, but started either on *C* as the 'natural' hexachord, or on *F* as the 'soft' hexachord, or on *G* as the 'hard' hexachord.

At first sight, it seems incomprehensible that two sets of notes in exactly the same arrangement should be distinguished as soft and hard. Actually, the two epithets did not derive from distinctive qualities of the hexachords themselves. They alluded rather to the two shapes of the letter *B* which were distinctive of the two hexachords: in the hexachord on *F*, the note *B*, representing the fourth of the scale, had to be flatted and was indicated by a rounded letter *B*, the *B rotundum*. In the hexachord on *G*, on the contrary, the note *B*, representing the major third of the scale, had to be natural and was indicated by an angular letter *B*, the *B quadrum*. The first sign was 'soft,' and the second, 'hard.'

The two forms of the letter *B* have survived; they still exist as the international symbols for flat and natural before the head of a note. And the two Latin names of the hexachords, *molle* and *durum*, or 'soft' and 'hard,' are still extant. The French call a flat *bémol*, the Spaniards *bemol*, and the Italians *bemolle*, and the Spaniards also speak of *becuadrado*. The Germans, on the other hand, call the major and minor modes *dur* and *moll*.

On page 64 is the marshalling yard, with, left and right, the modern letter names of the twenty notes (first column), the ancient letter names without specified octaves (center), and the medieval call-names of the individual notes, composed of their letters and the syllables of the one, two, or three hexachords to which they could belong (last column).

In this marshalling yard, the points could be shifted wherever it seemed practical in order to pass smoothly from hexachord to hexachord. The rule generally, though not always, accepted was to join the new hexachord on its *re* when the melody was *as*cending, and on its *la* when it was *des*cending. Our example, the Introit of the fourth Sunday in Advent, *Rorate coeli*, in the first mode, shows an exception in its first mutation, where the *hexachordum naturale* can obviously not be reached via its *re* and therefore must be joined on its *mi*. More important than this detail is the fact that so short a melody must avail itself of each one of the three hexachords, on account of its extended range as well as of the two different *B*'s that it needs.

e"	E							la	*E la*
d"	D						la	sol	*D la sol*
c"	C						sol	fa	*C sol fa*
b'	B						fa(b)	mi(♮)	*B fa* or *B mi*
a'	A					la	mi	re	*A la mi re*
g'	G					sol	re	ut	*G sol re ut*
f'	F					fa	ut		*F fa ut*
e'	E				la	mi			*E la mi*
d'	D			la	sol	re			*D la sol re*
c'	C			sol	fa	ut			*C sol fa ut*
b	B			fa(b)	mi(♮)				*B fa* or *B mi*
a	A		la	mi	re				*A la mi re*
g	G		sol	re	ut				*G sol re ut*
f	F		fa	ut					*F fa ut*
e	E	la	mi						*E la mi*
d	D	sol	re						*D sol re*
c	C	fa	ut						*C fa ut*
B	B	mi							*B mi*
A	A	re							*A re*
G	T	ut							*Gamma ut*

It now becomes obvious why medieval theory had to use hexachords, not octaves, as in the Church modes themselves. The reason-for-being of solmisation was that *mi–fa* served as a symbol of any semitone, wherever it stood. Therefore, the basic set of syllables would have been useless if it had contained more than one semitone. The maximum length of a one-semitonal stretch was a sixth; and extension upward to what is now *ti* would have left doubtful whether the note *B* had to form a semitone with *A* or with *C*.

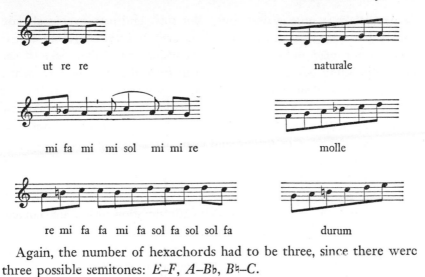

ut re re   naturale

mi fa mi   mi sol   mi mi re   molle

re mi fa fa mi fa sol fa sol sol fa   durum

Again, the number of hexachords had to be three, since there were three possible semitones: E–F, A–Bb, $B\natural$–C.

Guido's 'hand'—prefigured in similar systems of China and India—facilitated correct singing by adding tactile to audible memorization. It consisted of having the right index finger touch appropriate spots of the open left hand, to which the twenty notes of the musical range were allocated in a somewhat perplexing tangle, the lowest *gamma ut* having its place on the tip of the thumb, with the scale progressing down the thumb, across the metacarpus, up the small finger, across the finger tips, down the index, back to the third phalange of the ring-finger, and in an S-curve up to a place in the air above the tip of the middle finger for the highest note *E la*, since there was no space left for it on the nineteen phalanges of the hand. Though confusing rather than helpful, at least from our viewpoint, the Guidonian hand was in use far into the Later Ages as a symbol and sum total of musical pedagogics.

It also fits the interest in practical pedagogy of the eleventh century that, among its numerous treatises, we find an anonymous *vocabularium musicum*—the earliest dictionary of music.

POLYPHONY AND NOTATION.

The polyphonic form used to embellish the liturgy on festive days was still the *órganum*. This form, however, was changing its character thoroughly. We still hear of parallel lines, note against note. But this rigid pattern was already yielding to a freer counterpoint. The *cantus firmus* retreated to the lower voice part and left the more conspicuous higher part to the counterpointing *vox organalis*, which in turn liberated itself from the fetters of parallel motion and showed a growing tendency to answer ascending steps of the *principalis* by descending steps and vice-versa, in what amounted to contrary motion. The *vox organalis* did not hesitate to cross the *cantus firmus*, and even dared to oppose two or more notes against one note of the *cantus firmus*. In other words, the organum was steadily developing from a clumsy parallel setting to what our teachers call the first and second species of counterpoint. Unfortunately, the vagueness of neumatic notation makes any correct transcription of the extant sources quite impossible.

Even contemporaries were not able to achieve exactness and demanded a more reliable script. Heriman the Cripple, already mentioned, complied by adding small letters to indicate the sizes of steps: an *e* for *equisonus*, or unison, an *s* for *semitonium*, a *t* for *tonus*, a *ts* for the minor third (tone plus semitone), a *tt* for the major third (two tones), and so on.

But the pregnant improvement started from the single red reference line for *f*, some time around the year 1000. Not much later, a second, green or yellow line was introduced for the higher *c'*, and Guido of Arezzo is rightly or wrongly said to have developed these beginnings to a four-line staff for *d-f-a-c'*, with the spaces in between left for *e-g-b*.

At the same time, a system of four clefs was ready. A letter C on one of the three upper lines at the beginning of the staff would indicate whether the note *c'* was left on the highest line or else transposed to a lower one when the range of the piece was higher than usual. A fourth clef, a *c* preceded by a kind of note-form, gave *f* its place on the third line and therewith marked a transposition by one line upward.

The four staff lines with their four clefs have been preserved in the Catholic Church to this day.

The use of staff lines implied a special adaptation of the neumes. Simple dashes picturing motion gestures would no longer do. Converted into actual pitch symbols, the neumes were given reinforced endings where they met the lines or spaces of the staff that showed their pitches: head and stem, the *cauda* or tail, became distinctly separate parts of the note. Following local habits of holding the pen, these heads were given either a square form (the so-called Roman) or (plate V) a diamond shape (the Gothic). The *punctum* became a stemless head, and the *virga*, a head with a stem. The other, complex, neumes, in which one stroke of the pen depicted the melodic line of a single step or a group of steps, were kept as *ligatures* of contracted squares and oblique bars. They were used—as they still are in Catholic prayer books—to slur the two or more notes that are to be sung on one syllable of the text.

The notes themselves had been given letter-names as early as the end of antiquity. Only, the letters of the alphabet were not repeated from octave to octave, but continued throughout the range of music, until the modern usage was adopted in the tenth century, if not before. There was a difference, though: the first note of the octave, our modern *C*, was then more logically called *A*; and *B* was what today is *D*. The unfortunate shift to the modern names was caused by the monk Odo of Cluny, who also lived in the tenth century. Ignoring the secular major mode, which was already taking shape, he adapted the *A–G* series to the Church modes, in which not *C*, but *A*, the basis of the second mode or Hypodorian, was the lowest note, and *G*, the octave of the seventh or Mixolydian mode, was the highest one. Unbelievable as it seems, our modern practice is, after a thousand years, still the victim of forces that even then were reactionary.

The Church itself could not but open its gates to the major mode, at least where the liturgy allowed popular melodies to mingle with the Gregorian chant—in the sequence (*cf.* p. 49 ff). A few French sequences of the eleventh century, like *Laetabundus exsultet* and *Gaudete vos fideles*, extant in contemporary manuscripts, are not only marchlike and catchy, but also so definitely in major that they even show the characteristic leading semitone below the tonic, which was far from the modal ideals of the Church.

The only secular music of which we know is a special kind of song, in bloom from the end of the tenth to the twelfth century. Its poets and composers were the *goliards*, or wags—uprooted students and clerics who, gadding about all through the continent, expressed their love of woman, wine, and life, in a curious, half-popular, half-scholarly Latin poetry. Unfortunately, the small amount of preserved melodies is written down in staffless neumes, so that, once more, transcription is unfeasible. Only one of the love songs—*O admirabile Veneris idolum* (tenth century)—exists also in letter notation, which at least reveals a simple repetitive form and unmistakable major mode, without, however, betraying the rhythm.

READING

Gustave Reese, *Music in the Middle Ages*, New York, 1940. Joseph A. Dunney, *The Mass*, New York, 1942. Curt Sachs, *The History of Musical Instruments*, New York, 1940: Chapter 14. Curt Sachs, *World History of the Dance*, New York, 1937: Chapter 7. Curt Sachs, *The Commonwealth of Art*, New York, 1946: Cross Sections 1050 and 1120. Curt Sachs, *Rhythm and Tempo*, New York, 1953.

6

THE EARLY AND CENTRAL GOTHIC PERIODS

1150–1300

TROUBADOURS AND TROUVÈRES. The advent of the troubadours in the last years of the eleventh century marks a decisive change in knightly ideology. From an exclusive perfection in the rougher arts of fighting, hunting, and drinking, it had begun to rise to an ecstatic worship of the Virgin and of gentlewomen, to elaborate chivalrous ethics, stylized manners, and the appreciation of artful poetry and music.

Aristocratic poetry with its treasure of melodies was the work of *troubadours* or, in their native Provençal language, *trobadors*, inventors. They were either knights, courtiers, if not princes, or itinerant bards who travelled from castle to castle and occasionally met in *puys*, or contests.

Those who invented verses were not necessarily knights themselves; low birth by no means excluded a man whose verses conformed to the atmosphere of educated society. The sources list Guillaume de Poitou, who was a count, alongside Marcabru, who had been a foundling laid on the threshold of a rich man's house, and Bernart de Ventadour, who was the son of a furnace stoker.

Any caste-like seclusion was the less sought after or achieved in that the troubadour lived often in the company of some professional minstrel or juggler, who played the fiddle to his master's singing, wrote the verses down (since writing was not yet a compulsory part of knightly education), and possibly had a vital part in setting them to music. Such steady contact with folk musicians must have prevented the melodies of the knights from gliding away into either amateurish poorness or snobbish over-sophistication.

69

The following episode is characteristic of such contact. One day, around the year 1195, two professional fiddlers from France made their appearance at the margravial court of Montferrat in northern Italy, near Turin, and entertained the distinguished party with their popular dance tunes. The court enjoyed one tune particularly; a new *estampie*, a stately gliding dance in 4 × 3 beats. Only Raimbaut de Vaqueiras, a knight and Provençal troubadour in love with the sister of the margrave, remained silent and depressed. Thereupon the young lady asked him to be cheerful and to sing in his turn. Obedient, he rose and sang a couple of impromptu verses to the catchy melody just heard. The charming piece is preserved and has been recorded.

This recording, and for that matter any realization in sound or on paper, is to a certain extent arbitrary. For almost three hundred melodies of Provençal troubadours collected in beautiful *chansonniers* of the time are written in plainsong notation, which does not tell what the time values of the individual notes, and hence their rhythm, should be. In this predicament, two French historians of music at the beginning of our century, Pierre Aubry and Jean-Baptiste Beck, argued for a metrical interpretation. Since rhythm was not written out, so they argued, it must be implied, and it could be implied only in the unmistakable meter of the text (in a way similar to most Greek melodies). However, these meters were usually either iambic (short-long), or trochaic (long-short). The result was a tedious, limping triple-time throughout.

This is hard to take on musical grounds. And, if there is no other lead than the verses of the text, must these songs have had a compulsory, unequivocal rhythm at all? Why, then, did the composers or copyists not use the time values provided by the mensural notation (*cf.* pages 71 ff), which, after all, existed in the thirteenth century? And why did the most important musical writer around 1300, the Frenchman Johannes de Grocheo, expressly dissociate all secular music from precise time-beating: "*non ita praecise mensurata est?*" As matters stand, these songs may have been sung in whatever rhythm the singer preferred; indeed, they may have had no definite rhythm at all. And since they were Mediterranean, they may have been dissolved in a good deal of free and improvised coloratura anyway.

The songs of the Provençal troubadours were carefully classified. There were the crusader's song, or *sirventes*; the *planh*, or lament for a fellow-knight; the *tenson*, or song on a given topic for some *puy*, or contest, like that depicted in the second act of Wagner's *Tannhäuser*; the *pastoreta*, or modish shepherd's song; the *serena*, or serenade; and the *alba*, or morning song after a night spent with the sweetheart.

Similar in scope and essence was the northern French offshoot of the art of the troubadours, that of the *trouvères*, of which about 1700 melodies have been preserved. This art began with the poems of Blondel de Nesles (*c.* 1150–1200), who did *not*, as a legend has it, rescue King Richard Coeur-de-Lion by wandering from dungeon to dungeon and singing a song well known to both of them until he heard the king's refrain; and it ended with Adam de la Halle (1220–1287), the famous poet-composer of a pastoral play, *Le Jeu de Robin et de Marion*, which dates from either 1275 or 1285. The period of the *trouvères* thus extended over hardly more than a hundred years.

Altogether, the trouvères gave preference to firmer structures. More than in the songs of the southern troubadours, we find in the northern repertory the well-assorted stock of secular and partly secular vocal forms, to be discussed in the following section.

THE MUSICAL FORMS of secular songs in France have been classified into four principal types.

(1) The hymn or stanza type, represented by the *vers* and *canzo* forms, with a through melody for the whole stanza, to be used again for each consecutive stanza.

The *vers* had a through melody in a narrower sense, which covered the whole stanza without any repetition of phrases. A *canzo* stanza, on the contrary, followed the structure AAB: one first phrase covered two lines, and its repetition, the next two lines, while the two final lines were sung on a different melody. A possible seventh line used to take up the second part of phrase A as a coda.

(2) The litany type, in which each line was sung to the same short melody.

There was the ordinary form, as in the epics, or *chansons de geste*, where the (sometimes fifty) lines of a *laisse*, or section, repeated the same melody all over and over again, while only the last one broke loose and followed a concluding cadence. And there was the *rotrou-enge*, where a chorus took up the last, divergent line as a refrain.

(3) The sequence type with one melody to every two lines: AA, BB, CC, and so on.

The *lai* was the simplest sequence form, although in later times it also provided one melody for three or four lines in various combinations. The (instrumental) *estampie* in 4 × 3 time, a courtly gliding dance, did not repeat the musical phrase, or *punctum* (as it was called in dance music), in a strict form, but answered the *overt*, or half-cadence, of the first line by a *clos*, or full cadence, in the second line of each of its pairs.

(4) The round-dance (*carole*) or refrain type, in which a leader sang the stanzas, and the chorus of the dancers answered with the refrain. There were three forms, *rondeau*, *virelai*, and *ballade*.

The French *rondeau* was, in its oldest form (twelfth and thirteenth centuries), a song performed by those engaged in a round-dance. The leader acted as the soloist, and the chorus of the dancers responded by repeating his part. This was done in a curious way: the simple melody, covering the entire stanza, consisted of two phrases of even or uneven length (we call them A and B); the soloist sang the first one (A), which was at once repeated by the chorus; then, the soloist sang the whole tune (AB), which again was repeated by the chorus:

```
soloist:  A        AB
chorus:        A         AB
```

From the thirteenth century on, the final refrain of the chorus was anticipated at the beginning:

```
soloist:          A        AB
chorus:  AB            A        AB
```

The *virelai* and the *ballade*, on the other hand, had true refrains, with a melody different from that of the soloist.

The *virelai*, whose name, pronounced *veerelay*, stems from Old French *virer* (to veer) and *lai* (poem) and hints at the regular turning movement of round dances, had the same melodic phrase for each of its lines, however many there were, except for the last one, which anticipated the melody of the refrain:

```
refrain:  A              A
stanza:        BBB . . . A
```

The same form rules the famous Spanish *cantígas* in honor of the Virgin, more than four hundred melodies of which were written down for King Alfonso el Sabio and have been preserved in beautiful, illuminated manuscripts of the later thirteenth century.

The *ballade* of the *trouvères* must not be confused with the Italian *ballata* of the fourteenth century or, for that matter, with the epic ballad of the last two hundred years. It did not anticipate the refrain; it followed the AAB form of the Provençal *canzo* but added a refrain which ended the stanza on a melodic phrase of its own:

stanza: AAB
refrain: C

These descriptions do not mention the alternation of a soloist and a chorus as the singers of stanzas and refrains because the three round-dance forms had already begun to part from the dance proper, to become merely musical patterns (such as we find later in Chopin's waltzes, mazurkas, and polonaises), and to leave both stanzas and refrains to the same soloist.

THE MINNESINGER or *Minnesänger* (from *minne*, 'love') was the German counterpart of the *troubadour* and, in a way, even moreso of the *trouvère*. He and his art were modeled after patterns from France, like all the aristocratic culture of the later Middle Ages. At the beginning, the Germans even availed themselves of original melodies from France and adapted them to German words.

Still, the Minnesinger had features of their own. The texts leant more to the religious side, and also the melodies, less popular and dance-like, were closer to the style of the Church: not the merry major mode of the jugglers prevailed, but the solemn Dorian and Phrygian of the priests. Again, the leading form of Minnesinger music came from France: the *Bar*, or stanza, of two *Stollen* on the same melody and a concluding epode, or *Abgesang*, on a different melody derived from the *canzo* of the troubadours. The *Preislied* in Wagner's *Die Meistersinger* follows this typical AAB form.

The best known Minnesinger are the lyrical, passionate Walter von der Vogelweide (*c.* 1170–*c.* 1230) and Wolfram von Eschenbach, poet of the epics *Parzival* and *Titurel* (which served Wagner as the sources of his last work, *Parsifal*). None of Wolfram's melodies has been preserved, but we know a few of Walter's, one of which has become a Protestant chorale and is still alive in the Old Hundred.

Besides these courtly poets, naturalistic Neithart von Reuenthal (early thirteenth century) moved the scene from chivalrous, refined, and spiritual *Minne* to the drastic sex life of uncouth swains but also added a healthy infusion of brisk and simple tunes from the country-side.

The *Minnesang* lasted altogether from the times of Spervogel (*c.* 1200) to those of Hugo von Montfort (1357–1423) and the Tirolese Oswald von Wolkenstein (1377–1445); that is, it lagged behind the knightly singers of France by a hundred years.

Once more, it must be emphasized that there was hardly any barrier between the songs for knights and those for commoners. On the contrary: Johannes de Grocheo, who lived at the end of the thirteenth century, recommended expressly that the *chants de geste* "be sung before old people, working burghers, and low-caste men when they rest from their toil, so they might, on hearing about the misery of others, better stand their own depressing condition and with more cheerfulness resume their occupations. Hence this kind of song is important for the conservation of the State." Which, in a modest way, recalls Confucius' and Plato's musico-political theories.

In a similar naive utilitarianism, youths were required to sing *cantilenas* in order "that they may not entirely get lost in idleness." One form of *cantilena*, the *stantipes*, was so hard to perform that "it kept the minds of the boys and the maidens busy and took them away from evil thoughts." And another form of *cantilena*, the nimble, rapid *ductia*, "protected the hearts of girls and boys from vanity and, as they say, from the kind of passion that they give the name of love."

Singing and dancing were severed in the thirteenth century. Ballads and *rondeaux* became purely vocal forms detached from actual dancing, while dancing itself was accompanied on instruments.

THE JUGGLERS or Minstrels, in charge of instrumental dance music, were a motley lot. Some descended from the cosmopolitan vagrants of the disintegrating Roman Empire, some from Celtic druids,

Nordic scalds, continental bards. Runaway monks and uprooted elements from all strata of society kept joining the older stock. And motley was their trade. No rigid line separated the musician proper from the skilful acrobat who, with balls and missile knives, with dancing and rope-walking, amused both the courts and the villagers. But even within the musical field, the juggler was a Jack-of-all-trades. He was, as one troubadour stated, expected to play no less than nine different instruments.

Though indispensable and received with delight as entertainers—doubly welcome in a time without considerable communication from place to place—the jugglers were untouchables. The solidifying middle class, proud of their houses and crafts, frowned upon a shapeless class that lived on the highways and wandered from town to town, without a home, without the ties of an honest, sedate trade, without the kind of respectability that the burghers were building up. The Church, on the other hand, resented the high percentage of runaway clerics among the jugglers and the anticlerical trends that they nourished and expressed.

The jugglers answered with attempts at organization after the model of the craftsmen's guilds and with rigid professional statutes. In 1321, those in Paris founded a *Confrèrie et Corporation des Ménestrels de Paris* under a 'king,' *le roi des ménestrels*; and similar brotherhoods came to life in other countries.

But this striving for respectability did not help too much. The Church refused the sacraments, including matrimony. Nor did the civil law protect the jugglers: the one who had suffered tort was allowed to slap the offender's shadow only, since he himself had only a shadow of honor. As late as 1406, the municipality of Basel forbade the jugglers to wear trousers! The powers, spiritual and secular, came heavily down upon them.

Still, the juggler was one of the most important agents of medieval civilization. His poetry, his melody were an essential part of public and private life; he expressed what the Church in its aloofness was not able or willing to express; and he was admitted through a backdoor to the very liturgy to help in filling the gap between the earth and heaven.

Coronations, princely weddings, Church feasts and councils were the great occasions for the vagrant player. Courtly poets of the time delight in enumerating all the instruments that sounded together. One

German mentions 25, a Spaniard 29, and the Frenchman Guillaume de Machaut, a musician himself and therefore especially reliable, 36 kinds of instruments, some with many men playing the same part. Historians confirm these numbers. Four hundred players performed in 1340 at the court of Mantua, 450 during the *Reichstag* at Frankfurt in 1397, and the Church councils of the time are said to have attracted more than 1,000 each. Obviously the men played most often individually or in small groups. But the descriptions and contemporary paintings of heavenly orchestras leave little doubt that the players also performed in huge ensembles with *très grande mélodie* and *très grand noise*.

INSTRUMENTAL MUSIC as an independent art was, indeed, a creation of jugglers, and, so far, the thirteenth century yields the earliest evidences of it. Some motets written down without words in any of their voice parts were expressly meant for *viellatores*, or fiddlers, and the courtly poets of the time, whose predecessors had exclusively mentioned dances to which the dancers sang, speak now of dance tunes played by *videlaere* and pipers, or even by actual orchestras with strings and trumpets and drums.

The instruments themselves were manifold enough. Besides the long-established fiddles and harps, some lutes and kindred instruments had already been introduced from Muhammedan Spain, but were not yet essential in western music. Two oriental zithers, on the other hand, were given a remarkable welcome: the plucked psaltery from Egypt and the beaten dulcimer from Persia. Both of them were destined to live on with keyboards as the harpsichord and the piano. The Islamic world, in close touch with the West through the crusades and the Muhammedan conquest of Spain and Sicily, also provided oboes, trumpets, and small-sized kettledrums. Indeed, it presented the Christian world with the ordinary military drums and the tambourine, which had had no place in older European music.

The instrument that, according to literary and pictorial sources of the time, was, more than any other, in the center of musical life, was called *vièle* or *vielle* by the French and *fiddle* by the English (whence, later, *viola*). The reader will find illustrations on plate XIV and XVII in the author's *History of Musical Instruments*, pages 140 and 188.

Built in the size of a modern viola or even larger, the *vièle* was usually guitar-shaped, had a peg arrangement different from that of the violin (frontal), and was as a rule provided with five strings. We even know how the fiddlers tuned them. Jerome of Moravia, a Dominican friar who lived in Paris around 1250, relates that they did it in three ways:

$$d \quad G \quad g \quad d'd'$$
$$d \quad G \quad g \quad d'g'$$
$$G \quad c \quad g \, d'$$

As a hangover from the Orient, the *d* in the first two tunings was an unstoppable drone to be plucked with the thumb while the other strings were being bowed. The two *d'* in the first tuning stand without doubt for one double string, and the same is probably true of the group *Gg* in the two first tunings. As a consequence, the three tunings must tentatively be reduced to:

$$\begin{array}{ccc} & g & d' \\ & g & d' \; g' \\ G \; c & g & d' \end{array}$$

METER AND MENSURAL NOTATION. Before passing to polyphony, it must be made clear that any elaborate coincidence of several voice parts—two, three, or more—was impracticable without a careful organization of some kind. In the earlier órganum, the *vox principalis* held a note until the *vox organalis* had finished its coloratura, and then proceeded to the following note. The new style of polyphony, which will be discussed anon, required a more organic integration in the progress of the voice parts and found it in the concept of poetical meter, where syllables, long and short, were arranged in ever recurring, similar patterns, or feet, with a breathing spell at the end of a line.

A voice part in the polyphony of the thirteenth century proceeded in exactly the same way. Long and short notes formed in similar patterns—trochaic, iambic, dactylic, anapaestic, spondaic, or tribrachic. The patterns were uninterruptedly repeated (as in oriental music) until some rest marked off a section. The number of repetitions within a section was indicated by *primus ordo* for the solitary, unrepeated pattern, *secundus ordo* for one repetition, *tertius ordo* for two repetitions, and so on.

However, musical conditions caused difficulties unknown to the poets. Polyphony, for which the patterns were created, combined not only different voice parts, but often different metrical patterns to enhance their independence. But a combination of trochaic or iambic with dactylic or anapaestic patterns was not immediately possible, since the former two contained a long and a breve, or three time-units each, and the latter two, a long and two breves, or four time units each. As a way out, the dactyl and the anapaest were awkwardly stretched out to two times three or six units, three for the long syllable, and three, in the exact likeness of the iamb, for the two short syllables, the second of which was twice the size of the first.

The result was an official system of six metrical *modi*, in which all patterns, established on a three-unit basis, could perfectly well be combined.

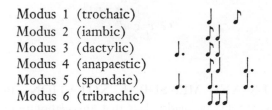

Modus 1 (trochaic)
Modus 2 (iambic)
Modus 3 (dactylic)
Modus 4 (anapaestic)
Modus 5 (spondaic)
Modus 6 (tribrachic)

This strict rhythmization, however, applied only to polyphonic music, to órgana, conducts, and motets. It did not apply to monophonic music, to the Gregorian chant or to troubadour melodies, nor, in general, to any music before 1150 or after 1300.

While plainsong notation with its neglect of time values was still being used for monophonic melodies, the complicated three and four voice-part polyphony of the Church needed a measuring, 'mensural' notation to secure the necessary coincidence of the singers.

Mensural notation developed around 1225 from plainsong notation by distinguishing between a stemmed square, as the *longa*, and a stemless square, as the *brevis*. The corresponding rests were a longer vertical dash across two spaces of the staff and a shorter vertical dash between two lines. The two forms of notes, of which the breve still occurs as the symbol of an 8/4 note, indicated at the beginning the rather brief values of a long and a short syllable in cantillation, that is, of a modern quarternote and a modern eighthnote.

The long and the breve were sufficient as long as polyphonic music clung to the first and second metrical modes. But with the adoption of the third and fourth modes, composers were confronted with two different sizes of longs, one of three and another of only two time-units, and in a similar way with two different sizes of breves, one of two time-units (like the smaller long) and another with only one time-unit. There were altogether four values of notes but only two symbols and two names. And, worse, the smaller long was actually the equivalent of the larger breve. This situation is at first sight unintelligible. Why not four or, better, three names and three symbols for as many values? The explanation is the irresistible spell of poetic meters from which the metrification of music had started. For a long time to come the poetic conception of syllables as nothing but long or short obstructed the seemingly normal way to an unequivocal notation and terminology on the basis of time-units.

With such equivocation, the mensural script in its older forms could not be read immediately, but only after the reader had carefully scanned a piece as a whole and found out what *modus* was intended. This imposition, incomprehensible from our modern viewpoint, must however have been acceptable in a time that cherished double meaning, enigmatic disguise, and esoteric mysteries in all the arts.

Some progress was made about 1250 with the introduction of a third symbol, the diamond-shaped *semibrevis* with its rest in the form of the modern whole rest. Coincident with this was a momentous shift in the time values of the older two symbols: the long drew nearer the modern halfnote, the breve became approximately an equivalent of the modern quarternote, and the semibreve, of the modern eighthnote.

Reading was facilitated in the second half of the century when Franco of Cologne, the author of an influential treatise on the *Ars cantus mensurábilis*, assigned definite (relative) time values to the various conventional forms of ligatures, such as breve-long, or long-breve, or long-long-breve. This, too, meant emancipation from the tyranny of the metrical *modi*.

The end of the century found even the semibreve insufficient to indicate the shorter values that the composers needed. Thus, the Frenchman Pierre de la Croix, or, Latinized, Petrus de Cruce, subdivided the breve into four, and later even into twelve semibreves, which, without for the time abandoning the name and writing-form of the semibreve, meant going beyond this smallest unit and preparing the acknowledgment of a still smaller unit, the *minima*.

The slow development of the mensural script, which eventually became our modern notation, will later be discussed.

The arrangement of polyphonic voice parts in notation was not unlike the modern vertical score with the parts in strict coincidence above each other. The score, however, was given up during the thirteenth century in favor of the so-called choirbook arrangement, which lasted far into the Later Ages. The voice parts were written after each other on two consecutive sides of the open book, generally with the two upper voices on the top of the left and the right pages, and the one or two lower parts at the bottom, so that all the singers were able to read their parts from the same book:

$$1 \quad 2 \quad \text{or} \quad 1 \quad 2$$
$$3 \qquad\qquad 3 \quad 4$$

The word *choirbook*, however, is misleading. The polyphonic forms— at least motet and órganum—were meant for soloists, not choirs, and the choirs themselves were supposed to sing from memory, not from the book.

POLYPHONY was increasingly dominated by strict mensuration in the patterns provided by the metrical *modi*. Indeed, the thirteenth century introduced a special name for all polyphonic forms subject to such mensuration: *discantus* (the same spelling in the singular and the plural).

The transition from free to measured polyphony occurred in the *Ars antiqua*. This was the name that the later Middle Ages gave to the musical styles before 1300. Although there has been disagreement as to how far back the term should be applied, it is generally accepted today as including the second half of the twelfth century. This means coincidence with the early and the central period of Gothic art and with scholasticism in philosophy.

In the center of the *Ars antiqua* stood the body of music connected with the cathedral of Notre Dame in Paris. Its first monument was the *Magnus Liber Organi* or Great Book of the Organum, a collection of about ninety órgana; and its earliest master was Leoninus who, in the enthusiastic report of a contemporary English traveller, was called an *óptimus organista*, that is, an excellent contrapuntist (not organist).

Leoninian órgana were sung at festive Masses and Offices to replace the plainsong of the soloist in Graduals, Alleluias, and other responsoriaᴶ sections. All the choral phrases of such sections were unchangeably chanted in the plainsong unison of the choir.

Within the organal parts, the upper voice, or *duplum*, was performed by a solo singer, and the lower one, or *tenor*, possibly also by a solo singer or, more probably, by an instrument, by preference an organ mixture. In these respects, the órganum of Leoninus did not differ from earlier órgana. But the dimensions had grown. Since the duplum flowed in ever freer and longer coloraturas, the tenor stretched out to solemn, longheld pedal notes, which often would drone for more than a dozen (what we would call) bars and thus exclude any actual pₑrception of its melodic progress (plate III).

Ｈowever, the growing trend towards a strict mensuration took possession of even so free a form as Leoninus' órganum was: from time to time, the master interrupted its boundless flow by a *claúsula* in *discantus* style. In these episodes, the duplum was subjected to one of the modal meters—iamb, trochee, dactyl, or any other—and even the tenor, aᵣoused from its torpor, joined the strictness of the duplum in shorter, even strides, one to every metrical foot.

Leoninus found a worthy successor in Master Perotinus, whom admiring contemporaries called "the Great." Characteristically, the anonymous Ｅnglish traveller described him, in contradistinction to Leoninus, as an *optimus discantista*, which epithet testifies to a victory of the spirit manifested in Leoninus' *discantus* parts with their greater strictness. Deploying "an abundance of color and beauty," in his words, replaced many of Leoninus' *claúsulae* by richer ones. But even outside the *claúsulae*, in the órganum proper, the younger master forced the duplum into an exact, consistent meter (plate III) and often added a *triplum*, or third part, indeed a *quadruplum*, or fourth part. Thus he increased the number of voice parts, with the third part, or the third and the fourth, joining forces with the duplum against the tenor.

A Perotinus *órganum triplum* or *quadruplum* starts on a long drawn-out chord. While the tenor holds on, the two or three upper voices proceed in clear-cut phrases instead of the older free coloraturas. They also proceed in an even meter, iambic, or trochaic, or dactylic, all at the same time and coincident, save for a few passing-notes. Melodically, however, they follow their own devices, so that, except for the strictly consonant cadences, all kinds of dissonances occur. Still, there were beginnings of coördination and melodic coherence. Excepting the canons of primitive tribes, we find in Perotin's órgana the earliest 'imitations,' that is, repetitions of some melodic phrase in other voice parts, which eventually, four hundred years later, led to the fugue.

The tenor, however, participated in the play of the upper voices only in the *claúsulae*. In the purely organal sections, it was still more stretched out than in Leoninian órgana; it might happen that forty or more measures were supported by the same almost endless note of the tenor. In view of such unnatural length, one must indeed consider the coöperation of an instrument rather than of a solo voice; and among the instruments at hand the only suitable one, again, would be the organ, which, as we recall, was a mixture organ without solo stops. The only possible alternative seems to be that a singer sustained the notes as long as he could and then simply waited until the next one fell due.

MOTET AND CONDUCT.

The órganum had an offshoot which proved to be the most important polyphonic form of the thirteenth century: the motet. It originated when the counterpointing voice or voices of the *claúsula* abandoned the text of the tenor, or *mot* (word), and sang a *motet*, or 'little text,' of its or their own. When the separation of the old and the new form had been perfected, the name *motet* passed from the text of the counterpointing voice to the whole form.

The tenor of a motet was left either to an instrument or to a vocalizing voice. It had no text but the *íncipit*, that is, the first word or words of the passage in the liturgy from which the melody was taken. In a strange way, this melody was bent into regular groups of three units with a subsequent rest instead of a fourth unit. Sometimes such a melody was long enough, with its groups of four units, to cover the motet in its full length; sometimes it covered only half or a third of it, so that it had to be repeated once or twice. Sometimes, again, the section from the liturgical melody was so short that it formed an ever repeated ground or *ostinato*.

The vocal upper voices, generally two, had originally one text and one meter, but later were given different meters and texts. Two texts made the motet 'double,' three texts, 'triple.' Different texts, however, expressed ideas similar or closely related. The first voice would sing *Ave virgo regia mater clementiae*, and the second, *Ave gloriosa mater Salvatoris*. The texts were not necessarily sacred. Many motets had secular texts, against the ecclesiastical melody of the tenor. Indeed, it happened that the texts were sung in different vernacular languages, in French, German, and English.

Thus, the motet could be polyphonic, polyrhythmic, polytextual, and polyglot. It was, in a typically Gothic way, unified in the spirit rather than in appearance. And typically Gothic also was the role of the tenor. It never formed a well-rounded melody, but rather a solid structure of equal, evenly spaced blocks to support the lighter texture of the upper voices.

The *conductus*, first mentioned around 1140, was a third type of early thirteenth century polyphony. It had two, three, or four voice parts, the lowest of which sang a Latin text on a freely invented, not liturgical melody, while the other voice parts—probably instrumental—accompanied 'homorhythmically,' that is, in chords exactly coinciding with the notes of the melody. The meaning of *conductus* is not quite clear; the current interpretation derives it from 'conducting' the priests in processions.

To summarize: the polyphony of the thirteenth century crystallized in three principal ways of writing:

> *Conductus*, with one text and one meter.
> *Organum*, with one text and different meters.
> *Motet*, with different texts and different meters.

Most of these polyphonic forms differ from modern polyphony in one essential point: the voice parts are not meant to represent the human ranges from the soprano down to the basso, but, instead, often keep within a similar range. They are *aequales*, to use a term well known from Beethoven's pieces for trombones of equal size. As a consequence, the impression is much lighter and less suggestive of spatial depth. In the twelfth century, a momentous influence on polyphony had come from the English *gymel*, or *cantus gemellus* (twin song), in which the melody was accompanied by quasi-parallel, now major now minor, sixths and thirds. Both intervals obtained, around 1200, their official recognition as *optimae concordantiae*, and soon found their way into continental forms of polyphony. Still, they were only timidly used for a long time to come.

The two new *optimae concordantiae* were combined to make triads in the *English discant*, in which some Gregorian melody was accompanied by parallel thirds and sixths *above* to form a trio. The three singers, performing a *discantus supra librum*, or counterpoint from the book, sang from the same one-staff notation, the first singer as it stood, the second in *meane-sight*, a third higher, and the third in *treble-sight*, a sixth higher. There was an exception only for the first and the last note of a piece; these were accompanied in the fifth and the octave, to make the beginning and the end perfectly consonant.

This way of singing, however, must not be confused either with the free counterpoint known as the French discant (*cf*. page 80) or with the *fauxbourdon* of the fifteenth century, which will be discussed later.

THE FIGHT for a consonant third seems to have been the cause of decisive changes in the medieval and post-medieval scale. So far, the Middle Ages had followed the '*cyclic*' system with its perfect fifths and fourths (*cf*. page 14). Its third was the result of moving two fifths up and two fourths down, as from C up to G, down to D, up to A, down to E, or, mathematically, $3/2 \times 3/4 \times 3/2 \times 3/4 = 81:64$. Simpler, and therefore more consonant, was the third that the *divisive* system provided: $5:4$ or $80:64$. However, a simple change from the cyclic to the divisive system would not have been feasible; it had the disadvantage, unbearable in polyphonic music, of exacting two different sizes of tones from the player and from the listener, such as $C–D$ in the ratio $9:8$ (or 204 cents) and $D–E$ in the ratio $10:9$ (or 182 cents).

The important *Speculatio musicae* of the Englishman Walter Odington (*c*. 1300) shows that, as a way out of this dilemma, the thirteenth century achieved the earliest *temperament*, or wilful alteration of the scale, that we find in the Western world. The divisive third, 5:4, was accepted, but cleft into two equal tones. The reader desirous of figures will easily realize that the tone was given (approximately) 386 cents divided by two, or 193 cents, as against the 204 and 182 cents in the orthodox divisive system.

These are the beginnings of the later *mean-tone* temperament which, before and along with the equal temperament, lived far into the nineteenth century.

READING

Gustave Reese, *Music in the Middle Ages*, New York, 1940. Curt Sachs, *The History of Musical Instruments*, New York, 1940: Chapter 14. Curt Sachs, *World History of the Dance*, New York, 1937: Chapter 7. Curt Sachs, *The Commonwealth of Art*, New York, 1946: Cross Sections 1140–1265. Curt Sachs, *Rhythm and Tempo*, New York, 1953. Willi Apel, *The Notation of Polyphonic Music*, 900–1600, 3rd ed., Cambridge, Mass., 1945. Heinrich Husmann, *Die drei-und vierstimmigen Notre-Dame-Organa*, Leipzig, 1940.

7

THE LATE GOTHIC PERIOD

1 3 0 0 – 1 4 0 0

A MOMENTOUS CHANGE occurred in Europe early in the fourteenth century. The authority of both the Church and the Holy Roman Empire weakened; the cities, the burghers, the common people came to the fore; and the arts turned to depicting the realities of earthly life beside the myths of heaven. A writer on music about 1300, the Frenchman Johannes de Grocheo, dared, as the first one, to discuss the *musica vulgaris* of Paris, with its songs and dances, along with the dignified chant of the Church. The age-old barrier between the popular and the "higher" music had been taken down.

Alas, the Church had reason to resent the merger. Pope John XXII, in a famous bull of 1324, denounced the artificial meters, new melodies, notation, rapid tempi, ornaments, rests, polyphony, and secular tunes of the "modern" school and made them responsible for the alarming distraction, intoxication, and perversion of the devotees.

Exactly who and what these objectionable moderns were is not quite clear; "new" and "modern" have always been poor targets, for the attackers as well as for the defenders. Did the Pope have in mind the motets of Petrus de Cruce, who, freed from the tyranny of metrical *modi*, had written in an almost rhapsodic polyphony on the threshold of the century? Or did he think of his French contemporary, Philippe de Vitry, who was much stricter in style and even reverted to the *ordines* of the *ars antiqua?*

All the same, Philippe de Vitry (*c.* 1325), whom Petrarch has called "the greatest, the only poet of the age," was the most influential composer of the early fourteenth century and a particularly modern one in his disregard of unadulterated church modes—"*musica ficta* is the

86

musica vera" (*cf.* page 98), he said—and in his acceptance, in polyphony, of the futuristic thirds and sixths, which even as progressive a musician as Johannes de Grocheo found rather "hard on the ears."

Polyphony—and this is another aspect of the reconciliation of the ecclesiastic and the secular styles—had conquered all the domains of music, the secular as well as the religious sphere. No doubt, the beginnings of such comprehensive practice must be sought in the thirteenth century. Some dances of that time had indeed a second or even a third part written down. But as a rule, such accompaniment must have been done without notes and often at random. The fourteenth century, on the contrary, took polyphony seriously enough to elaborate the voice parts in its secular forms as much as in its Masses, motets, and conducts.

One of these secular, popular forms, which Grocheo defines as "bending back on itself like a circle," was the *rotundellus, rota,* or *rondellus,* a familiar type of piece like our *Row, row, row your boat* or the almost global *Brother John,* which we officially call a canon, and colloquially, a round. The structure can be represented by the following graph:

```
First voice:   1 2 3 4 1 2 3 4 . . .
Second voice:    1 2 3 4 1 2 3 4 . . .
Third voice:       1 2 3 4 1 2 3 4 . . .
Fourth voice:        1 2 3 4 1 2 3 4 . . .
```

Again and again four voices sing the same short melody of four measures, but enter with a delay of one measure each, which is easily feasible if the four measures are devised to be harmonically and contrapuntally consonant. As a variation, all voices may start together with the appropriate measures, so that the entries are shifted, not delayed:

```
First voice:   1 2 3 4 1 2 3 4 . . .
Second voice:  4 1 2 3 4 1 2 3 . . .
Third voice:   3 4 1 2 3 4 1 2 . . .
Fourth voice:  2 3 4 1 2 3 4 1 . . .
```

In the thirteenth and fourteenth centuries, popular canons were written down — and therewith officially recognized — in Germany, Spain, and England. A German *radel* (wheel) dealt with a St. Martin's goose, the Spanish *caças* (or hunts) were devised for pilgrims wandering to the shrine of Montserrat in Catalonia, and one from England is commonly known by its text words *Sumer is icumen in, Lhude sing cucu* (Summer has come, loudly sing cuckoo), a catchy dance tune for four voice parts upon a *pes* (a foot or fundament) of two additional voices moving in a *ground* or *ostinato* form. Incidentally, Dr. Bukofzer has corrected its musical text in the light of a recent study of the original.

Out of the popular canon, the French created one of the most amazing art forms of the fourteenth century, the *chace*, and the Italians followed with the similar *caccia*.

THE *CHACE* (pron. *shahss*) of the French was a lengthy canon in unison, that is, with the voices following each other at the same pitch and in the same key. The two voices entered at a distance of at least four measures from each other and proceeded straight-away, without any repetition and without—to requote Grocheo's words—bending back on themselves "like a circle."

The Italian *caccia* (pron. kahtchah), whose name again denotes hunt, was similar in pattern, but had an instrumental *pes* in longer notes which served as a supporting bass.

Both the texts and the melodies of these straight-away canons were in the naturalistic taste of the age. They depicted with gusto the sports of hunting and fishing in every detail, and also fire alarms, market scenes with voluble bargaining, and the characteristic cries of street peddlers.

Such is the curious *caccia* of Master Zacharias of Florence. The poet abandons the usual sequence of eleven syllables and uses a genuine prose. A hunter suddenly finds himself in the noisy tangle of a market: "Crabs, new crabs!—Give me crabs for two!—Let us first take the shells off!—I want five!—Ann, go peel them!—I don't want any!—Good lemons!—Are they really fresh?—How much?—A nickel!" At last, a toothpuller recommends his services. The music, quite informal, follows the syllables faithfully; now high, now low, the cries and questions and answers, talk and backtalk leap from voice to voice, without a conventional, clean-drawn melody and often in a one-note *parlando* or patter. This is the oldest example of markets in music, a predecessor of Janequin's *Cris de Paris* in the sixteenth and Richard Deering's *Cries of London* and *County Cries* in the seventeenth century, of Gustave Charpentier's opera *Louise* (1900) and Ralph Vaughan Williams' *London Symphony* (1914). And we can safely assume that giant canons of this kind gave their contemporaries the same delight that we ourselves experience when a familiar subject is treated with the utmost economy of means in a few masterstrokes, with humor and spirit.

The leaping from voice to voice that talk and backtalk, question and answer required was technically known as *hoquetus* or *hocket*, "hiccup," a kind of openwork writing in which, in rapid alternation, a scrap of melody in one of the voices concurred with a rest in the other one. It is quite probable that the hocket was due to the same impulse to dissolve coherent masses and surfaces that urged the architects of later Gothic times to disintegrate their walls and spires into lace-like openwork.

The *caccia* is characteristic of the revolutionary changes in the later Middle Ages. Side by side with the emancipation of secular, popular art, we witness the liberation of rhythm from the strait jacket of the metrical *modi*, and its rapid evolution to modern freedom and characterizing power, indeed, to ultra-modern refinement and syncopation in what Philippe de Vitry proudly called the new art, *ars nova*.

Coincident with this liberation, we see the emancipation of the Italian spirit from the fetters of Gothic mentality.

For many a hundred years, Italy had been taking rather than giving. But around 1300 she began to compete with France and, in less than a hundred years, won so thoroughly that, although French art in the fourteenth century, with a few exceptions, is known to historians only, the contributions of Italy are still a part of our life, whether we think of Dante's gigantic *Divina Commedia* or of Boccaccio's audacious everyday tales, of Giotto's solemn frescos or of Simone Martini's lovely Virgins.

Music had an important part in this shift. True, the French composers of the *ars nova* were godfathers to the new Italian music. But the young Italians went their own way; little connected them with the culture of Paris, and nothing with the unworldly seclusion of Gothic art and scholasticism. Their songs were as realistic as was their painting. They dealt lovingly with life and nature and neglected the realm of religion almost as much as the preceding century had failed to heed the claims of the secular sphere.

But above all, the Italians turned their backs on the horizontal, anti-sensory polyphony of the Gothic age and consequently also on the *tenor*, or *cantus firmus*. The one or two accompanying voice parts were almost meant as harmonic supports—indeed, as basses in a modern sense.

THE TWO MAIN FORMS of Italian music besides the *caccia* were *ballate* and madrigals. The *ballade* and the *rondeau* were left to the French.

Madrigale, as a name, has as yet no certain derivation. Madrigalesque poetry was idyllic, bucolic, meditative.

As a form, the madrigal had usually two or three stanzas, each of three lines, with the same melody. The whole madrigal ended in a *ritornello*, which was *not* a refrain but a kind of Abgesang (*cf.* page 73) with a new melody in a different rhythm.

Stanza I	melody I
line 1	
line 2	
line 3	
Stanza II	melody I
line 4	
line 5	
line 6	
Ritornello	melody II
line 7	
line 8	

Madrigalesque music, written in two or even in three voice parts, was full of daring coloraturas in the upper voice, while the one or two accompanying parts were played on instruments in an almost harmonic, chordal spirit.

This early madrigal must not be confused with its very different namesake in the sixteenth century.

The Italian *ballata*, unlike the French *ballade* and rather like the *virelai*, was a chain of stanzas with refrains before, between, and after them. There were two melodic sections: one for the refrain, or *ripresa* (take up), and the other for each of the two first pairs of lines in the stanza, the third pair anticipating the melody of the following refrain.

stanza: B B A
refrain: A   A

All these forms were aristocratic chamber music, to be sung and played by educated amateurs. Some pieces must have been great favorites, to judge from the copies extant. One *ballade* by Pierre de Molins has been preserved in no less than six manuscripts of the time and, besides, on a figured tapestry, in the hands of an elegant gentleman who sings it to the accompaniment of a small-sized harp.

Church music played a minor role among the fourteenth century Italians. The spiritual world found its musical expression less in liturgical than in extra-liturgical, popular forms, such as the hymns of devotional fraternities in Italy, or *laude*—of a cast very close to the *ballata*—and of penitential brotherhoods—the flagellants—in Germany.

Two UNUSUAL MEN emerge from the mass of eminent composers of the time: the Frenchman Guillaume de Machault and the Italian Francesco Landino.

Guillaume de Machault (or -aut, pron. mahshów), who lived from about 1300 to 1377 as a contemporary of Petrarch, must be considered the greatest musician of the fourteenth century and one of the century's greatest geniuses in any field. A versatile spirit—cleric, courtier, poet, and composer—he served three rulers, John of Luxembourg (King of Bohemia), John of Normandy, and King Charles V of France, became a canon, wrote a number of outstanding epic poems, and was the musical leader of the Flamboyant Gothic.

He left a good many pieces of aristocratic chamber music—*ballades*, *rondeaux*, and *chansons balladées*, or *virelais*—in a refined and often over-sophisticated style which marks the ending of an age rather than a fresh beginning. While his *ballades* and *rondeaux* have two or three and even four voice parts, most of the *virelais* are unaccompanied melodies. But we learn from a letter addressed to Machault that two of them could be coupled as double *virelais*.

In the religious field, Machault has a unique place, with many motets and a powerful Mass, of uncertain date, in an archaic, isorhythmic motet style (*cf.* page 98), in fact, the earliest complete Mass ever composed by a single man.

Francesco Landino, or Landini, was born in Fiésole near Florence in 1325, went blind as a child, learned composition and the technique of several instruments, among which he favored the portative organ, was awarded the laurel crown of the *poeta laureatus*, and, admired and honored as few musicians had been before him, met his end at Florence in 1397.

Landino's name has been connected with a certain type of cadence, or concluding formula, in which the 'leading' note does not precede the final tonic directly, as *B–C*, but indirectly via the sixth, as *B–A–C*. He was by no means the first one to use it, though, and the formula may even go back to the old inherited northern chain of thirds discussed on page 56.

INSTRUMENTAL MUSIC was essentially restricted to dance melodies:

The *estampie*, a solemn, courtly gliding dance in 12/8 beat consisting of four or five different periods, or *puncti*, each of which was played twice, the first time with a semi-cadence, and the second time with a full cadence.

The *saltarello*, a vivid stepping dance either in triple time (Italy) or in duple time (Germany), with or without an upbeat.

The *trotto*, a form of *ballata* in imperfect *tempus*, that is, in duple time.

The energetic turn, so strikingly characteristic of the fourteenth century, away from the horizontal polyphony of the earlier Middle Ages towards a vertical, harmonic conception of music is neatly reflected in the creation of keyboards. For keys are prompted and justified only by the need of playing at least two notes or voice parts at the same time although no different tone-colors set them off against one another. Such playing, which necessarily resulted in vertical chords, or, in other words, in the blending of notes perceived simultaneously, was acceptable only in times that tolerated or even favored such a novel conception.

The organ had been given keys instead of its older, clumsy sliders as early as the thirteenth century.

Stringed keyboard instruments, precursors of the modern piano, followed at least at the beginning of the fourteenth century. The *Musica speculativa*, that the Frenchman Jean de Muris is said to have written in 1323, mentions not only one but various kinds of them; among them is a clavichord with nineteen strings and another stringed instrument, evidently plucked, in the shape of a grand—that is, a harpsichord.

The clavichord (plate XIV)—literally a monochord with *claves* (Latin, "keys")—had wire strings stretched from right to left within a small and shallow rectangular box three feet long and one foot deep. Each key had on its after end an upright metal tangent which, when the key was being pressed, would gently touch the string and thus produce a weak but charming tone. Its soulful character could even be enhanced by a violin-like *vibrato*, which the Germans later called the *Bebung*. It consisted of a shaking touch of the key and resulted in a rapidly changing tension of the string.

The harpsichord and its nearest relatives, on the contrary, were plucked by tiny, thornlike pieces of quills, which projected from jacks, or wooden hoppers, kept loosely upright on the after ends of the keys and tossed toward the strings when the keys were pressed (*cf.* the illustration on page 334 of the author's *History of Musical Instruments*).

There were three forms of plucked keyboard instruments:

1. Upright, with the vertical soundboard facing the audience.

2. The grand form, with the strings running from front to back, which was later called *harpsichord* in English, *clavicémbalo*, or, abbreviated, *cémbalo*, in Italian, and *clavecin* in French (*cf.* plates XXI and XXIV in the book cited above).

3. The square form, with the strings running from right to left (as in the clavichord), which later was called *virginal* or *spinet* in English, *spinetta* in Italian, *espineta* in Spanish, and *épinette* in French.

The word *harpsichord*, however, did not appear before the seventeenth century; the term *virginal*—which does *not* derive from the Maiden Queen Elizabeth—stood in Tudor times for both the square and the grand form. Incidentally, the official form was *virginals*, in the plural, or even a *pair of virginals*, the word *pair* denoting, not a couple, but one set of any number of parts. The fifteenth and sixteenth centuries understood the instrument as a set of individual tone-producing units, as, for instance, the *C* key with the *C* strings, the *D* key with the *D* strings, and so on. Furthermore, the virginals were very often described, in those centuries, as "single" or "double." These enigmatic epithets did *not* stand for instruments with one or with two keyboards. They referred rather to their musical range. English notation indicated the octave below great *G* (on the lowest line of the *F* clef) by double letters—*FF, EE, DD,* and so on. A single virginal did not and a double virginal did reach down into the double-letter octave.

In a similar spirit, the Italians distinguished between a *clavicémbalo* and a *gravicémbalo.* The latter descended to those notes that the Middle Ages already had called the *graves*—from *A* to *a.*

Almost in the same year, 1323, in which the *Musica speculativa* of Jean de Muris mentions stringed keyboard instruments for the first time, a manuscript in the British Museum (the Robertsbridge Codex, *c.* 1325) records the earliest intabulations, or tablatures (*cf.* page 20), for keyboard instruments of motets and *estampies.* To be sure, the choice of a keyboard instrument—whether clavichord, virginals, or organ—was up to the performer.

In almost four hundred years, right into the time of Bach, the northern organ was, indeed, to share its music with the stringed keyboard instruments. And this it was able to do because in the fourteenth century, the most fateful span in its history, it began to equal the virginal and the clavichord in agility and to outdo them in coloristic possibilities. By the end of the century, some organs already had two manuals and a pedal keyboard and, for the first time, characteristic, colorful solo stops, such as 'flute' and 'trumpet,' against the tinkling, uniform mass of its mixtures. Guillaume de Machault could rightly call the (northern) organ of his time "the king of all the instruments."

The invention of pedals is indicative of the special consideration that composers gave to the lower range of music, as always in dynamic times. We find it also in the bass shawms (somewhat like our modern baritone oboes), which were mentioned in 1376 as something novel.

NOTATION. The novel musical language of the time was beyond the means of the older, Franconian script and the rigid modal principles of the thirteenth century. The freedom and unprecedented authority of secular music and the rights accorded to duple time along with the typical triple time of the bygone era caused a revolution in the mensural script that one of its strongest promoters, Philippe de Vitry, proudly called the *ars nova* (plate IV).

The *ars nova* consisted mainly of two momentous innovations: the introduction of smaller time values and a wider scope of rhythmic expression. The new time values were the *semiminima*, the *fusa*, and the *semifusa*.

Their mere existence implied a general shift in time values. The older units became slower: the long was drawn-out to the length of a modern moderate whole note; the breve, to a modern half note; the semibreve, to a quarter note; the minim, to an eighth note. The standard was the semibreve at approximately 60 MM.

The greater subtlety in rhythmic expression showed in the red, and later, black, color of certain notes, which allowed for indicating triplets and kindred shifts in meter. But the most important concept was the possibility of subdividing each time-unit into either two or three smaller units. This system can be conveniently represented in only six lines.

Modus perfectus:	the long equals three breves
Modus imperfectus:	the long equals two breves
Tempus perfectum:	the breve equals three semibreves
Tempus imperfectum:	the breve equals two semibreves
Prolatio major:	the semibreve equals three minims
Prolatio minor:	the semibreve equals two minims

(A little mnemonic help: *mOdus* organized the *lOnga*, and *tEmpus* the *brEvis*.)

The two *modi*, two *témpora*, and two *prolationes* each had its signature:

A figure 3 after a circle or semicircle stood for the perfect *modus*, and a figure 2 (generally omitted) for the imperfect *modus*.

A full circle stood for the perfect, and a semicircle for the imperfect, *tempus*.

A dot inside the circle stood for the major prolation, while the circle was left empty in the minor prolation. Hence:

C 3 is *modus perfectus, tempus imperfectum, prolatio minor*, or, in modern terms, 3/2 rhythm.

O 2 is *modus imperfectus, tempus perfectum, prolatio minor*, or 6/4 rhythm.

C 2 is *modus imperfectus, tempus imperfectum, prolatio minor,* or 4/4.

⊙ is *tempus perfectum, prolatio major,* or 9/8.

O is *tempus perfectum, prolatio minor,* or 3/4.

Ȼ is *tempus imperfectum, prolatio major,* or 6/8.

C is *tempus imperfectum, prolatio minor,* or 2/4.

The last sign, an empty semicircle, or C, has survived in our present notation.

One of the oddest traits of medieval notation was the inconsistent key signature within the same polyphonic piece. Often, the upper voice(s) was left without any signature while the lower part(s) carried a flat. No definitive explanation has been given so far. Still, the curious custom was logical in an age unwonted and unwilling to think in terms of harmony, common keys, or even common Church modes. Let us not forget that medieval musicians considered a contrapuntal composition to be the simultaneous progress of individual melodic lines. Even as late a man as Glareanus (1547) defined the Church modes of such individual lines, but never of a polyphonic composition as a whole. In such a composition, two clefs at the distance of a fifth (such as the mezzosoprano and the tenor clef) would easily suggest two hexachords (which after all were still in use) a fifth apart, such as the *hexachordum naturale* and the *hexachordum molle*; the first, continued upwards, might require a natural B, while the B of the second was of necessity flatted.

THE FRANCO — NETHERLANDISH 'artifices.' Even today, cheap music 'history' would scorn the later Middle Ages for having strangled the soul of music in contrapuntal tricks and artifices. This is a unilateral, illicit judgment characteristic of romantic periods, in which the works of art are so exclusively expected to aim at emotion that any stress on structure is deemed a misdemeanor and proof of superficiality.

The art of the later Middle Ages sprang from other sources and cannot be understood or judged by the standards of romantic aesthetics. Gothic music was calculated and constructed in the truest senses of the words, just as Gothic cathedrals were calculated and shaped to display openly their structure from the basement to the finial of the spire—which was easily compatible with genius and inspiration, even if those words were not in the vocabulary of the time.

Thus, it would happen that an entire section of the Mass was written in a strict canon in unison, where the voice parts entered in a *stretto*, or 'narrow,' that is, at a small distance without waiting until the preceding voice had finished the theme (as in Master Dufay's *Gloria ad modum tubae*). But even this was too simple a device. Composers often wrote 'crab' canons, in which the second voice would read the melody of the first one backward, note by note, or 'mirror' canons, with the page turned upside down, so that the notes were read not only backwards but also inverted (for example, a last note *f″* on the highest line of the staff would become the first note *e′* on the lowest line). Or else, one voice part would have the same notes as the second, but stretched out to double time values, or, on the contrary, would have them compressed into halved values. Or each of four voices would sing the same notes, but in different rhythms. Guillaume de Machault once wrote a *rondeau* in which the second voice read the part of the first one backward while the tenor, with notes only up to the middle of the piece, supplied the second half by reading the first half backward.

In addition, the correct way of performing from a rudimentary notation was kept secret under enigmatic directions. Machault would notate a whole *rondeau* in one short line and expect the four performers to decode their parts, the cues being given in the words of the text: "My end is my beginning, and my beginning is my end. . . ." Somewhere else, the singers would find the texts "Suddenly, they turned their backs on me" or "I am undone unless you redo me," and in all three instances, they knew that the solution of the puzzle was a crab canon.

The tricks themselves and their disguise were not meant to be funny. Nor must they be bunched together as anti-artistic superficialities. Contrapuntal subtleties were the last fulfillment of the architectural, constructivistic mind that ruled the later Middle Ages. Their disguise was the reflection in music of the later Gothic trend to give works of art a secret meaning behind the outer, perceptible appearance and to reserve the key to the free-masonry of those initiated.

One of the artifices had nothing to do with riddles, but showed in a similar way a special interest in structure, even if the senses were little concerned. This was the famous *isorhythm*, or equal rhythm. Deriving from the *órdines* of the thirteenth century (*cf.* page 76), it implied, in its simplest form, a characteristic pattern of longer or shorter notes, which ruled all the sections of a melody, without any change. This can easily be understood when we think of the metrical organization of the verse of the national anthem of the United States, which is a true rhythmical pattern forced upon the melody from phrase to phrase: ♪.♪♩♩♩♩

But there was also a more complicated form of isorhythm: some melody repeated itself in equal sections (stanzas or verses) while the rhythmical pattern was shorter or longer than the melody and therefore did not coincide with the melody in its re-entries. If, for instance, the rhythmical pattern was one note longer, the melody, repeated for the first time, would set in on the last note of the not-yet-repeated rhythmical pattern, while its second note would be given the metrical value of the first note of the repeated pattern and consequently would shift the metrical values of all its notes by one digit. In its second repetition, the melody would set in on the penultimate note of the rhythmical pattern and hence would have all its metrical values shifted by two digits. All repetitions of the melody would have the identical sequence of pitches, but all in different time values. It was one of the most intricate attempts at unity in variation, at variation in unity, in an obvious disdain of sensuous perceptibility.

M USICA FICTA OR *FALSA.* The claims of polyphony, on the one hand, and the growing interference of secular music, on the other hand, were steadily disintegrating the white-key purity of the Church modes. To be sure, the so-called *musica ficta* or *falsa,* denoting the introduction of extra-modal flats and sharps either "by reason of beauty" or "by reason of necessity," had its seeds in the Church itself, where a B♭ was introduced in the first and the fifth mode before an A (*cf.* page 47).

The two technical terms come from the thirteenth century. And so does the official recognition of B♭ and E♭, and also of F♯ and C♯, which had become compulsory in order to avoid tritones (intervals of three consecutive wholetones, like F–B♮). But men of the thirteenth century had also begun to sharpen the leading (seventh) note before the tonic in the spirit of the advancing major and minor modes.

In the fourteenth century, *musica falsa* became, as Philippe de Vitry emphatically stated, the *musica vera et necessaria*. Still doubtful in its grip on melody, it was the unquestioned principle that ruled progressions in counterpoint and harmony. Here are the most important rules:

1. Diminished fifths, octaves, and twelfths that might originate in the current of voice progression must be made perfect.

2. Thirds opening into fifths, and sixths opening into octaves, must be major.

3. Thirds shrinking into unisons must be minor.

Since these simple, natural rules were self-evident in the later Middle Ages, the composers did not often care to indicate them expressly by sharps or flats. Many modern editors of medieval music, on the other hand, neglect to add the necessary accidentals because they want to preserve what they believe to be the authentic text. By such neglect, they create a romantically archaic but falsified picture, of which our readers should be warned.

Although the rules of *musica ficta* reflect a definitely harmonic conception, certain concluding formulas of the time disavow this attitude. The most important of these anti-harmonic features was the double leading note. Not only was the final octave preceded by the lower semitone, but the fifth, too, was reached from its lower semitone, so that the two voice parts formed strictest fourth parallels—a practice reminiscent of the gliding, bodiless sway of contemporary Gothic statues, in which the two hips bulge in and out in a parallel movement (*cf.* the author's *Commonwealth of Art*, page 85).

READING

Gustave Reese, *Music in the Middle Ages*, New York, 1940. Curt Sachs, *World History of the Dance*, New York, 1937: Chapter 7. Curt Sachs, *The History of Musical Instruments*, New York, 1940: Chapter 14. Curt Sachs, *The Commonwealth of Art*, New York, 1946: Cross Sections 1300–1400. Curt Sachs, *Rhythm and Tempo*, New York, 1953, Chapter 9. Willi Apel, *French Secular Music of the Late 14th Century*, Cambridge, Mass., 1950.

8

THE AGE OF DUFAY

1400–1460

ON THE THRESHOLD between the fourteenth and the fifteenth centuries, between the Middle and the Later Ages, between the worlds of Machault and Dufay, a powerful British composer and astronomer, John Dunstable (d. December 24, 1453), led Gothic music to a last impressive culmination. His Masses, motets, and antiphons flowed forth in long-drawn, passionate melodies, but a typically English predilection for the consonances of the third and the sixth and for a sensuous, full-set harmony gave them a denseness as uncontinental as that of the massive cathedrals of his country. Still, he was neither fully Gothic nor fully English. In the years that he probably spent in France, he made himself familiar with continental up-to-date techniques, with isorhythm and ornamental *cantus firmi* in the upper voice. Many of his works, indeed, acquired European fame, among them the isorhythmic motet *Veni creator spiritus* and the chanson *O rosa bella*.

The Renaissance—in the narrowest sense of the word—began in the early fifteenth century, in music as well as in the other arts. How momentous it was, how deeply the contemporaries felt that a new age had dawned, can be read from an audacious statement in the *Liber de arte contrapuncti* of the Flemish musician Johannes Tinctoris (1477): "There is no music worth hearing save only in the last forty years."

The word Renaissance seems to suggest a basically retrospective movement, namely the rebirth in form and spirit of classic antiquity. But the study of Greek and Roman authors, sculptures, and architectural ruins was hardly more than auxiliary within an infinitely wider scope of re-orientation. Actually, *rinascimento* implied a rebirth of the Italian spirit after centuries of "Barbarian," "Gothic" thought and form, and its ultimate goal was liberation from the fetters of the Middle Ages. Boldly, it established the right of the senses against the spirit, the right of personal experience and judgment versus authority, and hence, the right of individual against collective mentality.

Since this reaction against the spirit of the Middle Ages was at the same time a reaction of the Italian or Mediterranean against the Germano-Celtic spirit of the North, it showed in the arts as a victory of the classic ideals of balance, clarity, simplicity, and strictness in structure.

This occurred in architecture, sculpture, and painting, and it occurred in music, too. But the musical situation was rather unusual, for Italy concentrated on the visual arts with so much energy that in a hundred and fifty years she was not able to produce one single composer of world renown—not a single one between Landino and Palestrina.

The gap was filled by a long and steady importation of masters from Burgundy and the Netherlands who, while serving in the princely chapels of Italy—in Rome, or Venice, or Florence—adapted their native Gothic styles to the taste of the Italian Renaissance.

In making this statement, it should be explained that most singers in the princely chapels of that time were eminent composers with an all-around musical education, and also that the number of members was small. The Papal Chapel in Rome had, in the time of the Burgundians, in 1436, not more than nine singers, but grew to have twenty-four by the end of the century.

The outstanding monument erected to the music of that time is the gigantic anthology known as the Trent Codices, partly printed in the *Denkmäler der Tonkunst in Oesterreich* (the official publication of outstanding older music in Austria) in volumes 7, 11 i, 19 i, 27 i, 31, 40. They consist of seven manuscript volumes written not long before 1500 for a music-loving Austrian bishop and contain nearly 2,000 compositions of some seventy composers of the fifteenth century. Among them is a substantial part of the work of the generation which, coming from Burgundy, gave its genius to Italy and accepted the spirit of the Renaissance in return.

THE BURGUNDIAN LEADERS were Binchois and Dufay. Gilles Binchois (pron. -shwah), born about 1400 in the province of Hainaut, was at first a soldier and only later became a singer in the famous chapel of Duke Philip the Good, of Burgundy. He died outside Burgundy, at Lille in France. A few of his works belong in the spiritual sphere, but most are smiling, amiable melodies in the traditional secular forms of the *rondeau*, the *ballade*, and the *chanson*.

Guillaume Dufay (pron. -fahee), born about, or rather before, 1400 in the Franco-Netherlandish borderland, started out as a choirboy at the cathedral of Cambrai in northeastern France, which, according to a contemporary letter, surpassed all other churches of the world in the beauty of its singing; and he died in 1474 as a canon in the same cathedral. But in the middle of his life he spent nine momentous years as a singer in the Papal Chapel at Rome—from 1428 to 1437, with an interruption of two years—and there had adapted his Gothic, northern style to the spirit of the Italian Renaissance. It was Italy that taught him to conceal the musical framework, just as she had taught the architects to do without buttresses; it was Italy that smoothed the angular zigzag lines of his melodies and showed him the charm of limpid, clear-cut forms and of drawn-out, restful triads and sixth chords (A triad in root position has the tonic below, as in *C–E–G*; a sixth chord is the first inversion, *E–G–C*). A beautiful example is his Mass *Se la face ai pale*, "If I have a pale face." Indeed, most Masses of the fifteenth and sixteenth centuries had individual names, taken from some melody, either liturgical or secular, which, performed in long-drawn notes in the tenor part, supported all the sections of the Mass as the backbone. Where such is the case, we speak of *cantus firmus* or tenor Masses.

We have to look back to the motet of the thirteenth century, if not to the older órganum, to understand this curious practice. Medieval polyphony had started from liturgical, Gregorian melodies, to which adorning counterpoints were sung. The liturgical melodies, not the contrapuntal voices, had been the essential element. This basic dualism controlled the ways of polyphonic writing all through the Middle Ages, but the accent shifted. The counterpoint would musically get the better of the tenor, it would grow more alive, more flexible, more florid, and yet it needed the solid sub-structure of the sober, immutable Church melody and, in the true spirit of the Middle Ages, needed its unquestioned authority and meaningful presence.

This dualism was no less compulsory in the fifteenth century. The Burgundian masters, though influenced by the Italian Renaissance, were still a part of the longer-lasting northern Middle Ages. But the idea of unquestioned authority had gone. What remained was the meaningful presence and, besides, the delight in the playful interweaving of musical motives pre-existent and newly created, of the well-known and the novel, of gift and gain, a delight that music has preserved ever since in the variation form.

It was only natural that in this deterioration the sacred *cantus firmi* yielded to the more popular melodies of the *chansons*, and the more so as the fifteenth century loved to mix the spheres of heaven and earth. Composers did not hesitate to build their Masses and motets on worldly melodies, just as the painters replaced the unapproachable Queen of Heaven by the tender Mother of the Child.

However, one form of polyphonic Mass in Dufay's time refrained from any common *cantus firmus* for all the sections. Instead, it availed itself in each of the sections of a corresponding Gregorian melody, of a *Kyrie* for the *Kyrie*, of a *Credo* for the *Credo*, of a *Sanctus* for a *Sanctus*. This form is called a *missa choralis* or plainsong Mass.

In all these polyphonic compositions, the medieval equality in range of the various voice parts (*cf.* page 83) had begun to yield to an almost modern spacing of voices high and low by nature. One consequence was the conquest of bass regions not considered before. Again it was Dufay whom contemporaries credited with lowering the bass limit from G (Guido's *gamma*) to D below the staff in the bass clef.

Organ builders, at least in the north, followed laws of their own. For we hear, after 1430, of organ pipes thirty feet tall, which must have reached down beyond the lowest string of the modern piano.

From Italy we hear of no such thing. Far from joining the north in the development of multiple keyboards, pedals, contrasting solo stops, and thundering counterbasses, Italian organs still consisted of delicate, balanced mixtures of octave, double octave, triple octave, the fifth above, quadruple octave, the fifth above, and quintuple octave, such as

$$C \quad c \quad c' \quad g' \quad c'' \quad g'' \quad c'''$$

and sometimes even without disconnecting stops.

Vocal music was astonishingly light-colored. Only about six percent of all the voice parts in the extant pieces are true bassos, and all men's voices were given a strangely high tessitura.

The majority of compositions in Binchois' and Dufay's time were written for only three voice parts: the melodic *cantus* or *discantus*, the *tenor*, melodic as well, and, between the two, the *contratenor* or simply *contra*, an often entirely unmelodic part which, in order to form harmonic triads with the outer voices, jumped up and down to wherever the filling note was needed and did not hesitate to cross the tenor now and again.

Instruments played a vital role in this style, though no composer cared to demand and specify them in his notation. They often replaced or doubled the singing voice in the *cantus* and the *tenor* and were in exclusive charge of the *contra*, whose unmelodious character was not suitable for singing. The time liked motley, glittering colors in music just as well as in painting. No literary sources describe the customary combinations, but paintings of the time with musical scenes show that the instruments performing some piece belonged to different, contrasting families in order to keep the voices well apart. A frequent combination was a small or medium-sized harp, a bowed, five-string fiddle, and a portative organ, carried at right angles on a shoulder strap and played with the right hand while the left operated the bellows (*cf.* plate XVI in the author's *History of Musical Instruments*, page 272).

In dance music, on the contrary, the participating instruments were far more homogeneous, because they did not serve the interests of polyphony proper. Usually, the players performed their *basses danses*, *saltarelli*, and *pive* on two shawms or oboes and on one trumpet, which evidently had a long-throated, telescopic mouthpiece as a trombone-like slide to supply (artificial) melodic notes besides the few skeletal notes provided by overblowing (plate VII, *cf.* also Appendix).

In keeping with the strong harmonic trends of the time, the Renaissance did frequently (and doubtless also in dance music) renounce the contrapuntal style in favor of a *fauxbourdon*, or, as the English said, a *faburden*. Like the English discant of the twelfth and thirteenth centuries, this technique was a singing, or playing, in parallel thirds and sixths, but it placed the leading melody in the upper voice, so that the middle voice accompanied at the lower fourth, and the basal voice, at the lower sixth. So far, the earliest documents of *fauxbourdon* are Italian and date from about 1430. It seems to have reached England only after 1460.

For the rest, the traditional forms of secular music had not greatly changed. *Ballade, chanson, rondeau, virelai* were, on the whole, what they had been in the thirteenth and fourteenth centuries.

Even the motet, chiefly used for solemn occasions, both spiritual and secular, clung to the concepts of the thirteenth and fourteenth centuries. Dufay's most celebrated State motet, evidently commissioned by the City of Florence in 1436, has still the old instrumental tenor on a liturgical melody, and two *cantus* on different, closely related texts, *Salve flos Tuscae* and *Vos nunc Etrusca*, but he did add a *contra* in the style of the time in order to fill the chordal consonances; that is, to complete the triads of which the other two voices provided only two notes instead of three. This was done *below* the tenor, so that this latter was no longer the lowest voice part; the tenor had become what it is today, the higher of the two male voice parts. Dufay's earlier motets, written before the Italian influence, even preserved the Gothic principle of isorhythm in the form in which Machault had used it (*cf.* page 98).

N OTATION progressed during the earlier part of the fifteenth century both in the field of the mensural script and in that of instrumental tablatures.

The turn from the 'black' to the 'white' notation was a decisive step from the medieval to the modern script. Ligatures were less often used, and the larger symbols—long, breve, semibreve, and minim—which had been black before, were left unfilled, anticipating the unfilled heads of modern wholenotes and halfnotes.

The long had still the value of a modern wholenote; the breve, of a halfnote; the semibreve, of a quarternote.

A hundred years after the apparently first attempt at a keyboard tablature in England (page 94), a similar notation appeared in Germany in 1432. Subsequently, it was used there exclusively till 1624 and had not entirely disappeared even in the time of J. S. Bach, who occasionally availed himself of its facilities.

This so-called German keyboard tablature consisted of the letter names of the notes—*A*, *B*, *C*, and so on—with, above them, rhythmical symbols taken from certain forms of mensural notation, such as a vertical dash for the semibreve, a dash with one flag for the minim, with two flags for the semiminim, with three flags for the *fusa*. A loop-like flourish at the end of the letter—in medieval writing the customary abbreviation of the Latin ending *-is*—indicated the sharped notes, which in German terminology were, and still are, called *cis*, *dis*, *fis*, *gis*, *ais*.

One German organ tablature of 1448 is particularly remarkable for having the earliest bar-lines, which became general only in the seventeenth century. Four years later, Conrad Paumann wrote the most celebrated German organ tablature, *Fundamentum organisandi*, a systematic collection of counterpoint studies (*órgana*) for the organist.

INSTRUMENTS. The growing importance of keyboard instruments in the North, reflected by the mere existence of tablatures, is confirmed not only by the increasing number of pictorial representations in paintings, woodcuts, and reliefs, but also by the unparalleled interest in their construction. An impressive evidence of this interest is the illustrated treatise in the *Bibliothèque Nationale* in Paris, written about 1440 by a Netherlander, Henry Arnaut, and recently printed in facsimile.

Most clavichords and virginals of the time seem to have had only three semitones in the octave: B♭ as the changing note in the *D* and the *F* mode (*"una nota super la"*—*cf*. page 48), F♯ as the leading note of the *G* mode on its way to major, and C♯ as the leading note of the *D* mode on its way to minor. Many organs, on the contrary, had already the complete keyboard of today. A good evidence is the instrument of St. Cecilia on van Eyck's altar at Ghent (*cf*. plate XVI in the author's *History of Musical Instruments*, page 272).

Whether complete or not, the black keys, almost exclusively used as leading or changing notes, were tuned in some acceptable relation to their immediate neighbors, but not to the other keys. As their usual name *semitonia*, their smaller size, and their rear position implied, they were mere accessories, not keys in the proper sense. Nor were the white keys themselves submitted to any universally valid tuning rule.

Speaking of instruments, we might mention that in 1457 western Europe made its first acquaintance with larger kettledrums, struck by riders on horseback in the retinue of some Polish political mission. They impressed the listeners enough to be eventually received into the western stock of instruments as companions of the princely trumpets. Not everybody liked them, however. To use Sebastian Virdung's words in his *Musica getutscht* of 1511, the "enormous rumbling barrels trouble honest old people, the ill and the sick, the devotees in monasteries who study, read, and pray, and I think and believe the devil has invented and made them."

READING

Gustave Reese, *Music in the Middle Ages*, New York, 1940. *Music in the Renaissance*, New York, 1954. Curt Sachs, *World History of the Dance*, New York, 1937: Chapter 7. *The History of Musical Instruments*, New York, 1940: Chapter 15. *The Commonwealth of Art*, New York, 1946: Cross Section 1430. *Rhythm and Tempo*, New York, 1953: Chapters 10, 11. Charles van den Borren, *Guillaume Dufay*, Bruxelles, 1926. *Instruments de Musique du XVe Siècle. Les Traités d'Henri-Arnaut de Zwolle et de divers Anonymes*, ed. Le Cerf et Labande, Paris, 1932.

9

THE AGE OF OCKEGHEM

1 4 6 0 – 1 5 0 0

THE TIDAL LAW, manifest in aesthetic reversals from age to age (as the author explains in his *Commonwealth of Art*), interrupted the classical trends of the Renaissance in the 1460's. The arts went back to picturesqueness, haste, and stress on action and feeling. And music went with them.

The Burgundian composers, who had been in the lead before 1460, shared but little in this turn. The new men came from farther north, from the Lowlands, from Flanders and Holland.

The helmsman of the Netherlanders was Jan or Johannes Ockeghem (whose name has also been spelled Okeghem). Born around 1430 in the Flemish town from which he took his name, he served as a choirboy in the cathedral of Antwerp in 1443 and 1444, studied with Guillaume Dufay, probably at Cambrai, and after 1453 spent most of his life in France as the king's conductor. He died in 1495 at Tours on the Loire, mourned as "the prince of music."

He excelled in Masses and motets, canons and French *chansons* and wrote the first polyphonic Lamentations of Jeremiah (1474). Delightful as his smaller secular works may be, his greatest achievements are the larger liturgical forms, in which he turned his back on the short phrases of the Burgundians and their clean-cut cadences after every few measures. His was a truly polyphonic flow without interruptions.

Ockeghem's greatest musical contemporary was Obrecht, a Dutchman among Flemings.

Jacob Obrecht lived the typical life of a Netherlandish musician in the age of the Renaissance, singing and conducting in cathedrals of his homeland, joining one of the brilliant court-chapels of Italy, and returning to the North. But the concluding episode of Obrecht's life was unusual. After serving Duke Ercole of Este in Ferrara, he went back to his native Utrecht, where Erasmus, the illustrious humanist, was among his pupils. He accepted leading positions in Cambrai, Bruges, and Antwerp; but thirty years after his prior sojourn in Italy, he could not resist another call, went back to the Este court in Ferrara, and there met his death in the plague of the following year, 1505.

Obrecht's works include many Masses, motets, hymns, and French *chansons*. In one Mass, with the cantus firmus *Sub tuum praesidium*, Obrecht revived the archaic style of the Gothic motet: its six voices sang three different texts simultaneously (which, incidentally, was done at the same time by the German composer Adam of Fulda).

But most of his compositions show the triumph of the new harmonic (vertical) over the old contrapuntal (horizontal) conception. This triumph found a particularly strong expression in the cadence or concluding chords, which appear in Obrecht's and Ockeghem's works for the first time in the modern form. The older masters, thinking contrapuntally, had usually prepared the final octave chord (say, $c'-c''$) by a major sixth ($d'-b'$), so that either of the outer voice parts ended in a second-step—the upper voice ascending from b' to c'', and the lower voice descending from d' to c'. From the end of the fifteenth century on, we find, instead, the orthodox harmonic cadence via the dominant ('authentic') or the subdominant ('plagal'), that is, $b'/g' > c''/c'$ in the first, and $a'/f' > c''/c'$ in the second case.

Fond of a powerful harmonic density, Obrecht even gave his cadences full, triadic final chords instead of the empty fifths and octaves of medieval cadences.

His melodies had an incomparable vigor and breath. The tidy, clear-cut, shortwinded structures of the Burgundians were abandoned, and their smiling, kindly sereneness was lost. Ockeghem's and Obrecht's melodies, intense and passionate, stretched in far-flung, powerful arches; the voices reached to pitches high and low that had hardly been considered before, and the texture was compact.

The older trio style (*cantus, contratenor, tenor*), sometimes shunned even in the generation of Dufay, was little by little given up as too empty and sober. The modern four-part writing became the rule. Indeed, exceptional pieces went further: Heinrich Finck gave one of his Masses eleven voices; Antoine Brumel, a Fleming in Italian services, wrote a motet for twelve parts; Josquin des Prés, another one for twenty-four parts; and Ockeghem himself, a giant canon for no less than thirty-six voices.

The transition from the standard three-part to the standard four-part writing was momentous from the viewpoints not only of harmony and counterpoint, but also of terminology. For the *contratenor* was cleft into two different parts in order to provide the part to be added. One of them became the *contra altus*, or high contra, more or less stretched between the cantus and the tenor; the other one became the *contra bassus*, or low contra, which on the main kept below the tenor. Graphically:

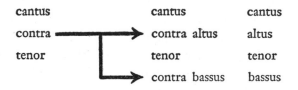

cantus	cantus	cantus
contra	contra altus	altus
tenor	tenor	tenor
	contra bassus	bassus

It was at that time that the word *tenor* began to shift from its original meaning of a held, sustained *cantus firmus* and to adopt the modern sense of a certain range and timbre of voice. However, as late as 1557 the Imperial chapel in Brussels still called its six men-singers *hault-contres*, *tailles* (tenors), and *bassecontres*, thus keeping the *contra* epithets for both the alto and the basso; and in the following year 1558, Zarlino expressly said that some people called the part above the tenor *contratenor*, some *contralto*, and some *alto*. The French preserved the word *hautecontre* as a translation of *contra altus* for centuries and—with the Italians and Spaniards—call the human alto voice *contralto* to this day. The English, on the other hand, clung long to the even older *contratenor* for the alto voice.

The *cantus firmus* itself was by no means given up. It appeared in the cantus as well as in the tenor. And with a similar unconcernedness as in the generation before, the *cantus firmus* would be taken from secular music, too—indeed, from erotic *chansons*, like *La belle se siet* (The belle sits down) or *Baisiez moi* (Kiss me). The song *L'homme, l'homme, l'homme armé* (The soldier) was, for reasons unknown, used more than thirty times as the tenor in French, Netherlandish, German, Spanish, and Italian Masses during the two centuries from Busnois to Carissimi, and even Palestrina is on the list.

Besides such so-called *cantus-firmus* Masses with a foreign tenor, the times offered parody Masses and freely invented Masses. The parody Mass, or *missa parodia*, took not merely the melody, but the whole polyphonic web from some *chanson* or motet, either complete and uninterrupted or only in sections, which had to alternate with freely invented sections. In the third form of the time, the freely invented Mass, the whole material, themes and texture, came from the composer himself. In short:

Tenor Masses, with foreign *cantus firmi*.

Parody Masses, with foreign polyphonic webs.

Free Masses, wholly invented.

Plainsong Masses (mentioned before) drew their melodic material from corresponding Mass sections of the Gregorian liturgy.

The motet itself had turned to the new ideals of the end of the fifteenth century. Not only had it given up the multiple texts, vernacular languages, and secular topics, but also, like the other polyphonic forms, it had done away with the distinction between the individual voice parts, which more and more were given equal weight and importance, although the *cantus firmus* was for a while retained.

The definition of this new type of motet is, in short: a polyphonic choral composition for four or more voice parts on a Latin text from the Scriptures.

Taking possession of a scriptural chapter untouched before, the motet gave its style to an unprecedented polyphonic *Passion* to supplant the mere Gregorian recitation of the Easter week Lesson on the sufferings and death of Christ.

The earliest examples of polyphonic Passions, in Italian and English manuscripts between 1480 and 1490, are anonymous. But around 1500, we find a composer's name connected with such a work: Jacob Obrecht allegedly wrote a Passion after the Latin version of St. Matthew, for four voice parts in the customary motet style without distinction of the narration proper, the words of Christ, or the interjections of the people.

GERMANY—for the first time in the Later Ages—was able to present a powerful master, Heinrich Finck. He was born in 1445 and educated in Cracow, Poland's capital. We do not know too much of his adult life—only that, as a mature and prominent master, he served the courts of Poland, Württemberg, and Salzburg. Almost eighty years old, he retired in 1524 to a monastery in Vienna and died there in 1527.

The none too numerous pieces that a benevolent Providence has preserved show two rather different styles: a number of predominantly melodic and harmonic, warm-hearted part-songs are connected with the earlier German *Liederbücher* (*cf.* below); while his polyphonic motets, written on a *cantus firmus*, are close to the up-to-date Flemish style.

A magnificent example of his Flemish polyphony—obviously in what his nephew and editor, Hermann Finck, calls the older, "hard" style—is the Easter chorale *Christ ist erstanden* (Christ has risen), in which four Gothic, angular voices zigzag around the granitic melody of Wipo's Easter sequence *Victimae paschalis laudes*.

To judge from the important collections written down around 1460—the *Lóchamer*, the *Glógauer*, and the *Münchner Liederbuch*—the *Lied* was indeed in the focus of German music.

The two latter *Liederbücher* also contain a number of dance tunes with curious titles, such as *Der Rattenschwanz* or *Der Bauernschwanz*. They are less curious, however, once we realize that the word *Schwanz* had not the modern meaning of "tail," but derived from an older verb *swansen*, "to swing oneself, to leap." The titles simply mean a rat's and a peasant's dance.

The importance of singing, though in other forms, shows also in the peculiar art of the German *Meistersinger*.

THE *MEISTERSINGER* (master singer, or, better, craftsman singer) symbolized the rapid shift of spiritual life from the degenerated chivalry to the working men in cities and towns. The last of the *Minnesinger*, Oswald von Wolkenstein, had died in 1445. Only a few years later, the Swabian Michael Behaim (b. 1416, assassinated 1474) marked the transition from singing knights to singing burghers—though he was not yet a sedentary artisan.

Despite the change of atmosphere, the Meistersinger created no altogether novel style; they were neither pioneers nor revolutionaries.

Greek dancer with clappers, from a vase in Cambridge.

Two kithara players and two pipers in a Greek procession, from a vase in Berlin.

PLATE I

Staffless neumes from a gradual of the twelfth century, manuscript in the New York Public Library.

PLATE II

Organum and trope in mensural notation, from Higini Angles, *El Codex Musical de las Huelgas* [thirteenth century], Barcelona, 1931.

PLATE III

French ballade in mensural notation of the later fourteenth century, after
Johannes Wolf, *Schrifttafeln.*

PLATE IV

Gloria Patri in Gothic plainsong notation of 1487, manuscript in the
New York Public Library.

PLATE V

The chapel of St. Mark's in Venice around 1496, after a painting by Giovanni Bellini.

PLATE VI

Courtly dance band in Martin Zasinger's "Decapitation of St. John the Baptist," c. 1500.

PLATE VII

Raphael, "St. Cecilia," c. 1515, Museo Civico, Bologna.

PLATE VIII

Angel with lute from Vittore Carpaccio's "Madonna" of 1510 in Venice.

PLATE IX

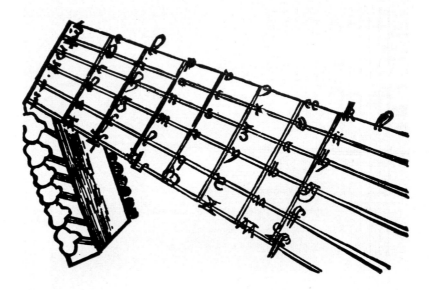

Fingerboard of a lute with the symbols of the German lute tablature,
from Sebastian Virdung, *Musica getutscht*, 1511.

PLATE X

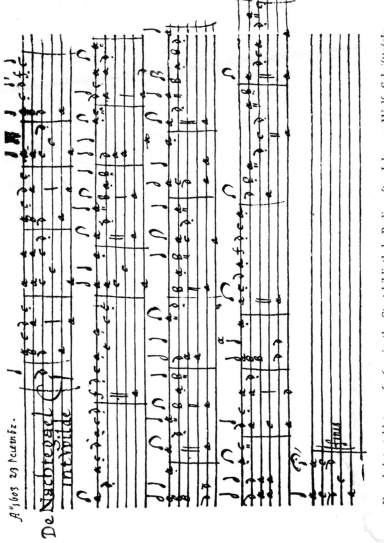

French lute tablature of 1603 in the *Staatsbibliothek, Berlin, after Johannes Wolf, Schrifttafeln.*

PLATE XI

PLATE XII

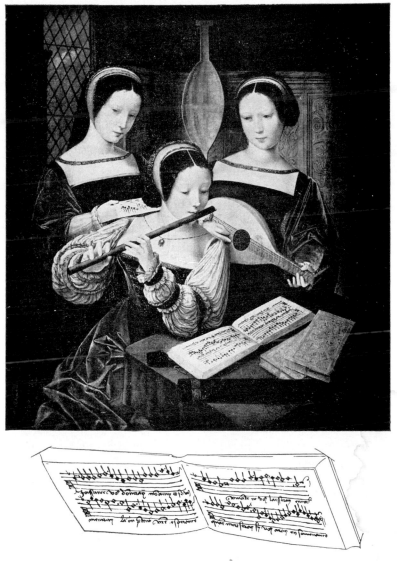

Three ladies performing a *chanson*, by a French master c. 1530, Harrach Gallery, Vienna.

PLATE XIII

Lady playing the clavichord, by I. C. Vermeijen, in the *Kunsthalle*, Hamburg.

PLATE XIV

Three trumpetists, from H. Aldegrever's series, "The Wedding Dancers," 1538.

PLATE XV

Francesco Ferdinando Richter's portrait of Francesco Maria Veracini
(1685–1750).

PLATE XVI

Their merit was to have saved a desiccating art through a transplantation to another soil, which granted it a second bloom for a century and a half. A great personality like the shoemaker Hans Sachs in Nürnberg (1494–1576), hero of Wagner's opera, was able to lift the art of the Meistersinger to a higher level, maybe under the impact of political events and the Reformation. But even the works of Sachs show the limited scope of these craftsmen who, mistrusting free, creative imagination, were satisfied with patchwork as long as it conformed with their narrow rules of composition. Any breach of these rules was pitilessly recorded with chalk by the *Merker*, or monitor, who, at the weekly singing meetings of the masters in one of the churches, had to safeguard petty correctness rather than power, beauty, or imagination.

"When," says a contemporary chronicler, "the singer has sat down in the singer's chair, and has been silent for a while, the first of the monitors shouts: Begin! Thus the singer begins, and when a stanza has been done, he pauses until the monitor once more calls out: Go on! Having finished, the singer gets up from his chair and cedes it to another one. Monitors are those (usually) four who as chairmen of the guild sit in a curtained booth at a table and a bulky pulpit. The oldest one has the Scriptures in Mr. Luther's translation on the pulpit before him, opens it on the page from which the poem has been taken, and eagerly watches whether the song agrees with the story as well as with the words of Luther. The second monitor, sitting opposite the first, watches out whether the poem conforms to the prescribed laws of the tablature, and wherever offence has been committed, he marks the fine with chalk on the pulpit. The third monitor writes down the rhymes and scores any incorrectness. And the fourth monitor is concerned with the melody, whether it is correct, and also, whether all *Stollen* and *Abgesänge* correspond."

Two similar *Stollen* (the term originally meant a pillar) and one concluding epode, or *Abgesang*, formed a stanza, or *Bar*, in the form AAB. Thus, even the exclusive principle of *Meistergesang* structure was taken over without any change from the art of the *Minnesinger*. The first *Stollen* was sung *mezzoforte*, the second, *piano*, and the *Abgesang*, vigorously *forte*.

During the early days of the *Meistersinger*, we hear of the first Italian societies for music performances independent of churches and courts. In 1482 an *accademia* was founded in Bologna, and in 1484 one in Milan. But our knowledge of their exact nature is none too certain.

THE MOVEMENT DOWN towards the bass register, which Dufay had started in a modest way, entered its decisive phase at the end of the fifteenth century. Some scores of the Ockeghem age extended as far down as the voices would carry, one even to C. The movement also showed in novel instruments of a lower range than had been considered before. Amazed musicians from Spain in 1493 exclaimed that in Italy they had seen some viols as tall as themselves—evidently double-basses. An Italian painter, Matteo di Giovanni, who died in 1495, depicted the first trombone in modern form save for a less expanding bell (and hence a more chamber-musical tone). The painting is in the National Gallery, London (*cf*. also plate XV).

A short time later, monographs on instruments—which became frequent soon after 1500—already record full families of wind and bowed instruments, of flutes and shawms, of rebecs and viols, in three or four well-graduated sizes each, as treble, alto, tenor, and bass.

The keyboard instruments, too, had to extend much farther down. This extension, however, implied augmented costs, especially for the organ, where any additional key meant the addition of not only one, but of quite a rank of pipes (*cf*. page 54) with their complicated machinery and the largest and costliest size. Hence the sellers and the buyers were interested in having only the strictly necessary pipes added, with the omission of those *semitonia* which would not be used in the bass range, as *C♯, D♯, F♯, G♯*, since they generally served as leading notes in the melody only.

This resulted in a so-called *short octave* at the lower end of the organ keyboard. The customary arrangement of white and black keys was preserved, and the eye was under the impression that the notes went straight down to *E*. But the keys operated other notes than those which their position suggested. The usual arrangement was:

in which the *E* key actually produced *C;* the *F♯* key, *D;* the *G♯* key, *E;* and the other keys, the usual sequence *F G A B♭ B♮.*

The stringed keyboard instruments, though not concerned with the high cost of many extra pipes, followed this arrangement since they shared their builders, their players, and their music with the organ. The full chromatic bass octave was not compulsory before the eighteenth century.

The organ itself maintained the contrast between the south and the north. The Italian mixture-organ with one keyboard was still in general use, and only a few builders were willing to add a *flute* as the earliest, though little contrasting, solo stop. The North developed the colorful "Gothic" organ with its many contrasting solo stops and multiple keyboards suitable for contrapuntal playing styles. As a novel addition, the builders introduced the "reeds," or sets of trenchant pipes with metal reeds not unlike those of the clarinet and the saxophone.

The pedal keyboard, invented not so long before (*cf.* page 94), became important in taking over one of the voice parts and therewith enhancing the contrapuntal possibilities. Indeed, the German organ tablature of 1448, mentioned in the preceding chapter, displays the practice of a double pedal, in which either foot plays a part of its own instead of coöperating with the other foot in the performance of one single part. (Schlick's *Spiegel* of 1511 mentions even three-part playing on the pedal.)

As another remarkable trait, the organ at Hagenau in Alsace was given, in 1491, the earliest *tremulant* as an interrupting device to produce sentimental slow vibrations when connected with one of the stops. Even so rigid an instrument as the organ accepted the emotional trends of the time.

These changes were the more significant as large collections of organ music, such as the *Buxheim Organ Book* of about 1470, show the growing importance of organ playing during the later part of the fifteenth century, both in church and in house music.

T EMPERAMENT. It was in keeping with this growing importance that Franchino Gafori's *Practica musicae* of 1496 mentioned the earliest thorough temperament of keyboards by way of shortening the fifths.

Not much later did Arnold Schlick describe this obviously common temperament in his *Spiegel der Orgelmacher* of 1511. Based on medieval beginnings (*cf.* page 85), the so-called mean-tone temperament had divisive thirds in the ratio 5:4, or 386 cents (*cf.* page 12), and subdivided them into mean or equal tones. Actually, it was a compromise between the divisive system with its welcome third and the cyclic system with its chain of fifths as a handy way to tune a keyboard.

This compromise works in the following way. The cycle of fifths yields a third by a Didymean comma, or 22 cents larger than the one of the divisive system. Taking a quarter of this comma, or 5½ cents, off each of the four fifths that lead to a third (an amount almost imperceptible to the ear) creates both satisfactory fifths and octaves, and divisive thirds of 386 cents:

$$C \ 696\tfrac{1}{2} \ G \ 696\tfrac{1}{2} \ D \ 696\tfrac{1}{2} \ A \ 696\tfrac{1}{2} \ E.$$

The distance from C to E is 2786 cents. But the E is actually two octaves too high; it is two octaves *plus* a third. Thus we have to deduct the cent number of two octaves, 2400, and arrive at the correct 386 cents.

The mean-tone temperament was an excellent solution, melodically and harmonically, when only white keys were used. But it did not work on the black keys: the note between G and A, for example, would be either $G\#$ or $A\flat$. As $G\#$, it would lie two major thirds above the lower C, that is, C–E and E–$G\#$, or $386 + 386 = 772$ cents. But as $A\flat$, it would lie one major third below the higher C, or $1200 - 386 = 814$ cents, which makes a difference of no less than 42 cents, or approximately a quartertone.

Only the radical 'equal' temperament was able to help. It will be described in Chapter 15.

INSTRUMENTAL MUSIC was to a great extent dependent on improvisation.

The outstanding example is dance music. The pieces to accompany the leading court dance—*basse danse* or *bassa danza*—consist of nothing but one staff with uniform breves from the beginning to the end under a tenor clef signature. Such skeletal, lifeless rows of notes can evidently not represent the actual music to go with the dance, and so much the less as most contemporary pictures of princely ballrooms show dance bands of three pieces, two shawms or strident oboes, and a slide trumpet not unlike a trombone (plate VII). This trumpet, probably the lowest (tenor) instrument of the group, must have played those tenor clef notes. But it could use them only as the raw material for a living melody which the player had to adapt to the ever-different step arrangement of the individual dance. The two shawms may have improvised either two higher parallels—in English discant or otherwise— or else two counterpoints *alla mente*, that is, without written-out parts.

Incidentally, whenever paintings of the time show musical performances, singers hold part-sheets, but players do without notation.

T IME AND TEMPO. Notation turned with growing speed away from the medieval traits of uncertain mensuration.

The *longa* was still what the wholenote is today, the breve corresponded to the halfnote, and the semibreve to a quarternote. Franchino Gafori, apparently the first one, indicated in 1496 that the semibreve corresponded to the pulse of a man with quiet respiration, that is, to MM 60–80.

It might be well to recapitulate, in the following diagram, the approximate time values of the mensural notes with c. MM 60–80 to the modern quarternote.

	longa	breve	semibreve	minim	semiminim
c. 1225:	♩	♪			
c. 1250:	♩	♩	♪		
14th and 15th centuries:	𝅝	♩	♩	♪	♪
16th century:	𝅝𝅝	𝅝	♩	♩	♪
17th century:	𝅝𝅝𝅝𝅝	𝅝𝅝	𝅝	♩	♩

In many modern editions, the bewildered reader is faced with curious slow-motion pictures which he cannot be expected to understand. There are two cases.

1. The editor, realizing that the forms of the ancient mensural symbols live on in modern notation, keeps them to preserve the original aspect as much as possible.

In doing so, he ignores the fact that the time values of these symbols have changed considerably. A breve of the thirteenth century looked like the breve of our time, but was about sixteen times faster; it corresponded, not to a double whole note of today, but to an eighthnote. In keeping the breve form, the editor has sacrificed musical, audible meaning to meaningless visible form.

2. Many editors, aware of such grotesqueness, give up the form of the older symbols, yet do not dare to be consistent. They stop somewhere in the middle of the road and reluctantly reduce—as they illogically say—a long to a breve or even a semibreve (wholenote) where the actual meaning is a quarternote. Thus they render neither form nor meaning.

The only acceptable way is to transcribe according to the meaning and to take care of scholarly needs by a simple indication at the beginning of the score: $\Box = \flat$

As long as this practice is, alas, not general, the reader cannot avoid transcribing himself what the editor has failed to transcribe for him.

How much the ancients themselves subordinated their symbols to the concept of a compulsory unit of speed—which to us is the normal quarternote as the measure of a natural step—shows in the general practice of the *tactus*.

TACTUS was for centuries the official name for the steady, almost metronomical tempo marked by the even down-and-up of the conductor's hand. The word lives on in the German terms *Takt schlagen, taktieren* for "time-beating."

Around 1500, the normal *tactus* covered a breve, and either one of its two beats, a semibreve. This means, in modern symbols, a quarternote down and a quarternote up. Since Gafori allotted the pulse-beat of a man with quiet respiration to the semibreve, a *tactus* must have covered a 2/4 allegro measure in MM 60–80.

To be sure, there was more than just one immutable tempo. But the differences in tempo were very far from the personal arbitrariness of modern performances, where a quarternote can have every possible duration from *adagio molto* to *prestissimo*. Any tempo different from the normal—the *tempo giusto* (as the Handel period called it)—derived from the standard by a strict multiplication of the unit. This was done in the so-called proportions:

Proportio dupla meant double tempo, with two, not one, semibreves to the beat.

Proportio tripla, triple tempo, with three semibreves to the beat.

Proportio quadrupla, fourfold tempo, with four semibreves to the beat.

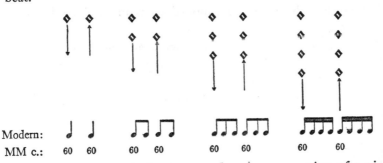

The tempo signature at the beginning of a piece or section of a piece expressed the *proportio* in an arithmetic fraction: 2/1 or 2, 3/1 or 3, 4/1 or 4, which must not be confused with the modern signature of two, three, or four wholenotes to the measure or with the older signatures of the *modus perfectus* and the *modus imperfectus*. The numerator of the fraction simply indicated how many time-units should take the place of the original one.

The *proportio dupla*—the only one to do so—often did without the numerical symbol and adopted instead a vertical dash through the C-like semicircle that stood for the normal fourbeat rhythm. This sign is still in use for a certain change of tempo for which we have stuck to the ancient mensural name: *alla breve*. Its meaning is that the piece has to be taken at twice the normal speed, with one beat to the halfnote, instead of the usual one beat to the quarternote, or *alla semibreve*.

A slightly more complicated case was denoted by the fraction 3/2 before a piece or a section. Again, this signature did not, as in later music, imply three halfnotes to the bar, but demanded that three notes be compressed into the time ordinarily given to two notes—in other words, that the time be increased by a half. This increase in tempo and reading in triple time was called the *proportio sesquiáltera*, a clumsy term that meant a ratio whose denominator was *áltera*, 2, and the numerator, one more, or 3.

This proportion explains what the Germans called a slightly faster *Nachtanz*, or after-dance, *proporz*. It often used the same melody as the quieter *Vortanz*, or opening dance, but in the proportion 3/2, that is, in triplets against the former duplets.

A warning to the reader: in the seventeenth century, the German *Nachtanz* is called *tripla* and has accordingly the time signature 3. But it is meant to be the old *sesquiáltera*, whose name has become as obsolete as the whole idea of proportions is meaningless in an age of free tempo.

As for the notes themselves, the once quadrangular heads were often triangular and sometimes even oval, and the stems, which till then had normally been drawn upwards wherever they stood, were drawn downwards from the middle staff line on, lest they reach into the staff above.

MUSIC PRINTING. Clarity and simplification of the script were the more indicated as music began to benefit from the portentous new invention of printing.

In the first decades of printing, theoretical books and liturgical incunabula left appropriate empty spaces for musical examples to be filled in by hand. And in the sixties some of the printers met the readers halfway by providing red staff lines so that only the notes themselves remained to be added.

The first attempts at actual music printing were made in Italian workshops in missals of 1476. It was a rather complicated process of double-printing, first of the staff lines and then, in a second treatment, of the notes—a process that easily allowed, and often was used, for combining black and red in the two procedures. This technique was so rapidly perfected that, after exactly a quarter of a century, it came to a climax in the famous *Odhécaton* or Hundred of Songs, a beautiful collection of ninety-six favorite pieces of the time, which the publisher

Ottaviano dei Petrucci (pron. -ootchee) printed at Venice in 1501.

It was quite definitely a step backwards when, after the first attempts of double-printing, an Italian introduced in 1487 a process of single-printing from wooden blocks into which the page was cut as a whole in the manner of the older woodcut picture books. Since delicacy is denied to woodcutting, the results were notably inferior to those of the double-printing process.

The usual arrangement of polyphonic pieces was still the old choir-book pattern, with all the voice parts written or printed in juxtaposition on two consecutive pages (*verso* and *recto*) of the oversized tome on a pulpit in front of the chorus. Scores in a modern sense, with the voice parts exactly below one another, were not yet considered.

The birthplace of musical printing and publishing was Venice, with its two patriarchs, Ottavio Scotto, from 1481 on, and Ottaviano dei Petrucci, who obtained a 'privilege of music printing' in 1498.

With printed editions and publishing houses, music entered an entirely new development. No longer dependent upon a few casual handwritten copies, it was able to overcome the limits of space and time as well as social and economic barriers.

READING

Gustave Reese, *Music in the Renaissance*, New York, 1954. Curt Sachs, *World History of the Dance*, New York, 1937. *The History of Musical Instruments*, New York, 1940. *The Commonwealth of Art*, New York, 1946. *Rhythm and Tempo*, New York, 1953. Otto J. Gombosi, *Jacob Obrecht*, Leipzig, 1925. Otto Kinkeldey, "Music and Music Printing in Incunabula," *Reprint from the Papers of the Bibliographical Society of America*, Vol. XXVI, 1932.

10

THE AGE OF JOSQUIN

1500–1530

THE HIGH RENAISSANCE also had two phases: one roughly from 1500 to 1530, and one from 1530 to 1565. And, once more as in the early Renaissance, the first phase was quiet and reserved, and the second, agitated, dramatic, and free. In the first, the object of this chapter, music went Raphael's way—the way of strictness and clarity in structure, of dignified sedateness, of moderate emotion. The boundless effusion of Ockeghem's days was gone. All music submitted to the laws of simplicity and discipline.

The leading masters were Josquin des Prés and Henry Isaac.

JOSQUIN DES PRÉS' name reflects the love more than the reverence of his contemporaries. It is the French spelling of the Flemish pet name Joskin, equivalent of our Joe. His last name—so often nonsensically misspelled with an *accent grave*—means "meadows" or "pastures," like the last name of his older countryman, the painter Roger van der Weyden. Josquin himself, though, used the archaic spelling *Prez*.

The master must have been born in Hainaut, Belgium, around 1450. He became Jean Ockeghem's pupil in Paris, spent at least thirty years —with an interrupting stay at Cambrai from 1495 to 1499—in Italian chapels in Milan and Rome, in Módena and Ferrara, lived once again in Paris, and died as the provost of the cathedral at Condé in his native country on August 27, 1521, a few months after Raphael.

His works include *chansons* in French, but mainly psalms, motets, and Masses, of which the ones surnamed *Ave maris stella*, *Pangue lingua*, and *Hercules* are best known.

The latter work is very strange in its melodic conception: the leading theme is not due to any creative imagination or inspiration and not even to the technical consideration of contrapuntal pliancy. It is *soggetto cavato* (pron. sodjetto), or "extracted subject," provided by the simple and apparently mechanical process of substituting for each syllable in the name of Josquin's employer Duke Ercole of Ferrara, the note (or one of the two notes) whose solmisation syllable has the identical vowel:

Her-	cu-	les	dux	Fer-	ra-	ri-	e
re	*ut*	*re*	*ut*	*re*	*fa*	*mi*	*re*
D	C	D	C	D	F	E	D

Josquin followed exactly the same principle in his curious polyphonic fanfare *Vive le roy*, Long Live the King, whose *cantus firmus* transforms the vowels $u(=v)$ *i u e e o i* into the notes *ut mi ut re re sol mi* or *C E C D D G E*.

The mystic spirit of the Gothic Middle Ages had not yet disappeared. Hidden, esoteric significance still weighed more than superficial, sensuous beauty—even if such a pregnant cohesion in the spirit is almost paradoxically found by way of a merely sensuous, superficial likeness.

We do not know, and perhaps will never know, how far this Gothic procedure had deteriorated in Josquin's mind to an amusing trick. Anyway, the master had otherwise conquered the spirit of the Middle Ages. Celebrated as "the prince of music" by contemporaries and as a beloved patriarch by at least two following generations, he was, in the years of his maturity, the chief representative of the high Renaissance, side by side with Bramante, Leonardo, and Raphael. As such, he dammed the ecstatic torrent of Ockeghem's style and shaped his quiet melodies out of the natural flow of the words. As once Dufay had done, he delighted in chains of restful perfect chords and molded his ideas in strict, transparent, symmetrical forms. To emphasize this symmetry, he would often repeat a phrase of the two higher voices in the two lower ones and thus anticipate, in a way, the antiphony of two choruses so dear to the Baroque.

Indeed, while the Burgundians and early Flemings had, under the sway of medieval ideas, allotted different tasks to each of the voice parts—to serve as a *cantus firmus,* or as a free counterpoint, or as a harmonic filler—the Netherlanders increasingly assimilated them in the spirit of balance that ruled the Renaissance, until they all were partners with equal rights and duties. Late in the fifteenth century, the process of assimilation went so far that the voice parts would present themselves, in the manner of a fugue, in successive entries with the same initial motive in each of the sections of a piece, although they were free to continue in their own ways.

Hugo Riemann ascribed this novel form of weaving the voice parts in a fugato technique to Ockeghem. The present generation of historians is rather inclined to give the honor to Josquin. The term that Riemann coined, *Durchimitierender Stil,* or, literally, "through-imitation," has no proper equivalent in English.

This imitative style is in itself only a part of a greater innovation—indeed, of the most essential innovation—in the concept of polyphony which is the real divide between the Middle and the Later Ages in music. While the medieval contrapuntists had composed the voice parts one after another—the *tenor* first, then the *cantus,* and lastly the *contra,* without the conception of a coherent, perceptible whole—the generation around 1500 began to conceive polyphonic pieces in the modern sense, as units in which the voice parts were meaningless elements without a life of their own. The earliest evidences appear in the writings of Pietro Aron, in *De Institutione Harmonica,* 1516, and *Thoscanello de la Musica,* 1523. After describing the outmoded method of successive writing, he says that from Josquin, Obrecht, Isaac, and Agricola on, composers considered all the voice parts *together.* But, he adds, "doing so is a very difficult thing and requires long training and practice."

In keeping with this new ideal of balance, but also in keeping with the much more austere attitude at the turn of the century, were the renouncement, at least in principle, of the older gay and motley mixture of voices and instruments within the same composition and the adoption, in its place, of the urge for an *a cappella* polyphony of unadulterated human voices. To a certain extent the time was feeling what St. Clement of Alexandria had felt some thirteen hundred years before: "We need one instrument, the peaceful word of adoration, not harps or drums or pipes or trumpets."

Raphael, the leading painter of the time, has left an unforgettable pictorial symbol of this reversal in his St. Cecilia in the museum of

Bologna (plate VIII). Flutes, a triangle, cymbals, drums are scattered on the ground in utter neglect, the viol has cracks and the skin of the kettledrum is burst, the very portative organ is dropping from her holy hands and losing its pipes. But she pays no attention. Rapt, she listens to the purer sounds from above, from the clouds where, freed from the earthliness of instruments, four angels bend over the choirbook and sing *a cappella*.

Hendrik, or Henry Isaac was the master closest to Josquin. Born in Flanders some time before 1450, he went to Italy and served now the Duke of Ferrara, now Lorenzo the Magnificent of Médici in Florence, then again lived in Innsbruck at the court of Emperior Maximilian I, returned to Florence and once more to Germany to work at Augsburg and Vienna, and died at Florence in 1517.

This life, beginning in the Netherlands and subsequently alternating between South Germany and Italy, is reflected in his works much less as a mixture than as a co-existence of styles: he expressed himself in Flemish music like a Fleming, in Italian music like an Italian, in German music like a German, and he even composed French *chansons*. Besides his songs in Latin, French, Italian, and German, he wrote many Masses and motets and also instrumental pieces. The most popular of all his compositions is the German Lied *Innsbruck ich muss dich lassen* (Innsbruck, I must now leave thee), which he probably wrote when his time in the capital of the Tyrol was up. The heartfelt melody of this secular song found a warm welcome in the Lutheran liturgy as a chorale with the title *Nun ruhen alle Wälder* (In peace now rest all forests), which later became an Anglican hymn with the text *O Lord how happy should we be*, and also an Episcopal hymn on the words *Come see the place where Jesus lay*.

Another fascinating pupil of Ockeghem, still little known, was Loyset Compère, a Franco-Fleming (d. 1518), to whom the *Odhécaton* gave no less than 22 of its 96 numbers.

The leading italian form was the *fróttola*: a lyrical song with, generally, the melody in the upper voice and an accompaniment of two or three lower parts which followed in chords rather than in counterpoints and were either played on one or several instruments or else sung. To be sure, the singers were soloists—choral rendition was not considered.

Its structure, like that of the *ballata* (page 90), consisted of a number of stanzas preceded, separated, and followed by *riprese*, or refrains. Each stanza had a melody in two sections, which may be called A and B. The *ripresa* availed itself of the whole melody, AB. In the stanza, two lines followed A; the next two lines, A as well; and the last two lines, B. Graphically:

ripresa: AB   AB   AB
stanzas: AAB   AAB

The last *ripresa* would end in an additional coda taken from the first half of A.

The Venetian publisher Ottaviano Petrucci printed no less than nine collections of *fróttole* in the four years between 1504 and 1508 and an eleventh one in 1514; the tenth book is lost. They were, indeed, in great demand, particularly in the courtly circles of Mantua and other north Italian city-states; and leading masters, such as Marco Cara and Bartolommeo Tromboncino among the Italians, and Henry Isaac and Josquin des Prés among the Flemings, placed their art at the disposal of the fashionable form.

This is important: it shows that regular structure, simplicity, and catchiness were at that time the usual traits not only of folk and popular music, but also of the refined music of the elite. They were characteristic of the classical-minded first generation of the sixteenth century.

Another favorite form of the time was the *lauda* (plur. *laude*), which, except for its devotional text, was related and indebted to the *fróttola* in its simple upper-voice melody and four-part setting. It should not be confused with either the late medieval form of this name (*cf.* page 91) or the popular *lauda* in Filippo Neri's prayer chapel after 1550.

A third preponderantly vocal form was the classical *ode*, for whose revival the humanistic, Latin trends of the century were responsible. Sometimes, as in Petrucci's three books of *fróttole* of 1504, the name implied strict, iambic songs with a curious rhyme arrangement (AAAB/BBBC/CCCD/DDDE/ and so on). In the main, however, the name denoted a Latin ode by Horace, or some other poet of a similar cast, set to music in "quantitative" meter. The term, discussed before, means that every short syllable was rendered by a short note, and any long syllable, by a note of double value, while the accompanying voice parts followed note against note in *stile famigliare*, as it was called. First suggested by the German humanist Conrad Celtes shortly before 1500, such beatless pieces were then written during two generations. Among composers in quantitative meter, we find the Germans Tritonius (1507), Paul Hofhaimer, famous organist to the Imperial court (1539), and the greatest Swiss musician, Ludwig Senfl (1532). France joined them a few decades later with her *vers mesurés* (cf. page 15).

A final pseudo-plebeian, popular form of the time was the *strambotto*. It had stanzas of eight lines, of five iambs each, with the curious rhyme arrangement AB AB AB CC, that is, two alternating rhymes for the first six lines and a fresh rhyme for the last two. The Italians called this arrangement *ottava rime*. The melody, in the upper voice, spanned only two lines in its two sections, A and B, and had to be sung four times. Graphically:

line	rhyme	melodic phrase
1	-ardenti	A
2	-serra	B
3	-accenti	A
4	-guerra	B
5	-tormenti	A
6	-terra	B
7	-core	A
8	-honore	B

THE PROTESTANT CHORALE was the logical issue of a Church reform that gave the congregation as a whole an active part in the service. As a congregational song, the chorale was bound to be simple and great, strong and impersonal.

As a German song, the chorale also needed a regular alternation of stressed and unstressed units, both in its words and in its melody, generally with three or four stresses in an iambic meter, as *Christ lág in Tódesbánden.*

In such regular alternation, the chorale was related to the German folksong, and the circle of musicians around Luther did not hesitate to avail itself of this treasure house. The melody was retained and only the secular words were replaced by religious poetry in a process that the ancients called a *contrafact* or *parody*.

But the regular iambic or trochaic alternation of stressed and unstressed units, so dear to German songs, was also the metric principle of the Catholic "hymn." And so it happened that quite a number of them were kept in the Lutheran Church. *Veni redemptor gentium* became *Nun komm der Heiden Heiland*, and *Veni creator spiritus* was given the new text *Komm Gott Schöpfer heiliger Geist*.

But the old, inherited stock was not sufficient, either in number or in spirit. The blooming of a new religious poetry entailed a blooming of composition. Admittedly, not all the melodies that we find in the early chorale books were divine inspirations; many were vamped up with melodic turns found here and there in folksongs and melodies of the Church.

Luther's own activity in composing or piecing together is doubtful; even the war song of the Evangelical Church, *Ein feste Burg ist unser Gott* (A mighty fortress is our Lord, or, originally, *Oure God is a defence and towre*), cannot be traced to him with any probability.

As early as seven years after the posting of the theses, in 1524, no less than four chorale-books with unaccompanied melodies were published in Wittenberg, Erfurt, and Strassburg. But the time, and Luther himself (who was a great admirer of Josquin des Prés), clung so much to the intricate weaving of Netherlandish polyphony that the chorale, with all its essential simplicity, could not elude elaborate setting in the imitative *cantus firmus* style. Thus, the reformer's musical adviser, Johann Walter in Wittenberg, edited, once more in 1524, a *Geystliches gesangk Buchleyn* with thirty-eight chorales for three, four, five, and even six polyphonic voice parts, the melody being in the tenor. As the climax of this early Lutheran polyphony, the printer Georg Rhaw, also in Wittenberg, published in 1544 *Newe Deudsche geistliche Gesenge*, or New German Spiritual Songs, with contributions of the leading masters, such as the Swiss Ludwig Senfl, the Silesian Thomas Stoltzer, and the probably Swiss Arnold von Bruck.

The difficulties of these sophisticated settings excluded the congregation as the performer. Only well-trained choirs would do. This need led to the establishment of two important forms of organization, the *Kantoreien* and the *Gymnasialchöre*.

The *Kantoreien*, or spiritual glee clubs, had their roots in pre-Reformation laymen's fraternities, many of which turned to the new faith. After Johann Walter had founded the first informal Protestant *Kantorei* in Torgau on the Elbe in 1529, the *Kantoreien* spread rapidly all over the country, singing for their own edification and helping in the church on Saturdays and Sundays.

In addition, music had a favorite place in the *Gymnasium* (the German secondary educational institution, somewhat between high school and college, with Latin as its backbone). It was often granted six periods a week, and the *cantor*, or singing teacher, stood next to the *rector*, or principal, in the faculty. But the other teachers were also expected to be musical: "A schoolmaster must sing; otherwise I would not look at him," said Luther. The singing classes prepared the repertoire of the services in the parish church—and not only the current liturgy. Rather, they were bound to have ready every Sunday, and often every Saturday afternoon, a couple of modern religious settings, a motet or, later, a cantata, whether written by the cantor himself—as we know so well from the life of Bach—or taken from the stock of older masters. The school regulations recommended expressly Josquin's works and, later, those of Orlandus Lassus.

Musical life in Germany owed its blossoming to the burghers. The active coöperation of princes and noblemen, so prevalent in other countries, was in general lacking. Shortly before King Henry VIII of England married Anne of Cleves in 1540, his emissary Nicholas Wotton reported to him: "Frenche, Latyn or other langaige, she hath none, nor yet she canne not synge nor playe enye instrument, for they take it heere in Germanye for a rebuke and an occasion of lightnesse that great ladyes shuld be lernyd or have enye knowledge of musike."

INSTRUMENTAL FORMS, as distinct from those of vocal music, were created at an increasingly rapid pace.

The *ricercar* (pron. reetcherkáhr) or *ricercare* (pl. *-i*) was a name rather than a definite form. The oldest known *ricercari* were pieces for the lute that Petrucci printed in 1507. They consisted of alternating groups of chords and passages, and closely resembled what at that time were called preludes and, later, toccatas. Of a similar kind were the older *ricercari* for organ (the first in 1523) and for viol (probably first appearing in Ganassi's *Regola Rubertina* of 1542).

Since the name belonged for several decades to non-imitative, non-polyphonic forms, it cannot, as often assumed, describe the re-seeking (*ri-cercare*) of the theme in each of the voice parts. It rather denoted—as it does in modern Italian—preluding, or striking the keys, which is also the meaning of the closely related *toccata*, or "touch" piece.

Not earlier than 1542 did the name denote polyphonic, imitative pieces for soloists or instrumental ensembles, which eventually led to the fugue. The pieces differed from the fugue, however, in that they were not integrated wholes that progressed to final climaxes, but were usually set in separate sections, each with a different theme, which was successively imitated in each of the voice parts and then abandoned. Thus, these *ricercari* were at bottom instrumental versions of the ordinary vocal motet.

They had counterparts in the Spanish *tientos* and the Portuguese *tentos*. Any *ricercar* less strict and less learned than usual was called *fantasía* and, later in England, *fancy*.

Besides the various forms of *ricercari*, instrumental music gave an important place to dance melodies.

In keeping with the dignified restraint of the generation of 1500, the *pavan* had a leading position. Ceremonious and even processional, it was one of the simplest and quietest dances ever performed: open couples did a regularly recurring step pattern of two 4/4 measures in about $\bf{J}$ = MM60, with mincing, well-measured steps, now drawing up to the other foot now gliding past it.

The earliest pavans appeared in tablatures for lute that the printer Petrucci in Venice published in 1508, but the pavan seems to have disappeared from courtly ballrooms as early as the middle of the century. However, it survived as a purely instrumental form of the pattern AA BB CC, that is, as a series of different periods, each of which consisted in a repeated phrase of four measures. Outstanding examples are the beautiful pavans by the Spaniard Luis Milán for *vihuela* (the larger guitar of Spain), printed in 1536 (plate XII).

Incidentally, Milán's publication *El Maestro*, with the two marks *a priesa*, or rapidly, and *a espazio*, or slowly, was the earliest work to prescribe a change of tempo within the same piece. The practice was unusual in the sixteenth century and, even with Milán, was used in instrumental music only.

Dances livelier than the formal pavan existed, to be sure, but they played an accessory role. The *galliard* did not appear before 1529 in prints, and the playful, circle-dances—*branles* in French and *brawls* in English—were so much below the dignity of the age that well-bred people did not do them in public unless they were masked.

The commonest player of dance music was the lutanist.

THE LUTE, rich in resources and easily carried, played an ever-increasing role in a time that strove for vertical rather than horizontal expression.

In its typical, elegant, almond shape, with a shell of slender staves, it had been brought from Persia at the end of the first millennium A.D., had originally been confined to the Arabian and Moorish parts of the Spanish peninsula, and then had slowly spread over the continent. During the Middle Ages, the Europeans had played it in the oriental fashion with a quill plectron; and they had performed on it one voice part only, either within a polyphonic piece or else in a free unison with a singer's voice.

Lute music with the use of multiple stops emerged only about 1500, after the example of keyboard styles. Its artistic value was still undeveloped. Besides impromptus, it consisted mainly of arrangements of polyphonic and chordal pieces in which all voices or notes that could not be easily fingered were skipped.

As an additional difficulty, the lute had no consistent tuning and changed its pitch according to the range of the accompanied singer, to its own size, and to the strength of its strings. As late as 1603, *The Schoole of Musicke* by Thomas Robinson gave the disconcerting prescription: "First set up the Treble, so high as you dare venter for breaking."

This made it hard to play from ordinary notation. The same notes required a different fingering on every lute and for each singer. Moreover, it was quite impossible to play from the separate part-books in which polyphonic music of the time was written or printed.

As a way out, the lutanists invented a tablature which allowed the player to neglect the absolute pitch and to prepare the pieces in an acceptable score form. Like any tablature before and after, the lute tablature indicated, not what the listener was to hear, but what the fingers were to stop on the fingerboard. Its staff lines stood for strings, and its figures or letters for frets or stopping places.

In the *German tablature* (plate X), six (originally five) lines represented the (single or double) strings, or courses, as they appear when the lute lies before the player with the pegbox to his left and the bridge to his right. As a consequence, the lowest string was represented by the lowest line. Figures on the lines stood for the open, unstopped strings: 1 for the lowest (of the original five) and 5 for the highest string. Other signs indicated the various stops; first the letters of the alphabet, then, after z, a few special symbols, and again the letters, with apostrophes, for the highest frets. Thus, *a* was the first stop on the (originally) lowest string; *b*, the first stop on the neighboring string; *c*, on the middle string; *e*, on the highest string; again, *f* meant the second stop on the lowest string; *g*, the stop next to *b*, while *k* stood for the second stop on the highest string; and so forth, proceeding stop by stop across the fingerboard from the lowest to the highest string. As a result, the symbols on the lowest string meant: *1*, the open string, however tuned; *a*, the semitone above; *f*, the wholetone; *l*, the minor third; *q*, the major third; *x*, the fourth; *a'*, the augmented fourth. Subsequently, the sixth (lowest) double string was indicated by a cross, and its frets, by capital letters.

The time values were indicated above the staff by the headless stems of the corresponding mensural signs: the whole note by a dot (since the corresponding semibreve had no stem), the halfnote by a bare stem, the quarternote by a stem with one flag, the eighthnote by a stem with two flags, the sixteenth by a stem with three flags (so that there was always one flag more than the modern notes have). When a letter of the tablature had no time symbol of its own, it repeated the last preceding value.

The earliest German tablature dates only from 1511 (not 1512, as has been said), to be sure. But the notation itself must be much older; the five strings for which it was devised testify to a stage of development that the lute had outgrown long ago.

The later tablatures—of the French, Italian, and Spanish lutanists—

kept the lines as images of the strings, but differed in marking the stops.

The French tablature, first printed in 1529, had no figures for the open strings and recommenced the alphabet on each line, so that, on whatever line the letter stood, *a* denoted the open string, *b* the first (semitone) fret, *c* the second (wholetone) fret, *d* the third (minor third) fret, *e* the fourth (major third) fret, *f* the (fourth) fret, and so on. This method was, from every viewpoint, so much simpler and easier that the French tablature triumphed over the German tablature even in Germany (plate XI). After 1584, however, the French, in their turn, began to change to the Italian tablature.

The Italian tablature—already printed in 1507, four years before the earliest available date of the German tablature—reversed the staff because, when played, the instrument turned its lowest string up. The stops were marked in a way similar to that of the French, but the letters were replaced by figures: *1* for the open string, *2* for the semitone fret, *3* for the whole tone, *4* for the minor third, *5* for the major third, and so on.

The Spaniards used the Italian tablature, but with the highest string up (plate XII).

Briefly, the four tablatures consisted of:

LETTERS

running across from string to string: German
running along each string: French

FIGURES

the lowest string uppermost: Italian
the highest string uppermost: Spanish

THE ORGAN continued developing at a tremendous pace. In 1511, a German organist, Arnold Schlick, gave it the earliest monograph, *Spiegel der Orgelmacher und Organisten* (Mirror of the organ builders and players), in which the fetters of medieval tradition are cut for good. He not only described an impressive number of solo stops, but even recommended—as something entirely unheard of—freely combining two or more solo stops in order to create tone colors unwonted and fascinating.

Such progress was made, however, in the North of the continent, not in the South. Italy, Spain, and southern France, and England also, lagged behind; they stuck to manuals, flue pipes, and mixtures, and used solo stops and pedals only as exceptions.

The sequence of nations was inverted when it came to creating a modern script for the organ and other keyboard instruments. As early as 1523, the Italians printed the first keyboard scores in modern form, with a right- and left-hand staff of five lines each and with bar-lines. The French soon imitated them, but England again lagged behind, and Germany did not follow until a century later (1624), and it did not abandon the older forms of notation for one hundred years more.

THE BOWED INSTRUMENTS bequeathed by the Middle Ages were in a state of chaos around 1500. But around 1510 they began to settle into the two essential families that the Later Ages used: the *viole da braccio* and the *viole da gamba*.

The family of the *viole da braccio*, or "arm viols"—equivalents of our violins, violas, and 'celli—were given the modern forms except for the highest string, which was added in the second half of the century. A fresco in the dome of the cathedral at Saronno in northern Italy, painted about 1535, rendered a complete trio of an actual violin, a viola, and a tenor violin (probably an octave below the violin), though with only three strings each.

Silvestro Ganassi's *Lettione Seconda . . . di sonare il Violone* of 1543 already mentions *vibrato* and *pizzicato*. The latter had probably been an old Italian practice dear to the land of mandolins and guitars; and the *vibrato* seems to have been introduced by Polish fiddlers,

> "Who, while their stopping fingers teeter,
> Produce a melody much sweeter
> Than 'tis on other fiddles done."
>
> Martin Agricola, *Musica instrumentalis Deudsch*, ed. 1545, f. 42.—Transl. C. S.

The *viole da gamba* (sing. -*a*), in modern English now called gambas, now viols (not violas!), were similar to the family of the violin or *viola da braccio* except for certain important traits:

1. The body was deeper, met the neck in sloping shoulders, and had a flat back.

2. The fingerboard was fretted, that is, provided with loops of catgut to mark off the notes of the scale.

3. Of the three chief members of the family, the treble had roughly the range of the viola, the tenor, the range of the now abandoned tenor violin (an octave below the ordinary violin), and the bass, the range of the 'cello. In addition, there were doublebasses.

4. The six or seven strings were thinner and had a lute-like tuning in fourths with a major third somewhere in the middle:

Treble	*d g c' e' a' d''*
Tenor	*A d g b e' a'*
Bass	*D G c e a d'*

5. The bass was held between the legs, like a 'cello, and the smaller sizes, vertically upon the legs (not horizontally against the shoulder). Hence the name *da gamba*, belonging to the leg.

6. The bow was held palm up, pushed forward on accented beats, and drawn back on non-accented beats.

7. The tone was more delicate, silvery, and reserved.

THE AGE OF INSTRUMENTS found its clearest expression in the printing of quite a number of fingering exercises, methods, and manuals for various instruments.

A few Germans made a beginning. In 1511, Arnold Schlick published the manual on organ building and playing just mentioned. In the same year, Sebastian Virdung, a Bavarian priest and Schlick's fellow-member in the court chapel of Heidelberg, printed a general treatise on the instruments of his time under the title *Mvsica getutscht*, or Music in German (*cf.* plate X), in the form, customary at that time, of a dialogue between some eager disciple and the master, and with numerous woodcuts. The two works were reprinted by Robert Eitner (*cf.* Bibliography).

Not much later, about 1516, the lutanist Hans Judenkunig published in Vienna an *Utilis et compendiosa introductio*, or Useful and Comprehensive Introduction for Lutes and Viols. The book had a respectable Latin title, to be sure, but in the subtitle, the author was obliged to call his subject *Lutinae et quod vulgo Geygen nominant*, Lutes and what they commonly call *Geigen*, which was a nice reminder that scholarly Latin did not too well agree with instrumental manuals. Indeed, about seven years later, in 1523, Judenkunig printed a German edition as *Ain schone kunstliche underweisung*, or Nice and Artful Instruction.

However, Virdung's book had had the advantage of being all-comprehensive and richly illustrated. Small wonder that a younger man, Martin Agricola (1486–1556), a cantor at Magdeburg in Saxony, availed himself of Virdung's woodcuts and general idea and wrote, in doggerel verses and a popular language, a *Musica instrumentalis deudsch*, or Instrumental Music in German (several editions from 1529 to 1545), "which comprises a method of learning how to play on various wind instruments, based on the art of singing, and how to play on organs, harps, lutes, viols, and all instruments and strings according to the correct tablature."

With regret, the reader leaves these honest, simple books on playing and instruments, to turn to the depressing treatises on general matters of music, which reflect the pitiless war in vilest form among the musicological chairs of North Italian universities, and particularly between the progressive party of the Spanish-born Bartolommeo Ramis de Pareja in Bologna and the conservative party of Franchino Gafori in Milan. While Gafori stuck to the Guidonian tradition of the Middle Ages, Ramis, two hundred years ahead of his time, postulated the abolition of Guido's obsolete hexachords and the recognition of a through octave, in which the teachers and the pupils could move without the pitfalls of mutation.

The greatest merit of both men was to draw the attention of contemporary musicians to the equal temperament with five perfectly even semitones per tetrachord that Aristoxenos had recommended. In so doing, they paved the way for the modern equal temperament.

MUSIC PRINTING was at first done in either one of the two procedures described in the last chapter: double-printing, as in Petrucci's *Odhécaton*, and the clumsier single-printing from woodcut blocks. The Italians, however, replaced the wooden blocks as early as 1516 by hand-engraved metal plates, used to this day. The English followed only a hundred years later with Orlando Gibbons' *Fantazies of three parts* for viols, of about 1609.

As an entirely novel process, music was printed with movable types for one note each, placed at the proper point of the staff, which in its turn was closely cut off left and right of the note, so that it met the neighboring sections as accurately as possible. To be sure, the junction could never be good enough to present an uninterrupted staff; the reader always faced a flickering mosaic. Besides, the movable types presented serious difficulties in keyboard music with its chords and polyphony. They were acceptable, however, where there was only one note at a time, in the old choirbook arrangement of polyphonic works with all the voice parts on two open pages, as well as in the new arrangement, which Petrucci first printed in motets of 1504, with all the voices in separate part books, one for the *cantus*, one for the *altus*, and so on.

The leading printer and publisher in this kind of type was Pierre Attaingnant in Paris, *rue de la Harpe*, who issued, from 1527 to 1549, an impressive number of collections of French *chansons*, motets, Masses, *pavanes*, *gaillardes*, and other music.

READING

John B. Trend, *Luis Milan and the Vihuelistas*, London, 1925. Lionel de la Laurencic, *Les Luthistes*, Paris, 1928. Carl Böhm, *Das deutsche evangelische Kirchenlied*, Hildburghausen, 1927. Knud Jeppesen, *Die mehrstimmige italienische Laude um 1500*, Leipzig, 1935. Curt Sachs, *World History of the Dance*, New York, 1937: Chapter 7. Curt Sachs, *The History of Musical Instruments*, New York, 1940: Chapter 15. Gerald R. Hayes, *Musical Instruments and their Music 1500–1750*, Vol. II, *The Viols, and other Bowed Instruments*, London, 1930. Walter H. Rubsamen, *Literary Sources of Secular Music in Italy (c. 1500)*, Berkeley, 1943. Willi Apel, *The Notation of Polyphonic Music 900–1600*, Cambridge, Mass., 1942, 3rd ed., 1945. Curt Sachs, *The Commonwealth of Art*, New York, 1946: Cross Section 1500. Curt Sachs, *Rhythm and Tempo*, New York, 1953. Gustave Reese, *Music in the Renaissance*, New York, 1954.

Sebastian Virdung, *Mvsica getutscht vnd aussgezogen*, 1511, ed. Robert Eitner, Berlin, 1882. Martin Agricola, *Musica instrumentalis deudsch*, 1st and 4th prints, Wittenberg, 1528 and 1545, ed. Robert Eitner, Leipzig, 1896. Arnold Schlick, *Spiegel der Orgelmacher und Organisten*, ed. Ernst Flade, Mainz, 1932 (older edition by Robert Eitner in *Monatshefte für Musikgeschichte* I, 1869). Josquin des Prés, *Werken*, ed. A. Smijers, 21 vol., Leipzig, 1924–1942. *Harmonice Musices Odhecaton*, ed. Helen Hewitt, Cambridge, Mass., 1942.

11

THE AGE OF GOMBERT AND WILLAERT

1530–1564

THE STRICTNESS, RESTRAINT, and sereneness of the Josquin-Raphael time had almost gone by 1530. The new generation—Michelangelo's age—strove once more for passion, exuberance, life, in often nearly baroque ostentation. As far as the traditional forms of Church music were concerned, the key personality of modern trends was Gombert "the divine."

Nicholas Gombert has a very uncertain biography. Born in Flanders before 1500, he is said to have studied with Josquin des Prés, was first a singer and later a master of the choristers in the Imperial chapel at Brussels, became in 1534 a prebend and, some time later, a canon, at Tournay. Then, he seems to have gone to Madrid in 1537 in the service of his emperor (both the Netherlands and Spain then being parts of the German Empire of Charles V), and died after 1555, possibly in Tournay.

Most of his works were motets and Masses. His only contribution to secular music was a book of French *chansons*. Like his religious music, they shunned the customary four-voice setting. Gombert's normal polyphony had five, if not six, parts.

This unusual number of voices testifies to a taste for compact writing. One of his contemporaries confirmed this taste when he commended Gombert for having done away with the many rests that composers of the preceding generation had cherished.

Gombert deviated from the musical language of the immediate past in many other respects, just as, two generations before, Ockeghem had deviated from the ideals of Dufay. He was uninterested in symmetry and the neat partitioning into sections, and often concealed caesuras between the sections in favor of an endless, even quarter note

138

progress of his contrapuntal melodies. Josquin's harmonic leanings and his chains of consonant chords were given up. In the polyphonic weaving of his parts, Gombert, with gusto, would violate the rights of the ear in reckless frictions.

This he did not do to illustrate some challenging word of the text. His attitude towards the text was a truly humanistic faithfulness, with due respect for correct and often syllabic enunciation of individual words as well as of sentences. But he carefully kept from word-description, just as he kept from *soggetti cavati* and other 'artifices.'

Gombert's delight in density, size, and weight was a common feature of the age. By the middle of the century, it led in Italy to the birth of a *polychoral* style.

The term denotes the massing and opposing of two or several choruses, either vocal or instrumental, or even partly vocal and partly instrumental. Contrasting in range and in color, placed on different sides of the room, and acting now together in a solid mass, now against each other in a light-and-shadow contrast, these *cori spezzati*, or split choruses, created an unheard-of power and that three-dimensional depth so dear to all the arts of the Baroque.

Though polychoral music can today be traced to the fifteenth century, its credit goes to Adriaen Willaert (d. 1562), Flemish chapel master of St. Mark's in Venice, who wrote a set of psalms for Vespers and gave them to two half-choruses placed upon the two opposite organ lofts of his cathedral. To avoid an obvious misconception, it must be said that in Willaert's time St. Mark's had not more than seventeen singers.

So much was the polychoral style in keeping with the taste of the Baroque that it lasted altogether more than two hundred years, into the age of Mozart in his Salzburg days. We shall in due time resume this subject.

TUDOR ENGLAND, despite the antimusical trends of the time, had her three great T's; Traverner, Tye, and Tallis. All three specialized in spiritual music and marked the confused transition from the Church of Rome to the Church of England.

John Taverner of Lincolnshire (d. 1545), organist at Oxford from

1526 to 1530, was imprisoned for Protestant heresy but subsequently freed because "he was but a musician." He introduced the Franco-Flemish polyphony into England, mastered it as well as any continental composer did, and gave it not only to Masses and motets, but also to a curious form of instrumental music which was received with favor and lasted from his time to the days of Purcell: the *innómine*. Meaning in the name (of God), it was a polyphonic composition either for the virginals or else for an ensemble, or *consort*, of viols, upon an unchangeable *cantus firmus* taken from a certain Catholic antiphon in the first Church mode, or Dorian, *Gloria tibi Trínitas*.

Christopher Tye (*c*. 1500–1572) was connected mainly with Cambridge, Ely, and Oxford, and was given the degree of Doctor of Music by both the universities of Cambridge and Oxford. He wrote *The Actes of the Apostles, translated into Englysche Metre* for four voices in a popular style (1553). And in a similar spirit he seems to have created the earliest anthems.

The *anthem* (a word that derived via Old English *antefn* from the Greek *antíphonon*) was an Anglican motet. It differed from the Catholic motet of the sixteenth century in its English text, syllabic diction, square rhythm, and a chordal rather than polyphonic style.

Thomas Tallis (*c*. 1505-1585), organist of Waltham Abbey, Essex, and, later, Gentleman of the Chapel Royal, has been called the founder of English cathedral music and was no doubt one of its greatest masters. Among his English anthems and Latin Masses and motets, one remarkable relic impressively shows the ties between the musical styles of England and Italy: a Catholic motet *Spem in alium numquam habui* for no less than forty voice parts in eight choruses, written at about the time when the Italian Alessandro Striggio gave the same number of voice parts to his motet *Ecce beatam lucem*. The gigantic motet of Tallis—never printed while the master was alive—is now available in an edition of the *Tudor Church Music* (1928).

IN THE SECULAR FIELD, the *chanson*, which the paragraph on Gombert has touched upon, was perhaps the finest contribution that France has made to music. Elegant, dainty, and lightfooted, never interrupting the even flow of melody, it closely followed an amorous and often indelicate text and rendered the words with a charm that musical forms have rarely achieved. One of its characteristic traits was a dactylic beginning—long–short–short—on one repeated note. In the decades of its bloom, between 1530 and 1560, its four voice parts were moderately polyphonic in an unscholastic way and often even chordal.

In modern concerts, *chansons* are usually sung by choruses. This is not correct, either historically or artistically. The majority are so nimble and transparent that only a rendition by four solo singers or, much better, by one singer and one or more instruments can do them justice.

Our plate XIII shows the typical performance of a *chanson* with photographic exactness and reliability. The music on the table (enlarged and inverted in the detail) is Claudin de Sermisy's *Jouyssance vous donneray*, which Pierre Attaingnant printed in 1531 in his *Trente et sept Chansons*. The transverse flute plays the upper part, the singer reads another voice, and the lutanist, without a part book, puts up with the two remaining parts.

Besides Sermisy (pron. -eezée), the outstanding composer of *chansons* was Janequin.

Clément Janequin or Jannequin (equivalent of Johnnie), very probably from the northeast of France, as the name indicates, was presented in 1544 for the curacy of Unverre not far from Chartres in the southwestern neighborhood of Paris, and acted as its curate at least in 1556. Three years later, he described himself as living in poor old age, a clue to his birthdate, which was probably late in the fifteenth century.

When the printer Adrien Le Roy in Paris published Janequin's works in 1559, he prefaced the collection with a sonnet that the famous poet Antoine de Baïf had made in honor of Janequin. It ended in the following six lines:

> When he composes motets with their mighty words,
> When he attempts to represent the din of battle,
> When in his songs he renders women's clack and prattle,
> When he depicts the chirping voices of the birds
>
> In all that Janequin has tried to design,
> He never has been mortal, but is all divine.
> —transl. C. S.

The first four of these lines sum up the essentials of his works: motets and *chansons* of a descriptive character, in which, among other subjects, the battle of Marignano (*La Guerre*), babbling women (*Le Caquet des Femmes*), twittering birds (*Le Chant des Oyseaux*) are depicted with incomparable skill and taste.

At that time, all nations shared in this delight in descriptive music. Lorenz Lemlin wrote a *Gutzgauch*, or Cuckoo, in 1540; Hans Neusidler a Battle of *Bafia* (Pavia) in 1544; Ludwig Senfl (d. 1555), The Bells of Speyer (*Kling klang*); Gombert, a *Chant des Oyseaux* in the same year 1544; Massimo Trojano, a Battle of the Cat and the Crow; Adriano Banchieri, a *Contrappunto bestiale alla mente*, representing a dog, a cuckoo, and an owl. And the list could easily be enlarged.

THE MADRIGAL, in a way the Italian counterpart of the French *chanson*, had little, if anything, in common with its older namesake of the fourteenth century except the freer character and form of its texts. Dealing with the beauty of nature, birds, and love, it had neither regular stanzas nor refrains. Musically, it was meant to be a refined vocal chamber music, not of accompanied soloists, but of three or four, and later five or more, amateur singers gathered around a table with their voice parts spread before them. The parts were in perfect balance without discrimination in importance, without a leading melody, a *cantus firmus*, or an accompaniment, and yet independent enough to catch the personal interest of the partners.

The earliest madrigals, written by the Flemings Philippe Verdelot and Jacob Arcadelt and by some Italian masters, were published by a Roman printer in 1533. In their predominantly homophonic texture and their emotional restraint, they show a certain relation to the older *fróttola*, which the generation before had used for the same purpose of refined social entertainment.

The style changed after 1540 under the leadership of the Flemish Venetians Philippe de Monte, Adriaen Willaert, and Cypriano de Rore. Their madrigals had, as an average, five voice parts, a more polyphonic, motet-like structure, and a growing emotional attitude.

In this emotional attitude, both masters, Willaert and Rore, pushed on to unheard-of, audacious chromaticisms. (*Chromaticism* is the use of more than seven notes per octave, unless the additional notes serve as modulation, or logical passage, into some other seven-note scale.) They invented chromatic melodies proceeding in semitones throughout the octave and wrote chromatic harmonies in strangely modulating chords.

It is hardly an accident that at the same time, around 1560, the composer and theorist Nicola Vicentino, who lived in Venice as a pupil of Willaert, designed a complicated keyboard for a super-organ or super-harpsichord (*arciórgano, arcicémbalo*) with thirty-one keys per octave on six manuals, in order to produce all the shades of the diatonic, chromatic, and enharmonic genders of the Greeks, who once again stood involuntary sponsors to modern developments. (The genders of Greece are explained in the third chapter of this book on page 29.)

The reader must be warned, however, that in the sixteenth century the term *madrigale cromático* often meant only a madrigal in which blackened notes and hence a faster tempo prevailed.

Our modern choral conductors should keep in mind that the madrigal was strictly chamber music of soloists and must not be performed by choruses—exactly like the French *chanson*. Would we tolerate orchestral renditions of Beethoven's string quartets?

Beside and after the madrigal, the Italians created, in the second third of the century, a vigorous antidote in their *villanelle* and *villote*.

The name (canzona) *villanella* or *villanesca*, which, from 1541 on, appeared as the title of a seemingly Neapolitan form of folksong, should not be translated as a rural, but rather as a loutish, song. Far from being rustic, *villanelle* were printed as an uncouth and often parodistic reaction against the sophisticated refinement of the madrigal, and they displayed so consummate a contempt of the rules of harmony and counterpoint that their three voice parts often proceeded in parallel triads (as, after centuries, in some scores of another Italian, Puccini). Indeed, as Thomas Morley said in his *Introduction* of 1597, these "countrie songs" were "made only for the ditties sake, . . . a clownish musicke to a clownish matter." A few years later, the *villanella* helped in creating the German drinking song.

The *villota*, printed from 1535 on, was, on the contrary, a true folk dance-song from various Italian provinces. Once more, the melody was in the upper voice, while the three lower (instrumental) parts followed strictly in chords.

The *fróttola* seems to have had its last publication in 1531.

The Spanish term *villancico* must not be confused with the similar Italian names. It denoted a song of several stanzas, or *coplas*, between refrains, or *estribillos*, in the exact form of a French *virelai* (*cf.* page 72). Although earlier *villancicos* had been written for three or four voice parts in a conduct-like note-against-note style, the masters around the middle of the sixteenth century—Miguel de Fuenllana, Juan Vásquez, Diego Pisadór, and Luis Milán, musician at the court of the viceroy of Valencia—transformed this rigid setting into what amounts to actual song melodies with the accompaniment of a *vihuela* (large guitar).

These Spanish songs are unique in the marvelous blend of aristocratic and popular attitude. On hearing them, one readily understands that in a country of an art so national in the best sense of the word, there was no room for French *chansons* or Italian madrigals.

Musica RESERVATA.　Altogether, vocal music was undergoing essential changes in the relation between text and melody. A glance at older works, especially Masses, shows more concern with writing good contrapuntal settings than with an adequate rendition of the text. Indifferent to the meaning and accents of the holy words, composers expected the singers to distribute the well-known syllables as they deemed best.

A different attitude set in with Josquin des Prés, the mature Renaissance, and humanism. The medieval conception that the mere presence of a holy text gave a voice part significance yielded to the modern conception that such practice had to give satisfaction to the ear. By 1552, when the Fleming Adriaen Petit Coclicus was publishing his often quoted *Musica Reservata*, it had become a serious prerequisite of respectable writing to apply the text to its proper place and to avoid setting a long note to a short syllable or vice versa; "for music has much in common with poetry."

William Byrd found a less wooden expression of the same idea when he printed his *Psalmes, Songs, and Sonnets* of 1611 "framed to the life of the words."

Shortly before him, another Englishman, Thomas Morley, had revamped the train of thought of the *Musica Reservata*. "If the subject be light," he said in *A Plaine and Easie Introduction to Practicall Musicke* (1597), "you must cause your musick to go in motions, which carry with them a celeritie or quickness of time, as minimes, crotchets, and quavers; if it be lamentable, the note must go in slow and heavy motions, as semibriefs, briefs, and such like." And he proceeds:

"Moreover you must have a care that when your matter signifieth ascending, high heaven and such like, you make your musick ascend: and by the contrarie where your dittie speaks of descending, lowness, depth, hell and others such, you must make your musick descend. For as it will bee thought a great absurditie to talke of heaven and point downward to the earth: so it will be counted great incongruity if a musician upon the words he ascended into heaven should cause his musick to descend." And later:

"We must also have a care so to applie the notes to the wordes as in singing there be no barbarisme committed: that is, that we cause no syllable which is by nature short, to be expressed by many notes, or one long note, nor so long a syllable to be expressed with a short note."

From this new deference to the word, as expressed in Coclicus and Morley, one way led to the *vers mesurés* of the French, the anti-polyphonic slogans of the Council of Trent, and the *stile recitativo*, and another way to the pedantic servile transcription and illustration of individual words and their meanings, which held the musicians of the Baroque spellbound from the motets and madrigals of the late sixteenth century to the sterile theory of affects (*Affektenlehre*) in the rationalistic eighteenth century: rendering the concepts of ascent and descent by rising and falling groups of notes, or 'cross' by two dovetailed melodic steps.

INSTRUMENTAL MUSIC. Adriaen Willaert, outstanding in Masses and motets, *chansons* and madrigals, also played a leading role in shaping a new instrumental form, the motet-like imitative *ricercar*, which has been described in the previous chapter. Since *ricercari* of this kind were printed in separate part-books, they certainly were meant for various instruments (of any kind).

Along with the strict, polyphonic *ricercar*, the organists and, at their head, the great master at the second organ of St. Mark's in Venice, Andrea Gabrieli (*c.* 1510–1586), created the free, homophonic *toccata*, or 'touch-piece,' in which full chords alternated with brilliant passages. The master at the first organ of St. Mark's, Claudio Merulo (1533–1604) merged the two forms by introducing imitative (*fugato*) episodes into the *toccata*.

Music for keyboard instruments and also for lutes reached its climax, however, in the truly instrumental form of the *variation*.

There can be no doubt that varying a given theme had been a customary practice of players long before the form appeared in prints and manuscripts. Variation is, after all, the only way for skilled musicians to stand a number of repetitions that the stanzas of a song or the consecutively entering couples of a dance impose.

A solitary, unprecedented, and unimitated set of *variations* on a song, the Mills of Paris, appears, indeed, sometime in the fourteenth century. In its uniqueness, it clearly shows that variation existed long before it became a written form. The innovation of the sixteenth century was not anything fundamentally new, but rather the generalization of the case of the Mills: careful planning instead of improvisation.

Variation appeared in the sixteenth century in its two basic forms, as *grounds* and as *paraphrases*.

The *ground*, or *basso ostinato* (obstinate bass), best known from later *passacaglias*, is the continual repetition of a short motive at the same pitch and, as a rule, in the bass while the other voice parts counterpoint with more or less freedom. It is foreshadowed in motets of the thirteenth century; the earliest sixteenth century example is a virginal piece by an English canon, Hugh Aston or Ashton (d. 1522), *Mylady Carey's Dompe* (an Irish lament, properly spelled dumpe).

The *paraphrase*, as we will call it, is a set of sections in which some popular dance or song appears first in its original simple form and subsequently disguised in ever changing paraphrases. The mature style of this type of *variation* is due to the Spaniards, who called it *glosa* or *diferencia*. Luis de Narvaez (1538) gave it to the lute, Diego Ortiz (1553) to the viol, and Antonio de Cabezón (1510–1566) to the organ, which, contrary to the situation in Italy, had developed in Spain to match northern color and versatility.

Songs and dances were, as a matter of course, just as well performed without *variations*. Numerous printed collections of the time for lutes or keyboard instruments abound in plainly harmonized notations of *Lieder,* dances, and *chansons*.

The *chanson*, though at first arranged for lute much in the original form, was destined for a more momentous future. For the time being, however, from 1542 on, it was translated into a specific type of keyboard music which shared with its vocal model the lightfootedness, clear disposition, and characteristic *fugato* beginning on a dactylic one-tone motive (long–short–short), but which was drawn out much longer than the singing form had been. As an instrumental form, it was called in Italy *canzone francesa* or *canzona da sonare*. (The Italians of the sixteenth century used two forms: *canzona*, plur. *-e*, and *canzone*, plur. *-i*.)

D ANCE MUSIC underwent decisive changes in the direction of sturdiness and jollity. The dignified pavan was given a lighter form in the *passamezzo*, or *passo e mezzo* (a step and a half), which was, from 1536 on, a favorite in collections of lute music. Seven years earlier, the bold and wanton *galliard* had appeared, a lively pattern of leg thrusts and leaps in 3/4 at about $\downarrow$ = MM 90, which reminded some spectator of a cockfight. And with the galliard came the lively, zigzagging *courantes* in 3/4, which Shakespeare's *King Henry V* called "swift corantos." Two other tempestuous dances were added in the 1550's: the tap-dance *canaries*, a play of heel and sole in a hasty dotted rhythm, was mentioned first in a Spanish source of 1552; and in 1556 the court of Paris introduced from Provence the boastful, strenuous *volta*, in which the gentleman turned and flung up his lady.

Besides this motley lot of couple dances, the time readmitted the playful, pantomimic circle dances, or *branles*, which had been taboo in the generation before; and the musicians—so we hear—played them in suites, one of every kind, in the order of increasing lightness and tempo: a sedate *branle double* for the older people, a brisker *branle simple* for the younger married couples, a rapid *branle gay* for the unmarried, and faster and faster up to the *branle du Hault Barrois* (called after one of the provinces), which "should be good to dance in the winter to make oneself warm," and to the hasty, skipping *gavotte*. This was a typically dynamic arrangement as opposed to the classical order of contrast in alternating tempi.

About that time, one kind of dance split off to lead a separate life: the *march*. In earlier times, the fifers at the head of military formations and the town pipers who played for civil parades and corteges probably availed themselves of dances and catchy songs in regular rhythm. We know from Thoinot Arbeau's excellent manual on the dance of his time, the *Orchésographie* (1588), that the pavan, for instance, served "when a bride of good family proceeded to church, or when priests, or masters and members of important corporations were to be escorted in dignified procession." Arbeau connects the march and the dance so closely that he gives not only a long introduction on the army-drum strokes and rhythms, but adds the proper drum meters, dactylic or otherwise, to every type of dance.

The earliest marches, as such, appear in *My Ladye Nevells Booke* for harpsichord in 1591: *The Marche before the Battell, The Marche of Footemen, The Marche of Horsmen, The Irishe Marche, The Marche to the Fighte.*

INSTRUMENTAL MUSIC proved to be so important that the various families of instruments were given playing methods. The player and manufacturer Hans Gerle in Nürnberg wrote a *Musica Teusch*, or Music (explained) in German (1532), for the use of violists and lutanists. But after him, the accent shifted to the south of Europe. The Italian Silvestro Ganassi of Fontego, near Venice, wrote in 1535 *La Fontegara* as a method for playing the recorder or whistle flute— which then was much more important than the transverse flute—and in 1542 and 1543 a *Regola Rubertina* for the viols. And after his contributions, the Spaniards took over. The monk Juan Bermudo published a comprehensive manual under the title *La declaración de instrumentos* in three editions between 1549 and 1555; Diego Ortiz, a chapel master to the Viceroy of Naples, printed a method for viols, the *Tractado de glosas* (1553); and in 1565, Tomás de Sancta Maria came out with a thorough method for keyboard and other instruments, the *Arte de tañer fantasía*.

The general, extra-instrumental theory of the time reached a climax in two personalities which have almost become symbols of their time: Glareanus and Zarlino.

G LAREANUS AND ZARLINO. Music had reached a critical point at which contrapuntal was yielding to harmonic conception, and the Church modes, to our modern major and minor. The crisis became manifest in two renowned theoretical works.

The earlier was the *Dodekáchordon* of the Swiss Henricus Glareanus (1547), a humanist who, under this learned title, presented a "twelve-mode" system by adding to the age-old eight Church modes, four additional modes: the Aeolian on *A* and the Ionian on *C*, and each with its *hypo* parallel, that is, Hypoaeolian on *E* and Hypoionian on *G*. This eleventh-hour addition of modes that the Church never did accept was nothing but a humanistic attempt to recognize the factual existence of minor and major by making peers of the two no-longer-avoidable commoners.

How far the major mode had driven back the modes of the Church appears from Glareanus' statement that Ionian was the *modus omnium usitatissimus*, the most current of all the modes.

The second work, more progressive and more important, was the epochal volume *Le Istitutioni harmóniche* (1558) of the great Gioseffo Zarlino (1517–1590), Cypriano de Rore's successor as the chapel master of St. Mark's in Venice. It established both the major and the minor third as the dual fundament of all harmony and determined their ideal sizes by the (mathematically so-called) harmonic and the arithmetic division of a vibrating string. The harmonic division consisted of the progression 2:1, 3:2, 4:3, 5:4; and the arithmetic division, in the progression 6:1, 6:2, 6:3, 6:4, 6:5. The following graph represents the two strings, their divisions, and the resulting intervals:

·	·	·	·	·	·
5:4	4:3	3:2	2:1		
C	E	(F)	G	c	
·	·	·	·	·	·

·	·		·	·	·	·	·
6:5		6:4	6:3	6:2	6:1		
C	Eb	G	c				

From Zarlino, the road of harmonic theory led directly to Jean-Philippe Rameau and his *Traité de l'Harmonie* of 1722 (*cf.* Chapter 16).

Although the minor third had been made reputable by Zarlino, this interval was not considered consonant enough to serve in the final chord of a piece. Down to the times of Bach, all compositions in the minor mode ended in an open fifth or else in a triad with the major third—which indeed adds to its finality, even from our modern viewpoint. This unexpected, startling major third has, for reasons unknown, been called the Picardian third. As late as 1757, Johann Christian Bach rebelled against this rule: "Why must one end a minor piece on a major chord?" he wrote to his old master Padre Martini.

READING

Gustave Reese, *Music in the Renaissance*, New York, 1954. Curt Sachs, *The Commonwealth of Art*, New York, 1946; Cross Section 1530. Joseph Schmidt-Görg, *Nicolas Gombert*, Bonn, 1938. Erich Hertzmann, *Adrian Willaert in der weltlichen Vokalmusik seiner Zeit, ein Beitrag zur Entwicklungsgeschichte der niederländisch-französischen und italienischen Liedformen in der ersten Hälfte de 16.Jahrhunderts*, Leipzig, 1931. Ernst H. Meyer, *English Chamber Music, the History of a Great Art From the Middle Ages to Purcell*, London, 1946. Alfred Einstein, *The Italian madrigal*, Princeton, 1949. Marcus van Crevel, *Adrianus Petit Coclico; Leben und Beziehungen eines nach Deutschland ausgewanderten Josquinschülers*, Haag, 1940. Edward E. Lowinsky, *Secret Chromatic Art in the Netherlands Motet*, New York, 1946. Curt Sachs, *World History of the Dance*, New York, 1937; Chapter 7. Thoinaut Arbeau, *Orchésographie*, English transl., London, 1925. Curt Sachs, *The History of Musical Instruments*, New York, 1940; Chapter 15. Curt Sachs, *Rhythm and Tempo*, New York, 1953. Silvestro Ganassi, *Regola Rubertina*, ed. Max Schneider, Leipzig, 1924. Diego Ortiz, *Tratado de glosas*, Roma, 1553; ed. Max Schneider (Berlin, 1913), Kassel, 1936. Henricus Glareanus, *Dodekachordon*, German translation by Peter Bohn, Leipzig, 1888.

12

THE AGE OF
PALESTRINA AND LASSUS
1564–1600

THE BEGINNING of a new age, generally called the Baroque, was marked by the foundation of the classical Academy of Poetry and Music in Paris, the classicism of the Florentine painter Angelo Bronzino and that of the poet of *Jerusalem Delivered*, Torquato Tasso, and the adoration of the strictly classical Vitruvian rules in the architecture of Italy and France, particularly in the works of Palladio. The details of this development can be read in the author's *Commonwealth of Art*, pages 125 ff.

All classicism and, for that matter, all neoclassicism, aims at clarity.

It was this aim that provided the uniting tie between the seemingly antipodic trends of music in the last third of the sixteenth century— between Palestrina's serene, unearthly Masses, Gastoldi's earthly *balletti*, Galilei's gloomy laments, and the beginnings of the recitative.

The common victim that all the 'modern' groups and masters immolated as the scapegoat on the altar of clarity was counterpoint, or, better, the monopoly and misuse of the polyphonic style. Counterpoint, to them, meant an involved technique for the sake of technique, skill at the cost of expression, confusion at the price of clarity; and they rejected it.

Paradoxically enough, the earliest among the great masters connected with this recession from counterpoint as an end in itself was the arch-contrapuntist to whom present-day teachers turn for advice and example: Pierluigi da Palestrina.

PALESTRINA'S LIFE is easily told. Born probably in 1525 in Palestrina, southeast of Rome, he was sent in 1534 to the pontifical church of Santa Maria Maggiore in Rome to serve as a choirboy and, sometime after his mutation (1539), as the *magister puerorum* to train the boys in the Cappella Giulia at St. Peter's. Next, he spent years as the organist and *maestro di cappella* in the cathedral of his native town. Then began the brilliant part of his career. He became chapel master at St. Peter's in Rome in 1551, and four years later, one of the twenty-five singers in the pontifical Sixtine Chapel—the highest honor that could be bestowed on a musician in Rome. After a few months a new, stricter pope, Paul IV, removed him from that august body for being a layman and married at that, but, again after a few months, gave him the position of a chapel master at the Lateran basilica. Resigning this post in 1560, he went on in the odd and restless circle of his life. In 1561, he was appointed *maestro di cappella* in Santa Maria Maggiore, only to retire in 1567. After four years spent outside the Church, he returned in 1571 as the chapel master to St. Peter's with the honorary title of *maestro compositore*. And this was the last stop in the narrow orbit of his professional life.

After the loss of several sons, his wife died in 1580. In his affliction, he applied for admission to the priesthood and was given the tonsure. However, as soon as the following year, he left the clerical state and married the widow of a well-to-do furrier, whereupon we find the most unworldly composer of Christendom engaged for years in the honorable but thoroughly worldly trade of pelts and furs in a managerial capacity. And it is only fair to add that during that time of selling and buying, he created some of his profoundest works.

He met his death on February 2, 1594.

Palestrina's world-wide fame was established by *a corpus* of one hundred and five Masses, two hundred and eighty motets, sixty-eight offertories, forty-five hymns, thirty-five *Magnificats*, and numerous lamentations, litanies, psalms, and madrigals, many of which are still in the active stream of Catholic music in and outside the Church, as the paragons of supra-personal sereneness, austere, uncompromising purity, and powerful simplicity.

It needed thirty-three tomes in folio and more than forty years (1862–1903) to reprint this gigantic life-work in a modern edition.

Palestrina's popular fame, however, was established by the legend that his intervention saved the music of the Church from the hands of fanatical purists. The legend, told over and over again and still used as the subject of Pfitzner's German opera *Palestrina* (1917), has connected the master and his work with the proceedings of the music committee within the Counterreformational Council of Trent (1545–1563).

It is true that all the members of the committee wanted a thorough purge of liturgical music. But while the extremists were ready to sacrifice polyphony in any form to the sober, single line of the Gregorian chant, their moderate opponents were satisfied with stripping polyphonic music of secular *cantus firmi* and 'artifices,' of unrest and confusion. Since a decision was not reached, the Pope appointed in 1564 a special congregation of eight cardinals and eight singers of the Papal Chapel to settle the fateful problem.

It is not true that, within this body, a victory of the radical wing was averted only because Palestrina, hastily composing a few Masses in a moderate style with the famous Marcellus Mass as one of them, stepped in and proved that dignified polyphony and orthodox religious attitude were perfectly compatible.

The legend, and even the authentic proceedings of the Council and the Congregation, disguise the actual issue: the time was ripe for a new outbreak of the age-old war between the classic Italian and the anticlassic northern spirit, between Mediterranean clearness and simplicity and 'Gothic' involution and obscurity. Of eight singers in the Congregation, five were Italians, two Spaniards, and only one was a Netherlander—nothing could more clearly show that the northern predominance in Italian music was drawing to a close.

One of the two Spaniards in the Chapel was the unforgotten Tomas Luis de Victoria (*c.* 1540–*c.* 1613), who added the ardent mysticism of his homeland to the solemn aloofness of the Roman style.

Most people who think or speak of the so-called Palestrina style are under a disastrous illusion. Alas, the solemn, ethereal chords and the simple, stately voice parts of Roman polyphony were never heard in the sober form that the scores suggest. The Romans counted on the art of melodic *diminution*, however little such practice seems, from our viewpoint, to be a logical one in Rome. The singers of the Papal Chapel were famous for their skill in dissolving the plain notation on their music sheets in fluent graces and coloraturas. Upon seeing the few of Palestrina's motets that contemporary masters wrote down in the form in which they were performed, we experience a disillusion about as great as the one that our fathers had when they realized that the temples and statues of the Greeks had not been white.

The old coloratura improvisation of the Orient and the Mediterranean had entered the extra-Mediterranean districts of Europe with the early Gregorian chant and did not part from them for a thousand years. Down to 1800, notation was a mere skeleton that the performer had to cover with flesh and skin and hair. For the West felt, like the Hindus, that "without graces, music is bald." Adriaen Petit Cóclicus, one of Josquin's disciples, expressed the idea picturesquely when he said in his *Musica Reservata* of 1552 that the composer's melody was always simple, commonplace, and crude, unless the singer made it elegant, indeed, unless he spiced the meat with salt and mustard.

NATURE, often prone to lift two different peaks instead of one to tower over the minor hills of an age, contrasted the contemplative Palestrina, who never traveled, hardly ever looked beyond the choir stalls of Roman basilicas, and practically never deviated from liturgical forms and the liturgical Latin, with the dramatic Lassus, a man of the world and a versatile master in all the forms of the time in any of the four leading languages.

Among the more than two thousand works of Lassus, there are no less than five hundred and sixteen motets, out of more than a thousand, united in the six volumes of his *Magnum Opus Musicum*, some of them overwhelming in the powerful polyphony of six and eight voice parts. There are the seven Penitential Psalms of 1565, which Duke William of Bavaria ordered copied in one of the most precious illuminated manuscripts of the sixteenth century. There are Masses, many of which were built on secular *chansons* although the Council of Trent had interdicted the parody form (*cf.* page 123). There are one hundred *Magnificat* settings. And there are his *chansons*, in which he spans the whole range between the boldest briskness and a tender intimacy.

Roland de Lassus, or Orlando di Lasso as the Italians named him, was born in Mons in Hainaut about 1532—approximately the time of Palestrina's birth. When he was a boy, the exceptional beauty of his voice allegedly led to three consecutive kidnappings. When twelve years old, he left his homeland and began to travel in the retinue of dignitaries. He saw Milan, Sicily, Naples, was for a time the chapel master at the Lateran in Rome, returned to the North to live in Antwerp, England, and (later) France, accepted in 1556 an appointment as the conductor at the ducal court of Bavaria, and stayed in Munich until, in 1594, the year that also took Palestrina away, a merciful death released him from the deep melancholy of his later years. Not many composers have been honored as Lassus was: Emperor Maximilian II conferred nobility upon him, and the Pope made him a knight of the Golden Spur.

THE HUGUENOT PSALTER. The antipolyphonic and antisecular austerity that appeared in the Counterreformation of the Catholic Church showed much more strongly in the liturgies of the Swiss reformers, of Zwingli and Calvin.

Even before the psalms of David had been appropriated by Calvin's Church as its only poetic and musical expression, Clément Marot—one of the most frivolous of poets not long before—had translated them into his mother tongue and dedicated his texts to:

> . . . the ladies and the maidens
>   Whom God creates to be his shrine,
>   But who, forgetting hymns divine,
> In halls and chambers entertain
> Their guests with words and airs profane.
> —transl. C. S.

The English Calvinists chimed in.

> Depart, ye songs lascivious,
>   from lute, from harpe depart:
> Give place to Psalmes most vertuous,
>   and solace there your harte,

we read in Archbishop Parker's Psalter, which was printed only in 1567 or 1568, but had already been finished by 1557.

Musicians abjured any music connected with licentious words in sentences no less energetic than those used by the poets. When—a while after the Dutch had published their *Souterliedekens*, or Psalter Songs—Claude Goudimel printed in 1551 the earliest French musical version of Marot's psalter, he emphasized in the preface that music was sacred, "although today we see it desecrated by lascivious, peppery, impudent songs."

This first version of the psalter must have antedated Goudimel's conversion to Calvin's doctrine, for he still published Catholic Masses as late as 1558. Anyhow, this version would hardly have been acceptable to the reformed liturgy proper. The austere and almost ascetic sobriety of Calvinism represses music as it condemns the painted or carved image—the words of God must not be pretexts for musical sophistication. Reformed churches often have no trained choirs; in unison, the congregation itself sings the psalms, which nameless composers have patched together out of scraps from popular songs.

But for use at home—*ès maisons*—elaborate forms were admitted and even encouraged. The singing of the psalter around the dinner table to keep the minds from worldly, futile thoughts did not shun the charm that polyphonic art conveys to the audience as well as to the performers themselves. It was on the ground of such religious chamber music that the greater masters were allowed to contribute to the reformer's work. They did so in two separate ways: on the one hand, in a simple, easy version, with a syllabic melody in the tenor and a chordal harmonization; on the other hand, in a rich and free polyphony for well-trained singers.

Of the two leading masters who again and again recomposed the one hundred and fifty psalms, the older, Claude Goudimel, was born at Besançon about 1505, spent his life apparently without a connection with either the court of Paris or with any church, and, assassinated in 1572 after the massacre of Saint Bartholomew's Night, paid the supreme price for his faith. The younger master, Claude Lejeune, "last polyphonist" and "Phoenix of Music" as the French called him, was born at Valenciennes near the Lowlands about 1528, became Royal Chamber Composer toward the end of his life, and died at Paris in 1600.

The religious reform was in itself, however, an outgrowth of a general French reversal, similar to the way in which the religious Counterreformation accompanied an Italian reversal in all the fields of art and mentality. It was not only the Huguenots who reacted against the "bad examples" and "dirty melodies" of the immediate past; Catholics, too, were in the opposition. In the 1560's, the poet Jean-

Antoine Baïf and the musicians Thibault de Courville and Goudimel took up the metric compositions of the humanists of around 1500, with a long note to a long, and a short note to a short syllable and with all the voice parts singing every syllable at exactly the same time. Claude Lejeune seems to have ended this series of composers with his post-humous psalms and the many *chansons* of his likewise posthumous collection, *Le Printemps*—at least so far as the use of the name *vers mesurés* is concerned; actually, even Lully's diction is still under the spell of 'correct' mensuration.

These metrical pieces, or *vers mesurés*, were not only a humanistic bow to the ancient Greeks and Romans in the spirit of the *camerata* in Florence, which will be discussed later, they were also a part of that fight against polyphony in which the Florentine debaters stood side by side with the Council of Trent. Indeed, they belong to the moral attitude of the Platonists in every land who postulate that all music ought to be controlled in the interest of the community—that disorderly music depraves the conduct of man, but orderly music improves it.

The English also availed themselves of the metric diction of the *vers mesurés* in their new Anglican chant, which, under the guidance of Tallis, Byrd, and Morley, squeezed the Catholic psalm tones into the framework of a simple four-part harmony. Moreover, William Byrd transformed the original concept of the anthem (*cf.* page 140) into the so-called *verse anthem*, where the choral sections alternate with solo sections.

Except for a few *vers mesurés* in French *chansons*, the reaction against polyphony and sophistication outlined so far belongs in the main to the field of religious music. But there was a typically secular reaction, too. It crystallized around the Italian concepts of *canzonetta*, *balletto*, solo madrigal, and recitativic monody.

THE *CANZONETTA* (plural -*e*) was a way out to those who wanted a well-made vocal chamber music but resented the refinement, complication, and stilted preciosity of the later madrigal. First printed in the 1580's (and again abandoned in the 1620's), the *canzonetta* was a simple three- or four-part setting of some unpretentious poem. Sometimes, the voices entered successively with the same motive in *fugato* style, but in most cases the melody, quick-footed, *staccato*, and even pattering, was seconded note by note in the other parts.

One further step led to Giovanni Giácomo Gastoldi's *Balletti per cantare, sonare & ballare*, which were first printed in 1591, often re-edited way down to the eighteenth century, and imitated with gusto all over Europe. In England, the first imitation was Thomas Morley's *Balletts to 5 voyces of 1595*, which were also published in Italian and German. *Balletti*, as the name implies, could be sung *ad libitum* or played on instruments or even danced to. They had, on the whole, the easy-going style of the *canzonette*, but differed in having catchy refrains on the playful syllables *fa la la* at the end of their stanzas.

France responded to the *canzonetta-balletto* reaction with the *air de cour*, which was *not* a courtly song but, on the contrary, the low-brow "vaudeville" of some soloist accompanied on a lute. England complied with the similar *ayre*, in which John Dowland particularly excelled (1562–1626). *Canzonette napoletane, villanelle*, and *balletti*, said Thomas Morley in his *Introduction* of 1597, "are by a generall name called ayres."

England was meanwhile adopting and adapting the madrigal itself. William Byrd had already imitated the Italian model on his own re-sponsibility, when an English publisher dared to print in 1588 a collection of original Italian madrigals in English translation under the title *Musica Transalpina*. These two impulses created, under the leadership of Byrd and Morley, the national English madrigal, which, despite its foreign origin, became truly British owing to the particularities of the English language and a greater emotional stress. The public response was extraordinary. Morley himself praised the gentry for singing difficult madrigals at sight as one of its noblest pastimes. This bloom, connected with the most eminent personalities in Tudor music, lasted till about 1630.

While this form of part-singing was having its earliest triumphs in England, the original, Italian madrigal had entered its final and most sophisticated phase around 1580 under the leadership of Luca Marenzio (*c.* 1550–1599). On a byway—as a forecast of the impending advent of the opera—it was even allowed to join a novel form, the madrigal-comedy, which reached its peak in Orazio Vecchi's *L'Amfiparnasso*, *comedia harmonica* (1594–97). The madrigal-comedy consisted of a prologue and a number of madrigals with five voice parts suggesting some dramatic development without any visible action or stage.

Now and then, however, the madrigal was converted into a solo melody with instrumental accompaniment. The outer and probably negligible reason for this change may have been the frequent want of five or six well-trained singers in the ranges required; one singer and one lute or a harpsichord were usually at hand. The inner, more decisive reason was the increasing trend towards monody: the simple melody of one accompanied singer moves the heart more than a polyphonic ensemble, Gioseffo Zarlino said in the *Istituzioni* of 1558.

The solo madrigal, to be sure, was nothing but a preparatory makeshift. Its setting was still polyphonic, the voice parts were still equal in importance, and, because they were skilfully interwoven, the self-styled soloist often had to withdraw from the listener's attention after a couple of bars, to allow one of the other voice parts to emerge and spin out the melodic line. Necessarily, wrote Lodovico Viadana in his One Hundred Spiritual Concerts (*Cento Concerti Ecclesiastici*, 1602), the solo part is often interrupted and lacks in regular cadence and cantability.

INSTRUMENTAL MUSIC for several instruments, such as the ensemble that Paolo Veronese depicted with an almost photographic exactness on his gigantic canvas of the Wedding at Cana in the Louvre, was still, in the main, a rendition of properly vocal music. Indeed, of the *Chansons musicales* that the Parisian printer Pierre Attaingnant published in 1533, those best suited for instruments were expressly edited for cross-flutes and recorders; Nicolas Gombert had his motets of 1539 and 1541 *accomodata* for viols and wind instruments; and not much later, many collections of appropriate pieces had the subtitle *da cantare ò sonare* (to be sung or played) printed on their frontispieces. More specifically, a reliable description of a ducal wedding at Munich in 1568, given by Mássimo Trojano, an Italian musician who was serving in the Bavarian court orchestra under Orlandus Lassus, relates that five *Zinken*, or cornets (short wooden horns with fingerholes), and two trombones played one of Lassus' motets at table, and that another polyphonic piece of the master, probably a motet, too, was performed by twenty-four instruments: eight viols, eight violins, and eight wind instruments.

But out of this current practice, the time was creating an exclusively instrumental form. Several times, Trojano himself had to record the performance of *canzone francesi*, which in his time had passed from lutes and keyboard instruments to chamber ensembles. This generation also knew *ricercari* of a somewhat freer style under the names of *capricci* and *fantasie*.

These musical forms may have constituted, to a great extent, the programs of the famous court ensembles of northern Italy and particularly of those of the Este in Ferrara, about which we read at the end of Hércole Bottrigari's dialogue *Il Desiderio overo* [or] *de' concerti di varij strumenti musicali*, Venetia 1594. There we learn what a huge and precious musical library the performers had at their disposal and how many instruments, which all, he says, "are always in playing condition and tuned, ready to be picked up and played on the spur of the moment."

At the same time, a convent in Ferrara had a celebrated nuns' ensemble of the highest quality. "You would," writes Bottrigari, "see them betake themselves in Indian file to a long table, upon one end of which a large harpsichord is laid [Italian keyboard instruments could be taken out of their cases]. Silently they entered, each one with her instrument, be it a stringed or a wind instrument, . . . and gathered around the table without the slightest noise, some sitting down, some standing, according to the nature of their instruments. At last, the conductress faced the table from the other end and, after having made sure that the other sisters were ready, gave them noiselessly the sign to begin with a long, slender, well polished baton. . . ."

England had a similar development in her *consorts* and their music.

The name *consort*, a misspelling of *concert*, appeared for the first time when the composer and publisher Thomas Morley printed in 1599 *The First Booke of Consort Lessons, made by divers exquisite Authors, for sixe Instruments* (two viols and four plucked instruments). Such an ensemble of different instruments was called a 'mixed' or 'broken' consort; a 'whole' consort, on the contrary, was meant for instruments of the same family, generally for viols, which then were held in a 'chest' or homogeneous set.

The form of music particularly written for consorts was *fancies* in a fugato style somewhat freer than the *ricercare* style of the Italian *fantasie*. "A musician," Morley said in 1597, "taketh a point at his pleasure, and wresteth and turneth it as he list, making either much or little of it according as shall seeme best in his own conceit."

M UCH MORE MOMENTOUS than the development of the consort was the English contribution to creating a true harpsichord music which, emancipated from the strictness of polyphony and regular voice-part setting, took the fullest advantage of the manifold chord and passage possibilities that the keyboard offered.

More than five hundred pieces by Elizabethan 'virginalists' have been preserved in special handwritten or printed collections of the time, which approximately span the production from 1575 to 1625. The oldest is the copy of forty-two of William Byrd's compositions in *My Ladye Nevells Booke* of 1591, and the most important is the famous handwritten *Fitzwilliam Virginal Book* in the Fitzwilliam Museum at Cambridge, England, which contains almost three hundred pieces and cannot have been copied before 1621. The *Parthenia or the Maydenhead* of 1611 was, on the other hand, as the title says, "the first musicke that euer was printed for the Virginalls."

Two generations of precursors, the first with Hugh Aston in England and the second with Antonio de Cabezón in Spain and a good many Italians, had provided the leading forms of Elizabethan harpsichord music: the *ostinato* ground and the coloratura variation of popular songs of the time. But when William Byrd took possession of these traditional forms, he gave them a mastery, power, and poetical charm that the earlier masters had hardly achieved. He also added to their interest by an almost imperceptible shift—in the mildest forms—from the realm of absolute music to that of descriptiveness.

A group of younger Britons followed Byrd's example, among them the organist Thomas Morley (1557–1603), the "Bachelor of Musick" Giles Farnaby (b. *c.* 1560), and the good-humored Dr. John Bull (*c.* 1562–1628), who did *not* write 'King's Hunt,' but did depict "Himselfe" in a remarkable piece with a few surplus notes which sound like a critical question mark. This is not a solitary self-portrait in Elizabethan music: Anthony Holborne, courtier and lutemaker, also published, in 1599, a consort *for Viols, Violins, or other Musicall Winde Instruments* under the title *My selfe*.

The English virginalists came to a peak and conclusion with a still younger master, Orlando Gibbons of Cambridge (1583–1625), upon whom the university of Oxford conferred the title of Doctor of Music. To this extraordinary man we are indebted for one of the most beautiful pavans ever written, *The Earl of Salesbury*.

These eminent names must not make us forget a little-known, imaginative pioneer, Nicholas Carlton, who wrote the apparently earliest keyboard duet "for two to play on one virginal or organ" and another virginal piece with the unprecedented key signature of four sharps.

It has been said that the players of the sixteenth century, and even those of the seventeenth, used a clumsy fingering in which the thumb and generally also the fourth and fifth fingers were left out. This is true as far as it goes. The front page of the *Parthenia* shows a player who obviously does without the last two fingers. But such index-middlefinger technique was probably confined to instruments with short keys which were touched on their front-edges with the tips of the longest fingers, thus excluding the other ones. Still, engravings of times before the *Parthenia* depict performers who avail themselves of all their fingers (plate XIV).

Much later, in 1753, Carl Philipp Emanuel Bach stated that his father had "heard great men in his youth who did not use the thumb except when it was necessary for large stretches" but had himself raised the thumb "from its former idleness to the position of the principal finger" (quoted from the translation in Hans T. David and Arthur Mendel's *Bach Reader*, page 254).

THE RECITATIVE was the true, revolutionary accomplishment of the time. Avoiding melodic organization in rhythm and form, giving—in principle—one note to each syllable of the text, and vaguely imitating the natural inflection and meter of ordinary speech, it rendered the sentence as a whole, hastened the words of minor importance, and thus became the ideal idiom for purely epic and dramatic episodes, which in their transitory character and rapid change of mood did not allow for the lyrical flow of melody proper.

Recitativo, however, had then a broader meaning than it had a hundred years later in operas, oratorios, and cantatas. The classics professor Giovanni Battista Doni, its petty, malicious, and arrogant herald, described it as any pleasant solo melody that allowed the words to be easily understood, on the stage as well as in church, in the prayer chapel, at home, or anywhere else. It could, he said, be adorned with grace notes which, although not likely to express emotion, please people of lesser taste and singers eager to display technique and knowledge.

The recitative had forerunners as far back as 1554 in Alfonso della Viola's pastoral play *Il Sacrificio* and, in one of the models of the *masque*, Baltasar de Beaujoyeux's *Ballet de la Reine*, that the court of Paris played in 1581 for a ducal wedding—the earliest ballet whose music is preserved. But, clumsy and stiff, these initial attempts at recitativic writing were still a far cry from the easily flowing recitatives that Italian masters wrote some twenty years later.

The novel style was born in Florence under circumstances unusual in the history of the arts. It was conceived by a *camerata*, or circle of artists and scholars, who gathered in the house of a Florentine nobleman, Count Bardi, and discussed the problems of science, poetry, and the arts. Ottaviano Rinuccini, a famous poet, Galilei's father Vincenzo, and the composer Giácomo Peri were outstanding members. Giulio Caccini acknowledged that he owed a better understanding of music to their scholarly discussions than to all his counterpoint lessons.

Those who believe in instinct rather than in intelligence will have some difficulty in accepting erudite arguments as the source of a creative revolution. They should understand that the birth of a new style can be facilitated by the purely intellectual process of eliminating inhibitions, questioning prejudices, and bringing the blurred outlines of a new trend into focus. But they also should understand that the *camerata* alone did not invent the style to come. It was one cog in the complicated organization that ended the Renaissance and prepared for the Baroque in all the fields of human activity.

For the reaction of the *camerata* was no longer a part of the Renaissance. That it started from the ideals of Greek culture and used to refer to Plato and Aristotle was only natural in an educated circle. All centuries have firmly believed that they have found their own dreams come to life in Greek and Roman antiquity: Gluck and, a hundred years later, Wagner, no less than Peri and Caccini, thought that they were recreating ancient tragedy. There is no trend in any period of history that humanists cannot legalize by a reference to classic antiquity, just as there is no way of thinking for which the preachers cannot find a corroborating Bible verse.

The road away from the Renaissance that the *camerata* opened led to emotionalism, individualism, illusionism, and the disintegration of music as an end in itself. It left behind the ideals of polyphony.

The official manifesto against counterpoint and the "modern" music as a whole was Vincenzo Galilei's *Diálogo della musica antica e della moderna* of 1581. There the author scorns those boorish, idiotic musicians who do not believe in the wonders of Grecian music and who measure that perfect and scholarly art by the standards of their own confused ignorance. "It is meaningless and ridiculous how they do justice to the words of the text and depict them, as children would do, with dotted notes and syncopation (as if they had the hiccup) when the text speaks of a limping ox; they mimic drums and trumpets; to the words 'he descended to Pluto,' the singers grumble as if to scare the little ones; to 'he ascended to the stars,' they scream as if they had the colic; indeed, they have their readymade symbols for crying, laughing, singing, shouting, clamoring, deceit, hard chains, harsh fetters, raw mountain, steep cliff, cruel beauty. Had Isocrates or any great orator stressed an individual word in a similar way, he would have been stopped by angry and laughing listeners."

Galilei's music, the first manifestation of the future, is lost. But we know its titles and, therewith, what he meant to express. In the first place, he composed the pathetic monologue, from the thirty-third canto of Dante's Hell, of the unfortunate Count Ugolino, who, starving in the tower of Pisa, watched his children also starve to death. Next, Galilei set to music the responsorial lamentations of Easter week, and in the third place, the lamentations of Jeremiah.

All three compositions were laments. And affliction remained the keynote for more than three generations. No delight in melancholy was the cause. At the bottom of these and all the following laments was the principal aim of Baroque art: to form a *stile rappresentativo*, as the musicians called it, and to create emotion in order to penetrate to the depths of human feeling. Music, in the words of Mersenne, should force its way into the listener's soul to possess and lead it whither the composer wishes. This was more than an empty phrase. Music

went the way of the greatest spiritual power of the seventeenth century, the Catholic Church, which, in the times of the Counterreformation, attempted to master the soul of man with all its means and
weapons: with the propagandistic order of the Jesuits, burning stakes,
a colorful service, and overwhelming architecture. And music went
the way of all the arts of the time, to naturalism, indeed, to illusionism.
It had its share in attacking the soul with irritation, flattery, and
intoxication.

The way through the lachrymal glands was the shortest and safest.
Tragic emotions are surer to reach the hearts than merry ones. Thus
we read in a diplomatic report of 1608 that, when Monteverdi's opera
Arianna was being performed at the court of Mantua, "many" shed
tears on hearing the heroine lament for Theseus, who had deserted her.
Indeed, exactly the same sentimental outburst occurred in Rome about
1630 when the *castrato* Loreto Vittori sang Mazzocchi's Lament of
St. Magdalen. Such reaction had hardly been reported in earlier days.

Even before the time of Galilei, Roland de Lassus and the German
Leonhard Lechner had composed—the contritest of laments—the seven
penitential psalms. William Byrd wrote *Psalmes, Sonets & Songs of
Sadnes & Pietie* for five voice parts in 1588. In 1605, the lutanist John
Dowland wrote *Lachrymae, or Seaven Teares, Figured in Seaven
Passionate Pavans* for lute, viols, and violins, of which both Byrd and
Farnaby made virginal versions. In 1613, one Angelo Patti printed
a Lyrical Plaint of the Virgin Mary Over the Face of the Dead Christ;
in 1623, the violinist Biagio Marini published *Le Lagrime d'Erminia;*
and in 1655, the same master came out with *Lacrime di Davide.*

At least from 1640 on, laments were composed as independent dirges
to the memory of some outstanding person. They were generally
given the French title *tombeau,* or 'tomb,' a custom apparently inaugurated by the great lutanist Denis Gauthier, who, in 1640, wrote one
for the organist Raquette. Most of them followed the form of some
solemn dance, a pavan, as in Dowland's case, or an *allemande.*

THE THOROUGHBASS. The musical revolution manifest in
the rise of solo singing, of the recitative, and of the monody had to
create the thoroughbass as a necessary substructure.

In the polyphonic style, the bass had been one among several voice parts, keeping mostly below the other parts, but at times ascending above the higher neighboring part and trespassing on tenor grounds when its natural progress imposed such a course. Indeed, on ending a phrase, it had rested for a few measures and allowed some other voice to be the lowest.

Against this polyphonic conception, the harmonic conception of a steady, permanent thoroughbass took shape. The movement quite naturally started with the key- and finger-board instruments, where the crossing of voice parts and their temporary interruption was indiscernable and therefore meaningless. As a consequence, the old conception of an individual bass among parts of equal rights was increasingly replaced by the new conception of a line connecting the actually lowest notes, whether or not they belonged to the same voice part. This bass, then, was no longer one of the voice parts, but an all-supporting *basso continuo*, or thoroughbass. Such an antipolyphonic attitude would not have been possible, of course, had not the growing sense of simultaneous hearing weakened the purely polyphonic conception of independent voice parts.

Under a similar influence, the polyphonic weaving had been subjected more and more to a logical progress of the con- and dissonances that the simultaneous voice parts formed. It was only a confirmation of such development that the accompanying players, unable or unwilling to perform the exact polyphonic weaving, interpreted it as an interesting form of movement from chord to chord and confined themselves to performing these implied chords instead of the contrapuntal weaving.

The players did not care to write the harmonies out, however, nor did the composers, for the density and range of the chords depended on the nature of the instrument on which they were played and also on the acoustic conditions of the room of performance. Instead of playing from written music, the accompanists 'realized' the chords *prima vista* from the bare thoroughbass, to which only a few figures were added, above or below the notes, to indicate what chords should be improvised over them—*3* for the third, *4* for the fourth, and so on, the *5* and the *8* generally being left out.

In this form, the figured bass or thoroughbass, realized on some organ, harpsichord, or lute, was an indispensable feature of all music until about 1760, whether it was instrumental or vocal, solo, chamber, or symphonic music. So important was this accompaniment that in all orchestral music the *maestro al cémbalo* acted as the conductor.

It was not the ordinary lute, however, that served as a bass accompaniment. Beside the usual strings, the thoroughbass lute needed a set of longer strings for the bass proper. But since these additional strings could not be arranged on the fingerboard without overtaxing the possibilities of the player's left hand, they were given a second, higher pegbox, from which they ran down to the bridge beside the fingerboard as unstopped drones. The two main models were:

(1) The *chitarrone* (pron. *k*-), a man-size lute, the neck of which continued straight above the pegbox proper and ended in a second one.

(2) The *theorboe*, which had the second pegbox only a little higher and slightly to the bass side, the two boxes being connected by a piece of neck in the shape of a flat S.

England had, besides her lutes, three specific instruments which often appear in the titles of printed music:

(3) The *cittern*, with a flat back, a pear-shaped outline, and usually nine wire strings in five courses.

(4) The *pandora*, or *bandora*, with a flat back, a scalloped outline, and seven double or triple strings.

(5) The *orpharion*, or *orpheorion*, with a flat back, an undulating outline, a slanted frontal stringholder, and eight double strings.

Illustrations of these five instruments, as well as of the ordinary lute, can be found in the author's *History of Musical Instruments* on pages 346, 371, and 373.

N OTATION in writing and print had not yet reached the modern stage. Bar-lines were rare, and the notes themselves still had, in general, the square and the diamond shapes of the mensural script. Once in a while, the bewildered reader meets the unwonted group of a stemless and a stemmed diamond, for which he finds no analogy in modern notation. It indicated a dotted semibreve *plus* a subsequent minim.

A much detested stumbling-block to modern score-readers is the (later so-called) *chiavette* (pron. kyahv-), or 'small clefs.' Bewildering from a modern viewpoint, it is an easy and logical form of script in the light of ancient practice. The following statements will explain its meaning and form.

(1) At a time when a voice part hardly exceeded the range of a tenth and therefore could be easily written within the five lines of the staff, the use of ledger-lines was rare and dreaded as an unnatural, unwonted, and confusing expedient.

(2) When a voice part was slightly higher or lower than usual, it no longer coincided with the staff and required ledger-lines. The best way out was to accommodate the voice part on the staff and to change the ordinary pitch by shifting the clef accordingly upward or downward—just as we do today when we pass from the treble to the bass clef, and vice-versa in piano and French horn parts. Plainsong notation had shown the way.

(3) Since, as a matter of course, the higher or lower range of any individual voice part entailed an accordingly higher or lower range of each of the other voice parts of a polyphonic piece, musical practice of the polyphonic era devised three principal sets of clefs to serve in keeping all the voice parts within the range of the staff, as shown on page 169.

This interpretation is confirmed and elucidated in Thomas Morley's *Plaine and Easie Introduction to Practicall Musicke* of 1597: all songs are "either in the high key or in the lowe key . . . but you must understand that those songs which are made for the high key be made for more life, the other in the low key with more gravetie and staidnesse." What Morley calls the low key is, however, the *chiave naturale*. The actual low *chiavette* were, according to him, used in men's ensembles only.

Key transposition has been thrown together, in a confusing way, with an entirely different change of key, which has very little to do with the 'high' and the 'low' key. Besides the written *chiavette*, which allowed doing without, or almost without, ledger-lines, an imagined *chiavetta* allowed the performer to transpose any piece upward or downward without a change in its written form. Suppose it seemed desirable to sing a certain piece a minor third lower than the composer had chosen to write it down. The altist, for example, could avail himself of the original notation, if he fancied the alto clef to be a tenor

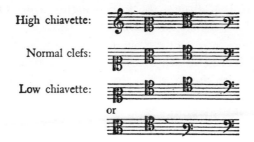

High chiavette:

Normal clefs:

Low chiavette:

or

High clefs: 1. treble:

2. mezzosoprano:

3. alto:

4. baryton:

Normal clefs: 1. soprano:

2. alto:

3. tenor:

4. bass:

Low clefs: 1. mezzosoprano:

2. tenor:

3. baryton:

4. counterbass:

(Slight modifications would occur.)

clef—that is, a *C* clef on the fourth, instead of the third, line of the staff. But he had to change the key signature, too. Otherwise, a *C* major phrase, for example, would become *A* minor, not *A* major. As a rule, performers seem to have been well able to make either change at first sight. But we also hear of the cheap expedient of glueing a scrap of paper with the new signature over the old one with a drop of wax.

The end of the sixteenth century witnessed the penultimate shift of time-values: the long, when still in use, came to approximate two modern wholenotes; the breve, one wholenote; the semibreve, a half-note; the minim, a quarternote; the semiminim, an eighthnote; the *fusa*, a sixteenthnote; and so on.

Polyphonic music was usually still written and printed in part-books. But something unprecedented happened in 1577; the printer Angelo Gardano in Venice published Cypriano de Rore's madrigals *spartiti*, or, literally, de-parted in score-form with bar-lines.

Bar-lines, nevertheless, did not necessarily mean in the sixteenth and seventeenth centuries what they do in modern music. Quite to the contrary, they often dangerously mislead the modern performer. For they did not indicate what we today call a measure—beginning on a heavy accent and ending directly before the following heavy accent—but rather the rigid, unconcerned, metronomical down- and upbeat of the *tactus*, which, according to the conducting rules of the time, conveyed the regular time-units whether the player had to arrange them in groups of two, three, or four beats, whether in a down-or an upbeat rhythm (*cf.* page 118). Thus, the seeming duple-time between the ancient bar-lines could easily conceal an actual triple-time. For instance:

Old notation:	♩ ♩ | ♩ ♩ | ♩ ♩ | ♩
New notation:	♩ ♩ ♩ | ♩ ♩ ♩ | ♩
Or even:	♩ | ♩ ♩ ♩ | ♩ ♩ ♩ | ♩

A final remark should touch upon the Spanish organ tablature, familiar from Cabezón's works and very different from the so-called German keyboard tablature. At first sight, it looks like a lute tablature. But its staff lines mean voice parts—two, three, or more—and the figures from 1 to 7, inscribed on the lines where they belong in the chordal or polyphonic texture of the piece, prescribe the notes of the *F* scale with the flatted or natural *B* according to the usual key signature.

READING

Gustave Reese, *Music in the Renaissance*, New York, 1954. Curt Sachs, *The History of Musical Instruments*, New York, 1940: Chapter 15. Curt Sachs, *The Commonwealth of Art*, New York, 1946: Cross Section 1567. Curt Sachs, *Rhythm and Tempo*, New York, 1953: Chapters 10, 11. Henry Coates, *Palestrina*, London, 1938. Charles van den Borren, *Orlande de Lassus*, Paris, 1920. Thomas Morley, *A Plaine and Easie Introduction to Practicall Musicke*, London, 1597; facs. edition by the Shakespeare Association, London, 1937; ed. Harman, London, 1952. Morrison C. Boyd, *Elizabethan Music and Musical Criticism*, Philadelphia, 1940. Charles van den Borren, *The Sources of Keyboard Music in England*, London, 1914. Margaret H. Glyn, *About Elizabethan Virginal Music and Its Composers*, London, 1924. Walter L. Woodfill, *Musicians in English Society from Elizabeth to Charles I*, Princeton, 1953. Edmund H. Fellowes, *William Byrd*, London, 1948. Edmund H. Fellowes, *Orlando Gibbons*, New York, 1952.

13

THE AGE OF
MONTEVERDI AND SCHÜTZ

1600–1630

THE *STILE RAPPRESENTATIVO*. Under the impact of a strong naturalism, the recitative had developed by 1600 into a rendition, not only of speech in general, but of all the passions, moods, and characters that speech expresses. Indeed, the new monody, avoiding melody in the proper sense of the word, followed the natural inflection of speech in order to make the audience almost forget that the singers were singing. Humanism, to be sure, had emphasized the prevalence of the words a hundred years before, but, with all respect for a clear enunciation of the text, the polyphonic style of early humanistic days had, in Giulio Caccini's own words, "stretched out or on the contrary compressed the syllables for the sake of counterpoint and thus destroyed meter and words." With the elimination of polyphony around 1600, the composer was at last in a position to comply with humanistic claims without restriction. In this spirit, Giovanni Battista Doni said: "The real delight in hearing a singer derives from a clear understanding of the text." Father Marin Mersenne, the Frenchman, even went a step further: "A singer's performance should have the effect of a well-made speech." Indeed, Monteverdi wrote: "Speech should be master of music, not its servant," and Caccini, who in the Florentine *camerata* had been trained to quote from the Greeks, referred to Plato's radical creed that "music was in the first place speech and rhythm and only in the last place tone." Logically, he claimed, in the preface to the *Nuove Musiche* of 1602, to have yielded to a noble disdain of melody, *una nobile sprezzatura del canto*.

The free addition of grace notes was no longer up to the singer.

The composer would prescribe them where they belonged without destroying the character of the role in question.

As a consequence of such ideas, Giovanni Battista Doni suggested that composers model their monodies after the speaking style of skilled actors. From them they would learn where the pitch goes up and where it falls, where the tempo is slow and where more rapid, and which of the words should be stressed. The actors would show them how a prince addresses his vassal or some petitioner and how a matron speaks differently from a young girl or a simple lad or a harlot.

It is hardly necessary to emphasize that so naturalistic and pregnant a recitative had little to do with the hasty, dry *parlando* of a hundred years later. Being *rappresentativo* and expressive, it was melodic enough in all its character and flexibility to demand the art of eminent singers and to captivate their interest. And the composer himself was often lured from the reserve of simple accompanying chords into a more elaborate and almost melodic accompaniment.

THE OPERA. The naturalness, tension, and emotion of the *stile rappresentativo* led inevitably to the form of the musical drama, or *dramma per música.*

The earliest opera, Jácopo Peri's *Dafne*, is lost. It was written on a text of Ottavio Rinuccini (pron. reenootcheenee) and performed, as an outstanding local and social event, during the Carnival of 1597, in Jácopo Corsi's *palazzo* on the Arno in Florence, in the presence of Ferdinand, grand-duke of Tuscany.

But the year 1600 has left us no less than three complete scores of first importance. Two, from Florence, are operas in a narrower sense. One was by Peri, and one, by Giulio Caccini, and both were on the same text, Rinuccini's *Euridice*, the drama of Orpheus. Jácopo Peri's score had been commissioned for the greatest social and political episode in the history of the Médici family: Maria's wedding with Henry IV, King of France. Caccini's was a rival score. In the forty years to come, all operas were intended to be given once or a few times in palaces at princely celebrations, and then to be put away for good.

In the same year, 1600, a Roman oratory congregation, Santa Maria in Vallicella (which San Filippo dei Neri had founded) performed a spiritual drama, *La rappresentazione di ánima e di corpo* (The play of the Soul and the Body), on a text of Laura Guidiccioni with the music of Emilio dei Cavalieri (d. 1602). As in the moralities of the fourteenth and fifteenth centuries, its *dramatis personae* were allegories or abstract conceptions—Time, the World, Life, the Intellect, the Body—and its attitude was strongly didactic and edifying rather than dramatic. And yet, its music adopted the modern dramatic *stile recitativo e rappresentativo*.

The three scores of 1600, their successors in the first third of the century, and doubtless also the lost *Dafne* of 1597, consisted of an endless recitativic melody over a thoroughbass, interrupted by a few melodic songs and choruses and ending in a short ballet. The orchestra, aligned on the stage behind the wings, not in a pit in front, 'realized' the figured bass. As we learn from a composer of the time, Agostino Agazzari (1607), every member of an operatic orchestra was expected to know enough counterpoint to improvise freely upon the figured bass—evidently, the sound was by no means as meager as the sketchy two-staff scores suggest. Agazzari himself had contributed the first of the operas after 1600, the school-drama *Eumelio* (1606).

More important was a second composition of Rinuccini's *Dafne*, written for the court of Mantua by the chapel master of San Lorenzo in Florence, Marco da Gagliano, and performed in 1608. Its lengthy preface shows how close the early opera stood to the ideologies of Gluck and Wagner. In an opera, says Gagliano, "the noblest treats unite: poetic invention, drama and thought, style, sweetness of rhyme, and musical art, concerts of voices and instruments, exquisite singing, nimble dancing and gesture, and even painting, both in the wings and in the costumes." Such conception is, after all, nothing else than the Wagnerian ideal of a *Gesamt-Kunstwerk*—a work embracing all the arts. Gagliano's preface even exhorts the singer to synchronize strictly the steps and gestures and musical beats, and gives him directions to the last details of performance—once more, just as Wagner did in 1852 in a pamphlet on Staging the Flying Dutchman.

MANTUA, the home of Gagliano's *Dafne*, had shortly before seen the birth of the two operas in which the early court opera reached a peak: Monteverdi's *Orfeo* (1607) and *Arianna* (1608), each written with an almost supernatural effort in the darkest hours of the master's life and in a deeply compassionate spirit. Years later, the master refused a few other mythological subjects suggested to him with the remarkable words: "A monster, a wind, cannot move. Arianna makes me cry, and Orpheus makes me pray; but what place would music have in such a piece?"

Claudio Monteverdi's dates are told in one short sentence: Baptized on May 15, 1567, in Cremona, Lombardy, he became a viol player and singer in 1590 and a conductor in 1601, both at the ducal court of Mantua, went to Venice as the director of music at St. Mark's in 1613, and died there thirty years later, on November 29, 1643.

His printed music, without including posthumous editions, spans no less than sixty of the seventy-seven years of his life. It begins with spiritual madrigals in 1583 and ends with the opera *L'incoronazione di Poppea* in 1642. The most remarkable of his numerous operas are *Orfeo* (1607), *Arianna* (1608, lost except for the famous lament), *Il ritorno d'Ulisse in patria* (probably 1630, but remodeled in 1641), and, as the last, the just mentioned Coronation of Poppea (1642). He also wrote seven books of madrigals, *canzonette*, a ballet called *Il ballo delle ingrate* (1608), several *intermedi*, or intermezzi, to be given between the acts of spoken dramas, and, in addition, Masses, motets, psalms, litanies, and a kind of oratorio, *Il combattimento di Tancredi e Clorinda*, on a subject of Tasso (1624), which has wrongly been claimed to be the earliest evidence of the violin *tremolo*.

Quite a number of these works have been reprinted in recent years, complete or abridged, and, among them, the *Orfeo* has appeared several times. Francesco Malipiero even endeavored to edit Monteverdi's Complete Works.

Monteverdi's position in history is uncontested. As one of the greatest geniuses of all times, inexhaustible in melodic, rhythmic, harmonic, and orchestral resources, he was alive and open-minded enough to follow, nay, to lead the changing trends of three successive generations.

Up to the age of forty, writing *canzonette* and madrigals only, he lived in the sphere of aristocratic chamber music in either one of the two aspects that it presented in the final years of the sixteenth century. On the one hand, he continued the evolution of the madrigal in an ever growing sophistication, which necessarily led from an intimate entertainment of cultivated amateurs to a concert form for skilled professionals. On the other hand, he had his share in the modish counterthrust against sophisticated madrigals by writing popular, light-footed *canzonette* in simple settings with catchy refrains and unsentimental words.

At forty, Monteverdi wholeheartedly joined the revolutionary movement of the rising Baroque, which, disregarding intimate chamber music, focused on the stage. Ten years before, the opera had been created and, with it, the *stile rappresentativo*, which, ignoring polyphony, modeled melody after the characteristic inflections of natural speech and filled it with a force capable of moving the audience that older times had not considered. Monteverdi, however, outdid the pioneers. Where Peri and Caccini had lost themselves in dry and tedious recitations, he, the leading master of the madrigal, knew how to give both force and beauty to such music and to express emotion in rare and daring modulations, and he, the master from the color-drunk Northeast of Italy—which had begotten Giorgione, Titian, and the Veronese—also knew the art of creating an emotional atmosphere by skillfully mixing the timbres of instruments. Peri's and Caccini's earlier operas had been precursors and have now hardly more than historical interest, but Monteverdi's *Orfeo* has great and lasting values.

NOT EVEN MONTEVERDI'S genius was able to give the musical drama an international, supranational significance. Spain produced a kind of courtly opera of her own, called *zarzuela*, after a royal country-seat near Madrid. But it had spoken dialogues—the recitative was not imported. Neither did Germany, France, or England show much interest in the new form of musico-dramatic entertainment.

The English, averse to the opera proper and more so to the recitative style, which did not suit the monosyllables and soundless vowels of their language, developed instead the age-old *masque* (or *mask*) to a peak. This was a sumptuous play of a mythological or allegorical character with spoken, vocal, and instrumental sections and with acting and dancing, partly after French and Italian models. It gave preference to the vivid forms of *ayres* and *balletti*. The poet most intimately connected with the masque in the times of James I and Charles I was Ben Jonson (d. 1637). For twenty-six years, it was his monopoly to write the masques for the court. Among composers, we find Alfonso Ferrabosco, and among the artists responsible for machinery, costumes, and scenery, the eminent architect Inigo Jones (1572–1651). The performers were aristocratic amateurs.

THE URGE OF THE TIME to convey emotion, so unmistakably apparent in the monodic *stile rappresentativo*, also reshaped the older madrigal and brought to a new height of sophistication and technical difficulty what had begun as a noble parlor entertainment, both in Italy and in England. Luca Marenzio was mentioned in the preceding chapter as the initiator of this development. In 1588 William Byrd gave the earliest evidence of an unprepared dominant seventh chord—before Monteverdi, who has generally been credited with this innovation. Monteverdi, however, continued and crowned Marenzio's work; Thomas Weelkes (d. 1623), like Gesualdo, delighted in novel harmonic clashes and shifts in his five sets of madrigals; and Gesualdo himself not only ended the over-refined period of the madrigal but brought the madrigal itself to an end.

Don Carlo Gesualdo, Prince of Venosa in South Italy, was born about 1560 and grew up as an almost fanatic lover of music and became the center of a brilliant circle of artists and scholars. A bloody family catastrophe ended the carefree years of his life in 1590: true to the pattern of the violent age, he caused the brutal deaths of his beautiful wife, her lover, and a child that he suspected not to be his, and fled to the court of the Este in Ferrara. He died in 1614 at Naples.

Although he was an excellent player of the bass-lute (*chitarrone* or *theorboe*) and other instruments, he published madrigals exclusively—madrigals rooted in the latest Marenzio-Monteverdi style, but boldly advancing beyond the innovations of these men. True, his polyphony, fluent and refined, followed tradition. But it ceded a good deal of its former dominating position to a harmonic style in which the simplest triads were in rivalry with unheard-of inversions of altered seventh chords in shifts and modulations of the weirdest kind, with appoggiaturas, changing notes, interrupted cadences, harshly dissonant entries, and chromatic progressions, which are always fascinating and often of irresistible beauty.

Contemporaries admired these madrigals as the inspirations of a genius, just as much as the critics of the nineteenth century scolded them as the amateurish experiments of "a cavalier stumbling about in the maze of modulation." Today, we know that he was one of the great masters and one of the boldest pioneers.

True, his modulation was 'illogical'; but only from the viewpoint of Rameau's harmonic system. It was not illogical as a floating harmony without a supporting thoroughbass. True, also, that Gesualdo did not strictly confine his unwonted chromatics to underscoring the Tristanic pangs of death in his love songs, with their ever recurring *io moro*'s (I die), or to other emotional climaxes. No doubt, Gesualdo overdid chromatics from sheer delight in eccentricity and abnormalcy. But, in this delight, he reflected one of the traits of the Baroque age—the one that popular terminology denotes as 'baroque.'

How these late madrigals of the seventeenth century were performed is largely unknown. But one important point is certain: the freedom of their tempo. Girólamo Frescobaldi (1583–1643), the greatest organist of his time, whose performances at St. Peter's in Rome were attended by tens of thousands of enthusiasts, is our witness. In 1614, the year of Gesualdo's death, Frescobaldi prefaced a collection of his own *Toccate e Partite* for harpsichord with the direction to the players not to stick to one persistent tempo, but, on the contrary, to change it within the same piece according to the changing character of the music. The players, he adds, should feel in this, as free as do the singers of modern madrigals.

Already, three years earlier, Adriano Banchieri had prescribed in the second edition of *L'órgano suonarino* six different tempo marks: *adagio, allegro, veloce, presto, più presto, prestissimo*.

The expressiveness of the modern style led to two further developments. In the first place, did the generation of 1600 depart from the earlier practice of keeping a musical piece in the same intensity throughout? Contemporaries said with pride that, while yesterday's singers did not know about forte and piano, the singers of today not only have a way to inflate and deflate the individual note [although, to be sure, not groups of notes or phrases], but they also alternate between piano and forte.

At least from Lassus's time, musicians and listeners had occasionally delighted in *echo* effects, with a whole phrase or the end of a phrase repeated in *piano*. Though the echo as such was retained up to the times of Mozart, the later sixteenth century developed the contrast of intensities on a broader basis.

Indeed, Giovanni Gabrieli wrote in 1597 a *sonata pian e forte* for two groups of instruments with the play of light and shade in a continual, carefully marked alternation of *forte* and *piano*.

But this sonata is also remarkable for another reason. Orchestration in a modern sense had hardly existed before: the selection of instruments had depended little or not at all upon the emotional character of a composition, and when subsequent pieces in a program were left to different groups of instruments, the idea was pleasurable change and contrast rather than significant meaning. As late as 1600, Emilio dei Cavalieri gave no special instructions in his *Rappresentazione di anima e di corpo*, but expected the conductor to make an appropriate selection and scoring of instruments, just as most of our organ music leaves registration to the performing organist, in order not to interfere with the special conditions of his church and his instrument.

It was in an entirely new spirit that Gabrieli's *sonata pian e forte* expressly prescribed a *zink* or *cornetto* and three trombones in the first, and a viola and three trombones in the darker, second chorus. The art of orchestration had been born.

THE INSTRUMENTS. The rise of orchestration was closely connected with a thorough change in instruments.

In the sixteenth century, instruments had been expected to provide a number of different, sharply contrasting colors; and the limited range that the voice parts had in the polyphonic style and their limited emotional quality had given a chance even to those instruments of the woodwind family which, due to wind-caps concealing the reeds and precluding any coöperation of the human lips, were unable to overblow into the higher octaves or to render shades of personal feeling.

The new monodic *stile rappresentativo*, on the contrary, needed instruments with the extensive range and the expressive qualities of singers. As a consequence, the rigid shawms, *sordoni*, *doppioni*, rankets, cromornes, *bassanelli*, *schryari*, and what not, disappeared from the scene (except for a few decades of continued life in German bands), and yielded their place to the more flexible wind instruments, such as flutes, oboes, bassoons, and, at the beginning of the century, the *zinken* or *cornetti*.

Again, as in most dynamic times, attention was given to instruments of a low tessitura: a musician in Berlin, Hans Schreiber, constructed a double-bass trombone and a double-bassoon.

Altogether, the seventeenth century—and Italy in particular—shifted the accent from the wind instruments to the stringed instruments. It was at that time that the manufacture of Italian violins had its first great period. Gásparo da Salò and Giovanni Paolo Maggini were working in Brescia, Lombardy, and Andrea Amati had founded the all-dominating school of Cremona near Brescia. The other nations did not yet participate in the manufacture of violins.

I NSTRUMENTAL MUSIC. Only a few years after the decisive victory of vocal monody, instrumental music, too, began to adopt the *stile rappresentativo*. A first move in the new direction was the book of *Sinfonie et Galliarde* (1607) by Salomone Rossi Ebreo (1572–1630), the 'Jew,' a violinist in the service of the Duke Gonzaga at Mantua and the celebrated composer of the Hebrew Psalms and the Song of Songs in polyphonic settings.

The term *sonata*, used in Rossi's third book of 1623, denoted 'trio' sonatas, that is, pieces for two melody instruments and a third instrument for the thoroughbass. The first book still left the choice between violins and *zinken* or *cornetti* for the melody parts; the later books were definitely meant for violins and nothing else. The figured bass was realized on a harpsichord or a *chitarrone*, if possible with the co-öperation of a bowed-bass—an instrument halfway between a 'cello and a doublebass, but not a gamba. These trio sonatas were actual monodies full of *affetto* and *cantabile*, and despite a good deal of imitative counterpoint, the two melodic parts often alternated at so long a distance that they formed consecutive solos.

This form, characteristic of the Baroque age down to the times of Handel and Bach, was brought to a first climax in the violin sonatas of the Brescian violonist Biagio Marini (*c.* 1600[?]–*c.* 1655). His earliest work, in 1617, had the timely title *Affetti musicali*, and contained, among sonatas for two violins, the oldest one for only one violin and accompaniment.

Incidentally, Marini's publication was called his *Opus* 1. Musical work-numbers date from that generation, although they were nothing less than general in the seventeenth and eighteenth centuries.

The common tendency in all the arts of the Baroque—to give their works a unity of matchless strength—led, in Rossi's instrumental monodies as well as in Monteverdi's vocal monodies, to a remarkable emphasis on variation in its two forms, either in ever new configurations over a 'ground,' or *ostinato*, or else as a set of paraphrases on the same melodic pattern (*cf.* page 161). Despite a general confusion of terms, the *ostinato* variation is generally given the name *passacaglia*, and the paraphrase on a steady succession of chords is called *chaconne*. As a rule, both have the triple-time in common. It must be stated, however, that the seventeenth century hardly knew of such classifications and used the two terms without any apparent discrimination. And the reader should also be warned that the French composers of the time allowed themselves to give either title to entirely different forms.

While the violinists were developing instrumental monodies, the organists clung to forms inherited from the preceding century. Girólamo Frescobaldi, already quoted, wrote *partite*, in their original meaning of variations, and *toccate* in a peculiar style, from which the polyphonic episodes, as well as the bravado passages, had disappeared.

A third form suitable for organ was the *ricercare*, which the preceding chapters have discussed. The unification that it reached at the beginning of the century made it almost a fugue. The master mainly responsible for this evolution was Andrea's nephew Giovanni Gabrieli (1557–1612), who first served the court of Munich under Lasso and then succeeded Claudio Mérulo to the first organ at St. Mark's in Venice (1586).

One part of his fame is due to the many-sided treasure of religious and secular music that he left for the organ, for orchestral ensembles, and for voices. The other part is pedagogical: two generations of young composers revered him and his uncle Andrea as their teachers, among them Hassler, Sweelinck, and Heinrich Schütz.

Hans Leo Hassler (1564–1612), fundamentally an organist, studied with Andrea Gabrieli in Venice, but spent most of his life in South Germany and attained an unusual reputation, culminating in the nobility that Emperor Rudolf II conferred upon him. Many of his compositions merged the Venetian style with German tradition. A curious example of these not-always-convincing mixtures is *Mein Lieb' will mit mir kriegen*, which sets a harmless, amorous madrigal text to the pompous style of Venetian state motets for two choruses. Truer to pattern are his typically German works: chorale-motets and such *Lieder* as *Mein G'müt ist mir verwirret von einer Jungfrau zart* (My mind is all confused about a tender maid), which later became one of the greatest Lutheran chorales with the texts *O Haupt voll Blut und Wunden* and *Wenn ich einmal muss scheiden*.

MICHAEL PRAETORIUS (1571–1621), although not a direct pupil of the Gabrieli, belongs in this group, too. For, no less than Hassler, did this great *Kapellmeister* of Brunswick graft the modern Venetian style upon his German heritage. A considerable part of his enormous number of compositions are polychoral, and many have the abrupt, exciting change of tempo and rhythm and the restless alternation of a chorus, solo singers, and instruments that Giovanni Gabrieli cherished so much.

To the modern world, however, he is much more important as the author of the most outstanding and comprehensive work on the music of his time: the *Syntagma musicum*, printed from 1615 to 1620 in three volumes, of which the second and the third are easily accessible in modern reprints. The first volume deals with the theory of music, especially counterpoint; the second is a complete manual of all the instruments of the time, with their ranges and their effigies in woodcuts carefully drawn to scale; and the third contains a detailed practice of music with all the forms of solo, choral, polychoral, and orchestral performance.

The name Praetorius is particularly familiar to the musicians of our time because, as the last chapter of this book will show, a number of modern organ builders have revived the German type of organ of about 1600 that Praetorius analyzes thoroughly in the second volume of his *Syntagma*. It has contrasting, hard, unbroken timbres with a special predilection for poignant, jarring reeds and four-foot stops (*cf.* page 196), which give it a lighter, more festive coloring than has the later organ.

An important Dutch disciple of Andrea Gabrieli was Jan Pieterszoon Sweelinck (1562–1621), organist at the Old Church in Amsterdam.

He wrote *chansons*, reformed psalms, and *cantiones sacrae*, that is, motets (his Christmas motet *Hodie hodie* is a favorite of our choral societies). But his incomparable eminence is based on gigantic fugues for the organ, the earliest—in the proper sense—ever written and, besides those of Bach, the peak of the form. A whole generation of German organists wandered to Amsterdam to be his pupils, among them Samuel Scheidt from Saxony, who will be discussed anon.

SAXONY can claim a section of her own in this short survey. Most German composers of all times have come from that Germano-Slavonian borderland. Late in the sixteenth century, she gave birth within two years to three composers whom contemporaries lovingly called their three great Esses.

Heinrich Schütz, the greatest among them and at once the greatest musician in Germany's seventeenth century, was born on October 8, 1585, a hundred years before Handel and Bach. Like many other men whom this book is to mention, he was for years undecided whether to become a lawyer or a musician. Not even the good luck of a grant to study the craft with Giovanni Gabrieli in Venice was able to bring a resolution. At last, his patron, the landgrave of Hesse-Cassel appointed the twenty-eight year old student court organist and therewith enforced a decision in favor of music. Soon the Elector of Saxony, more influential than the landgrave, took a fancy to him and 'borrowed' him as the *Hofkapellmeister* in Dresden, then Germany's musical center. Although the miseries of the Thirty Years War interrupted his stay repeatedly, he lived in his high position until he died, eighty-seven years old, on November 6, 1672.

Schütz has left an enormous amount of music—his *Complete Works*, printed around 1890, fill sixteen portly volumes. There, the reader will look in vain for instrumental music. Schütz wrote no keyboard pieces, no chamber music, and no dances, except, probably, in a court ballet *Orpheus und Eurydice* (1638), which is lost, as is Germany's earliest opera, *Daphne* (1627), composed by Schütz on Rinuccini's text, although in German translation. Even his *Symphoniae sacrae* and *Geistliche Concerte* were, despite their misleading titles, written for voices with instrumental accompaniment.

Thus, the *Complete Works* present exclusively vocal church music —Passions, oratorios, psalms, and motets, all set with a maximum of concentration and an unparalleled expressiveness. His style is not unified, and it could not be so. For, like Bach a hundred years later, Schütz's mission was to amalgamate German tradition and the latest idioms of Italy. He kept the polyphonic language of the sixteenth century and even found the way far back into a severe and vigorous archaism. In three (not four) Passions after the German versions of Luke, John, and Matthew (1665-1666), the octogenarian did completely without any instrument, and while a few dramatic choruses represented the people and the disciples, he reverted in the narration and the words of Jesus and other soloists to the austere psalmody of the Gregorian chant. Often he wove the powerful, festive polychoral style of Venice upon the sober web of traditional German counterpoint. But the modern *stile recitativo e rappresentativo* of Italy, shorn of its native theatricality, became his strongest medium to stress the meaning, grandeur, and intensity of the words of God in a truly Protestant spirit.

Johann Hermann Schein (1586-1630), one of Bach's predecessors as the cantor of St. Thomas' in Leipzig, formed in a way the complement to Schütz. His field was secular music, especially polyphonic songs and suites of dances. The titles of their collections, affected coquettish, are not quite to the taste of our time. His earliest set of secular songs was a *Venus-Kräntzlein, mit allerley lieblichen vnd schönen Blumen gezieret vnd gewunden* (Little Venus garland, decorated and wound with sundry lovely and beautiful flowers), and a later one, of 1621, *Musica boscarreccia, Wald Liederlein* (Little wood songs). The last of these secular collections, printed in 1626, is a *Studenten-Schmauss*, or Students' Banquet, for five voice parts and testifies to the role that German university students have played in the history of the German *Lied*.

The third of the three great Esses was Samuel Scheidt (1587-1654), disciple of Sweelinck and organist at St. Moritz's in Halle, Saxony. He, too, wrote part-songs in the older, pre-Italian and pre-monodic style. "I am astonished at the foolish music written in these times," one of his letters reads (1651). "It is false and wrong and no longer does anyone pay attention to what our beloved old masters wrote about composition. It certainly must be a remarkably elevated art when a pile of consonances are thrown together any which way. I remain faithful to the pure old composition and pure rules" (quoted from Norman and Shrifte, *Letters of composers*, New York 1946, page 17).

Scheidt's principal, widely influential work was the *Tabulatura Nova* of 1624, a weighty collection of organ music which (the earliest one to do so) established the contrapuntal art of paraphrasing the Protestant chorale melodies on the organ—an art that, via the Nürnberger Johann Pachélbel (1653–1706) and Georg Böhm from Thuringia (1661–1733), reached a climax a hundred years later in Johann Sebastian Bach's chorale-preludes.

T HE WORLD OF SCHÜTZ, Schein, and Scheidt can hardly be thought of without the specifically German and Netherlandish municipal bands. Descendants of medieval nomadic jugglers and minstrels who had settled in towns as respectable burghers, these bands were appointed by the municipal council, underpaid, and squeezed into the rigid social forms of medieval craftsmen's guilds. As a regular artisan, the master, or *Stadtpfeifer*, kept a number of *Gesellen*, or assistants—hardly ever more than four—and several apprentices. The little band, as a rule without the apprentices, played at all celebrations of the municipality, of the guilds and fraternities, and of the well-to-do families, on whatever instruments were required for the occasion— strings or woods, or brasses (*pl.* XV)—indoors or outdoors, down from the pipers' gallery in the city hall or from the tower, in the open market square, at processions and dances, at weddings and funerals.

The *Stadtpfeifer* played chorales—three times a day from the tower —and folksongs, but above all dances, solemn or lively (*pl.* XV). Such dances could be performed individually, one at a time. But it is more important, both from an artistic and a historical viewpoint, that the *Stadtpfeifer* took possession of the old idea of uniting several dances in some significant order and shifted such *suites*, as they called them, to the center of instrumental music. Our symphonies are their scions and acknowledge this parentage in their minuets and scherzos.

Schein and Scheidt played a momentous role in the early history of the suite. In 1617, Schein printed suites of pavans, galliards, *courantes*, *allemandes*, and *triplas*, or *Nachtänze*, in triple time, under the title

Banchetto musicale, or Musical Banquet, each of the five dances within a suite having not only the same key but also the same melodic theme. And Scheidt came out with similar sets in 1621.

READING

Manfred Bukofzer, *Music in the Baroque,* New York, 1947. Donald J. Grout, *A Short History of Opera,* New York, 1947. Curt Sachs, *The History of Musical Instruments,* New York, 1940. *The Commonwealth of Art,* New York, 1946. *Rhythm and Tempo,* New York, 1953. Leo Schrade, *Monteverdi,* New York, 1950. Michael Praetorius, *Syntagma Musicum,* vol. II, ed. Eitner, Berlin, 1884; facs. Kassel, 1929; tr. Blumenfeld, St. Louis, 1949. Charles van den Borren, *Les Origines de la Musique de Clavier dans les Pays-Bas jusque vers 1630,* Bruxelles, 1914. Hans Joachim Moser, *Heinrich Schütz,* Kassel, 1936.

14

THE AGE OF CARISSIMI

1630–1670

THE OPERA. After the 1620's, Italy, the land of form, experienced a mild classical reaction both in architecture and in painting. Music did not lag behind them. In 1626 the preface to Doménico Mazzocchi's opera *La Catena d'Adone* (The Chain of Adonis) spoke for the first time of the *tedio del recitativo*, the tedium of the recitative. The enthusiasm with which the modern musical language had been received a generation before was gone.

The changing attitude soon left its mark on the scores. The melodic qualities of the recitative could not be much enhanced without jeopardizing its speech-like qualities, and thus a splitting into two opposite forms was the natural way out. Melodic singing consolidated more and more in the well-wrought form of the *aria*, and recitativic singing became an ever quicker *parlando* without melodic ambitions.

The first chapter of operatic history had closed forever when Stéfano Landi, a papal singer, performed his *Sant' Alessio* in 1634. This half-religious opera kept equally aloof from the mythological subjects of the Florentine and Mantuan operas and from the pallid allegories of the earlier religious stage-works. Rather, it described the fate of a Roman of about A.D. 400, who forsook the opulent house of his father and after many years of Christian pilgrimage returned unknown to live under the stairs of his paternal mansion as a humble beggar. The score had wholly novel traits: melodious *da capo* arias, in which the first part was, after a contrasting second part, repeated "from the beginning"; two actual overtures before the first and second acts, in the later form with changing rhythms and tempi in several movements; a *castrato* who, being gelded, sang a woman's soprano with the

187

powerful resonance of a man's chest and added to the sensuous tonal beauty of sound at the cost of convincing naturalism; and a number of comic scenes and characters to provide the contrast—so dear to classical ages—with the serious, uplifting plot of the drama.

Claudio Monteverdi was once more in the modern camp. He, too, turned his back on the endless flow of recitatives and on the strict one-way progress of a drama in which no interrupting episodes allowed for contrasts. And he left the vagueness of subjects from myth and legend and resented the previous prevalence of drama over music.

His last opera, The Coronation of Poppea (1642; reprinted in 1931 in Volume 13 of Malipiero's edition), was still predominantly recita-tivic, yet it had parted from the ideals of *Orfeo*. The subject came from Roman history as the typical realm of classical operas, and a couple of *servi ridículi*, or comic servants, provided the customary contrast. The music often broke away into solid forms, like *ariosi*, duos, and even a *terzetto*; the harmonies were very simple; and the melodies, far from the chromaticisms of Monteverdi's early years, were mainly diatonic and even triadic. The master had re-established the supremacy of music.

Leader in three generations, Monteverdi was a symbol of the re-awakening Italian music after the Renaissance and its Netherlandish domination. But more than a symbol, he was one of the greatest masters of all times and, to us, probably the most 'modern' of those before Bach.

Five years earlier than The Coronation of Poppea, a far-reaching event in the history of the opera had occurred: in 1637, the first public opera house had been opened in the San Cassiano parish in Venice. The opera was no longer the exclusive property of courts, which performed a score for some dynastic celebration once and then put it away for good. It was now accessible to almost everybody who paid for his entrance ticket, and it was repeated as often as there was any demand.

From that decisive year we date the Venetian opera, which, after Monteverdi's last works, culminated in the scores of Cavalli and Cesti.

Francesco Cavalli (1602–1676) was successively a singer, organist, and chapel master at St. Mark's in Venice. Besides religious music, he wrote no less than forty-two operas, as a worthy heir to Monteverdi, and among them a much admired *Giasone* (1649), which has been partly reprinted by Robert Eitner.

Marcantonio Cesti was younger by half a generation. Born at Arezzo in 1618, he led the typical life of a seventeenth century conductor. *Maestro di capella* in a Florentine church in 1646, singer in the Sixtine Chapel from 1659 to 1662, he finally held the position of a vice-director of music at the Imperial Court of Vienna from 1666 to his death in 1669. Excepting a single early opera, all his dramatic works were written in the sixties. One of them—*Il Pomo d'Oro* (The Golden Apple), 1667—composed for the court of Vienna, has been reprinted in the *Denkmäler der Tonkunst in Oesterreich*.

The Venetian opera was in many respects much more 'classical' than the early Florentine, Mantuan, and Roman operas had been. The classical need for sharply outlined forms led to a distinct separation of recitatives and arias, to the use of clear-cut folksongs, and to a re-awakening, genuinely Italian delight in beautiful singing. But it also led the declivitous way to a more elaborate staging and to a continual contrast of dignified and vulgar persons, of serious and comic episodes, and of commonplace plots and counterplots, which often threatened to strangle the Venetian opera in an inextricable ravel.

To add to this ravel, it became more and more customary to interweave, act by act, a comic opera, or *intermezzo*, with the principal, serious one. Although this confusing practice was continued up to the eighteenth century, in 1639 Venice gave birth to the earliest *opera buffa* in its own right, Marázzoli's *Chi soffre speri* (Who suffers may hope).

ORATORIO AND CANTATA. In the age of the Venetian opera, and as a balancing factor against its worldliness, the Italians created the semidramatic, religious *oratorio*, which generally stressed the epic and lyrical sides of events, gave a preponderant role to the chorus—which the Venetian opera was neglecting—and suppressed the dialogue almost completely. Its origins can be traced back to the tropes, liturgical dramas, and mystery plays of the Middle Ages. But its immediate predecessor was the popular service in an oratorio, or prayer chapel, over San Girólamo in Rome. San Filippo dei Neri had instituted it not long before, "in order," as a contemporary says, "to attract the faithful and to entertain them with spiritual profit in those hours of the night which in the fall and the winter are the most dangerous, above all for young people."

In 1639, a French violist, André Maugars, attended oratorical performances in the Congregation of the Holy Cross in Rome. "It consists of the noblest gentlemen of Rome," he reports, "who are able to convene the choicest that Italy owns; and indeed, the outstanding musicians care to gather there, and the proudest composers deem it a privilege to have there performed the best they produce.

"The church is smaller than the *Sainte Chapelle* in Paris. It has, at the end, a platform with a middle-sized organ well suited for voices. Two other stages with excellent instrumental ensembles are placed on either side of the nave. To begin with, the voices sang a psalm in motet form, and the players followed with a beautiful symphony. Thereupon they sang some story from the Old Testament in the form of a dialogue: Susanna, Judith and Holofernes, David and Goliath. Each singer represented one personage of the tale and rendered the meaning of the words with perfect skill. After some famous preacher had delivered a sermon, the music recited the Gospel of the day, such as the story of the Samaritan woman, the wedding at Cana, Lazar, Magdalen, or the Passion of the Lord."

Stéfano Landi and Doménico Mazzocchi (pron. matzóckee), each a dramatic composer, had begun to graft these devotional forms upon the tree of the opera. But a greater man, with lyrical leanings, interfered and brought the theatrical development to a decisive stop. He was Giácomo Carissimi (1605–1674), a church organist and for some thirty years the chapel master at Sant'Apollinare in Rome. Doing away with action, costumes, and scenery, he established the later form of the oratorio.

Carissimi's oratorios are not exactly what the reader with Handel's gigantic works in mind would imagine. His twelve oratorios on texts from the Old Testament—among them *Jephte, Judicium Salomonis*, and *Baltazar* (Belshazzar)—last only fifteen or twenty minutes each. Since there was no visible action, a narrator—*históricus* or *testo*— related the happenings. As a rule, he was a soloist, but sometimes two soloists sang the *testo* in a canonic duet, or a whole ensemble sang it, or even the chorus itself. The *dramatis personae*—Jephte and his daughter, King Solomon, or Baltazar—sang recitatives, not arias. But the main role was given to the chorus, which, in vigorous, hammering, metrical chords with little polyphony, played the "ideal spectator" as in the tragedy of the Greeks. Instrumental music appeared, if at all, in the forms of short *sinfonie* and *ritornelli* without prescribed orchestration. Altogether, Carissimi's style was very simple, with resting basses and rudimentary harmonies, such as befitted a devotional form of art intended for a congregation rather than for a concert audience.

The *cantata*, a smaller, lyrical sister of the oratorio, slowly emerged in the 1620's as a third form of monodic singing. The name appeared first in Alessandro Grandi's *Cantade a voce sola* of 1620, which were monodic songs in stanzas, each stanza being a variation over the same 'strophic' bass or lengthy 'ground' spun out all through the stanza. Once more it was Carissimi who led the older cantata to a peak and established its standard form of two or more contrasting arias with their recitatives. There was, however, no chorus such as later in Bach's and other German, Protestant church cantatas.

T HE POLYCHORAL STYLE. St. Peter's Church in Rome, which had been planned as a circular, symmetrical structure fifty years before, was given a long nave in the twenty years from 1606 to 1626 and became, in its gigantic size, the largest church of the world. The first generation of the seventeenth century strove indeed for grandiose, colossal, overwhelming effects.

Music responded with the luxuriant growth of polychoral works. Willaert's modest double choruses of seventy and eighty years before would have little impressed the age of St. Peter's. Four, six, and more choruses were not exceptional, particularly in Rome. When the cathedral of Salzburg was inaugurated in 1628, two years after St. Peter's, the Roman Orazio Benévoli wrote a festive Mass for eight choruses, vocal and instrumental, with the accompaniment of two organs, and he doubtless was pleased on seeing it printed in a score nearly a yard in size.

Still, it should be realized that all these 'Roman' masters, however up to date in their trend toward the colossal, were strictly conservative; they had their roots in polyphony and almost ignored the monodic style with its *recitativo* and *rappresentativo*.

André Maugars, the French violist quoted before, described a poly-choral performance at Rome that he had attended in 1639:

"The church, in which two organs and music lofts are built in on either side of the high altar, was rather long and spacious. There were eight other lofts eight or nine feet high in equal distances along the nave, four on either side. Each chorus had its own portable organ.

"The conductor, in the midst of the best singers, beat time for the first chorus. Each other chorus had a sub-conductor who watched his gestures to keep time himself so that nobody lagged behind. The counterpoint was florid and full of beautiful melodies and pleasant recitatives. Now a soprano from the first chorus would sing a solo; now another from the third, fourth, and tenth chorus would answer. Sometimes two, three, four, or five voices from different choruses sang together, and sometimes all the choruses repeated a section after one another. Again, two choruses competed, and two others answered. Thereafter, three, four, and five choruses would sing together, and then one, two, three, four, or five solo voices; and all the ten choruses joined in the *Gloria patri*. I confess I had never before enjoyed anything as much as this performance."

G ERMAN AND ENGLISH SONGS. Germany's central figure was, in this as in the preceding generation, the venerable Heinrich Schütz. His contemporaries were of an infinitely smaller measure; and yet they played a vital role in preparing the modern *Lied*. They reached eagerly for the novel thoroughbass style of Italy, but, just like Schütz, they made it subservient to German ideas. Away from the operatic aria of the Italians, they resumed the tradition of the *Lieder-bücher* of the fifteenth century, of Heinrich Finck and of Hassler, in new monodic forms. And within a few years, they culminated in Heinrich Albert's *Arien oder Melodeyen* (1638–1650), Andreas Hammerschmidt's *Weltliche Oden oder Liebes-Gesänge* (1642–1649), and Adam Krieger's *Arien* (1657). In these titles the word *arie* is not meant in the sense of the Italian *da capo* aria, but rather denotes short, strophic songs similar to those that Giulio Caccini had called *arie* in his collection *Nuove Músiche* of 1602.

While these secular songs had a merely national scope, the powerful chorales that the cantor Johann Crüger (1598–1662) wrote in Berlin have reached the Protestant world in all the continents. His influential collection *Praxis pietatis mélica* (1647) had no less than forty-six editions in Berlin alone, and some of his melodies, like *Jesu meine Zuversicht* and *Nun danket alle Gott* and *Schmücke dich o liebe Seele*, have found their way into the liturgies of a great many denominations.

England, meanwhile, delighted in a peculiar form of part-singing known as the *catch*, a round or canon, very often with a text of the most robust indecency. The date of the earliest printed collection of catches is 1609, and the famous compilation *Catch That Catch Can* for three and four voices, edited and published since 1652 by John Hilton in London, represents about the zenith of this national form.

However, the England of audacious catches also had *The First Book of Selected Church Music* printed in 1641.

INSTRUMENTAL MUSIC. Italy's main instrumental contribution was the *concerto*. The name, originally denoting accompanied vocal music, monophonic or polyphonic, began hesitatingly to designate a new, instrumental form of *canzona*, in which a soloist, generally a violin player, performed in a free virtuoso style between the various ensemble sections. It was from this Italian one-movement *canzona concertata* (under whatever name it might appear) that the concerto in its modern form developed in the last quarter of the seventeenth century.

The *canzona* proper, once a motley serialization of short episodes in different tempos, rhythms, and styles, accomplished the transition to the *sonata*, in the later sense of the word, by reducing the number of episodes and increasing their length.

France, England, and Germany may be represented here by only one outstanding instrumental composer each: Chambonnières, Locke, and Froberger.

Jacques Champion de Chambonnières was born around 1600 and died in 1670 as King Louis XIV's chamber harpsichordist. The output of his pen is not impressive in quantity: he left only two collections of *Pièces de Clavessin*, both printed in the year of his death and recently republished in one volume. (A *rondeau*—one and the same *refrain* alternating with different *couplets*—is reprinted in the author's *Commonwealth of Art*, New York 1946, on page 145.) But these few pieces, generally shorter dance forms, have a dash, delicacy, and melodic breath that give them an incontestable place next to the greatest masters of the harpsichord; and the French are right in calling him the patriarch of the glorious school of *clavecin* playing.

Matthew Locke (*c.* 1630–1677), pugnacious court composer to King Charles II and organist to Queen Catherine (of Braganza), excelled in other fields. He wrote masques, the musical parts for several (spoken) dramas, among them Shakespeare's *Tempest* and, allegedly, Davenant's version of *Macbeth*, and numerous anthems and ayres. And he led the consort from the old phantasy form into the suite of dances. Moreover, Locke left a small treatise under the title of *Melothesia, or Certain General Rules for Playing upon a Continued Bass* (1673).

The composer was as unruly as the man. He had an angular, rugged, and often violent style. Indeed, in a time when expression marks were unusual in England and a steady crescendo or diminuendo unknown all over the world, he would prescribe "lowd, soft, softer" or "lowder by degrees" and climax this gradual crescendo with a "violent." No doubt, he was a highly gifted master and not, as one of his many opponents called him, "a frightful scarecrow, stuffed with straw."

In the field of instrumental chamber music, the old *diferencia* of the Spaniards was fully up to date in England under the name *division on a ground*. It still was a variation in increasingly rapid passages on an *ostinato*, which the player performed "as his Skill, and present Invention, do then suggest unto him." This quotation is taken from the outstanding source of that practice, Christopher Simpson's book *The Division-Violist: or, an Introduction to the Playing Upon a Ground* (1659).

In order to perform divisions in an adequate way, the player had to avail himself of a division-viol "of something a shorter Size than a Consort-Basse [the usual gamba], that so the Hand may better command it."

A still shorter size of gamba was assigned to playing *lyraway*, an expression that referred to a bowed instrument of the time, the short-lived *lira da gamba*, which was played in full chords.

The German Johann Jacob Froberger, of whom we know neither the year of his birth nor his home town, served as an organist to the court of the emperor at Vienna between 1637 and 1657, but he spent the first four years of that time in Rome studying with the greatest Italian organist, Girólamo Frescobaldi. He died in 1667 in a castle of his patroness, the Duchess Sibylla of Württemberg, in eastern France. Unlike Schütz, he specialized in instrumental, indeed, in keyboard music. He wrote a number of beautiful *toccatas* with a thoroughly personal stamp and created the dance suite for harpsichord (instead of individual instruments), which later culminated in the English, French, and German suites, or *partitas*, of Bach, but even earlier had been instrumental in giving birth to the sonata.

The arrangement that Froberger and Matthew Locke gave the suite was different from that of the generation of Schein. To the older stock—*allemande, courante, sarabande*—they added, as a fourth movement, the rapid *gigue* in 6/8 or 2/4 time, once the *jig* of merry old England, but they added it before or after the *courante* and not, as later, at the end, so that the two usual arrangements were:

allemande	*courante*	*gigue*	*sarabande*
allemande	*gigue*	*courante*	*sarabande*

Musicians should be warned against taking the modern slow and dignified conception of the saraband for granted. This Spanish-American dance, in its beginnings naughty rather than respectable, had been fast, not solemn, and as late as 1676 Thomas Mace still characterized it in his *Musick's Monument* as "more toyish, and lighter than Corantes." Indeed, in 1752, Johann Joachim Quantz, as Chapter 17 will show, gave it the tempo of the *gigue*: MM 80 to the quarternote.

The "corante" itself asks for a similar comment. The name denoted two very different dances in the seventeenth century. The Italian *corrente* was still a lively dance in 3/4, in keeping with the proper sense of the word: running. But the French *courante* changed its character sometime around 1630 and became a *danse très-grave* in six beats which were organized in fascinating shifts from 3/2 to 6/4. Hence the contradictory tempo indications in contemporary music and musical manuals; Bassani marked it *largo* in 1677, Johann Kuhnau, "rather quickly" in 1689, and Johann Joachim Quantz, MM 80 for the quarternote. Bach used either national type in his suites and *partitas*.

SCIENCE AND INSTRUMENTS. As a new trait, the time presents two portly, comprehensive tomes which extended the then modern enthusiasm for scientific research to the realm of music. One is the *Harmonie Universelle*, published in 1636 and 1637 by Father Marin Mersenne, a friend of the philosopher René Descartes; the other is the *Musurgia Universalis* of Father Athanasius Kircher, a German Jesuit in Rome. Mersenne wrote in French, and Kircher, in Latin. But each is a consummate scholar and scientist without any attempt to be popular, and each, as the two titles imply, had a universal, anti-specialistic attitude. Their approach to music, to the whole of music, was preponderantly mathematical and physical; therefore, they dedicated an essential part of their works to the instruments and the details of their mechano-technical construction, down to the materials and thickness of soundboards and strings.

The instruments themselves were progressing rapidly. The organ was substantially improved; equalizing double bellows and a wind gauge controlled the wind pressure, the number of stops was growing, and small-scale 'string' or 'bowed' pipes like the *gamba* were introduced. But the organ's timbre was still dominated by the light-colored four-foot stops.

Since some readers may not be familiar with the term *four-foot*, a brief explanation must be inserted here. The great or 'cello *C*, at one time the lowest key of the organ, provides the expected note if the corresponding pipe is just eight feet long; it provides small or viola *c* if the corresponding pipe is just four feet long; it provides counter- or doublebass *C* if the corresponding pipe is just sixteen feet long. Hence, organ registers, or 'stops'—complete sets of pipes—are given the title 8′ if they have an eight-foot pipe on the *C* key and thus agree with all the keys on which they are played; they are given the title 4′ if they have a four-foot pipe on the *C* key and therefore sound an octave above the normal; they are given the title 16′ if they have a sixteen-foot pipe on the *C* key and therefore sound an octave below the normal. Correspondingly, a 2′ sounds two octaves higher, and a 32′ sounds two octaves lower. In a figurative sense, our modern piano is exclusively an 8′ instrument, but the harpsichord had also a 4′ stop connecting a whole set of strings half the normal length and sounding an octave higher, and occasionally a 16′ stop connecting a set of strings double the normal length and sounding an octave lower.

Around the middle of the seventeenth century, the harpsichord was provided with the regular arrangement of two eight-foot stops and one four-foot stop, or 8′8′4′. That is, it had two sets of strings in normal length and pitch, and one set half as long and an octave higher. The two eight-foot stops did not serve merely as duplication and intensification; for two, three, or four stops needed actions placed behind one another, with the result that each of them plucked the strings at different spots and thus created divergent timbres. The motion imposed on the string by plucking (or striking, or bowing) was particularly strong at the point of attack and excluded the formation of nodes there. One result was the deficiency of certain partials (*cf.* Appendix) and hence a timbre different from that caused by an action on any spot nearby.

Sixteen-foot stops, sounding an octave lower, were not considered in either the sixteenth or the seventeenth century, and even in the eighteenth century were given only to a few German instruments and during a very short time.

Modern harpsichordists must also be warned against any lavish change of timbre within a piece. The stop-handles on ancient instruments could not be operated without interrupting the performance; and when a certain harpsichord-maker in London, whom Thomas Mace mentioned in his *Musick's Monument*, devised pedals to alternate between "several various stops at pleasure, and all quick and nimble, by the ready turn of the foot," nobody cared. Such alternation was not to the taste of the time.

Italy had yielded its forward position in harpsichord building to Flanders and the then leading dynasty of the Ruckers in Antwerp. Instead, she brought the construction of violins to a second acme under the headship of Girólamo's son Nicola Amati in Cremona (1596–1684). At the same time, Jacob Stainer in Absam near Innsbruck (1621–1683) and Thomas Urquhart in London (b. 1625) became the patriarchs of German and English violin making.

The earlier predilection for wind instruments had gone. They were not flexible enough for the new monodic, expressive style; and taste had drawn away from the motley alternation of glaring colors that the winds provided, toward a unified, neutral timbre.

Early violin players of rank were Biagio Marini (*c.* 1600–*c.* 1655), a native of Brescia who spent many years at German courts, and Carlo Farina from Mantua. Their dance tunes, sonatas, and trios required an accomplished technique including such refinements as the fifth and sixth positions, double and triple stops, *scordatura* (or irregular tuning), and bowing close to the bridge (*sul ponticello*) or with the wood of the stick (*col legno*). Double stops, by the way, had occurred at least as early as the mid-sixteenth century.

Germany, under the influence of Marini, gave rise to outstanding violin virtuosos who specialized in double stops and polyphonic playing, thus preparing for the technique of Bach's sonatas for a solo violin. One name may suffice: Thomas Baltzer, who went to England and became concert master of King Charles II.

England, however, was still opposed to violin playing. According to contemporaries, the *gamba* was a highly respected instrument, but the violin (except in the King's Band) belonged to "common fiddlers" only. Still, it made headway. Matthew Locke's *consorts* were written "for Viols or Violins. . . . either alone or with Theorbos & Harps."

France, welcoming the violin as the typical dance instrument fit to accompany her court ballets, created the leading orchestra of the time under the name *Les Vingt-Quatre Violons du Roy*, The Twenty-four Violins of the King. This ensemble consisted of:

> 6 first violins (*dessus*)
> 4 second violins (*quintes*)
> 4 third violins (*haute-contres*)
> 4 violas (*tailles*)
> 6 *basses* (between violoncelli and double-basses)

The French words added to the modern names above meant voice-parts, not instruments, and could be used for any combination of instruments. The *quinte* had nothing to do with the five-stringed violin *quinton* of the following century, but stood for the older Latin *quinta vox*, that is, the fifth voice-part added (anywhere) to the normal four parts.

Good as the Twenty-four were, the demands on violin playing increased so rapidly that Lully, himself an excellent violinist, was no longer satisfied with the older group and created (in 1656?) a competing elite orchestra of only sixteen under the name *Les Petits Violons du Roy*.

The lute, too, was having a golden age in France. The central figure was Denis Gaultier *L'Illustre* (*c.* 1600–1672), who gave his instrument the solid polyphonic structure that it had generally lost for the sake of easy technique. His principal work (*c.* 1655) is a collection of suites under the title *La Rhétorique des Dieux*. After him, Charles Mouton (*c.* 1626–*c.* 1710) closed that brilliant era.

While the Germans clung to the lute for another hundred years, the French turned brusquely to the less assuming guitar with five double strings, which was being brought into fashion by the then modish Italian comedians in Paris and the great virtuosity of Francesco Corbetta, or Francisque Corbett (d. 1681), a favorite at the court of Louis XIV in Lully's time. He and his disciple Robert de Visée charmed the court to such an extent that a contemporary made fun of "the universal strum" that they conjured up in the palace.

A T LONG LAST, manuscripts and prints of the time take on the familiar, modern forms of our notes and, with the forms, the familiar, modern time-values. Since the seventeenth century, the breve, not the long, has corresponded to a double wholenote; the semibreve, to a wholenote; the minim (once a diamond with cauda), to a halfnote; the semiminim, to a quarternote; the *fusa* (once a black diamond with cauda and flag), to an eighthnote; and so on.

The English, Italians, and Spaniards have persistently used the Latin terms, which, as we have seen, were obsolete and wholly inadequate as early as the end of the thirteenth century. They do not hesitate to call the largest current unit, the wholenote, a 'half-short'; the halfnote, 'smallest'; and the quarternote, 'half-smallest.' The United States has followed the German example in taking the 4/4 bar as the unit of length and simply dividing it into halves, quarters, eighths, sixteenths, thirty-seconds, and so on.

Although the traditional terms denoted different time values, the tempo had not changed. Christopher Simpson and Henry Purcell both state that the semibreve should last "as long as you can moderately tell four"—which is more or less what had been, two hundred years before, the value of the long, then equivalent to the modern wholenote.

READING

Manfred Bukofzer, *Music in the Baroque*, New York, 1947. Henri Prunières, *Cavalli et l'Opéra vénitien du XVIIe siècle*, Paris, 1932. Walther Vetter, *Das frühdeutsche Lied*, 2 vols., Münster, 1928. K. Seidler, *Untersuchungen über Biographie und Klavierstil Johann Jacob Frobergers*, Diss, Königsberg, 1930. Curt Sachs, *World History of the Dance*, New York, 1937: Chapter 7. Curt Sachs, *History of Musical Instruments*, New York, 1940: Chapter 16. Curt Sachs, *The Commonwealth of Art*, New York, 1946: Cross Section 1642. Curt Sachs, *Rhythm and Tempo*, New York, 1953.

15

THE AGE OF
LULLY AND PURCELL

1670–1710

THE LAST PART of the seventeenth century belonged mainly to the Italians, the French, and the English. The French were beginning to export their orchestra players, and the Italians were exporting their composers, conductors, and singers to almost all the courts of Europe.

THE VENETIAN OPERA reached a last climax outside Italy in the noble style of the North Italian Carlo Pallavicino (1630–1688) and of the Venetian Agostino Stéffani (1654–1728), who produced their masterworks in the same year, 1687: the former, *La Gerusalemme liberata* (Liberated Jerusalem), and the latter, *Alarico*. Both men lived at German courts; both operas were performed in Germany, one in Dresden and one in Munich.

In Italy herself, however, the Venetian opera degenerated to the so-called machine opera, in which the tricks of the stage—all imaginable kinds of apparitions from the sky and the underworld (the famous *deus ex máchina*), audacious, fanciful transformations, and incredible sceneries—became the essential ingredients of the performance with precedence over music and poetry, and in which the chief engineer was the most important and best-paid figure of the cast. A contemporary description of a few amazing tricks can be found in English translation in the author's *Commonwealth of Art*, New York 1946, page 229.

N O LONGER did the Venetian opera monopolize the musical drama. Another style of operatic art had been established in Naples. This so-called Neapolitan opera derived from scores that Francesco Provenzale, of Naples, had written in the 1650's, and it celebrated its earliest triumphs with the works of the Sicilian Alessandro Scarlatti (b. 1658 or 1659, like Purcell, d. 1725 at Naples), one of the most prolific musicians, who composed no less than one hundred and fifteen operas, almost seven hundred cantatas, and two hundred Masses, not to mention oratorios, motets, and harpsichord pieces in various forms.

The Neapolitan operas were opened by overtures in a new form, named for Scarlatti or simply called 'Italian' overtures. Differing from Lully's 'French' overture, they had three sections, in the arrangement allegro-adagio-allegro.

Apart from the overture, the 'Neapolitan' masters were not much interested in instrumental music, nor in dancing, machines, or sumptuous display. But they were not much interested in truly dramatic action either. Giving predominance to music, they developed the only extra-musical trait that music was able to enhance: description of human characters, heroic, generous, or vile. And eventually such description could not avoid the fate of early stereotyping—not even in the hands of the most influential and probably the most celebrated of librettists, Pietro Metastasio (1698–1782), who provided texts for a century of composers, for Scarlatti, Handel, and Mozart.

The recitative, once the backbone of the opera as the carrier of all dramatic and epic phases, lost more and more of its character, descended to an unemotional, hasty, matter-of-fact *parlando* with a few routine chords on the harpsichord—the so-called *recitativo secco*, or 'dry' recitative—and was eventually left to the haphazard improvisation of the singers themselves. The aria, in the *da capo* form ABA, was given almost exclusive rights—so much so that contemporaries sneeringly spoke of the Neapolitan opera as a "bundle of arias." With the undramatic stress on well-wrought, lyrical, and heavily ornamented melodies, the interest inevitably shifted to the sensuous beauty and acrobatic virtuosity of the voice—the *bel canto*—and to the singers themselves, *castrati* and divas who, incredibly arrogant, imposed their will and whim on conductors, stage-directors, and even the composers.

THE ENGLISH stood close to the Italians, with Purcell, composer to the Royal court, as their greatest master.

Henry Purcell was born in London in 1658 or 1659, died, only thirty-six years old, on November 21, 1695, and was buried beneath the organ of Westminster Abbey, which he had played since 1680. This is about all we know of the man and his life and death.

Like Mozart's, this pitifully limited life sufficed for a musical production astonishing in depth and versatility. It included a true opera, incidental music for forty spoken dramas—among them Betterton's *Dioclesian* (1690) and Dryden's *King Arthur* (1691)—the anthems, services, and hymns that his connection with Westminster Abbey demanded, the odes and welcome songs on sawdust texts for the Royal family, much chamber music, such as fantasias, sonatas, and Lessons for the harpsichord, and a good number of catches (whose robust words are sanctimoniously purged in all reprints).

Charles II had brought back from his exile in France (1660) a strong partiality to everything French, including music. On his return, he established The King's Private Band of twenty-four pieces in imitation of the twenty-four *Violons du Roy*, and made no secret of his aversion to the "heavy" music of England. Purcell condemned this sort of courtly music as dance-like and superficial. In opposition to the taste of his sovereign, he followed, as he expressly stated in the preface to his earliest sonatas (1683), the most celebrated Italians for the inspiration of their austere gravity in order to retrieve the almost lost tradition of England with its sense of noble, sedate dignity. In this he found himself in the company of Elizabethan musicians, with their madrigals and church polyphony, and of Chaucer and Shakespeare, who also had looked to the South for models and standards. Italian influence is particularly evident in his almost Corellian sonatas for two violins, bass, and harpsichord, but no less in his only real opera, *Dido and Aeneas*, which he wrote as an amateur play for a fashionable girls' school graduation. Seen from its important choral parts and its dances, the work is very English, no doubt. But its climax, the beautiful, moving lament of the dying queen on a solemnly striding *ostinato* or ground, has a truly Monteverdian cast.

In the religious field, Purcell, as well as his teacher John Blow (1649–1708), gave the Anglican anthem the festive high-Baroque form that Handel brought to a climax a little later. They introduced the sparkling color of instruments and added a jubilant *Alleluia* in a majestic choral fugue as a grandiose ending. And grandiose he was also in his hymns and *Te Deum*'s restoring the forceful polyphony of the Tudor masters, which the Puritan revolution had almost destroyed, and paving the way for Handel.

THE GERMAN OPERA had little significance. Most poets, composers, singers, and players for the princes' stages were imported from Italy; indeed, as late as the mid-eighteenth century, King Frederick the Great of Prussia could in all seriousness say that he would rather be neighed to by his mare than listen to a German singer.

The only permanent and public opera with German plays and German personnel was kept at Hamburg between 1678 and 1738. Its inauguration with Johann Theile's *Adam und Eva* and, in general, its marked predilection during the first dozen years for subjects from the Old Testament, promised a respectable level. But later, the Biblical themes made way for mythological banalities and for local sensations with ghastly execution-scenes and genuine blood from pigs' bladders. Alas, one of the worst, with the pirate *Störtebeker* (1701) as its hero, was written by a master whose genius knew better—Reinhard Keiser (1674–1739), a highly gifted, prolific composer and a charming adventurer who would now shock the respectable Hamburgers with princely ostentation, now disappear from the sight of cheated creditors.

THE OPERA IN FRANCE was late because her great ballet tradition and the flowering of spoken tragedy retarded the beginnings of a style that exacted drama of the musical stage and lyricism of the dramatic stage. As late as 1636, in his *Harmonie Universelle*, the

Frenchman Father Mersenne could mention as an unusual and remarkable fact that Italian singers used to perform with so convincing an expression that the listener might confuse the passion they were rendering with their personal emotion.

No less than three-quarters of a century after the advent of the musical drama in Italy, numerous futile attempts and serious setbacks on the stage led at last to an opera in France. The first important step was taken when two native Frenchmen, the poet Pierre Perrin and the composer Robert Cambert, performed the 'pastoral' *Pomone* at Paris in 1671. However, associated with a couple of rascals, they became insolvent, went to jail, and, in all their misery, were glad enough to sell to Lully their royal privilege for performing operas.

GIOVANNI BATTISTA LULLI, born on November 29, 1632, in Florence, was brought to Paris as a fourteen-year old boy, under somewhat questionable circumstances, to "keep company" with the nineteen-year old Duchess of Montpensier, one of the leaders of the *fronde*, or opposition against the king (Louis XIV). In 1653, however, Lulli left the Duchess, went over to the royal camp, danced in the court ballets, and was appointed— once more we do not know exactly why—composer of the king's instrumental music. Eight years later, the favorite of fortune got the title and position of a superintendent and composer of the royal chamber music and at the end of the year became a French citizen under the name of Jean-Baptiste Lully.

Admirable musicianship and energy, a genius for anticipating the needs of the Parisian public, the unwavering affection of the king, and the ruthless disposal of competitors granted him successes such as few musicians ever had, in his art as well as in his financial dealings. On the crest of his career, making an ostentatious display of devotion to his monarch in a solemn *Te Deum* after the king's recovery from an illness, he himself contracted a sepsis from hitting his toe while beating time on the floor with the pounding baton used by French conductors of his age, and died on March 22, 1687.

After having devoted twenty years to writing court ballets, Lully turned to real opera at the mature age of forty and left sixteen scores in this field. Outstanding were:

Cadmus et Hermione 1673
Alceste 1674
Thésée 1675
Atys 1676
Isis 1677
Bellérophon 1679
Persée 1682
Phaéton 1683
Acis et Galathée 1686
Armide 1686

The privilege that he had bought from Perrin allowed him to show these operas first at court and subsequently in the public opera house called the *Académie Royale de Musique*. There, some of them were kept on the repertoire for a hundred years—until Gluck's works replaced them.

The character of Lully's operas was thoroughly French. Frenchmen have always worshipped the spoken word, its accent, meter, and timbre, and have never permitted it to yield either to music or to pantomime. As a consequence, the melodic material of their musical dramas has had a reserve almost unknown to Italians. Lully complied with this national respect for the word, not only with his own intelligence and adaptability, but also with the guidance of his librettist Philippe Quinault and his friend Molière. After early experiments with recitatives to the dry accompaniment of a bass and a harpsichord, Lully achieved in the court ballet *Le Triomphe de l'Amour* (1681), a recitative accompanied by the orchestra which allowed for so thorough a unification in style that the verses ran smoothly from scene to scene, the recitative becoming ariose and the arias almost recitativic. Moreover, this 'endless' melody was carefully modeled after the inflection and accents of the greatest actors, whom he studied in the *Comédie Française*.

No less French than Lully's attention to the individual word and the cadence of the spoken sentence were the moods and images depicted in his works. Early French opera would be unthinkable without emotions like those expressed by raging tempests and the miracles of enchanted gardens or moonlight nights, of which the Florentine master has given the classical models.

Again, Lully stressed the significance of purely instrumental episodes and, above all, of the overture. His 'French' overture, in opposition to the so-called Italian overture of the Neapolitans, had a majestic and somewhat strutting first section in a sharply dotted, indeed double-dotted rhythm, a second section in quick *fugato* with the successive entries of all the instruments, and a coda in the first tempo, all without interruption.

With such a stress on instrumental music, Lully restored the orchestra—which had some forty pieces in his time—to an importance in French opera that it was steadily losing in Italian scores. In doing so, he became the patriarch of modern orchestration, and his ingenious, delicate coloring has provided even as late a master as Berlioz with characteristic examples for his Treatise of Instrumentation.

The opera in a narrower sense was only a part of Lully's activities. Before writing operas, he had written numerous court ballets, which were however so amply interspersed with singing and independent instrumental music that they must be considered as important steps towards the inevitable opera. Molière took the last step but one when in the year 1661 he introduced a comedy-ballet with a play, as he said, "sewn on a ballet." Such were *Le Mariage forcé* (1664) and *La Princesse d'Elide* (1664). Lully continued to write ballets after having veered to opera. In 1681 he dared even open the stage to female dancers as an unheard-of innovation. And his operas, themselves, gave a prominent place to dancing.

T HE NEW MINUET was the central dance of the time. In its dainty, mincing, reserved steps, it represented the last sublimation of the wooing couple dance that the age of the troubadours had created. Lully, musician and dancer, had a dominating position in its development.

Musically, the minuet had a fascinating counterrhythm, the steps contradicting the accompanying music: the latter proceeded in 3/4 time, while the steps—right-left, right-left—asked for duple time:

steps:	right	left	right	left
	1	2	3	4
music:	*1* *2* *3*	*1*	*2*	*3*

This counterrhythm was certainly attractive, but not without risks. Hence, contemporary dance manuals asked the accompanying musicians not to stress the strong beats of the even-numbered bars, lest the dancers get confused. This is why syncopated minuets, such as the one in Mozart's last *G*-minor symphony, are not "stubborn" but, on the contrary, true to the pattern of the steps.

The French often wrote minuets for a trio of two oboes and one bassoon, and, for the sake of contrast, Lully gave this limpid, brisk orchestration to the second of two successive minuets—*Menuet en trio*. In the eighteenth century, the term *trio* passed to the middle episode between the minuet and its repetition in the typical symphony, even if its orchestration did not justify the title; and in a similar way, the nineteenth century kept the name for the corresponding episode in the scherzo.

The minuet was dignified but fast: writers of the seventeenth and eighteenth centuries called it "rather rapid" and gave it the tempo MM 70-80 to the whole measure.

INSTRUMENTAL MUSIC. The main repository of the dances—both those up to date and those no longer performed in the ballrooms—was the instrumental *suite*. Around 1670, it still followed the arrangement of Froberger's and Locke's suites, with the *gigue* somewhere in the middle. But the taste of the end of the century gave preference to another sequence, and in 1693 a Dutch publisher deemed it prudent to reprint the late Froberger's suites, as the title says, "in a better order." Since then, the lively *gigue* has invariably stood at the end to serve as a sweeping Sir Roger.

In the same decade, it became an accepted practice to give the suite one or more additional movements from the current dance repertory, such as the *bourrée*, the *gavotte*, the *minuet*, the *passepied*, or the *rigaudon*.

The suite of the French was still, as it had been before, an optional set of dances without a definite order. On the other hand, it pushed forward to the later symphony by merging with the so-called French overture, which headed a series of dances or dancelike movements, such as *airs*, *ballets*, marches, minuets, in a motley order and often with *doubles*, or repetitions, in richer ornamentation.

Many movements of the French suite had characteristic headings, such as *La Coquette*, *Harlequin*, *La Pastourelle*, which must be interpreted as labels rather than as programs. It has been suggested that such titles expressed relations to the court ballet. This, however, cannot be true, since they also occur in instrumental pieces totally different from dances, as later in Jean-Philippe Rameau's *Pièces de clavecin en concerts*. It would probably be more justifiable to trace them to the rationalism of the French, who have always preferred concepts definite and concrete to the impalpable vagueness of untitled music. Lionel de la Laurencie, eminent historian of French music, was certainly right in saying that the Frenchman, "thoroughly intellectual, does not stand sonorous emotion unless it is associated with a precise idea and feels at ease only when the sentimental merchandise is covered by the intellectual flag."

THE OUTSTANDING FIGURE of French instrumental music was François Couperin, surnamed *le Grand*. He was born in Paris on November 10, 1668, became harpsichordist to the court and teacher of the princes, also played the organ at the church of Saint Gervais (which has been preserved in its original form), and died at Paris on September 12, 1733.

As an organist, Couperin wrote organ music to accompany the Mass. He also composed a famous vocal work for alternately one and two voices under the title *Leçons de Ténèbres*, to be sung at Matins and Lauds on the 'dark' days of Easter week when the candles were extinguished one after another (the word *leçon* having just as little didactic meaning as the English word *lesson* when used in religious services).

Couperin also created instrumental chamber music; the *concerts* in honor of Corelli and Lully (*Le Parnasse ou l'apothéose de Corelli*, 1724, and *Concert . . . composé à la mémoire immortelle de l'incomparable monsieur de Lully*, 1725). For the informal Sunday afternoon receptions in the palace of Versailles shortly before the death of Louis XIV (1715), he wrote four *Concerts royaux*, which were later appended to the fourth book of his *Pièces de Clavecin*.

Couperin's most important works, though, were devoted to the harpsichord, either as a solo instrument or in a chamber ensemble with a crossflute or a few bowed instruments. He carried the harpsichord to a summit of delicacy, inventiveness, and humanity. Now majestic, now tender, playful, pastoral, melancholy, humorous, exuberant, he was ever different and ever the same—The Great.

His finest harpsichord music was printed in four volumes of *Pièces de Clavecin* between 1713 and 1730. The proper way to perform them, and particularly the skilled and tasteful treatment of the graces, was so vitally important that the master himself found it necessary to publish a special method of playing under the title *L'Art de toucher le Clavecin* (1716).

THE ITALIAN SUITE, generally called *sonata da cámera*, was neither written for outdoor ensembles, as in Germany, nor for keyboards, as in France, but for some chamber combination with a thoroughbass. The term itself appeared first outside Italy in suites of the Veneto-German Johann Rosenmüller (1620–1680). Outstanding examples are the two dozen of Arcangelo Corelli's sonatas for violin and harpsichord published in 1685 and 1694. As a rule, they were in four movements with a *preludio* at the beginning and a *giga* or *gavotta* at the end.

Incidentally, it is rewarding to have a look at Volume 1 of the *Zeitschrift für Musikwissenschaft* (1918/19) on pages 292f and to realize in what almost incredible ornamental distortion the familiar melodies of these sonatas were, or could be, played around 1700.

Corelli's name has also been connected with a certain kind of cadence or concluding formula, the so-called Corelli clash, which, however, can be traced back at least a whole generation to Stéfano Landi's opera *Il Sant' Alessio*. In a harsh collision, the upper voice anticipated the final note on the upbeat, say *C*, while the second voice played the leading note *B* before it turned to *C* on the downbeat.

Opposed to the *sonata da cámera* was the *sonata da chiesa*, which was by no means restricted to the church as the name implies. In this form, composers dropped the dance titles of the individual movements, and gradually also their dance-like character. Instead, they prepared the free movements of the later sonata, as we know it, under tempo titles —*Adagio* or *Allegro* or *Presto*.

A second instrumental type that Italy created was the concerto.

Concerto, a name denoting both 'to agree' and 'to compete,' was given in the sixteenth and seventeenth centuries to different forms of instrumental and vocal music, but survived as the title of a symphonic form in which one or several soloists competed with an orchestra, the Italian verb *concertare* meaning 'to agree.' Where there were several soloists, the form was more specifically called *concerto grosso*.

In the contrasting movements of the *concerto grosso*, a group of soloists with an accompanying harpsichord formed the *concertino*, or small concerto. As a rule, it consisted of two violins and a violoncello. Its partner was the full orchestra, *concerto grosso* or *ripieno* ('filling'). Alessandro Stradella (*c.* 1645–1681) seems to have been the initiator; Giuseppe Torelli (1650–1708) and Arcangelo Corelli (1653–1713) created the first masterworks in this novel form around 1680. The *grosso* was, as a rule, very small compared with modern orchestras, but as an exception, Corelli's *concerti* were performed at Rome in 1682 with no less than a hundred and fifty pieces.

We speak of a solo concerto, on the contrary, as one in which only one soloist acts against the orchestra. The form is somewhat younger than the *concerto grosso*, just as the solo sonata is younger by a few years than the trio sonata. Not much before 1700 did Tommaso Albinoni (1674–1745) and Giuseppe Torelli compose the earliest concertos for one violin and orchestra. Concertos for keyboard instruments originated in the subsequent generation; Bach and Handel broke the ground, the former with thirteen concertos for the harpsichord and the latter with eighteen concertos for the organ.

WHILE THE BULK of German composers depended on French or Italian models, two masters embodied the spirit of the later Baroque in Germany without any foreign interference. They were Buxtehude in the North and Biber in the South.

Dietrich Buxtehude (1637–1707), a native of Helsingborg in Sweden, was by far the greater of the two. Organist at St. Mary's in Lübeck on the Baltic Sea since 1668, he conducted annually the celebrated *Abendmusiken*, or Evening Concerts, in Advent, to which young Bach, then twenty years of age, made a reverent pilgrimage. As a composer, Buxtehude left a large stock of organ pieces, choral cantatas, motets, and chamber music, in which he achieved a truly German Baroque, fantastic and powerful, flickering, restive, and angular, with florid, often bombastic coloraturas and sudden changes of tempo.

Heinrich Biber (1644–1704) from Bohemia, a violinist and conductor at the court of Salzburg's archbishop, was baroque in a different way, less fantastic and angular, but rather in search for means and aims abnormal or singular. He wrote polyphonic church music, sophisticated pieces for one unaccompanied violin, sonatas for harpsichord and a violin, and duos for two *viole d'amore* (the next chapter will discuss these instruments). The violin was often used in *scordatura* or 'distuning,' with all four strings, or only some of them lowered or raised by varying intervals, so that they created new possibilities of chord fingering and also timbres now softer, now sharper than the wonted colors of the violin. One set among these sonatas describes scenes of the Passion of Christ and adds a title vignette to each one in an unusual combination of visible and audible illustration.

DESCRIPTIVE MUSIC flourished indeed, in Germany as well as in France. One Johann Fischer tried to depict nothing less than the salt-working process in the pits of Lüneburg in a suite consisting of an overture, an *entrée*, an *aria*, a minuet, and two ballets for one violin, four oboes, and *basso*. In 1700, Bach's predecessor at St. Thomas' in Leipzig, Johann Kuhnau, published six Biblical sonatas for clavichord or harpsichord (which, incidentally, were *not* the earliest keyboard compositions under the title of sonatas). One of them, The Combat between David and Goliath, describes in seven short movements Goliath's bravado, fear and prayer of the Israelites, David's courage, the duel—in which you hear the stone hurled at the giant and his collapse—the helter-skelter flight of the Philistines in an amazing fugue, the triumph of the Jews, and general dance and rejoicing.

If Kuhnau did not hesitate to describe the violent paroxysm of Saul in parallel fifths and violations of Church modes in another of these sonatas, or, in still another, Laban's fraud in the misleading cadences that musical terminology calls 'deceptive,' he found himself outdone when Marin Marais, French gamba player, depicted, in a piece for this instrument, a complete operation for stone, including the sight of the surgical apparatus, the patient's shuddering on seeing it, and all the following episodes in minute details and with pedantic explanations within the musical text in almost every one of its measures. A few lines of this curiosity are reprinted in the author's *Commonwealth of Art*, New York, 1946, page 222.

INSTRUMENTAL MUSIC, except organ and outdoor pieces, was mainly performed at court and in homes of the nobility and the gentry. However, one generation after the establishment of a public opera house in Italy (1637), the English evolved the earliest regular concert-going. For six years, from 1672 to 1678, the excellent violinist John Banister, once conductor of the King's Private Band, arranged performances of music in London in a rented room "over against the George Tavern in White Friars" with "a large raised box for the musicians, whose modesty required curtains," as a contemporary puts it.

It was a young coal merchant in London, Thomas Britton, nicknamed "the musical small-coal man," who, after Banister, organized weekly concerts in a loft over his storehouse in Jerusalem Passage, at first free of charge, and later for a yearly subscription *plus* a penny for coffee. These concerts were given both by advanced amateurs and by England's best professionals, like Handel. They lasted for thirty-six years until Britton died in 1714.

THE INSTRUMENTS underwent decisive changes. The French took interest in improving the (transverse) German flute, which had been cylindrical and in one piece and therefore not tunable. And the oboe, which had been a shrill and noisy shawm, was so much refined in the hands of the French that it eventually found its way, together with the improved flute, from dance and military bands into the orchestra—at first, apparently, into Lully's orchestra. It was then that the French name *hautbois* (pron. oboè), or 'high wood,' conquered the world but in the correct phonetic spelling that the Italians used for the instrument. Another important acquisition of the French orchestra, operatic and symphonic, was the *horn*, which the English call the French horn, and the French, *cor allemand*. Whoever the reformer and whatever his nationality, the instrument, once a hunter's horn not too different from a bugle, was given a long, narrow, and partly cylindrical tube with a widely expanding bell and, as a consequence, a wide overblowing range.

While the nationality of the French horn is not altogether certain, the *clarinet* was without a doubt developed in Germany. Originally a cylindrical folk-instrument with a single reed, known under the French name *chalumeau*, it became an art instrument in the workshop of the Denners—father and son—in Nürnberg, but struggled during a full hundred years for a permanent seat in the orchestra.

The Italians, meanwhile, reduced the clumsy half-bass of the violin family to the elegant size of the modern 'cello. The smaller dimensions and the consequent tone allowed the admission of the 'cello to solo performances. One Doménico Gabrielli (with double *l*) in Bologna wrote the first two sonatas for violoncello and figured bass and in 1689 *Ricercarj per violoncello solo*.

AS A CONSEQUENCE of the growing importance of keyboard instruments, the time saw at last the realization of an idea that the Spaniard Ramis de Pareja had anticipated two hundred, and the Chinese, one hundred years before: the *equal temperament*. Older, unequal systems, such as the one described on page 85, were imperfect and became unbearable when the harmonic orientation of the new time needed free modulation into remoter tonalities and, therefore, the integration, with equal rights, of the previously shunned, uncertain black keys, or *semitonia*.

The evolution was slow. Andreas Werckmeister, a Saxon organist (1645–1706), did *not* invent the equal temperament. True, his pamphlet *Musikalische Temperatur* of 1691 and later writings describe a mathematically founded and viable method of tuning all kinds of keyboard instruments so that a player could easily and satisfactorily transpose into remoter keys. But *Werckmeister's temperament was still unequal*.

Not before 1724 do we find the description of an actual equal temperament with twelve perfectly even semitones per octave in Johann Georg Neidhardt's *Sectio canonis harmonici*.

As a consequence of the nearly and the truly equal temperaments, Johann Caspar Ferdinand Fischer (1650–1746), *Kapellmeister* at the court of Baden, wrote in 1715 a cyclical keyboard work under the title *Ariadne Musica*. (Ariadne, daughter of King Minos of Crete, revealed to Theseus the way out through her father's labyrinth—the labyrinth here being the tangle of tonalities.) The work contained twenty fugues with their preludes in nineteen different keys.

A few years later, Johann Sebastian Bach materialized the same idea in the first part of his *Wohltemperiertes*, or Well-tempered, *Clavier* (the usual English title *Clavichord* is a dangerous misnomer). More thorough than Fischer, he gave it preludes and fugues in each of the twelve major and twelve minor keys in the sequence *C* major, *C* minor, *C♯* major, *C♯* minor, *D* major, and so forth. About twenty years later, he wrote a similar cycle in a second part, so that the entire *Well-tempered Clavier*, "The Forty-Eight," goes twice through all the major and minor keys.

NOTATION of this age still clings to the diamond shapes of mensural notation but is essentially, including barlines, the script of our time. The stemmed white-note corresponds to the modern halfnote, and the stemmed black-note to the modern quarternote. The stemless black diamond has disappeared, and dotted groups are written out.

Nevertheless, the dotted notation of the time is a thorny problem to the modern musician who believes in the unequivocal meaning of symbols. To us, the dot implies a lengthening of the preceding note by a half of its value. Late in the seventeenth and early in the eighteenth century, its meaning was, on the contrary, far from certain. It might be what it is today; it might also, as in the slow introductions of French overtures, stand for the stronger form of lengthening that we denote by a double dot; and it might, though not compulsorily, give the first note two, and the following note one out of three units, to coincide with a triplet in the other hand of the player (most readers will have tripped over such passages in Bach's works). The amount of lengthening was not accurately fixed, and the modern player, in performing music of that time, is free to do what he deems best.

Nor had the key signature around 1700 the logic and consistency of today. As a rule, there was a sharp or a flat less than we would expect: one flat for *G* minor, two flats for *C* minor, three sharps for *E* major. One reason was that the signature was not meant to symbolize the key at first sight, but rather to save the trouble of a continual repetition of those signs which had to be used all the time.

Another reason was that, since the early Middle Ages, the sixth in the first mode (Dorian)—*una nota super la*—had been flatted without adding the flat as a key signature. Accordingly, all minor scales, being identical with Dorian in their descending phase, were given a flat less than they have today: *G* minor had one flat, *B*, while the second flat, *E*, was, as the minor sixth, not put in the key signature. And this is why *C* minor had only two, and *F* minor, only three flats.

In a similar way, the sharp tonalities were given one sharp less than today. The *musica ficta* had admitted, and even required, the sharped 'leading' note without adding it to the key signature, since it was, properly speaking, against the key.

Not the least reason for such curtailing practice was the curious abhorrence of complicated key signatures in the sixteenth and seventeenth centuries. Even in the very simple case of *B* flat major, Morley's *Plaine and Easie Introduction to Practicall Musicke* (1597) took offence at "the verie sight of these flat cliffes (which stand at the beginning of the verse or line like a paire of staires, with great offense to the eie, but more to the amasing of the yong singer)." Foreigners, he continues, put only one flat in the signature and add the other ones as accidentals at their proper places.

G RACES. Once more, the delicate subject of ornamentation must be touched upon. Once more, it must be emphasized that music, vocal and instrumental, and particularly that for keyboard, was 'bald' and lifeless without graces in a time that did not use shades of intensity to stress and enliven the notes of importance.

Grace notes, or, as the French said, *agréments*, were expected from the performer as a matter of course, whether the composers took care —as did the French—to denote every single one of them by a special symbol, or were—as in Germany—rather negligent in writing them down. The numberless graces in common use were mainly of two kinds.

(1) One kind of grace conveyed particular life and breath to single notes, such as the

Appoggiatura, in German *Vorschlag*, which was the accented touch *on* the beat (not, as today, the unaccented, fleeting touch before the beat) of a neighboring, non-harmonic note, to be slurred over to the note that the harmony actually required.

Mordent or 'biter,' a rapid, unrepeated to-and-fro between the main note and one of its neighbors.

Trill, a continued prestissimo alternation of the main note and one of its neighbors, beginning with the latter.

(2) The other kind of grace smoothed the passage from note to note. Such were the

Turn, on which a group of notes—four or five—circled rapidly around the first note as if winding up for attacking the following one.

Tirata, or 'slur,' which softened a large melodic stride or leap by a slurring scale-passage from note to note.

Profuse ornamentation with graces is only a part of the glittering sound that music presented around 1700. While the harpsichord player was bound to his notes and only embellished them with *agréments*, the singers and players of melody instruments were required to dissolve their parts, in slower movements especially, into an uninterrupted flow of coloratura, similar to the diminutions in Palestrina's time.

READING

Manfred Bukofzer, *Music in the Baroque*, New York, 1947. Curt Sachs, *World History of the Dance*, New York, 1937: Chapter 7. *The History of Musical Instruments*, New York, 1940: Chapter 16. *The Commonwealth of Art*, New York, 1946: Cross Sections 1675 and 1690. *Rhythm and Tempo*, New York, 1953: Chapter 12. Edward J. Dent, *Alessandro Scarlatti*, London, 1905. A. Westrup, *Purcell*, London, 1937. Lionel de la Laurencie, *Lully*, 2nd edition, Paris, 1919. Julien Tiersot, *Les Couperins*, Paris, 1926. Mario Rinaldi, *Arcangelo Corelli*, Milano, 1953. Wilhelm Stahl, *Franz Tunder und Dietrich Buxtehude*, Leipzig, 1926. Wilhelm Dupont, *Geschichte der musikalischen Temperatur*, Kassel, 1935. Edward Dannreuther, *Musical Ornamentation*, London, 1893–95.

16

THE AGE OF
BACH AND RAMEAU

1710–1750

THE YEAR 1685 was fraught with destiny. It gave birth to two illustrious Saxons, Handel, February 23, and Bach, March 21, and to one Italian, Domenico Scarlatti, October 26. Two years earlier, the Frenchman Rameau had been born. In an incomparably short time, Providence had the leading actors ready to close the past and to open the future.

Two of these masters, Bach and Handel, were glorious enders of ancient traditions rather than pioneers, in spite of all their innovations. Scarlatti and Rameau, freed of bounds that the past imposed, anticipated the future.

JOHANN SEBASTIAN BACH, the son of a prodigious dynasty of Thuringian cantors, organists, and town pipers, was born in Eisenach at the foot of the Wartburg on March 21, 1685, lost his parents at the age of ten, and was reared in nearby Ohrdruf by an older brother, who tried in vain to bridle his dashing advance. He locked away a book with copies of 'great' music, by Froberger, Buxtehude, and others, which the eager boy at last secured and secretly recopied by moonlight, only to have his manuscript confiscated upon discovery.

In 1700, Bach was sent away to finish his education at the *Gymnasium* of Lüneburg, Hanover. He occasionally journeyed to Hamburg for Jan Reinken's famous church music and to the little capital of Celle, Hanover, where an excellent French court orchestra made him familiar with the latest foreign style.

After three years in Lüneburg, he graduated from the Gymnasium and began the traditional life of a Thuringian musician. He served for a short time in the ducal orchestra in Weimar, and in the same year (1703) as an organist in Arnstadt. From there he took a momentous leave of absence to study Dietrich Buxtehude's church music in Lübeck. During those weeks he changed his style so much that on his belated return to Arnstadt he was taken to task not only for the neglect of his duty but also for his turgid playing, in which the congregation was at a loss to find the familiar chorale melody. In 1707, he became the organist at St. Blasius' in Mühlhausen, Thuringia, and married his cousin Maria Barbara Bach.

Only a year later, as the second phase of his professional career, he entered the service of Thuringian courts. At that of Weimar he was organist and chamber musician from 1708 to 1717, and at that of Cöthen director of chamber music from 1717 to 1723.

In the latter year he settled in Leipzig as the cantor, or director of music—with some Latin teaching thrown in—at St. Thomas Church and School. Later he became also director of music in the university. "At first," he wrote to a friend, "it was not wholly agreeable to me to become a cantor after having been a *Kapellmeister*, and for this reason I delayed making a decision for three months." Far from the worldly splendor of the great *Hofkapellmeister* and virtuosos, he led the somewhat provincial life of a respected small-town man in comfortable though narrow circumstances. Married twice, he had twenty children, of whom only nine survived their father.

Bach was no pioneer—his very sons turned away from him and sailed for coasts unknown. He was the colossal summit of centuries of musical energy—with him the polyphonic language in fugue and canon, the chorale cantata and the chorale prelude, Passion and Mass, suite, concerto grosso, and toccata reached their climax and ultimate fulfilment. But neither was his art retrospective; towering masters finish and crown, they do not repeat.

This musical climax coincided, in time and in spirit, with the final peak of the German Baroque. Bach's incomparably forceful expression, his urge to pile up structures of unheard-of dimensions in densest polyphonic weaving and a final unification, are all typical of the closing Baroque in his country. And more so is his mystic absorption in things transcending reason. Through the often feeble, pompous, redundant words of contemporary Protestant poetry, he looked into the last, unutterable depths of religious awareness, and both in his nearly two hundred cantatas and in his chorale preludes, which freely widened and deepened the Sunday's chorale on the organ, he gave expression to religious wisdom at the eleventh hour, when the rationalism of the dawning Enlightenment was blocking its way.

Still, there is no unified Bach style. No easy formula can cover the riches of his work and his genius.

He crowned the mighty polyphony of the German Baroque in the forty-eight fugues of the *Well-tempered Clavier* (part I, 1722, part II, c. 1742) and those for the organ; in the breathtaking choral fugues of the *B* minor Mass (1733), in the canons of the thirty *Goldberg Variations* (1742) (called after a harpsichordist of this name), and in the last bequest of his pen, *The Art of the Fugue* (1750).

He amalgamated with his German heritage the finely chased art of France in his *French Suites* for the harpsichord (1717) and also in the luxuriant ornamentation of his chorale preludes for the organ.

To Italian music he paid his respects in the numberless recitatives and *da capo* arias of his cantatas and of the two Passions after St. John (1723) and St. Matthew (1729). He also did so in his concertos, in those of the *grosso* form, as in the six *Brandenburg Concertos* for Christian Ludwig of Brandenburg (1721), in those for one, two, three, and even four harpsichords with orchestra, and in the *Italian Concerto* of 1735, where he gave the solo and the accompanying *ripieno* to the two keyboards of the harpsichord. Indeed, several of his harpsichord concertos are transcriptions from violin concertos of the Italian master Antonio Vivaldi, with sevenths added to the simple triads of the original score, with greater importance and action of the basses, and sometimes with the rigid lines of Vivaldi's style dissolved in sparkling fireworks.

A few traits, however, hint at the future. One of them is the timid appearance in the concertos, of a second, contrasting theme, which was to play a decisive role in the sonata form of the 'classic' masters. Another unexpected trait is the beautiful, affectionate first melody of the soloists in the Brandenburg Concerto in *D* major, which anticipates the characteristic *allegro cantabile* of the later eighteenth century, of his youngest son Johann Christian, and even of Mozart.

In the forty-seven tomes of Bach's complete works—which, in view

of many losses, are by no means complete—we find whatever forms
the time provided: Masses, Passions, cantatas, and motets; suites, concertos, preludes, and fugues; sonatas and variations, toccatas and phan-
tasies; from the freest, almost shapeless, rhapsodic forms of the latter
to the strictest weaving of the fugue, from the miniatures of the
Clavier-Büchlein to the gigantic size of the Mass in *B* minor.

Here is a short list of Bach's principal works:

ARNSTADT 1703–1707
   Capriccio sulla lontananza del fratello diletto 1704
MÜHLHAUSEN 1707–1708
   Cantata *Meine Seele rühmt und preist* 1707–1710
WEIMAR 1708–1717
   Organ passacaglia in *C* minor
   Organ toccatas
CÖTHEN 1717–1723
   Brandenburg Concertos 1721 (commissioned by a Margrave of Branden
      burg)
   Chromatic Fantasia and Fugue
   English Suites
   French Suites
   Inventions
   Violin sonatas
   Violin concertos
   Well-tempered Clavier I 1722
LEIPZIG 1723–1750
   Magnificat 1723
   St. John's Passion 1723
   St. Matthew's Passion 1729
   St. Mark's Passion 1731
   Clavierübung I 1731, II 1735, III 1739, IV 1742
   Christmas Oratorio 1733–1734
   B minor Mass (*Kyrie* and *Gloria*) 1733
   Italian Concerto 1735
   Easter Oratorio 1736(?)
   Goldberg Variations for the harpsichordist Johann T. Goldberg 1742 (in
      Clavierübung IV)
   Four Masses 1737–1740
   B minor Mass (from the *Credo* on) 1738
   Well-tempered Clavier II *c.* 1742
   Musical Offering (*Musikalisches Opfer*) 1747
   The Art of the Fugue (*Die Kunst der Fuge*) 1749
   Six motets
   Most cantatas

A few obsolete instruments in the scores of Bach require a short
explanation.

The *violino piccolo*, prescribed in the first Brandenburg Concerto in *F* major, is a three-quarter violin tuned a minor third higher, and sharper in tone, than the usual violin.

The *viola pomposa*, often discussed, was very probably a viola with the *e″* of the violin as a fifth string.

The *viola d'amore* (or, in French, *viole d'amour*) was a modish instrument in viola size and *gamba* form, held and played like a viola, against the shoulder and with a palm-down bow. It had six or seven bowed, catgut strings in an arbitrary triadic tuning, *A d f a d′ f′a′* or otherwise, and, behind them, a set of delicate wire strings, which, taking up the vibrations of the bowed, gut strings, resounded 'sympathetically,' as the physicists say, made the tone fuller, and even gave it a silvery echo. The reader should, however, consult the author's discussion in *The History of Musical Instruments*, pages 364–367 with the illustration on page 364. This instrument, which had but a small, insignificant literature of its own, was mainly used for solos; to cram it into an ensemble of modern old-music performers is a mistake, both historically and artistically.

The *violoncello piccolo* had the usual tuning but was, in size at any rate, smaller than the customary German 'cello, which served the purpose of duplicating the thoroughbass rather than that of solo playing.

The greatest problem has been posed by the so-called *Bach trumpet*, which climbed high up in the range of ledger-lines—*e‴*. Modern performers play the delicate parts on extra-small, high-pitched trumpets and do achieve the most precarious notes, to be sure, but, with a midget tube too short to provide a satisfactory timbre, deprive them of all their brilliance and charm. That in the time of Bach these parts were played—and probably well played—depended on other factors than shortness; we actually know that they were played on trumpets twice as long as the alleged Bach trumpets of our day. The most important of these factors was the strict division of labor in the "Knightly Guild of Trumpetists and Kettle-drummers," which allowed—and forced— a *clarino*, or first-part player, to specialize all his life in the highest range, without ever spoiling the high-range adjustment of his lips by descending into the lower registers of *principal* trumpetists, which the modern orchestra trumpetist cannot avoid doing all the time. In such specialization, the player availed himself of a suitable mouthpiece with a very shallow basin and a broad, lip-supporting rim—not of the deeper, small-rimmed compromise mouthpiece of the modern trumpet-ist. And we must assume that the few highest, almost acrobatic parts in the scores of Bach were certainly 'tailored' for one or two outstand-ing virtuosos, just as operatic arias were written in those days for the personal abilities of individual stars.

A variety of the trumpet, used by Bach to double the chorale, was the *tromba da tirarsi*, or *corno da tirarsi*. The epithet meant 'to be pulled.' The mouthpiece had so long a throat that the instrument could easily be drawn out and in while playing, in order to produce those notes not yielded by overblowing.

The *corno* itself, usually called the *corno da caccia*, or 'hunter's horn,' was more or less what the French horn is today. However, it was played by trumpetists, apparently on trumpet-like mouthpieces, and held bell up, the modern "pocketward" position being due to the later technique of stopping. The effect was therefore much gayer and brisker.

Finally, a few words may be added on two unusual oboes: the *oboè d'amore* and the *oboè da caccia*. Both had the pear-shaped, so-called *d'amore* bell—well-known from the modern *cor anglais*—which, on account of its narrow opening, softened the tone. The former in-strument was an oboe in *A*; it was so much longer than the ordinary oboe that the fingerholes usually producing a *C* scale would yield an *A* scale instead. The *oboè da caccia*, being an oboe in *F*, was the an-cestor of the *cor anglais*, or English horn. The inappropriate name 'horn' may find an explanation in the curious sickle form of some of the old 'hunting' oboes (illustration on page 382 of the author's *History of Musical Instruments*).

G EORGE FREDERICK HANDEL (German spelling: Hän-del) was born in Halle, Saxony, on February 23, 1685, only twenty-six days before Johann Sebastian Bach and not far from his birthplace.

One might say that, in order to sum up the cyclopean work of Baroque music, Destiny had to create two giants of equal powers, but of different and even opposed temperaments: one sedentary, firmly rooted in his native Saxony, the other a man of the world, at home in Halle, Hamburg, and Hanover, in England and Italy; one in constant friction with church and town and school authorities, the other wrestling with *castrati* and divas, with managers and audiences; one avoiding, the other seeking, the dramatic forms of the opera and the oratorio; one introvert and the other extrovert.

Handel spent his early years in Halle and there received a solid training in organ playing and polyphonic writing. The important part of his career began at the age of eighteen in Hamburg, as a violinist, a conductor, and a composer of four German operas. Three years later, he went to Italy, forgot his German tradition, and became a successful composer of Italian operas, oratorios, and cantatas. After less than four years of Italianization, he followed an invitation to conduct the music of the Electoral Court at Hanover, but took a leave of absence in the very same year (1710) to visit England and perform his opera *Rinaldo* in London. Two years later he returned to London to stay for good—against the wish and will of his monarch. But the Elector, too, exchanged his Hanover for London: in 1714, he was crowned King of England. Handel is said to have reconciled the grudging prince with an orchestral outdoor suite, the *Water Music*, performed on a barge next to the king's at a court gala on the Thames in 1715. But this is a legend.

Handel did not re-enter the service of the court, although he accompanied the king on a travel back to Hanover in 1716. There he wrote a last composition on a German text: the *Passion* after a poem by Brockes. In England, he quietly worked for three years as a guest and chapel master of Duke Chandos—whence his two Chandos *Te Deum*'s and twelve Chandos anthems. Thereafter, he engaged in the management of opera houses in London and was caught in an inextricable maze of cabals, rivalries, public opposition, singers' intrigues, and bankruptcy. His superhuman struggle led to a stroke and a palsy. But because of an iron constitution and an incomparable energy he recuperated and lived to the age of seventy-four. Death came on April 14, 1759.

The works that made his name immortal were the English oratorios. Handel had tackled this form as a young composer in Italy. When he reverted to it in the maturity of his fifties, he created an unprecedented type of music. Very far from Carissimi's devotional oratorio addressed to the congregation of an *oratorio* or prayer chapel, Handel wrote for a large, diverse, and anonymous public and overwhelmed it with the epic grandeur of his Biblical heroes and the dramatic vigor of his choruses, with the size and weight of his means and the very dimensions of his scores. In fact, the renditions of some of Handel's oratorios were among the earliest mass performances in the sense of nineteenth-century music festivals.

Most important are:

> *Israel in Egypt* (1738)
> *Saul* (1738)
> *Messiah* (1742)
> *Judas Maccabaeus* (1746)
> *Joshua* (1747)
> *Jephtha* (1751)

Besides oratorios, Handel left an enormous amount of *concerti grossi,* chamber, harpsichord, and organ music. Both the oratorios and the chamber music have wrongfully overshadowed his dramatic work. From 1704 to 1740, Handel wrote no less than forty-six operas in the Italian language and in the lyrical style of Naples with the predominance of *da capo* arias. Best known are *Ottone Rè di Germania* (1723), *Giulio Cesare in Egitto* (1724), *Rodelinda* (1725), and *Serse,* or Xerxes (1738). One of the arias in the latter work has been held in the heart of the public in the disguises of all imaginable instrumental combinations as Handel's so-called *Largo.*

It took Friedrich Chrysander almost half a century to complete the *Gesamtausgabe* of this gigantic life work, which he had begun on the centenary of Handel's death. And its one hundred volumes still leave gaps unfilled.

I TALIAN OPERAS written for the English by a German present a strange, though highly characteristic, picture. Handel was not the only one. Gluck did the same thing in London, Copenhagen, and Vienna as "the famous master of Italian music"; and Johann Adolf Hasse (1699–1783), the "dear Saxon" or *caro Sássone* as the Italians called him, wrote more than one hundred Neapolitan operas. The international triumph of this musico-dramatic form had come to its peak.

Nevertheless, a countercurrent is visible in the time of Handel's greatest operas. Benedetto Marcello in Venice (1686–1739), celebrated composer of fifty psalms, printed, and often reprinted, his renowned *Teatro alla moda*, which pitilessly lampooned the poetic and musical weaknesses of the current opera pattern with its falsity and stilted pompousness.

This was criticism from outside; but the stage itself reacted, too. The rising middle-class could not but feel frustrated when forced to attend the serious opera with its stale mythology and Graeco-Roman history, with its Armidas and Didos, Caesars and Xerxeses, with heroes and heroines, ideal characters, patterned virtues, theatrical pathos, and grandiose gestures. The public got bored with a genre so far from reality—had they no right to comprehend, to relax, and to laugh?

As a way out of this crisis, the stage directors would interrupt the opera proper by some *intermezzo*, or 'in-between,' which was played act by act between the acts of the *seria*—a procedure quite unable to deepen the impression of the opera in any idealistic sense, but in return well able to reconcile the listeners with the tiresome duty of attending recitatives and *da capo* arias during the continual alternation of *seria* and *buffa*. The most famous example of an early comic opera, Giovanni Battista Pergolesi's *La serva padrona* (The Servant Mistress) of 1733, had been an intermezzo, before, shaking off the framework of serious operas, it became a *buffa* in its own right.

While the Italian *buffa* was an actual musical comedy, the *opéra comique* of the French was a play in which the spoken dialogue was interrupted by songs in the lighter vein with a definite accent on ridiculing the serious opera. After more obscure predecessors, this novel genre descended from Alain-René Le Sage's *Télémaque* (1715).

In a similar spirit, England opposed to the foreign *seria*, meant for aesthetes and connoisseurs, a domestic, popular, catchy *ballad opera*. It included a number of simple songs in the lighter vein, but for the most part it was spoken without any attempt at a recitative. John Gay, the poet, said in a preface of 1728: "I hope I may be forgiven, that I have not made my Opera unnatural, like those in vogue; for I have no recitative." The beginning was made in 1725 with Allan Ramsay's pastoral comedy *The Gentle Shepherd*. Not more than three years later, John Gay came out with his epochal *Beggar's Opera*, for which John Christopher Pepusch (1667–1752) had arranged appropriate melodies. With its musical hits and the open satire of a social and political character, it constituted a serious challenge to the musical plays of the court and a decisive victory of the *style bourgeois*. Another *ballad opera* of the same year, 1728, Charles Coffey's *The Devil to Pay*, with music arranged by a certain Seedo, and his later *Merry Cobbler* (1735) became the fundaments of the German *Singspiel* and will be mentioned again in the following chapter of the book.

THE SLOGAN *STYLE BOURGEOIS* leads us straight into the central problem of the time.

When Louis XIV died in 1715, the heavy, majestic style branched out in two directions. In one, generally called the Rococo, majesty and heaviness were dissolved in light-footed elegance and light-hearted eroticism, albeit the atmosphere and spirit of the court were kept. The other direction—for which there is no adequate term—led to the province of the *bourgeois,* to honest simplicity, and to the stress on soul and sentiment generally known by the German word *Empfindsamkeit*.

In music, the Rococo was known as *le style galant*. The other way led to the realm of what we rashly and deceptively call 'classical' music.

Each style turned its back on the austere polyphony of the preceding generation. That Johann Joseph Fux in Vienna printed in 1725 his famous bible of counterpoint, the *Gradus ad Parnassum* (Steps to Parnassus), which contains the definitive classification of the five species, indicates, as the publication of comprehensive manuals so often does, the end rather than the climax of that language.

Both styles strove for lightness and limpidity and put the stress on melody proper with little care for the bass-line and still less concern for the voice parts in between. The musical *style galant* joined the architectural Rococo in its profuse decoration with grace notes; the *style bourgeois* dropped most of the graces except for the *appoggiatura*, which served its tender expressiveness. The *appoggiatura* was in Stamitz's time characteristically called the 'Mannheim sigh.'

In the first half of the century it is easy to juxtapose Couperin as *galant*, and the ballad operas and German *Lieder* as *bourgeois*. But later it is hard, if not impossible, to label the masters of the time as either *galant* or *bourgeois*. They all draw inspiration and vitality from both sides and attempt to fuse them in their own way.

J EAN-PHILIPPE RAMEAU, the leader in France, was baptized in Dijon, Burgundy, on September 25, 1683, two years before Bach, Handel, and the younger Scarlatti, but he outlived them by several years, dying in Paris on September 22, 1764. Far into maturity, he earned his living as an organist in various churches, until an influential protector enabled him to give most of his time to writing.

Rameau might well have been the greatest composer of France in the eighteenth century. Though he wrote religious music and harpsichord pieces, too, the emphasis of his work was on operas and ballets. But when he turned to the stage he was already fifty years old, and Lully's most important successors in the field of opera and ballet, André Campra and André Cardinal Destouches, had laid down the quill.

Among Rameau's *tragédies lyriques*, or operas, *Castor et Pollux* (1737) and *Dardanus* (1739) were the best known in their time: the latter work was played till 1785. Among his ballets, four are outstanding:

> *Les Indes galantes*, 1735
> *Les Fêtes d'Hébé*, 1739
> *Platée*, 1745
> *Zaïs*, 1748

Rameau's dramatic truth, equally far removed from the frigid pompousness of the late Baroque and the pastoral playfulness of the *style galant*, placed him in a no-man's land, before the French were ready to demand or even tolerate a personal feeling in music. This gap between the composer and his audience was aggravated by the weakness of his texts.

Rameau's far-reaching influence upon the generations after him is probably due less to his scores than to an epochal *Traité de l'Harmonie* of 1722 (the year of Bach's *Wohltemperiertes Clavier* I). This earliest manual of harmony, though bold and ingenious, contained a good many errors and inconsistencies that his later writings had to correct.

After a hundred years, Berlioz still spent his nights studying, as he said in his autobiography, this "treatise of harmony digestible only by those who already know harmony."

In his approach to harmony, Rameau was a typical Frenchman of the eighteenth century, distrusting mere experience and imagination and calling in the all-powerful *raison*, "indispensable for any sane decision." Music "depends on reason, nature, and geometry" and is "a physico-mathematical science."

The gist of the *Traité* is the recognition that sixth and six-four chords are merely inversions of the triad in root position. For the rest, Rameau believed that the major triad was the basis of all harmony. It begot not only its direct inversions and, by addition, the seventh and ninth chords, but even the minor mode. The minor, mirroring the major scales in descending order, was in a way an inversion of the major. Since the conception of inverted chords implied a stress on the root, Rameau quite naturally formed the idea of what he called a 'fundamental bass' fictitiously connecting the roots of all the chords. It is necessary to mention this fictitious bass because an unprepared reader is prone to mistake it for the figured bass.

Harmony dominates Rameau's entire invention to such a degree that his melody is often nothing but a broken chord. Hence, he complains that "music is ordinarily divided into harmony and melody although the latter is only a part of the other." And four years later, in a *Nouveau Système de Musique théorique,* he affirms "that melody stems from harmony."

DOMENICO SCARLATTI, Alessandro's son, was born in Naples on October 26, 1685, and died in the same city in 1757. As a disciple of his father, he wrote a few operas for Rome and also conducted the music at St. Peter's. Then he went abroad and spent the greatest part of his life as a harpsichordist in England, Portugal, and Spain.

For his favorite instrument, he wrote many hundreds of sonatas in a wholly novel, progressive style. Witty and spirited, limpid and brisk, they were short and free in form, changing in tempo, and thoroughly, exclusively harpsichordistic, with glittering arpeggios, audacious leaps, crossed hands, and other resources of modern keyboard technique. Any contrapuntal respect for individual voice parts had completely disappeared.

In this modern, anticontrapuntal attitude, Scarlatti found an important brother-in-arms in Giovanni Battista Pergolesi, who died in 1736, only twenty-six years old. Pergolesi's universal fame was founded on the intermezzo *La Serva padrona* (1733), a melodious *Stabat mater* for two women's voices, strings, and organ (1736), and a number of trio sonatas for two violins, bass, and harpsichord. The turn to a new instrumental melody, to a cantability even in the faster movements, to contrasting themes, and to almost buffonic repartees is nowhere more obvious than in these sonatas.

I N GERMANY, the turning point of the Baroque style became evident in the works of a man even older than Handel, Bach, Rameau, and Scarlatti: Georg Philipp Telemann.

He was born on March 14, 1681, in Magdeburg, Saxony, and died in 1767 in Hamburg, where he had been Carl Philipp Emanuel's predecessor as the director of church music. He probably wrote more than any other composer, so much that, merely because of their number, he is not likely ever to have his complete works republished. At a rough estimate, there are, among his compositions, six hundred suites for orchestra, forty operas, forty-four Passions, and twelve complete annual sets of cantatas and motets for the Protestant service, not to mention oratorios, his music for special occasions, and the gigantic amount of his chamber music.

Though much of this writing inevitably followed routine, his contemporaries considered him the outstanding German master of the time and far superior to Johann Sebastian Bach. He was, indeed, more 'modern.' Though trained in the same tradition as Bach—"He could write a motet in eight parts as easily as someone else could write a letter," said Handel—he presently gave up his weighty German church polyphony for the fashionable *style galant*, and succeeded so well that his famous chamber music collection of 1735, the *Tafelmusik* had a surprising number of French subscribes.

His form has shown little change; thematic imitation is still the essential means of melodic weaving, and often enough one finds a true *fugato* in the bygone style. But the old solemnity and heaviness has disappeared; the melodic line is sprightly and gracious, and the instrumental ensemble, perfectly limpid. The thoroughbass, indispensable in the seventeenth century, seems already to be doomed; instead of doubling the harpsichord bass, the 'cello is often set free to join the melodic instruments, and, to avoid marring the texture, the harpsichord rests during several bars.

THE EMOTIONALISM inherent in the modern *empfindsame* style, which eventually led into an actual 'sentimental' style in the subsequent age, was heralded in unprecedented forms of changing sound-volume as against the simple contrast of rigid fortes and pianos.

The epochal, pregnant invention of the time was the *Gravicémbalo col pian e forte*, which allowed playing softly and loudly by the mere pressure of the fingers. The new instrument, whose complicated original name was subsequently abbreviated to *pianoforte*, *fortepiano*, or even *piano*, was first designed in 1709 by a harpsichord maker in Florence, Bartolomeo Cristófori. The outer form he took from the old harpsichord, but the old jacks or springers with their plucking tongues were replaced by the complicated lever-action of our modern pianos, in which each key flings a hammer up against the strings and releases it to fall back to its original position before the finger leaves the key, by means of an automatic releaser, or *escapement*. The Metropolitan Museum owns one of the two preserved Cristófori pianos, though its action is not the original.

Cristófori was the earliest and most excellent, but not the only, inventor of pianos. An English monk, Father Wood, in Rome, built one in 1711, possibly upon hearing of Cristófori's invention; a Frenchman, Marius, in Paris, another in 1716; a German, Christoph Gottlieb Schroeter, in Saxony, a fourth in 1717. Their models were very different, but they agreed in allowing for an unlimited number of shades of intensity and a smooth passage between them. In a similar spirit, the English organ builders Abraham Jordan & Son devised in 1712 the earliest organ-swell by enclosing a group of pipes in a box which could be gradually opened or closed by a pedal. Representatives of a whole generation in the leading musical countries were acting against the older ideal of constant intensity.

At exactly the same time, Roman orchestras are said to have inaugurated an unheard-of novelty which today we take for granted: "the gradual diminution of tone little by little, and then returning suddenly to the full power," not a *decrescendo* of individual tones, as around 1600, but of phrases, indeed of whole melodies. The Neapolitan opera composer Nicola Jomelli (1714–1774) brought the new technique to Stuttgart when he conducted the orchestra of the Duke of Württemberg. Witnesses relate how the audience rose irresistibly from their seats on hearing the swell of the orchestra.

The institution especially connected with the devices of gradually changing intensity and sudden *fortissimi* as means to stir emotion was the orchestra of the Count Palatine in Mannheim on the Rhine. Charles Burney, who had come from London to study the musical situation in Germany, lent in his interesting diary the most admiring words to this finest orchestra of the time: "an army of generals, equally fit to plan a battle, as to fight it." And the contemporary German poet, Daniel Schubart, wrote enthusiastically, "Their *forte* is like thunder, their *crescendo* a cataract, their *diminuendo* the rippling of a crystal stream, their *piano*, the soft breath of early spring." Franz Xaver Richter (1709–1789), Johann Stamitz (1717–1757) and, in Mozart's time, Christian Cannabich (1731–1798) created in Mannheim the modern art of orchestral playing and conducting and successively contributed to developing the modern symphonic style, of which the following chapter will outline the principal features.

It should not be assumed, however, that *crescendo* and *diminuendo* were altogether victorious. As late as 1748, the new practice was so completely unknown in France that Jean-Philippe Rameau, who needed it in his ballet *Zaïs*, was forced to describe it in a roundabout way: "Here, each instrument sets in, at first softly and then imperceptibly swelling to an extreme *forte*." Indeed, the most complete of German treatises on musical performance, the method of flute-playing by Johann Joachim Quantz, *Versuch einer Anweisung die Flöte traversiere zu spielen* (several editions between 1752 and 1789), dealt with the proper use of *forte* and *piano* on five full pages without so much as mentioning *crescendo* or *decrescendo*. But then, the taste of Quantz, as Burney said in 1772, was "that of forty years ago."

THE EMOTIONALISM, leading to flexible intensity, to *crescendo* and *decrescendo*, was no longer 'Rococo' or *style galant*. Rather, it was a decisive turn away from the cool atmosphere of aristocratic life to the warmer climate of the *bourgeoisie*, the middle class.

Perhaps the strongest, and certainly the strangest, contact of the dying Baroque and the dawn of the burgher age in music was old Bach's curious *Coffee Cantata*, in which the then still recent incursion of the stimulating drink from Arabia was given a perpetual monument in the form of a Protestant, German cantata with recitatives and arias. It is open to question whether the master paid a somewhat facetious tribute to the novel, burgher style by conferring upon it the pompous idiom of the church cantata and the *opera seria*, or whether, the other way around, he delighted in caricaturing his own style in all its majesty by laying the scene of this secular cantata in a middle-class party. We may visualize him sitting comfortably down with a broad, good-humored smile to do both at one blow.

But in a deeper sense, the Coffee Cantata is even symbolic. Coffee parties in private homes—*salons*—and public coffee houses became debating places where musical currents and works were discussed when the burghers had assumed the responsibility for the arts that the courts and the Church were giving up.

The conception of music as a public concern was enhanced by the barely precedented rise of musical criticism as a profession. Critical columns were printed in Paris in the *Mercure de France* (1672–1825), and in London in *The Tatler* (1709–1711) and *The Spectator* (1711–1712). In Germany, Johann Mattheson published a *Critica Musica* (1722–1726), Johann Adolf Scheibe a *Critische Musicus* (1738–1740), and Friedrich Wilhelm Marpurg, a *Critische Musicus an der Spree* (1750). These German critical essays, printed as serials and short-lived, were timid beginnings of music-magazine publishing. Germany continued with Lorenz Mizler's *Musikalischer Staarstecher*, or Musical Cataract Cutter, of 1739 and 1740, France with Abbé Marc-Antoine Laugier's *Sentiment d'un Harmoniphile sur divers Ouvrages de Musique* (two numbers), and England with *The New Musical and Universal Magazine* of 1775.

In organizing public concerts, the Londoners had taken the lead some decades before (*cf.* page 255). Germany and France followed in the time of Bach and Rameau. In 1713, Telemann founded the *Wöchentliche Grosse Concert im Frauenstein* at Frankfurt-on-the-Main, and in 1720, a similar institution in Hamburg; shortly after, in 1725, Anne Philidor—a man!—established the famous *Concerts spirituels* in the Tuileries at Paris. The earliest American concert on record was given in 1731 at Boston, without, however, becoming a regular institution. In Vienna no public concert existed before 1740.

T HE INSTRUMENTS, at least in the North, were still under the domination of the organ. It no longer was the organ of Praetorius. Gottfried Silbermann in Freiberg, Saxony, and his fellow builders unified and dimmed the glaring colors of its stops, but gave them transparence and a silvery lustre. The stress went down from strident four- to the more majestic eight- and sixteen-foot registers, from denser mixtures to slender solo stops, from jarring reeds to milder labial pipes.

Strings and wind instruments changed even more, particularly in Italy and in France.

Antonio Stradivari, most famous among the makers of violins, died in 1737, almost a hundred years old, and two other masters of Cremona, Carlo Bergonzi (d. 1747) and Giuseppe Antonio Guarneri "del Gesù" (1687–174?) held the standard for a few more years before decline set in.

However, this highest peak was not the ultimate phase of violin making. Even the most precious and best preserved instruments of the Stradivari generation have since been submitted to important alterations which have changed their tone. The neck has become longer by about a quarter of an inch in order to facilitate the modern technique of playing in higher 'positions' of the hand, that means, of shifting the stopping hand way up on the fingerboard in the interest of a higher range. Moreover, the playing plane has been slanted by wedging up the fingerboard to slope away from the body and, consequently, by heightening the flatter bridge of the originals. Lastly —not to mention changes in the strings—the bass-bar, a slender ledge inside, below the G string, resisting the pressure from above and increasing the tension of the soundboard, proved to be too short and too weak in times of a rising pitch and was replaced by a longer and stiffer bar (plate XVI).

While deterioration set in both in its homeland and in Germany, the violin was not yet recognized in France as a chamber or solo instrument, although it had a firm position in dance and operatic orchestras. As late as 1740, Hubert le Blanc, a lawyer, thought it necessary to publish a bellicose *Défense de la Basse de Viole* [the gamba] *contre les Entreprises du Violon et les Prétensions du Violoncel*. Upon the death of Jean-Marie Leclair (1764), the leading magazine, *Mercure de France*, stated in a eulogy that the violin owed its acceptance by "decent people" only to the deceased master. Not before the early nineteenth century did France have any violin maker of rank.

Together with the decline of the viols and the final rise of the violin family, the time witnessed the descent of the recorders and the final rise of the transverse or cross-flute. Both events were unmistakable symptoms of a change from cool reserve to a more and more expressive, emotional style. Bach still meant the old recorder wherever he simply indicated *flauto;* otherwise he prescribed *flauto traverso*. And even after Bach's death, the leading flute-pedagogue in Germany, Johann Joachim Quantz, saw fit to call the instrument distinctively a *Flöte traversiere* on the title page of his famous *Versuch einer Anweisung*. The French had long ago given up the recorder or *flûte douce* and were leading in the manufacture and performing style of the *flûte*.

The time also put an end to the long career of the lute, even in its stronghold, Germany. The instrument was costly to keep and difficult to handle. John Dowland (d. 1626) had already stated sadly that as the lute "of all instruments that are portable is, and ever hath been most in request, so is it the hardest to manage with cunning and order, with the true nature of fingering," and Bach's friend Johann Mattheson once said that a player eighty years old must have wasted sixty of them in tuning. Unassuming songs were just as well accompanied on the simpler guitar, and elaborate solos found a more proper place on clavichords, harpsichords, and pianos. When, shortly after 1750, the thoroughbass was at last given up, the lute lost its reason for being and disappeared.

The pitch of the lute was still relative, according to the voice to be accompanied and the strength of the strings ("First set up the Treble, so high as you dare venter for Breaking").

THE ABSOLUTE PITCH of the time was generally lower than today. Between 1720 and 1730, Italy had an $a' = 395$–404 vibrations per second, which, compared with our 440 v., was 187–148 cents (*cf.* page 12), or approximately a whole- or a three-quarter-tone, lower. Germany's pitch was slightly higher; two organs close to Bach's time and town had 415 and 420 v., they were 102 and 81 cents, or approximately a semitone lower.

READING

Manfred Bukofzer, *Music in the Baroque*, New York, 1947. Philipp Spitta, *J. S. Bach*, tr. Bell and Fuller-Maitland, London, 1951. Charles Sanford Terry, *Bach*, London, 1928. Hans T. David and Arthur Mendel, *The Bach Reader*, New York, 1945. Edward J. Dent, *Handel*. Frank Kidson, *The Beggar's Opera*, Cambridge, 1922. John Gay, *The Beggar's Opera*, New York, 1948. Lionel de la Laurencie, *Rameau*, Paris, 1908. Paul-Marie Masson, *L'Opéra de Rameau*, Paris, 1930. Ralph Kirkpatrick, *Domenico Scarlatti*, Princeton, 1953. G. Radiciotti, *Giovanni Battista Pergolesi*, 3rd edition, Roma, 1935. Rosamond E. M. Harding, *Origins of the Piano-Forte*, Cambridge, 1933. Curt Sachs, *The History of Musical Instruments*, New York, 1940. *The Commonwealth of Art*, New York, 1946. *Rhythm and Tempo*, New York, 1953.

17

THE AGE OF
HAYDN AND MOZART

1750–1791

WHEN JOHANN SEBASTIAN BACH died in 1750, the novel trends had reached maturity in all the fields of art. Wherever the masters tried to say in words what they thought the goal should be, they spoke, again and again, of nature, simplicity, passion. These slogans were heard in the creeds of architects, sculptors, and painters, in the critical columns of leading magazines in Paris, in the *drama bourgeois* and the *comédie larmoyante;* they were heard when the French ballet-master Noverre attacked the lifeless, stiff ballet of yore; and they appeared when the moderns fought for the rising waltz against the punctilious minuet.

IN THE OPERA, the three slogans—nature, simplicity, passion— appeared with greatest authority in the reform of Gluck.

Christoph Willibald Gluck was born as the son of a game-keeper in a village of Bavaria (*not* Weidenwang) on July 2, 1714, the year of Carl Philipp Emanuel Bach's birth. The scope and circumstances of his early education are unknown. After a few years of irregular musical studies and activities in Prague and Vienna, a Maecenas enabled him to go to Italy and learn the craft from the great teacher Giovanni Battista Sammartini in Milan, and soon he was engaged in writing an amazing number of Italian operas in the usual Neapolitan style. So overwhelming was his success that he was invited to England in 1745, and a little later to Germany, Denmark, and Austria. Here, in Vienna, he settled in 1750 and was four years later appointed Imperial *Kapellmeister* without conducting duties. On the whole, he lived as a free man, able to travel abroad wherever his presence was desired. His repeated stays in Paris in the 1770's were the most significant: his later operas played so important a role there that the French consider him almost as one of their own composers. On November 15, 1787, a stroke felled him in Vienna.

Gluck's universal fame is founded on the 'reform' operas of the 1760's and 1770's. It is only fair, however, to acknowledge that in his fight against the traditional opera he was by no means a preacher in the wilderness. The composer Tommaso Traetta (1727–1779) in Parma tried in a similar spirit to renew "the miracles of that art which the Greeks so much prized"; the Vienna of Count Durazzo, manager general of the opera, was wide-awake to such a reform; and Paris had never been a stronghold of Italian opera, even though one of the two hostile parties of opera fans played off the typical Italian Nicola Piccini against the reformer Gluck.

And it is also fair to acknowledge that Gluck's librettist of the 1760's, Raniero Calzabigi (1714–1795), rather than Gluck himself, was the motive power in fighting the pattern of Naples and leading the opera back to the dramatic spirit of 1600, indeed to the ideals of Lully. Once more, it was felt that the drama should be paramount, and music for the sake of music must not be allowed to interfere with the action on the stage or to attract attention in its own right. Rather was it the duty of music to express the characters and emotions of the *dramatis personae* with the strongest intensity without dwelling on beautiful but antidramatic arias. Thus, "I begged him," wrote Calzabigi, "to banish *i passaggi, le cadenze, i ritornelli* and all the Gothick barbarous and extravagant things that have been introduced into our music"—an admonition that can be fully appreciated by only those who know to what incredible extent the celebrated singers distorted and diluted the original melodies with chains of scales and trills so insipid and empty that the driest finger exercises of Czerny appear imaginative in comparison.

Gluck himself, who gave the credit to Calzabigi, professed the same ideals, although the words he signed with his name might have been penned by his poet. In the preface to his opera *Alceste*, printed in 1769, he wrote: ". . . I have striven to restrict music to its true office of serving poetry by means of expression and by following the situations of the story, without interrupting the action or stifling it with a useless superfluity of ornaments. . . . I did not wish to arrest an actor in the greatest heat of dialogue in order to wait for a tiresome ritornello, nor to hold him up in the middle of a word on a vowel favorable to his voice, nor to make display of the agility of his fine voice in some long-drawn passage, nor to wait while the orchestra gives him time to recover his breath for a cadenza. . . ." (transl. by Eric Blom).

His contemporary Charles Burney, mentioned before, could rightfully say: "He aspires more at satisfying the mind, than flattering the ear. . . . It seldom happens that a single air can be taken out of its niche, and sung singly, with much effect; the whole is a chain, of which a detached single link is but of small importance."

This is indeed the spirit of Gluck's reform operas:

Orfeo ed Euridice (Vienna 1762) in Italian, with an alto *castrato* as Orpheus
Alceste (Vienna 1767) in Italian (Paris 1776) in French
Paride ed Elena (Vienna 1769–70) in Italian
Iphigénie en Aulide (Paris 1774) in French
Orphée et Euridice (Paris 1774) a French revision with a tenor as Orpheus
Armide (Paris 1777) in French
Iphigénie en Tauride (1779) in French

Don Juan (Vienna 1761) was a reform ballet. Far from the earlier ballet *divertissements* with their meaningless *poses* and *pas*, the master created an actual dance-drama. It was the ideal, pantomimic ballet that the French revolutionary dancing-master Jean-Georges Noverre postulated in his famous *Lettres sur la Danse et les Ballets*, at exactly the time at which Calzabigi and Gluck were turning to an actual music-drama.

Among the one hundred and nineteen dramatic and semi-dramatic works of Gluck, there are a few French comic operas for the Viennese court, such as *Le Cadi dupé* (1761) and *La Rencontre imprévue*, or The Mecca Pilgrims (1764),which led directly to Mozart's *Abduction*. The existence of these delightful plays shows that courtly circles, too, could be honestly bored when the heroes were stiltedly singing their *arias* and deploying their magnanimous characters, and that the movement away from the *seria* was no longer *bourgeois*.

In Paris, the rift between the two genres and the factions that backed them came into the open when the unprecedented success of Pergolesi's *Serva padrona* in 1752 incited the hot-headed *Guerre des Bouffons*, or War of the Comedians, between the adherents of the traditional serious opera gathered around the king and the enthusiasts of the comic opera gathered around the queen—a battle fought with passionate pens and clever intrigues at court and in town.

Since one of the slogans in this battle was 'natural' versus 'learned' music, it was only logical that an amateur played a momentous role in the life of the *opéra comique*—Jean-Jacques Rousseau, the glory of literary France.

Rousseau's *Devin du Village*, or Village Seer (1752), had an incredible, lasting success, although, or because, the plot and the music are, to say the least, rather simple. Shepherd Colin forsakes shepherdess Colette; the fortune-teller promises to help her, and on his advice Colette, playing the flirt, tells Colin that she is in love with a city gent. The ruse succeeds, the lovers are reconciled, and everybody is happy. The subject is so meager that Colette's four airs practically summarize the play. The music was in the lightest vein, artless, and even amateurish.

Rousseau's leading successors, Monsigny and Grétry, were superior musicians. Pierre-Alexandre Monsigny (1729–1817) assured with *Le Déserteur* (1769) the first enormous popularity of the French *opéra comique;* the Belgian André-Erneste-Modeste Grétry (1742–1813) beat all records: his *Caravane du Caire* (1784) was performed more than five hundred times, and his *Richard Coeur-de-Lion* (1784) is still on the repertoire of theaters in Paris.

Rousseau, the dilettante, was also the pioneer of the *melodrama*. The word should not mislead. The reader must not think of the sweetish, sentimental connotation that the word has in modern English. The original melodrama of the eighteenth century was a genuine spoken drama with either one single actor (*monodrama*) or two actors (*duodrama*). To their speech, an orchestra contributed the hidden depth of the soul beyond man's actions and words—that depth that only music can give.

Jean-Jacques Rousseau's monodrama *Pygmalion* of 1762, although not quite unprecedented in the decades before, was the point of departure. Georg Benda, *Kapellmeister* to the Duke of Gotha, thought the work important enough to arrange it for piano. He himself tried his hand at two melodramas, musically better and probably more successful than Rousseau's: *Ariadne auf Naxos* (1775) and *Medea* (1778).

After its early triumph, the melodramatic form was not often revived but was never forgotten, either. Its later history stretches from the prison scene in Beethoven's *Fidelio* to Richard Strauss' *Enoch Arden* (1898), Schoenberg's *Erwartung* (1909) and *Pierrot Lunaire* (1912), to Honegger's *Roi David* (1923) and *Jeanne d'Arc au Bûcher* (1935) and Stravinsky's *Persephone* (1934).

Whereas the German melodrama derived from France, the German comic opera or, as they called it, the *Singspiel*, went back to the two English attempts of Charles Coffey: *The Devil to Pay* (1728) and *The Merry Cobbler* (1735). The former, far more successful, was first translated by the German ambassador to London, von Brocke, and publicly performed by a caravan troupe at Berlin in 1743. Nine years later, in 1752, Christian Felix Weisse remodeled the text of the two operas, and a little-known musician, Johann Standfuss, wrote a new score. Not before 1766 did the laborious process of assimilation come to an end, when Johann Adam Hiller, a leading figure in the concert life of Leipzig (1728–1804), replaced Standfuss' music by melodies of his own. From then on, the destiny of the German *Singspiel* was secured.

Hiller, like Monsigny in France, concentrated on composing *Singspiele*. One of them, *Die Jagd* or Hunt (1770) was so full of life and dash that two generations later, Hiller's last successor, Albert Lortzing in Berlin (1801–1851), saw fit to re-adapt it to the then modern stage. Charles Burney, travelling through Germany, was impressed by Hiller's popularity: "His music was so natural and pleasing that the favorite airs, like those of Dr. Arne in England, were sung by all degrees of people; and the more easy ones had the honor of being sung in the streets." In fact, a number of tunes today mistaken for German folksongs were composed by Hiller and his followers.

The delight in *Lieder*, deeply rooted in Germany, was greater than ever in the time of the *Singspiel*. In that age, the ideals of nature and simplicity that placed the *Singspiel* in opposition to the Italian *opera seria* also set the domestic *Lied* in opposition to the formalistic *aria* in Italian style.

The earliest center of German *Lied* composing, the so-called First

School of Berlin, included outstanding masters like Carl Philipp Emanuel Bach and Carl Heinrich Graun, but hardly rose above the level of rationalistic, pedantic dryness. Not until 1780, in the so-called Second School of Berlin, another North German composer, Johann Abraham Peter Schulz (1747–1800), was able to create a kind of *Lied* which, in all its simplicity, did justice to the poetical mood of the text in anticipation of Schubert.

The flight into utmost simplicity, manifest in all the *Singspiele* and *Lieder*, led inevitably to the domain of the child. Hiller's *Kinderlieder* were the first attempt to fill the need for songs that children could grasp and even perform—not a surprising trend in the age of Pestalozzi.

Meanwhile, the English *glee* (from Anglo-Saxon *gleo*, 'music') became a well-bred successor to the naughty *catch*. It was a short and secular song for amateurs in three or more men's solo voices (alto, tenor, basso) without instrumental accompaniment. Samuel Webbe (1740–1816) and Richard J. S. Stevens (1757–1837) were its finest representatives.

The numberless modern glee clubs go back to an original *Glee Club*, which met in a private house in London from 1783 onwards to sing *a cappella* ensembles after dinner—catches and glees, madrigals, motets, and canons.

T HE SERIOUS CRISIS of the mid-century is reflected in the strange development of two of the sons of Bach, Carl Philipp Emanuel and Johann Christian.

Carl Philipp Emanuel, third of the sons, was born in Gluck's year, 1714, at Weimar, and died in 1788 at Hamburg. He spent almost thirty years of his life in or near Berlin, mostly as a chamber musician to King Frederick the Great—whence he has been called the 'Berlin' Bach—and the remaining twenty-one years as the director of music in the six principal churches of Hamburg—whence he has been called also the 'Hamburg' Bach. Few musicians of the eighteenth century exerted an equally strong influence: Bach, to his contemporaries, was Philipp Emanuel, not Johann Sebastian, and Mozart said of him, "He is the father, we are the boys."

Philipp Emanuel wrote twenty-four Passions, two oratorios, many cantatas, chamber music, and odes. But most of his works were devoted to his cherished *clavier*, a term that, in principle, covered all keyboard instruments, but, by preference, the clavichord. He gave it more than two hundred short pieces, and a great number of sonatas in three movements, among them the 'Prussian,' the 'Württemberg,' and the Sonatas for Connoisseurs and Amateurs (*Sonaten für Kenner und Liebhaber*). And when, in 1781, he had to part with his dearly loved Silbermann clavichord, he said farewell in a deeply moving rondo, which anticipates the style of Beethoven's earlier sonatas and gives an idea of the inspired improvisations for which he was famous.

In the astounding affinity to a master almost sixty years his junior, he concluded a musical life that had begun in the strict polyphonic training of his father and had passed through the opposite ideals of the *style galant*.

J OHANN CHRISTIAN BACH differed from his father more than the other sons—in personality, life, and musical style. The youngest son of Johann Sebastian and Anna Magdalena, he was born on September 5, 1735, when his father was already fifty years old. After the father's death, fifteen years later, he was brought up in Berlin in the house of his stepbrother Carl Philipp Emanuel, who was his senior by twenty-one years. At the end of four years, he turned to Italy, to become a pupil of the most celebrated music teacher of the time, Padre Giambattista Martini in Bologna.

Johann Christian's Italianization was rapid and thorough. The son of the greatest musician of the Protestant world was converted to the Catholic faith, was appointed organist of the cathedral in Milan, and was much sought after as a composer of genuine Italian operas. To sharpen the contrast, this son of a sedentary man who had never left his native Germany and seldom the Saxo-Thuringian land, was too restive to stay in Italy and left for London in 1762. The so-called 'Milanese' Bach became the 'English' or 'London' Bach. He was entrusted with the musical education of the young queen, Charlotte Sophia; the focus of his life and interest, however, was in the public subscription concerts, of which he became the most prominent figure. After twenty years in his second adopted homeland, he died on January 1, 1782.

Two events in his English career were particularly momentous. The earlier was the English concert tour of the Mozart family. We know that in 1756 Wolfgang and his sister played a composition for four hands on the harpsichord and that the combination of two players on the same keyboard was a novel treat (although it had been known to the Elizabethan virginalists). Johann Christian subsequently published a number of sonatas "for two performers on one pianoforte or harpsichord." Did the master learn from the boy? Be that as it may, it seems more important that Johann Christian made a deep, indelible impression on the eight-year-old child with the melodious *cantabile* style which seems to anticipate the best and most essential of Mozart's language.

The second event in Johann Christian's English career was his piano recital, the earliest to be given on the new instrument. Some details will be presented later.

His quintet in *D* major for flute, oboe, and strings is a particularly charming composition. But it also interests us from another viewpoint: the two first editions have a figured bass, but the third edition does without figures. The middle voices, entirely neglected in the preceding *style galant*, became once more so vital that the harpsichord with its filling chords could be dropped from orchestral and chamber performances. This implied another important change: since the harpsichord withdrew from the orchestra, the conducting harpsichordist yielded time-beating to the leader of the violins.

At the same time, composers of *Lieder* began to write out the full accompaniment of the piano instead of a mere figured bass.

BOTH SONS OF BACH represent an age that endeavored not only to be simple and natural, but also to show emotions that a little earlier had been restrained or playfully steered around. Emotion was not, as in the age around 1700, confined to heroic passion or to religious absorption; on the contrary, it admitted with equal rights the unheroic moods of the *empfindsame* soul, of its melancholy, sentimentalism, and tearfulness, and it carried their expression far beyond the timid beginnings in the generation before.

In a number of books of the time, the intangibles of 'passion' are carefully classified and treated according to the recipes of an *Affekten-lehre*: melodic ascent expresses cheerfulness, melodic descent, dejection, and so forth. But this Theory of the Affects sprang less from the emotional trend or *affect* itself than from the often pedantic rationalism of the time. We still cherish some leftovers of this rationalistic system in the alleged characteristics of major and minor and of the keys, such as the 'heroic' quality of *E* flat major, though the *Eroica* sounded actually in *D* when Beethoven performed it.

Affect, melancholy, sentimentalism, and tearfulness were the soil in which the *musical glasses* throve. This name denoted sets of drinking cups, tuned by means of a greater or lesser amount of water and rubbed along their rims with wet fingers, in melodic sequence. In the immaterial vagueness of their tones, which transported the listener and carried him to the land of blissful dreams, they complied with the mood of the time so well that even as serious a man as Gluck saw fit in 1746 to entertain his audience in the Haymarket Theatre in London with "a Concert upon Twenty-six Drinking Glasses, tuned with Spring Water, accompanied with the whole Band."

Indeed, Benjamin Franklin, who, around 1760, represented Pennsylvania in London, found it worthwhile to convert the primitive device into a carefully fashioned *glass harmonica*. The player, sitting at a stand not unlike a sewing machine, touched the rims of glass bowls fitted into one another on a horizontal axle so that only the rims were accessible, while the foot was on a treadle to keep the axle rotating.

No wonder that another ethereal instrument became a favorite, too— the *aeolian harp*. A fancy contraption for romantic dreamers, it consisted of a framework with a number of thicker and thinner gut strings which, placed on a roof or in a window, sounded under the impact of the wind and united in mysterious, ever-changing chords—airy, bodiless, floating in the infinite. The changing was caused by the greater or smaller number of harmonics that the varying force of the wind generated.

Symptomatic as the glass harmonica and the aeolian harp might be, the two contrivances moved on by-ways rather than on the main road. The truly essential conflict in the field of instruments rose among the harpsichord, the clavichord, and the piano.

While the harpsichord was still the leader in all the countries of the West and the South, the intimate character of German music in the age of *Empfindsamkeit* found a more adequate expression on the clavichord, which, though small both in size and in the range of its expressiveness, nevertheless allowed for an *espressivo* and even a *vibrato* that the rigid harpsichord could never grant.

A German poet of the day celebrated the clavichord in these verses:

> *Sei mir gegrüsst, mein schmeichelndes Klavier,*
> *Was keine Sprache richtig nennt,*
> *Die Krankheit tief in mir,*
> *Die nie mein Mund bekennt,*
> *Die klag' ich dir.*

Johann Timotheus Hermes (1738–1821)

> Hail, thou, caressing clavichord,
> My wounded heart's distress,
> That language does not know to word,
> That never does my mouth confess,
> May on thy strings be poured.

—transl. C. S.

And: "The one who dislikes noise, rage and fuming, whose heart bursts in sweet feelings, neglects both the harpsichord and the piano and chooses the clavichord," said the critic Schubart (d.1791). Carl Philipp Emanuel enthusiastically shared in this affection. And for some decades, Germany witnessed a second bloom of the clavichord almost unique in history.

But no second bloom can last. The piano, in grand and square and upright forms, was recovering from the inertia in which it had existed since the days of Cristófori, half a century ago, and showed the world that delicacy of touch could be combined with power. And in the wake of this recovery something unheard-of happened: Johann Christian Bach, brother and pupil of the declared herald of the clavichord, gave the first piano recital at London in 1768 on a square instrument that J. C. Zumpe's factory had sold him for fifty guineas. And in the same year Mademoiselle Lechantre played the piano in the *Concerts Spirituels* of Paris. In vain, the English harpsichord-makers tried to rescue their age-old, menaced instrument by giving it a horizontal Venetian blind above the strings which, opened or shut by a pedal, produced a kind of forte and piano and even a modest transition between the two. The days of the harpsichord and, for that matter, of the clavichord too, were rapidly, irrevocably going.

PIANO MUSIC and other instrumental forms were conquering grounds never dreamed of before. Coping with the melodious flow of singing, instrumental music meant renouncing any intricate polyphonic weaving as well as the ties that had connected it with the dance. It aimed at cantability, even in rapid movements, and it became dramatic.

The leading form in which this happened was the *sonata*, a concept that covered not only the sonata proper for piano solo or for violin and piano, but also the usual forms of chamber ensembles, such as trios, quartets, and quintets, and even the symphony and the concerto.

This sonata has very little in common with earlier forms of the same name. It consists, as a rule, of four movements differing in character, tempo, and partly even in tonality:

A rapid first movement, often with a slow introduction inherited from the French overture.

A slow movement in the subdominant (lower-fifth key) or the parallel minor key.

A minuet, as the last remainder of the ancestral suite of dances, repeated after a more intimate *trio*.

A rapid last movement, often in *rondo* form (*cf.* page 194). Properly speaking, only the first movement—sometimes, also the last—is written in what musicians call the sonata form. It begins with an 'exposition' of some energetic, masculine theme in the principal key, followed by a contrasting, tenderer, feminine theme in a related tonality. In the eighteenth century, this exposition of the two themes had to be repeated; and subsequently, in a second section, its thematic material was playfully tossed about, until the first theme re-appeared triumphant in a 'reprise' and ended in a concluding formula or *coda* (Ital. 'tail'). The playful section between the exposition and the reprise, however, was slowly elaborated to form a 'development,' in which the themes, no longer treated as integers, were decomposed into characteristic fragments or motives which had sufficient driving force. The theme no longer *was*; it *acted*.

The typically classical features—two contrasting themes and a repeated, symmetrical exposition—seem to have been an essentially

Italian contribution. But the dramatic 'development' and the progress of the new instrumental style were almost exclusively German—for reasons that the author has pointed out in his *Commonwealth of Art* (pages 380 f). The only non-German symphonist of the time was the Franco-Fleming François-Joseph Gossec or, in another spelling (and correct pronunciation), Gossé (1734–1829). Living mostly in France, he excelled as the organizer of the *Concert des Amateurs* in Paris (1770), the re-organizer of the older *Concerts Spirituels* (*cf.* page 234), and the founder of the *Ecole Royale de Chant*, which later was transformed into the present *Conservatoire National de Musique*.

A freer style, in which the additive form of the older suite survived without the integration and dramatic urge of the sonata, was the *divertimento*, *serenade*, or *cassation*, a typically Austrian set of shorter movements (as in Mozart's *Haffner Serenade* and *Kleine Nachtmusik*), generally in the lighter, though never vulgar, vein for small ensembles, to be played on festive occasions in private homes and parks.

Haydn WAS, with sixty-six scores, the most prolific composer of *divertimenti*.

But the *divertimenti*, unassuming and retrospective, were certainly not the central part of his work. Our interest is rather focused on his one hundred and four symphonies and an incredible amount of chamber music in all imaginable combinations from fifty-two piano sonatas to duos, trios, quartets, quintets, and a sextet.

In these compositions—more than in the works of his contemporaries —evolved the 'modern' mobile, driving style of writing: the sonata form with its dramatic 'development' which has just been described; the rehabilitation of fluent (though free) polyphony enlivening all the voice parts as against the purely melodic attitude of the *style galant* with its lifeless middle voices; and even the delicate openwork technique in which a melodic idea leaps from part to part and allows the just abandoned part to rest for a moment.

And it was in these compositions, too, that the symphonic style and that of chamber music, giving up the older noncommittal playfulness, grew to an almost Beethovenian depth, dramatic power, and conflict of tragic passions. Even the most playful spot in the symphony, the minuet, lost its courtly, smooth connotations of elegant dancing and became a true, hobnailed Austrian *Ländler* along the back-to-nature line of the period. Excellent illustrations are Haydn's Fifth Symphony of 1761 and the Surprise Symphony written thirty years later.

In the face of so weighty an instrumental music, we are apt to forget that Haydn also composed twenty-four operas, a number of Masses, and other vocal pieces both religious and secular, and that, two generations after Handel, Haydn gave a fresh, momentous impulse to the oratorio in his *Creation* of 1798 and *The Seasons* (1801).

The man who thus emerged as one of the geniuses of the time was neither a pompous nor an altogether retiring man. He was born in narrow circumstances in a small town in Austria near the Hungarian border on March 31, 1732, sang as a chorister at St. Stephan's in Vienna, and made a scanty living by giving private lessons and accompanying in Porpora's singing studio. Ten years of hard studying went by. They were not without fruit. Harpsichord sonatas were composed, a string quartet in 1755, and a few symphonies in 1759.

In the same year, Haydn began his career as a conductor of the typical Austrian and Hungarian house-orchestras. He was employed by Count Morzin first, and in 1761 entered the service of the Hungarian Eszterházy in Eisenstadt and Eszterháza.

It was during this period that his compositions assumed a very personal character under the sway of the German Storm-and-Stress movement, which, laying emphasis on passion and individuality, tried to prevent the arts from sliding down into the levelling *genre bourgeois*. His main contributions of that time were the *Farewell* symphony and the *Sun* quartets of 1772.

When he published his *Jungfernquartette*, or 'Maiden' quartets, in 1781, he announced them as being written in a "new and special manner"—the 'development' had been born. The novel conception had ripened when he created the six great *Paris* symphonies (1786), including *L'Ours*, *La Poule*, and *La Reine*.

The fateful turn in Haydn's life came in 1790 when on his patron's death the orchestra was dissolved, although the master retained pension and title. Haydn was now free. He left Hungary and moved to Vienna, but in the same year accepted John Peter Salomon's urgent invitation to perform his compositions in London. The call was characteristic of a decisive change in musical life: performances in private houses and with the essential coöperation of amateurs had yielded to permanent professional concerts for paying audiences with a stress on international celebrities as guests. Such was the nature of Salomon's famous concerts.

Haydn stayed in London from 1790 to 1792 and again from 1794 to 1795. There he wrote the famous twelve *London* symphonies Nos. 93–104, among them the *Surprise* (1791), the *Military* (1794), the *Clock* (1794), the *Drum Roll* (1795). (However, these twelve are also nicknamed *Salomon* symphonies, the name of *London* being reserved for only one of them.)

Haydn returned to Vienna as the grand master of symphonic music. But, though he had finished his symphonic work, he was prepared to open new ways of expression. Under the deep impression of the English Handel-festivals that he had attended, he turned to choral music, to Masses first, well known under the names *Heilig*, *Pauken*, *Nelson*, *Theresien*, *Schöpfungs*, and *Harmonie Messe*, and above all to Handel's essential form, which had utterly degenerated, the oratorio. The two oratorios that he wrote around 1800 emerge like lonely peaks in a plain: the *Creation*, or *Schöpfung*, of 1798, after Milton's *Paradise Lost*, and the *Seasons*, or *Jahreszeiten*, of 1801, on a poem of James Thomson's.

Not much later, his creative powers weakened. He spent a peaceful old age in Vienna and died on May 31, 1809.

H OW DEEP THE CRISIS of instrumental music was and how uncertain composers and players felt at the time when Haydn's generation set forth on its pioneering work, appears from the astonishing fact that almost at the same time three excellent musicians, squeezed between a rapidly vanishing past and a timidly outlined future, sat down to write about correct performance. The titles, although longwinded and clumsy, pretend that the books are simply methods for flute, *clavier*, and violin. Johann Joachim Quantz, repeatedly mentioned on earlier pages, published his *Versuch einer Anweisung die Flöte traversiere zu spielen* in 1752. Leopold Mozart printed a *Versuch einer gründlichen Violinschule*, or Essay of a Thorough Violin Method, in 1756. And Carl Philipp Emanuel Bach, a *Versuch über die wahre Art das Clavier zu spielen* (1753–1762), or Essay on the True Style of Playing the Clavier—"the school of schools," as Haydn called it.

Actually, the three alleged instrumental methods were complete manuals of general performance way beyond the provinces of their title-instruments, with all the intricate details of tempo, accents, intensity, accompaniment, grace notes, conducting, organization of orchestral ensembles and chamber music. Conscientious modern musicians should not fail to study these books. Without them, they will necessarily see the whole of music between Bach and Mozart in a distorted light. Particularly in the field of grace notes, on which the melody of the eighteenth century depended to a degree almost inconceivable in our days, they cannot rely on their notorious 'instinct,' which is a milder word for ignorance.

Quantz, in particular, has made the momentous attempt to fix the average tempi by using a pulse beat of eighty per minute as the unit. Thus, the value of the quarter note was:

MM 80 in the tempi *Allegretto, Allegro ma non tanto, non troppo, non presto, Moderato*

MM 160 in *Allegro assai, Allegro di molto, Presto*

MM 40 in *Adagio cantabile, Cantabile, Arioso, Larghetto, Soave, Dolce, Poco andante, Affettuoso, Pomposo, Maestoso, Siciliano, Adagio spiritoso*

MM 20 in *Adagio assai, Adagio pesante, Lento, Largo assai, Mesto, Grave*

Exacter and more detailed metronomic directions can be found in the author's recent book, *Rhythm and Tempo*.

In the dances of France, Quantz adds, there were basically two tempi only:

MM 80 for *Canaries, Courante, Entrée, Gigue, Loure, Sarabande*

MM 160 for *Bourrée, Chaconne, Furie, Gavote, Minuet, Passecaille, Passepied, Rigaudon, Rondeau, Tambourin*

Do not overlook the fast tempo of the Minuet. As a matter of course, however, all these indications are approximate and must not be taken too literally.

The moderate attitude of the French showed in their pitch no less than in their tempo. As a rule, the French preferred a low, the Germans a medium, and the English a high pitch. Nothing is known about the Italian pitch. The medium, German pitch—was $a' = 422$–423 vibrations per second, which, compared with our 440 vibrations, was from 68 to 72 cents, or approximately a third of a wholetone lower.

WOLFGANG AMADEUS MOZART led that magnificent, scintillating age to a peak.

He was born in Salzburg on January 27, 1756 and carefully brought up under the closest guidance of his father Leopold, who was a well-educated violinist in the service of the Archbishop of Salzburg and the author of the aforementioned *Versuch einer gründlichen Violin-schule*. As a child prodigy, the son was taken to Munich and Vienna in 1762, to Paris in 1763, to London in 1764, and to Italy in 1769. The Germans and the French, the English and the Italians, received him with open arms, admiring the perfection of his harpsichord playing, the maturity of his compositions, and loving the warmth of his heart, his unassuming modesty, and his excellent manners. He himself, perhaps more than anybody else, could steadily widen his musical horizon in the closest contact with foreign masters and styles in the leading countries of Europe.

His adult life did not keep the promises of a glorious career that his younger years had made. Unable to find any adequate position, equally unfit to cope with the cabals of stage and concert life, and far from the blessings of an orderly domestic establishment, he created the greatest of his works in ever more troubled circumstances, died, only thirty-five years old, on December 5, 1791 in Vienna, and was buried in an anonymous common grave.

Without listing his earlier compositions, in which the Italian influence is particularly strong, we will confine ourselves to the principal scores of the last and truly Mozartian decade of his life, from 1781 to 1791.

In mentioning them, I must warn the reader that Mozart gave no opus numbers to his compositions. Their modern numbering with a capital *K*, as K.100, refers to Ludwig Koechel's *Chronologisch-thematisches Verzeichnis sämtlicher Tonwerke W. A. Mozarts* (1862), which was revised by Alfred Einstein in 1937 (1947).

Turning the pages of this portly volume, we are confronted with a tremendous, nay, unbelievable output for so short a life. It embraces all kinds of operas and cantatas, of symphonies and serenades, of chamber music, sonatas, *Lieder*, and Masses. Of operas from his last ten years, we mention:

Die Entführung aus dem Serail, or Abduction from the Seraglio, a German *Singspiel* on a text by Stephanie, 1781

Le Nozze di Figaro, or The Marriage of Figaro, an Italian *opera buffa* on a text by Da Ponte, 1783

Don Giovanni, a *dramma giocoso*, on a text by Da Ponte, 1787

Così fan tutte, an Italian *opera buffa* on a text by Da Ponte, 1790

Die Zauberflöte (The Magic Flute), a German opera on a text by Schikaneder, 1791

La Clemenza di Tito, an Italian *opera seria* on a text by Mazzolà after Metastasio, 1791

As representatives of the larger instrumental forms, let us add the three great symphonies in *E* flat major, *G* minor, and *C* major ('Jupiter'), all written in 1788, and, as a representative of the smallest vocal forms, the Lied *Das Veilchen* (The Violet) on a text of Goethe. It would be grotesque to juxtapose this miniature and the titanic frescoes, were it not that Mozart's genius makes mere size an invalid quality. The chamber music in between—as well as his serenades and concertos for piano, violin, harp, flute, clarinet, bassoon, French horn—are so overwhelming in number and quality that one would be at a loss to pick out a few characteristic examples. But one work, to which old Bach seems to have stood godfather, must be singled out: the *Requiem*. When death overcame the master, only the first half was completed, up to the *Lacrimosa*; Franz Xaver Süssmayer, a disciple, continued and finished the whole in Mozart's style.

In all these works, we face an equipoise unique and beyond discussion. In Mozart's operas, music does not merely serve the drama without any right of its own, nor, on the contrary, is the action sacrificed to undramatic melodies or mere virtuoso technique. He did not renounce the beauty of well-wrought form for significance, nature, or character, nor did he immolate the truth of nature and character to empty, sensuous charm or ingratiating elegance. He did not hesitate to give his *opera buffa* all the wealth and weight of the opera *seria* or, the other way around, to ease the tension of tragedy. On his instruments he bestowed the soul and breath of human voices, so that the slower movements of his symphonies often look like arias, and the faster ones, like the spirited finales of operas. Again, he led his voices with the skill of the well-experienced symphonic composer. He was the never-surpassed poet of rounded, heartfelt, smiling melodies, and yet he knew when the iron discipline of strict polyphony was needed. In vain, would you look for the typical German in him, in vain for an adopted Italian. Reconciling beauty and character, German and Italian spirit, the tragic and the comic, drama and music, voices and instruments, melos and counterpoint, he was graced in a blissful moment of history to hold the scales of style in perfect balance.

READING

Curt Sachs, *The History of Musical Instruments*, New York, 1940. *The Commonwealth of Art*, New York, 1946. *Rhythm and Tempo*, New York, 1953. Alfred Einstein, *Gluck*, London, 1936. Otto Vrieslander, *Karl Philipp Emanuel Bach*, München, 1923. Charles Sanford Terry, *John Christian Bach*, London, 1929. Karl Geiringer, *Haydn*, New York, 1946. Johann Joachim Quantz, *Versuch einer Anweisung die Flöte traversiere zu spielen*, ed. Schering, Leipzig, 1906. Leopold Mozart, *Versuch einer gründlichen Violinschule*, Wien, 1922. Carl Philipp Emanuel Bach, *Essay on the True Art of Playing Keyboard Instruments*, ed. Mitchell, New York, 1949. Francesco Geminiani, *The Art of Playing on the Violin* (1751), facs. ed. Bovden, London, 1952. Percy A. Scoles, *The Great Dr. Burney*, London, 1948. Alfred Einstein, *Mozart*, New York, 1945. Ludwig Koechel, *Chronologischthematisches Verzeichnis sämtlicher Tonwerke W. A. Mozarts* (1862), rev. by Alfred Einstein in 1937 (1947) Edward J. Dent, *Mozart's Operas*, London, 1947. Karl Geiringer, *The Bach Family*, New York, 1954.

18

THE AGE OF
BEETHOVEN AND SCHUBERT

1791–1828

THE FRENCH REVOLUTION of 1789 found the arts all over the West in a turn toward strictest classicism. The architects were working on a Roman revival; feminine dresses were imitating the fashions of the earliest times A.D.; and Canova's statues, Louis David's paintings, and Goethe's dramas were drawing their inspiration and laws from antiquity. Music, though paying a short tribute to the nightmare of the Revolution in a few 'horror' operas, was, for the rest, united with its sister arts in a classicism that imposed the iron rule of balance, structure, and restraint upon expression.

Luigi Cherubini (pron. *k*), a Frenchman of Italian descent (1760–1842), who became director of the new Conservatory of Music in Paris, was the oldest master in the classical line. He wrote very excellent church music and, above all, two Requiem Masses, one for mixed, and one for men's, voices. His dramatic creations, descended from Gluck, were noble and successful. But the curse of short-lived existence, so common in the world of opera, has buried in oblivion even his greatest masterworks, *Médée* (1797) and *Les deux journées* (1800). At least it should not be forgotten that the overture preceding *Médée* set the pattern of the noble, heroic style that Beethoven, ten years later, gave to his *Coriolan* overture.

LUDWIG VAN BEETHOVEN, scion of a Flemish family, was baptized on December 17, 1770, and born probably on the day before, in Bonn on the Rhine. His father and grandfather were, or had been, singers and conductors, and he himself was from the age of eight prepared for the career as a child prodigy of Mozartian cast. But less lucky than Mozart, he grew up in a rather dissolute house, went to public school only to the age of eleven, and had at home a kind of musical education which was strenuous, sketchy, and inferior, to say the least. Only with the arrival of Christian Gottlieb Neefe, who had been appointed organist of the Electoral court in 1779, did Beethoven find himself under the care of a well-trained, open-eyed musician who, realizing the genius of the boy, gave him systematic instruction and got him positions as an assistant organist in the church, as a harpsichordist in the court orchestra, and as a viola player in the theater.

As early as 1783 a few of his compositions were printed. Three years later, he traveled to Vienna in order to meet his idol, Mozart, but hastened back to Bonn when he learned that his mother was fatally ill. He found her still alive, but it was not long before he had to bury his "good, lovable, best friend." After her death, the distinguished house of the von Breunings gave him a second home and gentle guidance.

Nevertheless, when Haydn happened to stay over in Bonn on his way back from London, Ludwig decided to break away from the narrow conditions of the small, provincial residence and, twenty-one years old, moved to Vienna, the new capital of the musical world and home of Haydn and Mozart. Mozart had been dead for some months. But Ludwig found teachers in Haydn, Schenk, Salieri, and Albrechtsberger. He also was well received in the houses of music-loving aristocrats, whose names appear in the dedications of his works—Archduke Rudolph, Prince Lobkowitz, and Prince Lichnowsky who let him live in his palace for two years. Even his none-too-rare ill-mannered outbursts could never seriously disturb his good relations with the social elite, who sensed in him not only a matchless genius, but also a profoundly good, kindly, and noble character.

Beethoven's life, alternating almost rhythmically between the city in the winter and the country during the summer, was hardly ever interrupted by outer events. But seen from within, it spanned the whole gamut from trivial adversity to actual tragedy. The smaller, though telling, mishaps may be left to the master's biographers. They hinged on money, distrust of publishers, tailors, and charwomen, and an inborn restlessness. Worse was the burden of a vulgar, troublesome brother who embittered many years of Beethoven's life. The brother's death gave little release; against the claims of a disreputable mother, he tried to gain, and finally was given, the custodianship of the surviving son, only to find the nephew just as disappointing as the parents had been. But the worst affliction came from a disease of the ears, which appeared as early as 1798 and led gradually to total deafness. From 1819, he kept conversation books where visitors wrote down their part of the talk. Deafness barred him from hearing his own music; it isolated him socially, making any contact with people excruciating; and it excluded marriage. Two early evidences, the Heiligenstadt Testament of 1802 and the Letter to the (still unidentified) Immortal Beloved of 1807, both deeply moving, give a vivid idea of his growing loneliness. "My very best to your wife," he wrote in 1816 to Ferdinand Ries; "I have none, alas; I never found or will ever get one; this does not mean that I am a woman-hater."

On March 26, 1827, eleven years later, more secluded than ever, he died from a fibrosis of the liver.

The years of boyhood excepted, he never held any of the positions at court or in a church that, till then, had supported the best musicians and in turn had exacted from them routine composing for daily consumption and often swift oblivion. More than any composer before him, he wrote only what an inner urge enforced; and more than any composer before him, he waited for inspiration. It took him eight years, from 1815 to 1823, to finish the Ninth Symphony, and he composed no less than four different overtures to his opera *Fidelio* (II in 1805, III in 1806, I in 1807, all under the name of *Leonore*, and a fourth in 1814 under the name of *Fidelio*).

As a consequence, he left fewer compositions than earlier men like Haydn or even Mozart, whose life had been so much shorter: one opera, *Fidelio*, against Mozart's twenty; two Masses, against Mozart's fifteen; one oratorio, *Christus am Oelberg* (1803); nine symphonies, against Mozart's forty-one or, including his *divertimenti*, seventy-two; one violin concerto, against Mozart's six. Each of these works is an entity in itself, momentous, weighty, unprecedented in earlier pieces and never repeated in years to come.

This personal way of creation brings Beethoven close, suspiciously close, to romantic ideals. And he has, indeed, often enough been called a romanticist—even by his romantic contemporaries. True, he found the subjects of his art deep in the personal experience of the heart; true, he used to describe his own confusion and conflict. Hence the many violent outbursts, brusque interruptions, and stubborn syncopations in which his works abound.

But in confessing the troubles of his soul, he never yielded to romantic sentiment or dreaminess. His art, as probably no music before him, hardly left the realm of a relentless struggle for character, strength, freedom, and ultimate peace. He was and remained the conqueror, the master of himself. In this purposeful, masculine attitude, he acted as a true classicist, raising the conflict in himself to the conflict of mankind, dissolving the individual in the general, and finding the way from the accidental and accessory to a last sublimation and essence. As a classicist, he did not allow any extramusical concept to interfere with the inner logic of music—even his almost programmatic Pastoral Symphony (No. 6, *F* major) was not intended to be descriptive; "rather an expression of feeling than a picture," he defined it himself. But his inner logic was far from following conventional patterns; on the contrary, each one of his works has a form of its own. And, against and beyond the structural trends of his predecessors, he increasingly strove for the strictest integration, in which some work of gigantic size would develop from one melodic idea. The *C* sharp minor quartet (Op. 131, 1826) is a good example. And like Mozart, he drew, in his ripest style, quite close to Bach and embodied the most closely woven of forms, the fugue.

Since Anton Schindler's *Biographie* of Beethoven (1840) it has become customary to divide the master's work into three successive periods—a procedure helpful in orientation, but dangerously deceptive in its oversimplification. His divisions—which later authors slightly modified—are:

First Period up to 1800, "the time of learning and preparation," ending with the Septet.

Second Period up to 1814, which we might call the time of maturity, including all the symphonies, except the Ninth.

Third Period from 1815 on, which we might call the time of fulfillment, with the *Missa solemnis*, the Ninth Symphony, and the last quartets.

It is difficult, if not impossible, to single out the pieces of greatest importance and beauty from so exceptional a lifework. Conductors

would point at his nine symphonies and at a couple of overtures—
Coriolan, *Egmont*, the three *Leonores*, or *Fidelio*; pianists would think
of five concertos of a truly symphonic cast and of thirty-two sonatas,
among them the so-called *Emperor Concerto* in *E* flat major and the
Appassionata in *F* minor (Op. 57, 1806); violinists, of his *D* major
concerto (Op. 61, 1806), sixteen string quartets, and sonatas; and
'cellists, of five sonatas.

They all, however, agree on one important point: Beethoven's
greatness becomes manifest in his instrumental music in whatever form,
while his oratorio, *Lieder*, and other vocal compositions, excepting the
Missa solemnis (1818–1823), are rather on the periphery of his (and
of our) interest, although the master called the voices in to climax his
symphonic work with the solos and choruses at the end of the Ninth.

The seeds that Haydn had planted bore their ripest, ultimate fruit
in Beethoven's symphonies. "The depth, dramatic power, and conflict
of tragic passions" that the preceding chapter of this book has claimed
for Haydn, reached their highest peaks in Beethoven's symphonies.
Not that all his symphonies are 'profound.' Some are smiling, gay, and
even playful. But these are fertile, idyllic valleys between the craggy,
towering alps of the Third, or *Eroica*, the Fifth, in *C* minor, the Seventh,
in *A* major, and the all-human, supra-human Ninth, in *D* minor.

The nine symphonies are:

> First, *C* major, Op. 21 (1800)
> Second, *D* major, Op. 36 (1802)
> Third (Eroica), *E* flat major, Op. 55 (1804)
> Fourth, *B* flat major, Op. 60 (1806)
> Fifth, *C* minor, Op. 67 (1808)
> Sixth (Pastoral), *F* major, Op. 68 (1808)
> Seventh, *A* major, Op. 92 (1812)
> Eighth, *F* major, Op. 93 (1812)
> Ninth, *D* minor, Op. 125 (1823)

The Nine—despite their greater freedom and size—continue and
intensify not only the powerful significance that Haydn had given
to his instrumental works, but also the characteristic sonata form of
Haydn with its dramatic 'development.' It was even in keeping with
Haydn's transformation of the minuet as the third symphonic movement
into a genuine Austrian *Ländler* (though still under the conventional

name) that Beethoven dropped the inadequate name of the courtly dance and introduced the Italian title *scherzo* (pron. skertso) which allowed him to preserve the lightfooted three beats, but to free it from dance limitations and to make it now gay (as the name implies), now exuberant, now full of expectation.

In a similar way, the concertos and the chamber music followed in the wake of Haydn, to take the lead when the older master laid down his pen. The concerto, once designed to show the virtuoso's brilliant technique without much care for 'content,' became in Beethoven's hands a symphony with solo piano or violin, which was no longer merely accompanied by the orchestra, but blended and vied with it as an individual behaves in a group. His chamber music started from the older concept of a noble parlor entertainment, but became increasingly meaningful and esoteric and culminated in three almost mystic quartets —in *C* sharp minor, in *A* minor, and in *F* major—of 1825 and 1826, which were beyond the comprehension of Beethoven's contemporaries.

In his one opera, *Fidelio* or *Leonore* (in three versions of 1805, 1806, and 1814), Beethoven wrote the drama of the faithful wife who, hiding her sex in a man's attire, has taken a lowly position in the jail where her husband is held as a political prisoner and saves his life from the assassin through her courageous intervention. Such breath-taking drama would have called for a heroic opera in the vein of Gluck. But the librettists, Joseph Sonnleithner and Georg Friedrich Treitschke, spoiled the work by drawing freely from the opposite styles of the French *opéra comique* and the German *Singspiel*. It was this unfortunate hodgepodge of the great and the banal, of the sublime and the ridiculous, that caused its failure and forced the composer twice to transform the original score.

THE OPERATIC SITUATION was sounder in France, where the styles were neatly kept apart. Gluck's grandeur was alive in the works of the organist Etienne-Nicolas Méhul (1763–1817), particularly in *Joseph* (1807) which however had the spoken dialogue of the *opéra comique*, and in two earlier works of the Franco-Italian Gásparo Spontini (1774–1851), the incredibly successful *Vestale* (1807) and, preshadowing the *grand opéra* of Paris, *Ferdinand Cortez* (1809). Spontini's later scores, however, like *Olympie* (1819) and *Nurmahal* (1821), written shortly before or during his twenty-two years as the Musical Director General of the Royal Opera in Berlin, descended to a showiness which more and more disgusted the public, until he was forced to quit his post in 1841.

Besides Méhul and Spontini, both masters in the wake of Gluck's heroic style, the French could boast of two accomplished composers in a lighter vein: Boieldieu and Auber. François-Adrien Boieldieu (1775–1834) had the curious fate to see his two greatest successes separated by twenty-five years, *Le Calife de Bagdad*, in 1800 (and still alive in its overture) and *La Dame blanche* (The White Lady) in 1825, which reached a thousand performances within forty years. Daniel-François-Esprit Auber (1782–1871), master of the graceful, light-footed comic opera, achieved recognition with *Le Maçon* (The Mason) in 1825 and a lasting triumph with *Fra Diavolo* in 1830.

The overwhelming international success of the time, however, was *Il Barbiere di Seviglia* by a young Italian, Gioacchino Rossini (1792–1868), so truly international that only three years after its first performance in Rome (1816) it had already reached the stage in New York. Like the libretto of Mozart's *Figaro*, its text was taken from Caron de Beaumarchais's comedy *Le Barbier de Séville* (1775) and Rossini wrote the music in the incredibly short time of thirteen days. The Barber was the last important work in the style of the older Italian *opera buffa*, with sweetish arias, brilliant coloraturas, and witty, catchy ensembles. And it was the very last one with a *recitativo secco*, or rapidly pattered recitative without accompaniment except for the dry and commonplace harmony of piano chords. In the same year (1816) he replaced it for good by orchestral recitative accompaniments in his *Otello* (which, as an *opera seria*, required them anyway).

THE GERMAN OPERA, very far from the glittering, playful sensuousness of Rossini's scores, was thoroughly romantic, with the particular theme of relations between immortals and mortals on the stage and the expressive power of chords and modulations in the orchestra. Two momentous works of this type appeared in 1816, the very year of the Barber and of Otello: one, *Undine*, by the poet-musician E. T. A. Hoffmann (1776–1822), and the other, *Faust*, by Ludwig Spohr (1784–1859). They prepared the path for the two greatest romantics of the stage before Wagner: Weber and Marschner.

Carl Maria von Weber (the *von* being his father's self-conferred knighthood), born in December 1786 of an old family of Austrian musicians, lived the restless life of the stage, became *Kapellmeister* of the opera at Prague in 1813, and of the Royal Opera at Dresden, Saxony, in 1816, where he also became the leader in a ten years' fight against the predominance of Italian opera companies in Germany. Forty years old, he died on a triumphal tour to London on June 4, 1826.

Weber wrote cantatas, choruses, *Lieder*, piano and chamber music. But the focus of his work was on the stage. Three of his operas deserve the attention of the world. The first, and in a way revolutionary, one is *Der Freischütz* (The Freeshooter), written in 1821 on a text by F. Kind as an ingenious blend of the simple, heartfelt *Singspiel* in the wake of Hiller and of the fairy-opera with all the romantic requisites of rustling German woods and hunting horns, of spooky nights and haunted glens, of the devil and magic bullets against the power of innocence, piety, and love—a play immortal in Germany, though little accepted abroad, where the magnificent overture, however, has a favorite place in concert programs. Richard Wagner was right when, at the master's reburial in Dresden in 1844, he said of him, "Behold, the Briton now is full of admiration, the Frenchman bows in praise, yet no one but the German can adore thee."

The second of the great three operas was *Euryanthe* (1823), on a text by Helmina von Chezy, typically romantic, too, in its dependence on supernatural forces, but turning its back on the simplicity of the *Singspiel* and its spoken dialogue, and in a way foreshadowing the world of *Lohengrin*. With a last, heroic effort, while consumption and ulcer of the larynx were shortening his life, Weber composed the third of the great operas, for the Covent Garden Theatre in London— *Oberon* (1826), on a text of Planché after C. M. Wieland's poem, arch-romantic once more, and laid in a motley world of medieval chivalry and elves, of oriental glare and a magic horn.

Weber's concert, chamber, and solo music, showy rather than profound, is more or less forgotten. One piano work lives on, however, the *Aufforderung zum Tanz*, or Invitation to Dance, either in its original form or in one of its subsequent orchestrations by Berlioz or by Felix

Weingartner. The brilliant piece is remarkable as the earliest musical evidence of the novel Viennese *waltz* in its fiery tempo and dash with an exclusive stress on the first beat of the three—"the Viennese waltz surpasses everything in wild fury," says a contemporary—as against the many waltzes and *Deutsche* of the time, in which the weightier, hobnailed nature of the ancestral *Ländler* had not yet been discarded.

There is in all the works of Weber a remarkable contrast with the style of Beethoven. He is quite unconcerned with polyphony, symphonic development, or the problems of form. On the other hand, he has an astonishing *cantabile* in the popular vein (the word is meant in its best sense), and also in the higher realms of expression, though even there he takes his themes by preference from broken chords. Above all, he has the ability of the true dramatist to shift suddenly from sereneness to fear, from mirth to despair.

Weber would not have been a real romantic without a stress on the emotional atmosphere of sound as such, and, therefore, on the colorful language of harmony and orchestration. When in the *Freischütz* overture the tranquil quartet of the horns leads to the terrifying diminished-seventh chord of the *tremolo* strings with the fearful 'celli groaning above, the simple passage loses nothing of its gooseflesh effect on the listener.

Weber's name is also connected with an entirely unromantic by-way in the musical field. As a boy, he became interested in Aloys Senefelder's recent invention of 'lithographic' printing from plates of polished stone on which an artist had drawn with greasy ink or pencil. And Weber claimed to have improved it, for the benefit of music, to replace the costlier process of engraving. He was hardly fourteen years old, in 1800, when he lithographed his own Variations for the Piano Op. 2.

Heinrich Marschner (1795–1861), closer to the *Freischütz* than to Weber's two later operas, opened, with *Der Vampyr* (1828) and *Hans Heiling* (1833), the path into the ominous world of Wagner's Flying Dutchman.

FRANZ SCHUBERT, the greatest early romantic outside opera, died two years after Weber, and one year after Beethoven. His life had been tragically short and uneventful. He was born on January 31,

1797, in Vienna. His father was a school teacher, and his parental home, though poor, a meetingplace of serious musical friends and quartet players. At the age of eleven, he became, like Haydn, a choirboy, though in the famous Imperial Chapel in the *Hofburg*, or palace, not in St. Stephen's, and found an outstanding master in its conductor Antonio Salieri (1750–1825), who had also been one of Beethoven's teachers. After his mutation, he toiled for four years as an elementary-school assistant—but *not* in order to escape from military service, for which he was too weak and too short anyway (he measured less than five feet). Once more, his biography converged with Haydn's when, twenty years old, he accepted (and soon gave up) a position as a teacher in the Eszterházy family. He spent the short remainder of his life without any position, supported by the good will and the modest means of his friends, until, only thirty-one years old, he died on November 19, 1828. Upon his express desire, he was interred not far from the tomb of his idol Beethoven, who had preceded him a year before.

Although a faithful admirer of Beethoven, Schubert was in many ways his antipode. To the preponderantly instrumental imagination of the older master, he answered with a basically vocal attitude; to concentrated motivic elaboration, with broadly stretching, song-like melodies; to Beethoven's steely masculine energy and discipline, with an almost feminine submissiveness to the constant flow of inspiration. This yielding was romantic; and romantic, too, was Schubert's un-Beethovenian delight in the sensuous beauty of sound, in the characterizing force of modulating chords, in the juxtaposition of cheerful major and saddening minor. But above all, he was a romantic in finding the gravitational center of his work in the *Lied*, for which he drew inspiration from extramusical sources, without, however, sacrificing any of the laws of musical form.

We possess no less than six hundred and three *Lieder*, many of which form coherent cycles:

Die schöne Müllerin or *Müllerlieder* (1823), twenty songs on texts of Wilhelm Müller;

Die Winterreise (1827), twenty-four songs on texts of the same poet; while

Schwanengesang, 'Swan song' (1828), fourteen songs on texts of Heine, Rellstab, and Seidel, were collected at random after his death.

His most dramatic and powerful songs are among the more than seventy that he composed on words of Goethe, whom he had adored when still a boy. Such are *Erlkönig* (1815), *Ganymed* (1817), *Prometheus* (1819)—all matching greatness with greatness.

The "rational, pedantic dryness" of the First Berlin School has disappeared. Schubert does not yield to the poet nor does he domineer; as his peer, he renders the words in a musical language easily switched from lyrical, leisurely melody to power and pathos; and the piano, no longer toiling in the uniform clatter of broken chords, becomes itself the peer of the voice, interpreting, deepening, clarifying what the poet wants to convey, without interfering with the leading role of the voice.

Of Schubert's nine symphonies, only two have reached universal fame: the last, in *C* major (1828), "heavenly long," as its discoverer, Robert Schumann, praised it, and the tragic *B* minor symphony (1822), which he left unfinished after the first two movements. The numbering however, is so confused that a table should be added:

1. *D* major, 1813
2. *Bb* major, 1815
3. *D* major, 1815
4. *C* minor, 1816, The Tragic Symphony
5. *B* minor, 1816, The Symphony without Trumpets and Drums
6. *C* major, 1818, The Little Symphony
7. *C* major, 1828, The Great Symphony
8. *B* minor, 1822, The Unfinished
— A lost symphony, 1825.

Correctly, the last three symphonies should have the numbers 9, 7, and 8.

Of his numerous chamber music works—among them no less than twenty string quartets—at least four pieces have become common property of the musical world: an octet in *F* for strings, clarinet, horn, and bassoon (1824), a quintet for piano and strings in *A* (1819) with the surname *The Trout* because one of its movements is taken from a *Lied* of this name, a string quintet in *C* (1828), the string quartets in *A* minor (1824), in *G* (1826), and in *D* minor, the latter surnamed *Death and the Maiden* (1826) again because its slow movement is a set of variations on one of his early *Lieder* of this name. One might add to this list a piano trio in $B\flat$ (1827) and no less than twenty piano sonatas.

Schubert's unusual pleasure in making variations on his earlier songs, also evident in his *Wanderer Phantasy* for piano, shows how much his inspiration was vocal even in purely instrumental works.

It is hardly believable that beside this titanic work the thirty-one year old master left us fifteen dramatic compositions, among them the operas *Alfonso and Estrella* and *Fierrabras* and the incidental music to *Rosamunde*, all three in 1823. While these stage compositions are of minor importance, a good number of his many works for the church are still alive: seven complete Masses and twenty-two pieces of smaller dimensions, such as *offertoria, graduals,* and *tantum ergo* settings.

AS AN ESSENTIAL TREND of the time, musicians grew increasingly fond of physical power and volume. It would be a cheap expedient to make the outer facts responsible; namely, the public concert halls which replaced the smaller music rooms of princely palaces and the new conception of mass and grandiosity inseparable from the French revolution and the Napoleonic wars. An inner, and certainly more important, reason was the urge, characteristic of the age between 1760 and 1910, to get away from the often playful and always moderate spirit of yore, an urge to attain the extremes of expression, to achieve the most esoteric chamber music in almost inaudible *pianissimi*, or a clamorous, over-heated, overwhelming orchestral music in *fortissimi* on the verge of deafening the audience.

Monster performances became *à la mode*—and years before the revolution. In 1784, the English celebrated the memory of Handel in a festival at Westminster Abbey, in which five hundred and twenty-five players and singers participated, among them ninety-five violins, twenty-six oboes, and twenty-six bassoons; and it seems that the number was increased in subsequent years. The first performance of Haydn's *Creation* in 1798 used an orchestra of a hundred and eighty pieces; a performance of Handel's *Alexander's Feast* at Vienna in 1812 included an orchestra of about three hundred men, with a hundred and twenty violins, thirty-seven violas, thirty-three 'celli, and twenty-one doublebasses; a later production of Haydn's *Creation* in Vienna (1843) piled up a chorus of six hundred voices and an orchestra of three hundred and twenty pieces, with a hundred and eighteen violins. Obviously, Berlioz's famous dream orchestra, mentioned on page 279, was not far from reality. To be sure, such monster performances were exceptions; the current orchestras of the time, in opera houses and concert halls, necessarily kept within reasonable limits, with from twelve to forty violins, as compared with our usual modern maximum of thirty-two violins.

THE INSTRUMENTS themselves, even more than exceptional orchestras, give an unequivocal picture of the increasing fondness for physical power and volume. Most of them were improved in the direction of greater intensity; and quite a number of them, so far excluded from a regular and unimpaired role in the orchestra because of their incomplete range, submitted to radical changes and were accepted as equals.

The best example of increasing tone-volume is the evolution of the piano.

Invented two generations before and admitted to the concert stage in the sixties, the piano was given a front position and its modern 'pianistic' spirit, playing technique, and construction around 1800. The spirit was mainly due to Beethoven's predecessor, Muzio Clementi (1752–1832), the playing technique and fingering to Clementi and to the prolific etude-writer Carl Czerny (1791–1857), whose printed works—not pieces!—number almost one thousand.

The instrument itself reached a second peak with Johann Andreas Stein in Augsburg (whom Mozart praised in a letter of 1777 as one of the very best masters) and his son-in-law Johann Andreas Streicher in Vienna. But while the delicate, easy Viennese piano, sailing still in the wake of ancestral clavichords and harpsichords, was well in keeping with the easy technique of the native masters of Vienna, the Czerny, Herz, or Hünten, it was unfit to render the weight and power of Beethoven's sonatas and piano concertos. That Beethoven owned an English Broadwood, not one built by Streicher (who was his friend, though), symbolizes the victory of the recent western piano, which was developing away from the past toward the new ideals of orchestral volume. Thus, it is surely untrue that the master had written for clavichords and harpsichords before he designed his sonata in *B* flat major in 1817 expressly for the *Hammerklavier*. He himself explained the sudden appearance of this unprecedented title: he wrote to his publisher that henceforth he wanted the word piano to be replaced by *Hammerklavier* in works with German titles.

The pioneers of the powerful western piano were John Broadwood in London, Sébastien Erard in Paris, and John Isaac Hawkins in Philadelphia. Broadwood was the first builder to cut the ties with the clavichord and the harpsichord in the outer shape as well as the inner construction. In 1800 Hawkins invented the earliest metal braces between the wrestplank with the pegs and the soundboard in order to counteract the thicker strings of the time with their ever-increasing tension. In 1821, Erard created the modern, fully reliable action with the double escapement, or automatic backfall, of the hammers to a position midway between rest and stroke, which allowed for a ready repetition of tones.

Four years later, in 1825, the piano-builder Alphaeus Babcock in Boston designed the earliest full cast-iron frame to take the tension of the strings entirely off the soundboard and the outer case. At last, the same Babcock devised in 1830 the so-called over-strung scale. In this modern arrangement, the bass strings stretch diagonally across and a little above the higher strings. This allows them to profit from the better-resounding middle of the soundboard instead of being left to the ineffectual margin, and it also allows them to arouse better the sympathetic co-vibrations of the higher strings and thus to increase the intensity of partials.

Indeed, the modern piano originated in the three decades from 1800 to 1830.

The harp, too, was then given its definitive form. The harp in use during the eighteenth and early nineteenth centuries had had a 'single action.' Tuned in diatonic, 'white-key' sequence, it had been able to sharp each of the seven notes in the octave by a semitone with the help of one out of seven pedals. But despite these seeming chromatic possibilities, it had been unable to play in any of the flat keys: even *F* major, with only one flat, required the open *A* string *and* the sharped *A* string which had to supply the *B*♭.

Sébastien Erard in Paris solved the problem by giving the seven pedals a 'double action': an open string in C flat, for example, was shortened to C natural by pressing the corresponding pedal halfway down, and to C sharp, by pressing it all the way down. As a consequence, most black-key notes could be provided by two different strings. Clarifying diagrams can be found on pages 400 and 401 of this author's *History of Musical Instruments.*

THE WIND INSTRUMENTS, in their turn, hastened to complete their families. The clarinets appeared in all sizes, as sopranos, altos, basses, and even double-basses. Bands and orchestras were given solid fundamentals in the forms of serpents and bass-horns (illustrations in the same work on pages 421 and 423), which were clumsy, wide-bored wooden horns in double-S or bassoon form with open fingerholes and keys derived from the age-old *zink* (*cf.* page 159). Military bugles and the somewhat narrower cornets of postilions were developed into complete sets of sopraninos, sopranos, altos, and tenors.

The fingerholes and keys of serpents and bass-horns led to the central problem connected with the orchestral use of brasses. Far from having a complete scale from semitone to semitone, the horn and trumpet instruments had depended upon the few and incoherent 'overblowing' notes. This term indicates a steady increase of tension given to the player's lips, which results in producing other, higher notes than the 'fundamental' note produced by the weakest possible tension of the lips. Any taps sounded by an army bugle show the principle. They also show that the overblowing notes are in a natural, immutable relation: coinciding with the acoustical 'partials' of the fundamental, they are its octave, twelfth, double octave, double octave *plus* major third, and so on (*cf.* Appendix). How many of these overblowing notes can actually be produced, depends upon the bore and mouthpiece of the instrument as well as upon the skill of the player.

The first step in adding artificial notes to this natural skeleton had been taken many centuries before with the adoption of slides. Trombones and certain trumpets were made telescopic, so that the changing length of the tube provided a sufficient stock of fundamentals—up to seven in semitone distance—with their overblowing notes.

French horns, indispensable in the orchestra of the later eighteenth century, were unfit for slides for reasons of form and bore. Instead, in the 1750's they had submitted to 'stopping.' Changing from their older bell-up position to a bell-down position, they allowed the player's right hand to reach into the bell and therewith to lower the individual overblowing notes by a half- or a wholetone. But the stopped notes were muffled, inferior in timbre, and the players were seldom able to cover the embarrassing difference of stopped and open notes. And anyway, if stopping was possible on circular, wide-belled horns, it was impossible on other, straight and narrow-belled instruments.

It was more promising to try as a way out the key-covered finger-holes of the serpent. 1801 saw a keyed trumpet, and 1810 a keyed bugle (ill. *ibid.*, page 425). Within a few years, the latter developed into a family in alto, bass, and *monstre* sizes, which became well known for a short time under the grotesque name of *ophicléides*, or serpent-keys, although the instruments had the more conservative shape of a bassoon and not the fancy form of the serpent.

All these keyed instruments were discarded within a few decades. For in the meantime, from 1813, two German players had produced an infinitely better and definitive chromatization with their invention of valves and pistons (ill. *ibid.*, page 427ff). Instead of the required extra lengths being added in the form of a telescope-like slide, as in the case of the trombone, they were held in readiness in three U-shaped 'crooks' branching off the main tube. By the light pressure of a rotary valve or a vertical piston, these were switched on or off in order to lower the original set of 'natural,' or 'open,' notes, one for a semitone (usually, for reasons of space, between the two others and hence, properly speaking, the second, but, for the sake of better understanding, called the first in the following table.) Another valve served for two semitones (our second), and a third for three semitones. Indeed, two or even all three of the crooks could be switched on at the same time and thereby would lower the original set of overblown notes by a major third, a fourth, or a tritone. Altogether, three fingers on three valves were able to produce so many artificial notes that the result was an uninterrupted, uniform chromatic scale:

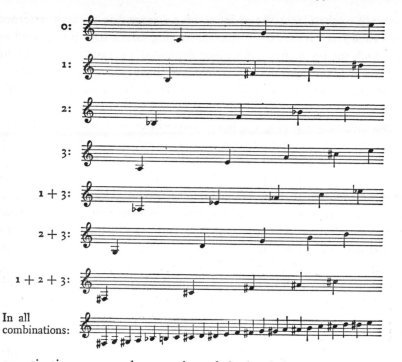

Chromatization even took possession of the kettledrums, though without a lasting success. In 1812, a kettledrummer in Munich, Gerhard Cramer, devised the earliest instrument of its kind to be tuned from semitone to semitone by a single movement, obviating the necessity for successive operation of six or eight individual tuning-screws.

TWO TEMPO REGULATORS, though not musical instruments in the usual sense, deserve a few short remarks in this context.

The first is the *metronome*, which was patented by Johann Nepomuk Mälzl (1772–1838) but was actually invented by the Dutchman Winkel. The apparatus consists of a ticking double-pendulum with a movable weight which, shifted up or down, determines its speed. The speed may be regulated according to a scale behind the pendulum: shifting the weight to, say, the mark 60 causes the pendulum to tick out sixty beats per minute. As a consequence, the composer's symbol at the beginning of a piece ♩ = MM 60 (Mälzl Metronome) conveys to the player the order to give a second to every quarternote. In a time from which the old, even-beating *tactus* had disappeared and in which the right effect of a piece depended a great deal upon finding out what tempo the composer had had in mind, the metronome became an almost indispensable companion of the composers as well as of the performers.

Beethoven was among the first masters interested in the possibility of prescribing the tempo of their compositions (although his MM's are not always reliable). As early as 1817, he returned to the scores of all his previous eight symphonies in order to metronomize them. And it is well known that, as a musical joke, he introduced evenly ticking eighthnotes in the scherzo of his Eighth in honor of Mälzl. Chronology, however, poses a question: the date of the metronome is 1816, and that of the Eighth is 1812. How could the master have celebrated the apparatus of Mälzl four years before it was invented? The answer is that in 1812 Beethoven had in mind an earlier, different contraption of Mälzl's, the *chronometer*, in which a little hammer struck an anvil.

As for the other time-beating device, the conductor's baton, in use long before, was given exclusive rights after 1800, although it was in a form much shorter and thicker than the modern one and was often grasped in the middle like a marshal's baton. François-Antoine Habeneck, conductor of the concerts of the *Conservatoire* in Paris (1781–1849 seems to have been the last to lead a symphonic orchestra with a violin bow.

READING

Alfred Einstein, *Music in the Romantic Era*, New York, 1947. Curt Sachs, *The History of Musical Instruments*, New York, 1940. *The Commonwealth of Art*, New York, 1946. *Rhythm and Tempo*, New York, 1953. Ludwig Schemann, *Cherubini*, Stuttgart, 1925. Alexander W. Thayer, *The Life of Ludwig van Beethoven*, New York, 1921. Leo Schrade, *Beethoven in France*, New Haven, 1942. Francis Toye, *Rossini*, London, 1934. Otto Erich Deutsch, *Schubert, Thematic Catalogue*, New York, 1951. *The Schubert Reader*, New York, 1947. Rosamond E. Harding, *The Piano-Forte*, Cambridge, 1933. *Origins of Musical Time and Expression*, Oxford, 1938.

19

THE AGE OF MENDELSSOHN, SCHUMANN, BERLIOZ

1828–1854

HE OPENING of this period at the year 1828 is justified not only as the year of Schubert's death and of Berlioz's Op. 1, Eight Scenes from Faust, but also as the year in which Auber inaugurated the unprecedented form of the *grand opéra* and made Paris once more the center of the musical world.

Grand opéra meant originally an opera with sung dialogue as against the spoken dialogue of the *opéra comique*. But from 1828 it had a narrower sense. Betraying the noble ideals of Gluck's heroic drama, it thrilled the senses with tumultuous choruses, pompous marches, heroes on horseback, conspiracies, prayers, clattering battles, murder, erupting volcanos, and burning palaces, with noisy orchestras, grandiose arias, and glittering ballets in places unexpected and unjustified. Grand opera meant, in Richard Wagner's biting words, "effect without cause" (although his own *Rienzi* and *Tannhäuser* were grand operas as well).

Auber's work, *Masaniello* or *La Muette de Pórtici*, dared present, as an operatic heroine, a dumb girl gesticulating to the accompaniment of the orchestra and at last leaping into the erupting Vesuvius; and the dotted rhythms of one of its arias were fiery enough to rouse an enthusiasm that unleashed the Brussels revolution of 1830 and helped in creating the Kingdom of Belgium.

The success of this new concept of opera was, alas, so great that in the year after *La Muette*, 1829, even Rossini, leader of the Italians, changed his style and wrote a French opera with *Guillaume Tell*, the national crossbow shooting hero of Switzerland, as the title figure and an unforgettable overture in the richest orchestral timbres.

273

It was another foreigner to Paris who lifted this pseudo-dramatic style to its peak, Giácomo (Jacob) Meyerbeer (1791–1864) a native of Berlin and a child prodigy on the piano. He was carefully educated in both Germany and Italy. An excellent musician and probably the best music psychologist as far as the expectations and receptivity of the public were concerned, he found in his famous librettist Eugène Scribe (1791–1861) of Paris an accomplished virtuoso of stage technique and an indefatigable inventor of ever new "effects without cause." Neglecting three unsuccessful German and seven successful Italian operas, the student might concentrate on the operas of Meyerbeer's Parisian period, which, owing to a superior technique, many a passage of greatest beauty, a brilliant, effective stage, and a truly dramatic genius, gave him his world fame and domineering position. Their sequence began with *Robert le Diable* (1831), culminated in *Les Huguenots* (1836) and *Le Prophète* (1848), and ended in *L'Africaine*, which Meyerbeer began in 1838 and only completed twenty-two years later in 1860.

Closest to Meyerbeer in style and time, and also with a libretto by Scribe, stood the still remembered opera *La Juive* (The Jewess), which the Parisian Froment Halévy (1799–1862), Bizet's father-in-law, wrote in 1835. Thirty-six more of his operas are forgotten.

The Italian opera of the time—which Rossini had prematurely abandoned in 1828—found two younger masters of importance: the Sicilian Vincenzo Bellini (1801–1835), whose *Norma* (1831) and *La Sonnambula* (1831, too) succeeded in maintaining the noble line of Gluck, although with a strong Italian flavor; and the North-Italian Gaetano Donizetti (1797–1841), who, in the serious *Lucia di Lammermoor* (1835) and the comic *Don Pasquale* (1843), followed in the less distinguished footsteps of Rossini.

Besides these westerners, one should not forget the earliest Russian-national composer, Michael Glinka (1804–1857) and his long-lived opera, *A Life for the Czar* (1836), which was not of a very outspoken national cast but enough so that the cosmopolitan Russian aristocracy sneered at it as "coachmen's music." Glinka's last opera, *Russlan and Ludmilla* (1842) was by far more national and, incidentally, anticipated Debussy's wholetone scale.

The symphonic music of the time expanded between two poles, between Mendelssohn and Berlioz.

FELIX MENDELSSOHN—later called Mendelssohn-Bartholdy—was born on February 3, 1809 in Hamburg, where the family, native of Berlin, stayed for a couple of years. Grandson of a famous philosopher and son of a wealthy banker, he marked a new step in the social history of music: not the scion of a dynasty of cantors or organists, not a musical incident in an indigent family, not the music student against his father's will, he was the first prepared to become a musician by well-to-do, highly cultivated parents. But to him the musical training was only part of a thorough, many-sided education, rounded off in the spirited social life of which the Mendelssohn house had become a center. Indeed, he was privileged to enjoy the hospitality and friendship of Goethe, who was sixty years his senior.

After his school years, he visited Switzerland, Italy, England, Scotland, and France, playing the piano and the organ, composing, and making friends everywhere. An enormous amount of delightful, affectionate letters reflect the happiness of these *wanderjahre*.

A strictly professional life began at the age of twenty-four. After brief activities as a conductor in Düsseldorf and Cologne, he accepted the direction of the *Gewandhauskonzerte* (Drapers' Hall Concerts) in 1835 and founded the Royal Conservatory of Music in 1843, both at Leipzig, making this city almost at one blow a capital of the musical world. Shortly later, his health began to fail. Only thirty-eight years old, he died on November 4, 1847.

The most popular of his numerous works are probably the shorter chorus songs, now at home in untold churches, and, in the wake of Schubert's *Impromptus* and *Moments Musicaux*, the short and lyrical *Songs without Words* (around 1830) which have been on every music student's piano. Concert-goers are particularly familiar with the overture for Shakespeare's *Midsummer Night's Dream*, written at the age of only seventeen, and the incidental music for the same play, including the perennial *Wedding March*, which he wrote when he was thirty-four. Hardly less known are the overture known as the *Hebrides*, or *Fingal's Cave* (1830–1832, after a stay in Scotland); the *Italian Symphony* (1833) and the *Scotch Symphony* (1842); the oratorios *St. Paul* (1836) and *Elijah* (1846), and a choral cantata *The First Night of St.*

Walpurgis (1832–1843); the *E* minor concerto for violin (1844); and all kinds of chamber music (a string octet, two string quintets, seven string quartets).

Balanced in his character and happy in his life, Mendelssohn found little to tell of passion, struggle, despair. His was the classic serenity of an aristocratic soul and the polished diction and well-chased form of a man of the world. His works were born of a loving, not a bleeding, heart; they were neither titanic nor violent, but always sunlit, blissful, and pure. (As this page goes to press, Dr. Eric Werner's newly won access to unpublished materials might cast new light on Mendelssohn's personality.)

From early childhood on, his parents imbued him with the love of Bach, and Bach became the great ideal from which he never swerved. As a boy, he introduced even Goethe into the magic world of the *Well-tempered Clavier*. Twenty years old, he discovered the lost manuscript of the Passion After St. Matthew and, against all resistance, performed it for the very first time with the chorus of the Berlin *Singakademie* on March 11, 1829, exactly one hundred years after Bach had written it.

THE EVENT was indicative of two different developments. The first one was the glorious evolution of middle-class choral societies at a time when the church choirs of all denominations were nearing the lowest level. Attemps to develop choral societies had been made before in the eighteenth century, particularly in England and Germany. But the movement became momentous only after the ex-harpsichordist of Frederick the Great, Carl Friedrich Fasch (1736–1800), had founded the earliest choral society with more than a local impact: the *Berliner Singakademie* (1791). From twenty-seven original members, it grew under Carl Friedrich Zelter, Mendelssohn's teacher, to nearly five hundred in Mendelssohn's time and to more than six hundred after 1840.

The other German cities followed at a rapid pace with similar laymen's choral societies—Stettin in 1794, Königsberg in 1799, Leipzig in 1800.

London underwent an analogous development. Earlier in the century, weavers and other craftsmen had founded *The Madrigal Society*, conceding to their members one glass of porter and one pipe of tobacco as a maximum of extra-musical entertainment. In the 1790's, the movement became general with the *Long-Acre, Titchfield, Handelian*, and *Surry Chapel Societies*.

The typically Swiss concept of all-men's societies for singing, as established by Hans Georg Nägeli in Zürich (1773–1836), made considerable headway after 1805, at first in Switzerland and later in South Germany.

The United States, incidentally, had anticipated the latest events in Europe. Andrew Adgate founded an *Institution for the Encouragement of Church Music* in 1784. Three years later, it adopted the name *Uranian Academy of Philadelphia*, and not only gave vocal concerts, but also provided free singing lessons to its members.

WHILE THE CREATIVE WORK of their time was focused on instrumental rather than on choral music, these societies revived music of those periods productive of choral styles. They went back to Bach and Handel, and even to Palestrina and Lassus. In so doing, the choral movement converged with the second movement of which Felix Mendelssohn's resuscitation of the Passion was indicative: the return to older music.

The resurrection of the Passion was indeed the prelude—though hardly the cause—of an amazing awakening of interest in the music of the Baroque. In the 1830's, Dr. Carl Proske, originally a physician, collected an impressive library of sixteenth and seventeenth century works, published Palestrina's Marcellus Mass in 1850 for the first time, and began in 1853 to print an important series of ancient church music in ten volumes under the title *Musica Divina*. In 1837, the publishing house C. F. Peters in Leipzig began an edition of the complete works of Bach, and in 1839, Franz Commer in Berlin began a rival anthology of church music, in thirty-eight volumes, under the title *Musica Sacra*. Meanwhile, the Prince de la Moskowa founded in 1843 a *Société des Concerts de Musique Religieuse et Classique* in Paris and printed the pieces performed there in a *Recueil . . . de Musique Ancienne* in eleven volumes embracing two hundred years of music, from Arcadelt early in the sixteenth century to Handel and Bach. At last, the year 1850 witnessed the foundation of the *Bach Gesellschaft*, which began in the following year to print the authoritative edition of Bach's complete works, the earliest of a long, comprehensive list of *Gesamt-Ausgaben*.

H ECTOR BERLIOZ (pron. -ose) was born on December 11, 1803, near Grenoble in the southeast of France. His father, a doctor, planned a medical career for him; but he soon gave up anatomy and began to study composition, at first privately under Lesueur and later at the *Conservatoire* under Lesueur and Reicha. Once admitted, he applied for the coveted Rome prize; but his unorthodox writing brought him failure after failure, until the fifth attempt, in 1830, was successful. After Rome, his life in Paris was only occasionally interrupted by invitations to conduct his works abroad. He lived as an indefatigable free-lance composer, with a regular column in the *Journal des Débats* and an insignificant assistant librarianship at the *Conservatoire* as the only mainstays of a regular income. Demonic, fiery, tempestuous, he challenged critics and public again and again with his unconventional scores; triumphs and failures alternated; his private life was far from happy. A lonely fighter, he succumbed in Paris on March 8, 1869.

His numerous works include the operas *Benvenuto Cellini* (1837), *Les Troyens* (1863), and *Béatrice et Bénédict* (1862), all on librettos by himself, the last one from *Much Ado about Nothing*; the actual symphonies *Phantastique* (1830) and *Harold en Italie* (1834); the half-symphonic *Roméo et Juliette*, a 'dramatic symphony with choruses, vocal solos, and prologue in chorale recitative,' and, as a continuation of the *Phantastic Symphony*, *Lélio ou le Retour à la Vie* (Lelio [Berlioz himself] or Return to Life), written in 1831 in the form of 'a lyrical monodrama with orchestra, choruses, and invisible soloists'; the choral works *Requiem* (1837), *Te Deum* (1849), *La Damnation de Faust* (1846), and *L'Enfance du Christ*, Christ's Childhood, 1854.

Intimate music, for chamber ensembles or keyboard instruments, does not occur in Berlioz's works.

Like so many romantic composers of the time, Berlioz left a good number of literary works. The most important is the *Traité de l'Instrumentation et d'Orchestration* (1844), the earliest and still consulted manual in the field, which Richard Strauss revamped in 1905. A volume of critical essays was re-edited in 1862 under the punning title *A travers Chants* ('songs' instead of the consonant *champs*, 'fields'); and two volumes of *Mémoires* were published a year after his death.

Thinking of Berlioz means thinking of wild imagination, an enormity in sizes and ideas, and fascinating colors—an iridescent, dazzling color that often outshines form and line; an imagination that stops short of nothing, neither of bizarreness nor of morbidity; an enormity that finds an end in itself in gigantic proportions and the piling-up of masses never heard before. In the second section of his Requiem, he renders the trumpets of Doomsday with four *fortissimo* brass bands in addition to the orchestra and sixteen kettledrums; on his arrival in Rome, he planned to match the gigantic dimensions of St. Peter's with a "colossal" oratorio, *The Last Day of the World* (which was never written); and he dreamed of a utopian orchestra of 465 pieces, with 120 violins, 40 violas, 45 'celli, 37 doublebasses, 30 pianos, 30 harps—which, incidentally, was not entirely utopian (*cf.* page 267). In his *Phantastic Symphony*, Berlioz allows the hero—who was none other than Berlioz himself—to be dragged to the scaffold. In a second part, the half-symphonic monodrama *Lélio* or *Return to Life*, he awakens from an unsuccessful attempt to take his life. His was a self-centered extravagance that did not hesitate to trespass against the natural claims of musical expression.

Still, this picture should be modified. It certainly applies to the works he wrote before 1850; but the later creations, *Christ's Childhood, The Trojans*, and the comic opera, *Beatrice and Benedict*, show a remarkable, almost conservative moderation.

By the same token, his older admiration for Wagner turned in the later period of his life to a complete lack of understanding. Far from Wagner's strictly dramatic ideals, he found satisfaction in the concepts of grand opera. This is true not only of his dramatic works. Even the choral compositions and symphonies are, in the spirit of grand opera, full of fascinating episodes far-fetched and "without cause." There is the gruesome march to the scaffold in the *Phantastic Symphony*, the *Ronde des Pifferari* in the *Harold Symphony*, the scherzo *La Fée Mab* in the choral symphony *Roméo et Juliette*, the Hungarian *Rakoczy* march in *La Damnation de Faust*. This intrusion of music for the sake of music without inner, poetical necessity is particularly odd in the work of a master who took his inspiration so often from extra-musical provinces that ignoramuses have called him the 'father of program music.' This he was not. Nor was he the 'inventor' of the *leitmotiv* (*cf.* Chapter 20), although he availed himself of ever-recurring ego-symbols, both in the *Phantastic Symphony*—there, under the excellent title of *l'idée fixe*—and in the autobiographic viola solos of the *Harold Symphony*, which, in a way, broke the ground for the later *leitmotive* of Wagner.

Berlioz was indeed a pathfinder—the great pioneer of 'modern' music —who severed the ties with the past and reached for goals unknown before he came, who widened the scope of music to horizons never unveiled before he set his eyes on them, who gave the orchestra riches and significance of which no man before him had dreamed.

T HE WORD *VIRTUOSO* has appeared several times in the pages of this chapter. Virtuosity, indeed, had its heyday in the eighteen thirties and forties.

Virtuosos in the sense of accomplished masters of the voice or some instrument had always existed. All the great composers of whom the history of older music speaks were admirable singers or players, but their ability was in the service of creative work. (I am not speaking of the *castrati* and divas of the opera around 1700.)

The instrumental virtuosos of the earlier part of the nineteenth century were different. They concentrated on playing, and composed their pieces of doubtful musical value in the service of boastful bravura technique. Incredibly spoiled, adored, deified, they toured from country to country, from city to city, exhibited the glittering, empty passages of their *études brillantes* and paraphrases of popular operatic melodies, and distracted the interest of music lovers from creative art to dazzling, acrobatic dexterity.

Three out of many hundreds of names resounding all over the world may represent that curious epoch of nimble-fingered heroes, intoxicated, fanatic audiences, and red-ribboned laurel wreaths: in the field of the violin, the almost legendary, demoniacal Niccolò Paganini (1782–1840), and in the field of the piano, the Viennese Sigismund Thalberg (1812–1871) and young Liszt, who, disgusted, gave up his virtuoso career towards 1850 to turn to the higher aims of a composer and educator.

FREDERIC CHOPIN was, in a way, the strongest typically romantic master—thoroughly self-expressive, sensitive in the extreme, unbalanced, melancholy. Morbidly delicate as a man and a composer, tearful, desperately changing and rechanging every single measure, and pining, as Shelley would say, "for what is not," he was exclusively pianistic and gave his best in the smaller forms of preludes and ballades, nocturnes and impromptus, waltzes, mazurkas, and polonaises. Of greater forms, he wrote nothing but two concertos and four sonatas, one, in Bb minor, with the world-famous funeral march. He was entirely unpolyphonic and concentrated on melody, which he often dissolved in the foam of coloraturas that we would be tempted to relate to Italian arias, were they not so airy, sublimated, and poetic that any thought of boastful virtuosity seems out of place.

Out of his pining, painful struggle arose a musical world that, in a hundred years, with all its limitations, has lost nothing of its irresistible charm. Hardly any other of the earlier romantic generation has survived in equal freshness; hardly any other is equally convincing, whether he admits us to his fleeting dreams or chivalrous visions, to his hope or despair. And hardly any other of that age of rising nationalism is so supranational, so all-human.

Chopin was born in Warsaw on February 22, 1810, the year of Schumann's birth. Only his mother was Polish. His father was French, and a teacher. A child prodigy, he gave his first recital at the age of seven and studied composition with Elsner from 1822. In 1830, he left his country, never to return, stayed a year in Vienna and then reached Paris, which remained his permanent residence for the rest of his life. After years of professional successes as a composer and a teacher, he had a severe attack of laryngeal tuberculosis in 1838 and, accompanied by his friend, the authoress Georges Sand, tried, in vain, the milder climate of the Balearic Islands. His last ten years were spent in a depressing alternation of triumphs, sickness, and misery. Not yet forty years old, he died in Paris on October 17, 1849.

ROBERT SCHUMANN, born a few months after Chopin, on June 8, 1810, in Zwickau, Saxony, studied law at his mother's request but left the university after two years to become a musician. His career as a piano virtuoso found a premature end before it had started, when an ill-fated treatment, undertaken for the sake of greater mobility, resulted in a crippled hand (1832). Forced to give up all hope for public playing, he concentrated on composition and, with enthusiasm and masterly skill embarked upon musical criticism. In order to be financially independent, he founded the *Zeitschrift für Musik* to serve the cause of modern music against routine and frigid academicism and stayed for ten years at its helm. In a genuine romantic spirit, hard reality was disguised in fictional concepts and persons: the 'cause' was in the hands of the *Davidsbündler* or 'Leaguers of David,' who fought against the Philistines, and Schumann himself let the ardent impetuous side of his character appear as *Florestan*, and the mild, sympathetic side as *Eusebius*.

Romance and marital life, as a rule excluded from this book, must be mentioned here, where they are an integral part of music history. The heroine was Clara (b.1819), young, enchanting, and a gifted pianist and composer. Friedrich Wieck, her father and Schumann's piano teacher, was the 'villain' of the drama. He opposed the match, not without good reason, but at last, on Clara's majority, a court decision made the marriage possible.

Courtship and a few blissful years of marriage gave Schumann's composing an almost incredible impetus. But only two years after the wedding, in 1842, a nervous breakdown heralded the fatal depression of the time to come. Schumann became more and more tight-lipped and lost contact with the outer world. Although a lovable person, Schumann could never hold a position. Mendelssohn, a devoted friend, appointed him as a teacher in score-reading at the Conservatory in Leipzig; but after a few months, Schumann resigned. Another chance opened when, at the age of forty, he was called to Düsseldorf on the Rhine as the Municipal *Musikdirektor* (1850). Discharged three years later as a hopeless mental case, he jumped into the Rhine. He was rescued and confined in a sanitarium near Bonn. There he died, forty-six years old, on July 29, 1856.

Schumann wrote only four symphonies:

1. *B* flat major ('Spring'), 1841
2. *C* major, 1846
3. *E* flat major ('Rhenish'), 1850
4. *D* minor, 1841-1851.

He composed *Das Paradies und die Peri* (1843), Scenes from Goethe's *Faust* (1844–1853), *Der Rose Pilgerfahrt* (1851), and other choral works; an opera, *Genoveva* (1848), which the public received without enthusiasm, and incidental music for Byron's *Manfred* (1849), with a soul-stirring overture; among excellent chamber works, a driving piano quintet in *E* flat major, three string quartets, and a piano quartet, all in the year 1842; and a great number of beautiful *Lieder*, almost all in cycles, as *Liederkreis* and *Dichterliebe*, on poems by Heine, and *Frauen Liebe und Leben*, on pocms by Chamisso, written in the year of his marriage.

But nearest his heart was piano music. True, his piano pieces were written mainly in his twenties, between 1829 and 1839, and his one piano concerto, in *A* minor (1845)—perhaps the most Schumannesque of his works—was already a bridge to orchestral writing. But he never became a genuine orchestral composer, either in handling the instruments or in symphonic inspiration and technique. In all his scores, one senses the pianist.

His piano compositions shun the classical form of the sonata. He created, for the most part, what might be called poems, with the *Phantasie* in C major (1836) in the lead. The typically romantic predilection for smaller, lyrical character-pieces, apparent in Beethoven's *Bagatelles* and Schubert's *Impromptus* or *Moments musicaux*, in Mendelssohn's *Songs without Words* and Chopin's innumerable dances, preludes, and *nocturnes*, reappears in Schumann's work, onward from the time of the *Papillons* or Butterflies (1829–1831). Indeed, in the full romantic spirit of obsession with the night, Schumann matched Chopin's *Nocturnes* with *Nachtstücke* (1839).

But not until Schumann were such character-pieces published in homogeneous sets with related ideas and common titles, such as the *Davidsbündler Tänze* (1837–1850), the *Carnaval* (1835), the *Kinder-szenen* (1838), the *Kreisleriana* (1838–1850), and the *Faschingsschwank aus Wien*, or Carnival Fun from Vienna (1839), with an incognito appearance of the *Marseillaise*, then prohibited in reactionary Austria.

THE HISTORY OF INSTRUMENTS has a few remarkable dates during this period of 1828 to 1854.

The organ took the decisive step toward a modern action with two English inventions of the greatest import. Joseph Booth's fully pneumatic action of 1827 did away with the delicate, uneven 'mechanical' system which connected the keys and the pipes by wooden trackers, stickers, and hooks, and thus made playing easier, more even, and more dependable. Charles Spackman Barker (1806–1879) followed around 1832 with a more successful *pneumatic lever*, which preserved part of the mechanical-tracker system but added a wind-fed conduit to transmit the pull pneumatically by the aid of a relaying system of valves or pallets, the last of which opened the pipe (illustrations in the author's *History of Musical Instruments*, pages 442 and 443).

In a roundabout way, the organ conquered chapels and homes in the form of a cheap and small *ersatz* instrument with reeds, without pipes, and generally without pedals: the *harmonium*, which owes a great deal of its perfection to American manufacturers, although it comes from France. In 1836, A. Prescott & Son in Concord, New Hampshire, contributed the curious *rocking melodeon*, in which the rocking motion of the whole case operated the bellows.

The wind instruments of bands and orchestras, too, underwent revolutionary changes.

In 1832, the year of Barker's pneumatic lever, Theobald Boehm of Munich produced the earliest Boehm flute. In this model, the misplaced, equidistant, smallish fingerholes of older flutes yielded to holes of sufficient size and acoustically correct positions regardless of easy fingering, which was cared for, however, by an ingenious system of keys and levers (illustration in the same book on page 409). Certain features of the Boehm flute, in particular the ring-keys over open holes which, on being pressed down, operated accessory, tone-correcting keys, were given to the clarinets as well from 1839 on.

In the family of clarinets, the bass, hardly ever used before, obtained its modern straight form and its perfect quality in 1836, and in the same year found an important place in Meyerbeer's opera *Les Hugue-nots*. The builder of this new bass-clarinet was Adolphe Sax of Brussels, who later moved to Paris.

However, it was not to the bass-clarinet but to an entirely new family of instruments that Sax owed his world renown—to the *saxophones*. They left his workshop around 1840 and appeared for the first time in a French score of 1844, but were on the whole so little successful outside France that Richard Strauss added a careful *ad libitum* to their four parts in the score of the *Sinfonia Domestica* (1903) and had to leave the parts unperformed because he could not find the proper players in Germany. Their belated bloom in the twentieth century is due to the rise of jazz.

Saxophones have a parabolically widening metal tube, with the bell up, in the shape of a tobacco pipe (excepting the soprano size). They follow the clarinet in their beak-shaped mouthpiece with the single reed, but the oboe in their key arrangement. Their versatile sound is too familiar to require description.

The name of Sax is also connected with a movement to fuse the features of cornets, bugles, and tubas in one complete, homogeneous family of horns, from the smallest size an octave above the usual *B*-cornet to the double-bass in *C* or *B*, or even to more gigantic sub- and double-sub-basses a fifth and an octave below. Most of these instruments were devised in some form and were introduced here and there in the twenty years following 1828—as, for instance, cornets, tenors, baritones, bass-tubas. Thus, the *saxhorns* of 1845 were not unprecedented instruments. But they were an equalized family, where the various althorns, euphoniums, and tubas had once been heterogeneous, independent instruments with timbres hard to blend. Illustrations can be found in the author's *History of Musical Instruments* on pages 429–433.

All the trumpets and horns—except the sliding trombones— accepted valves of either the rotary or the piston system, during the 1830's in the bands and during the 1840's in the orchestras.

Pitch had generally an upward trend and reached the modern standard or even exceeded it. A first attempt at international standardization at $a' = 440$ vibrations, made by a congress of physicists in Stuttgart, had no success. A quarter of a century later, in 1858, under the pressure of an evergrowing international exchange of traveling artists, a committee appointed by the French government decided in favor of 435 vibrations. But it took thirty more years before a special conference held in Vienna in 1889 confirmed this decision and recommended its universal acceptance. Alas, pitch is today as arbitrary as ever and is certainly above 435 vibrations.

Speaking of general regulations, we should mention that in 1831, fifty-five years before the international convention at Berne, an American Act of Congress granted the first musical copyright and therewith paved the way for the independent work of the modern composer, who is hardly ever supported, as his ancestors were, by courts, churches, or townships.

READING

Alfred Einstein, *Music in the Romantic Era*, New York, 1947. Curt Sachs, *The Commonwealth of Art*, New York, 1946: Cross Section 1819. *The History of Musical Instruments*, New York, 1940: Chapter 17. *Rhythm and Tempo*, New York, 1953: Chapter 14. Grove's *Dictionary*, art. "Mendelssohn." F. Niecks, *Robert Schumann*, London, 1925. Robert Schumann, *On Music and Musicians*, ed. Konrad Wolff, New York, 1946. John F. Porte, *Chopin*, London, 1935. Hector Berlioz, *Mémoires*, Paris, 1897. Jacques Barzun, *Berlioz*, Boston, 1950.

20

THE AGE OF
WAGNER AND BRAHMS

1854–1886

THE THREE DECADES from 1854 to 1886 saw an almost paradoxical marching under the flying banners of realism and of unrealism, of materialism and of idealism. Men of all tenets and temperaments joined the marchers, those who believed in the senses rather than in emotion and ideas, and their opponents who, in search of passion or profundity, despised the reaction of the senses, those who accepted, shaped, and interpreted the merciless world of then and there, and those who created imaginary worlds of saga and fairytale in a dreamy, romantic escape.

But in one thing they shared, in the intensity, indeed, in the violence of their expression and the almost total lack of unconcerned playfulness, serenity, or naive simplicity. Different as they were, they all acted as pioneers, fighters, apostles.

No wonder that the poets left the quieter forms of lyrics and contemplation and concentrated on tragedy, as Hebbel and Ibsen did. No wonder that music did the same. Again it was a natural process that musical tragedy in a naturalistic age should challenge the supremacy of music in favor of dramatic power and intensity, that the separate, self-sufficient *arias*, *cavatinas*, and ballets should be looked at distastefully as undramatic, delaying episodes to be replaced by an 'endless' melody, and that this melody, though often rising to pure and beautiful lines in the older sense of the word, should be, on the whole, an almost speech-like recitative in the spirit of Monteverdi, Lully, and Gluck.

The man who, conquering the older 'number opera,' created this new, inevitable 'musical drama' was Wagner.

287

RICHARD WAGNER was born on May 22, 1813 in Leipzig, of uncertain parentage: his father was either the police officer Wagner or the actor Ludwig Geyer. In his younger years, as a *gymnasiast* and even as a university student, he was attracted by poetry rather than by music—a characteristic attitude in a man who later wrote his texts himself, often long before setting them to music, and who hardly ever composed music for the sake of music outside the stage. After an abortive attempt at music studies during his school years, his actual musical education was confined to a six months' course with the Thomas cantor Weinlig in 1831. His piano playing never amounted to much. Yet he was able to enter a musical career, going through the mill of coaching and conducting in a number of provincial theaters until, after toiling for six years, he could no longer resist seeking his luck in the musical capital, Paris.

When he arrived in 1839, he had already tried his hand at two operatic scores, *Die Feen* ('The Fairies'), 1833, and *Das Liebesverbot* ('The Ban on Love'), 1835. Indeed, two acts of *Rienzi* were in his trunk. But he had not yet found himself: the German magic opera, the Italian singers' opera, the Parisian *grand opéra* had been his models indiscriminately. Even *Rienzi*, the tragedy of an Italian leader in the fourteenth century, the earliest of his works still in the repertoire of opera houses, was in spirit and style a 'grand' opera with all appurtenances—excited choruses, clattering marches, prayers, conspiracies, and a final collapse of the burning palace. In his few, unhappy Parisian years (1839–1842) he became a musical personality all his own. With *Rienzi* finished and, upon Meyerbeer's recommendation, accepted in Berlin (though first performed in Dresden 1842), he was already writing another opera, *Der fliegende Holländer* ('The flying Dutchman'), after one of Heinrich Heine's tales, the tragedy of the cursed seaman who sails for all eternity but is allowed to go ashore every seven years until a faithful woman redeems him. Contrary to the ideals of the grand opera, the *Dutchman* goes straight through a dramatic development, from the hero's arrival in a small Norwegian port to his death and salvation, without any digression, so much so that it has sometimes been given in one act by suppressing the intermissions and gliding from the end of one act into the first measure of the following one.

The performance of the Dutchman at the Royal Opera House in Dresden (1843) provided Wagner, for the first time, with a tenure, as a *Hofkapellmeister* at the same theater.

The two following Dresden operas, *Tannhäuser* (1845), the drama of a *Minnesinger* lost in carnal sin, and *Lohengrin* (1847), in which the Grail saga is interwoven with an episode from early German history, were not basically different from the older concept of romantic opera. They still had their duets, prayers, choruses, finales, but these were organically embodied in 'scenes' instead of forming separate 'numbers.' There was still romantic delight in supernatural forces—the lust and the spell of Tannhäuser's *Venusberg*, the miracle of the budding crosier, the swan that tugged the boat of Lohengrin, the mysterious knight who must not be asked who he is and whence he comes—and there is also, at least in *Tannhäuser*, as in the *Dutchman*, redemption through the faithful love of a maiden. There also was *grand opéra*, with brilliant marches, to the castle hall or to the minster, with clattering swords, and with prayers. Yet, there is no "effect without cause"; the acts flow from scene to scene without any anti-dramatic parceling-out in musical 'numbers'; and the two works are realistic in the sense that all the persons are fully alive, human, convincing, and very far from the usual operatic stereotypes.

The revolutionary years of 1848 and 1849 found Wagner as a radical leftist. Living as an exile in Zürich, Switzerland for twelve years, he filled a momentous pause in his musical creativeness with writing aesthetic and pseudo-aesthetic pamphlets, the most important of which was *Oper und Drama* (1851).

When he returned to his music-paper, he had broken with the past. A new style had taken shape. The first work in the novel language was truly gigantic; it took him more than twenty years to complete, and it formed a four-night cycle (or, properly, a cycle of one preluding play and three nights): *Der Ring des Nibelungen*, the disastrous ring of the demon of the underworld.

Drawing from Nordic and German mythology and forcing his poem into archaic alliterations, Wagner described the doom of the gods under the curse of gold and lust for power, from the day the giants build the towering castle of Valhall to the Twilight of the Gods, when the flames from Siegfried's pyre consume the world of Wotan.

In the Ring of the Nibelung—as in Monteverdi's works and those of Gluck—the drama became paramount; indeed it was promoted to the rank of *Gesamt-Kunstwerk*, a 'work absorbing all the arts,'—poetry, music, gesture, and stage-painting,—which obey the progress of the drama without a life of their own. And again as in Monteverdi's works, a kind of *stile recitativo e rappresentativo* rules the singing; with the exclusion of *arias* and other self-sufficient forms, the voices carry on in an 'endless' melody without caesuras, which adapts itself flexibly to the ever-changing actions, thoughts, and moods of the *dramatis personae* and yet is able to dwell on lyrical climaxes in a broad and beautiful stream.

The orchestra, weighty, rich, and eloquent as never before, was not confined to mere accompaniment. It stressed and deepened the action and conveyed what text and gestures were not able to say. The words of this unique orchestral language are the *Leitmotive*, or 'leading motives,' concise melodic turns, descriptive, significant, and expressive, which follow the drama with its outer and inner action, narratives, and emotional outbreaks as the ever-present beholder and herald.

Realizing that no stage would accept a work extending over four nights and requiring an enormous orchestra, a normal singing style, and a musical language foreign to all expectations and habits of the public, Wagner interrupted his work at the *Nibelungen* scores in 1857 to write two other dramas of a very different nature, which probably represent the climax of his creative life: *Tristan und Isolde* and *Die Meistersinger von Nürnberg*.

So different were the new styles that it might be admissible to suppose that for inner reasons, too, the master had to abandon the *Nibelungen*: his development as a composer jeopardized the stylistic coherence of the four scores.

While the melodic language of the *Ring* was preponderantly diatonic, and even triadic—with the motives forming in tonic-third-fifth-octave patterns—*Tristan und Isolde*, the actionless drama of longing for love and night and death, refined melody and harmony to the utmost with an unprecedented chromaticism. The logical enchaining and modulating from chord to chord was often abandoned for breathtaking illogical shifts—illogical from the viewpoint of school harmony. *Tristan* was the peak in the evolution of romantic harmony and the beginning of its disintegration in the hands of the impressionists.

Wagner began to write the Tristan book in 1857 and completed the orchestration in 1859. Attempts to perform the difficult work were given up after a few rehearsals. It did not come to life until young King Ludwig of Bavaria ended Wagner's exile, called him to Munich in 1864, and ordered Tristan to be given at the Royal Opera under the careful direction of Hans von Bülow.

Six months later, cabals forced the master to leave Bavaria. He settled in Hof Triebschen near Lucerne in Switzerland and composed *Die Meistersinger*. Completed in 1867, the score was performed in Munich in 1868.

Compared with the *Ring*, and with *Tristan*, the score of *Die Meistersinger* is almost a reversal to older ideals on which the master had seemed to turn his back, to diatonic melody and 'correct' harmony, to the overture form, given up since *Tannhäuser*, to self-sufficient solo songs, and even to a magnificent, regular quintet. But the matchless perfection of the *Meistersinger* precludes any such oversimplification. Was it not rather that after having done his pioneering work with iron consistency to the end of the road, he stopped for a blissful moment to rest from tragedy, saga, and magic potions, from chromatic refinement and melodic austerity?

In the meantime, 1865, Wagner had resumed work at the *Ring*. Having carried chromaticism to the maximum that his inner growth required, he had been free to write the diatonic *Meistersinger* and was equally free to readapt himself after eight years to the older giant scores. The whole work was finished in 1874 and came to life in 1876.

The first performance of the *Ring* occurred in Bayreuth not far from Nürnberg, northern Bavaria, in a theater built for Wagner's works exclusively and according to his plans: amphitheatrical without circles, with equally favorable seats throughout, and with a sunken orchestral pit halfways below the stage (which was at that time unprecedented). Far from commercial interests and the routine of ordinary theaters, this *Festspielhaus* was intended to give model performances of Wagner's works in summer festivals. After a life of hardship and disappointment, he saw the most ardent of his wishes fulfilled. Making his home in Bayreuth, he devoted the last years to composing a mystic, semi-religious drama taken from the Grail saga: *Parsifal*, whom, incidentally, he had mentioned some thirty years before as Lohengrin's father. *Parsifal* was finished and performed in 1882 but withheld from any other stage until the rights of Wagner's heirs expired in 1913, thirty years after the master had died in Palazzo Vendramin in Venice on February 13, 1883.

Altogether, Wagner's dramatic works, excluding the earliest attempts, are:

Die Feen (1833)
Das Liebesverbot oder die Novize von Palermo (1835)
Rienzi (1840)
Der Fliegende Holländer (1842)
Tannhäuser (1845)
Lohengrin (1847)
Das Rheingold, first part of the *Ring* (1854)
Die Walküre, second part of the *Ring* (1856)
Tristan und Isolde (1859)
Siegfried, third part of the *Ring* (1865)
Die Meistersinger von Nürnberg (1867)
Die Götterdämmerung, fourth part of the *Ring* (1874)
Parsifal (1882)

Of non-dramatic works, only two are important: *Eine Faust-Ouverture*, written first in 1840 and rewritten in 1855, at the time of the *Walküre*, and the *Siegfried-Idyll* (1870), a symphonic poem for a small, almost chamber-music orchestra on motives from *Siegfried*.

Interested in the characterizing force of orchestral color and in particular need of majestic hues for the world of gods that the *Nibelungen* score conjures up, Richard Wagner introduced a few additional brasses in the *Ring:* a so-called *bass trumpet* in the range of the tenor trombone (used in Bavarian and Austrian cavalry bands since early in the century); a *double bass trombone*, an octave below the tenor trombone and usually built in the (outer) shape and size of the latter with a twofold tubing which allows the various positions of the slide to agree in both instruments; and the *Wagner tubas*. These are tubas, two in *B* flat (tenor) and two in *F* (bass), of slightly different parabolical bore and with a kind of French-horn mouthpiece, which render a solemn, less explosive tone than other tubas. Later, they were scored also in Bruckner's Seventh and in Strauss' *Elektra*.

At the time Richard Wagner was heaping up his massive *Ring* orchestra with sixteen woodwinds and seventeen brasses, the organ, too, moved towards an unparalleled power. The number of stops exceeded a hundred in larger works; and the organ builders not only exaggeratedly increased the general wind pressure, but also devised high-pressure stops, like *tuba mirábilis* or *ophicleide*, which demanded three or four times the average pressure. To cope with these innovations, Charles Spackman Barker in London improved his pneumatic lever, making it an electro-pneumatic instead of a mechano-pneumatic action.

America paid a curious tribute of her own to colossal trends in the sensational concerts that Patrick Gilmore, "the supersalesman of music," conducted between 1864 and 1892 with a band of one thousand pieces and a chorus of ten thousand, with fifty anvils, and a battery of cannon outside firing on the beat.

THE FRENCH mainly persisted in their concepts of grand opera, besides, despite, and against the music drama of Wagner. Moreover, they had a few immeasurable successes with works that we cannot fully, or at all, connect with the typical grand opera of Auber's and Meyerbeer's time, but rather with the older, melodious *opéra comique*. They all share in the curious fate of being dubbed 'Wagnerian,' which seems to have been the critics' handy rubber stamp for 'untraditional.'

An older group is still alive in the works of Thomas and Gounod. Charles Gounod (1818–1893) conquered the operatic stage with a quite un-Faustian, lyrical *Faust*, after Goethe's drama. First performed in the Tristan year 1859, it now looks back to almost three thousand nights at the Paris opera alone. Gounod's *Mireille* of 1864 is much less well known.

Ambroise Thomas (1811–1896) composed his *Mignon*, after Goethe's *Wilhelm Meister* in 1866, and two years later a rather un-Shakespearian *Hamlet*.

Georges Bizet (1838–1875) gave us in 1872 the incidental music to Daudet's *Arlésienne*, which in the form of an orchestral suite has become a favorite of hearers and players alike. In 1875, shortly before his premature death, he transformed Mérimée's novelette *Carmen* into a racy play of passion and jealousy, of soldiers, smugglers, and bull-fighters under the parching sun of Andalusia, which with its exotic scene, its simple, human plot, its easily caught yet never trivial melodies, is unmatched in popular appeal in whatever country it appears on the stage. Unbelievable as it seems, the first performance in Paris was a failure, and the critics condemned the lack of melody!

Camille Saint-Saëns, to be mentioned later as a basically instrumental composer, contributed to the history of opera with *Samson et Dalila* (1877), of all these works the closest to the concept of grand opera, with its famous alto aria in *D* flat major.

Alexis-Emanual Chabrier (1841–1894), less well known outside France, but in his harmonic language more interesting than the men before him, created in 1887 a lasting work with *Le Roi malgré lui*, 'The King in spite of himself.'

Jules Massenet (1842–1912), one of the most prolific masters of French opera, may conclude this short survey with his sentimental *Manon* of 1884 and a miracle play, *Le Jongleur de Notre Dame* (1902).

In the year of *Mignon*, 1866, the operatic stage, so far dominated by masters of Germanic and Romanic countries, opened for the first time to a Czech, Bedřič (Frederick) Smétana, and his immortal, comic, peasant opera *The Bartered Bride*, with its inexhaustible stock of sparkling rhythms and melodies. Eight years later, another Slav, Modest Mussorgsky (1839–1881) gave the world a work of an entirely different cast: *Boris Godunov* (1874), the tragedy of a tsar. Audacious and colorful though somber and national, too, in the modal and often nonmetric melodies that Russian folksong and liturgy have inspired, it is equally distant from French delight in pleasing melody and Wagnerian pathos, claiming a position all its own. Its style was hardly precedented, nor did it conform to the standards of the time. Pioneering in novelty, it was not fully understood before the impressionistic turn of the twentieth century. This change in attitude is reflected in the two facts that Rimsky-Korsakov made, in 1896, a more 'professional,' orthodox, and polished revision of the score, and that today's performances reach for Mussorgsky's unadulterated version.

WHILE ALL THESE MASTERS created only one single successful opera and had, more or less, to stand in the shadow of Richard Wagner's domineering work, there was one man to counterbalance the power of Bayreuth with a long succession of operas in a different, opposite style: Giuseppe Verdi.

Verdi was the son of an innkeeper in a village not far from Parma, Italy. He was born on October 10, 1813, only a couple of months after Wagner, just as Bach and Handel had been born in the same year.

And just as in Wagner's work, Verdi's extra-theatrical compositions are the least important. We have to except, though, a *Requiem* (1874) and four *Pezzi sacri* (Sacred pieces), 1898, in which Italian melody and blissful serenity have found a supreme expression.

Verdi's world was the musical stage, which allowed him to blend the two gifts that nature had conferred on him, a genius for melodic invention and an infallible instinct for dramatic action and character. From 1839 on, he composed almost thirty operas at a pace unusual in the nineteenth century. But only two successes rewarded his early attempts: *Ernani*, after Victor Hugo's romantic drama *Hernani*, in 1844, and *Luisa Miller*, after Friedrich Schiller's *bourgeois* tragedy *Kabale und Liebe*, in 1849.

Then, exactly at the time of Wagner's break with the past after *Lohengrin*, Verdi entered maturity with the three most popular of all his works: the gruesome story of the hunchback *Rigoletto* and his daughter (1851), after Victor Hugo's historical drama *Le Roi s'amuse;* *Il Trovatore* (1853), after a play by Garcia Gutiérrez; and *La Traviata*, 'She who lost her way' (1853), after Alexandre Dumas fils' play *La Dame aux Camélias*, one of the earliest operas with its scene laid in modern life.

With all their dramatic force, these works made the texts subservient to music and were organized in separate numbers as *arias* and *cavatinas*, duets and *terzetti*, choruses and finales. For Verdi, uncontested heir to a great Italian tradition, wrote Italian operas, even when his librettos followed Schiller, Dumas, Hugo, or Shakespeare—operas full of Italian singing and passion. Indeed, beyond their musico-dramatic impact, they were interpreted as testifying to the Italian struggle for freedom and unity under the house of Savoy; and to his fellow countrymen his very name became a symbol of national longing and fulfilment: *Vittorio Emanuele Rè D'Italia.*

Despite an attitude so old-Italian, Verdi turned in *Aida* to thorough-bred grand opera, with the scene laid in ancient Egypt, a brilliant triumphal march, a colorful ballet, and, at the end, immurement of the guilty lovers in the catacombs of the temple seen in the upper half of the stage. This exceptional character resulted from the international atmosphere of the first performance: *Aida*, on a text by A. Ghislanzoni, had been commissioned to celebrate the inauguration of the Suez Canal in 1871. In the concluding phase of Verdi's life, the master converged with Wagner's ideals when he accepted continuous scenes instead of separate numbers, though he did not accept chromatic harmony, or the system of *leitmotives*, or, for that matter, any of the intellectual approach of Wagner. The last wonderworks took an unusual time to complete—an indication of how far they were from the routine. *Otello*, on Arrigo Boito's text after Shakespeare's drama, was completed only in 1887; and *Falstaff*, again on a book of Boito's after Shakespeare's comedy *The Merry Wives of Windsor*, was finished in 1892 with a whirling fugue of all participants—*Tutto nel mondo è burla*, 'Life is a practical joke.' Verdi was seventy-nine years old when this last, incredibly lightfooted, transparent opera crowned the work of his life. Eighteen years after Wagner, he died on January 27, 1901.

THE SERIOUS OPERA, and even more the exalted music drama, profound and presumptuous, produced an antidote, just as, a hundred years earlier, the heroic stage of Gluck had coincided in time and space with the French comic opera and the *Singspiel* of the Germans. This antidote was the *operetta*, a comic opera in the lightest vein, with spoken dialogues, but often original, dashing, and witty.

It began in its characteristic form with the poignant, satirical Parisian operettas of Jacques Offenbach (1819–1880)—*Orphée aux Enfers* (1858), *La Belle Hélène* (1864), *La Vie Parisienne* (1866)—which range in spirit with the contemporary caricatures of Daumier and Gavarni. *Les Contes d'Hoffmann* (posthumously performed in 1881) with its popular *Barcarole* is an opera rather than an operetta.

In the year of *La Vie Parisienne*, the Viennese entered the ring. The earliest was Franz von Suppé (1819–1895) with *Leichte Kavallerie* (1866) and *Fatinitza* (1876) and more than two hundred other scores for the stage. His greatest successor in Vienna was the Waltz King Johann Strauss, Jr. (1825–1899), composer of the ever-young, dance-provoking 'Bat' or *Fledermaus* (1874).

A few years later, the European leadership went to England's Sir Arthur S. Sullivan (1842–1900). While he wrote mostly church and incidental music in his earlier years, his world-wide fame—shared with his librettist William S. Gilbert—derives from numerous operettas, among them *Trial by Jury* (1875), *H.M.S. Pinafore* (1878), *The Mikado* (1885), and *The Yeoman of the Guard* (1888).

The American successors, Victor Herbert (1859–1924), with *Naughty Marietta* (1910) and forty other operettas, and the younger Jerome Kern (1885–1945) belong in the following generations.

SYMPHONIC MASTERS. Estranged from the classical forms of the sonata and the symphony, the orchestral and chamber types of music underwent changes no less incisive than those of the opera. Their pathfinder and leader was Liszt.

Franz Liszt, the closest friend and the herald of Wagner, was a cosmopolitan counterpart of the nationalistic master of Bayreuth. He was rooted in Hungary, Austria, Germany, France, and Italy. He was a child of this world and yet an ecstatic son of the Church, an influential, pioneering composer, a famous teacher, writer, conductor, and the greatest pianist of his time.

Born in Hungary, on October 22, 1811, he learned at an early age to master the piano and was taken to Vienna to study with Carl Czerny and Antonio Salieri. Not much later, from 1823, he completed his education in Paris under the guidance of Ferdinando Paer and Anton Reicha. Both taught him composition—he no longer needed a piano teacher—and he began a brilliant international career as a virtuoso.

But gradually he lost interest in mere virtuosity and the unrewarding life of concert halls and *salons*. For the time being, he gave his last public concent in Elisabethgrad, Russia. He had already accepted the position of a *Hofkapellmeister* at Weimar, Thuringia, at first in a visiting capacity. A resident since 1848, he indulged in almost feverish activity as a composer, teacher, conductor, player, and writer, but left Weimar in 1861 because his progressive taste met with ever-increasing difficulties at court and in the theater. The futile efforts of his lady friend to obtain from the Pope an annulment of her marriage to the Prince Sayn-Wittgenstein brought him to Rome; and the resulting impossibility of marrying the princess caused, or precipitated, his taking the first four degrees in the Franciscan Order. The remaining years of his life were spent alternately in Weimar, Rome, and Budapest. On July 31, 1886, he died peacefully in Bayreuth near the Wagner family.

His works reflect his life and character. His was an international style, in which the German, French, and Italian elements were blended —Faustian stress and sentimental pining, the chivalrous and the Catholic, profundity and showmanship, Bachian polyphony and Verdian *bel-canto*, Palestrinian harmonies and fiery *csardas* rhythms. Chamber music, however, had no place in his work; intimacy was alien to him. There are piano and orchestral works by Liszt, oratorios, Masses, and songs, but neither trios nor quartets.

In his earlier years he had written many empty, "effect-full" paraphrases of favorite operatic melodies. But his emphasis shifted radically to the meaningful side in his Weimar days.

In less than ten years, he made his most important contribution to music with a set of twelve *symphonic poems*—a new name and a new form. They are comparatively short orchestral pieces, which do not follow the pattern of the classic symphony, but rather the train of thought in some work of poetry or painting that provided the creative inspiration. Their titles are:

> *Ce qu'on entend sur la montagne*, What One Hears on the
> Mountain (1840, 1857)
> *Prometheus* (1850)
> *Festklänge*, Festive Sounds (1853, 1860)
> *Orpheus* (1854–1856)
> *Les Préludes* (1856)
> *Tasso* (1856)
> *Hungaria* (1856)
> *Die Hunnenschlacht*, The Battle of the Huns (1856)
> *Héroïde funèbre*, Heroic Dirge (1857)
> *Mazeppa* (1858)
> *Hamlet* (1859)
> *Die Ideale*, The Ideals (1859)

At the same time, in the fifties, Liszt wrote two symphonies which, just like the symphonic poems, disown the classical pattern and obey a poetic program. One might call them symphonic poems in several movements. It is revealing that he named the three movements of his *Faust Symphony* (1853–1861) — *Faust, Gretchen, Mephistopheles* — "character pictures." They describe but do not develop. At the end of this symphony, he called in a male chorus for the mystic, last verses of Goethe's drama; and in a similar way, he crowned his second, *Dante Symphony* (1856), with a Gregorian *Magníficat* for a women's chorus.

Also in the Weimar period, he composed his outstanding piano music, in which virtuoso technique is made subservient to forceful expressiveness: the first of his two concertos, in *E* flat major (1857) and the *Totentanz* (1849–1855), a concerto itself, fifteen of his twenty Hungarian Rhapsodies, and the *Années de Pélerinage*, or Years of Pilgrimage (1848–1852), the sonata in *B* minor (1853), and the *Etudes d'Exécution transcendante* (1854). And, still within that time of unbelievable fertility, he composed the *Missa Solemnis*, or *Gran Mass*, for the Hungarian city of Gran, and the Thirteenth Psalm, with a fervent tenor solo, both in 1855.

The time of his deepest religious experience, the sixties, gave us his two oratorios, *The Legend of Saint Elizabeth* (1862) and *Christus* (1866), the two Legends for piano (1866), the Hungarian Coronation Mass (1867), and, as his swan song, a *Missa choralis* (1886).

ANTON BRUCKNER, born in Upper Austria in 1824, was a teacher and organist in straitened circumstances before, at the age of forty-four, he was called to Vienna as a professor of organ, harmony, and counterpoint. After a quiet life devoted to teaching and composing, he resigned in 1894, died on October 11, 1896, and was buried in the abbey of St. Florian on the Danube, where he once had been a choirboy and, later, the organist.

His main contributions as a composer are nine (properly eleven) symphonies:

First   C minor 1866

Second   C minor 1872

Third   D minor 1873 ('Wagner')

Fourth   E♭ major 1874 ('Romantic')

Fifth   B♭ major 1876

Sixth   *A* major 1879

Seventh *E* major 1883

Eighth   *C* minor 1885

Ninth   *D* minor 1894

The peak among the nine is probably the solemn, far-stretching Seventh. The Ninth was left without a last movement and is sometimes performed with the Te Deum to replace it. This Te Deum (1881) and three Masses are among the greatest religious works in the second half of the nineteenth century. Beside them, one prominent work of chamber music, a quintet for strings (1879) should not be forgotten.

Bruckner's art is deep, monumental, powerful, but its scope is not wide. It expands between a festive, typically Austrian and Baroque Catholicism and hearty peasant dancing. He has nothing of the ascetic restraint and chamber-music texture of Brahms, whom he profoundly disliked. Instead, he has much of Wagner's heroic attitude—one of the symphonies is even dedicated to the master of Bayreuth—without, however, transplanting Wagner's dramatic style into the symphonic form. His thematic ideas are great, majestic, exalted, but he lacks structural discipline and often falls a victim to that repetitiousness which has barred him the way to countries outside Germanic Middle Europe.

Despite this want of formal economy, the mere fact that, ignoring the new form of the symphonic poem, he concentrated on the classical symphony and by-passed all the descriptive, extramusical trends of the time, gives him a place in the least romantic wing of romanticism.

J OHANNES BRAHMS, son of a doublebass player, was born in Hamburg on May 7, 1833. He began his piano studies at the age of eight and at thirteen played in taverns to bolster the modest budget of the family. Fifteen years as a teacher and a concert player, here and there, are of minor importance for this brief sketch of his life. In 1863, he settled in Vienna, whose gayer temperament attracted the austere North German as it once had attracted Beethoven. For a while he conducted the *Singakademie* (1863–1864) and the *Gesellschaft der Musikfreunde* (1872–1875). But he preferred independence in the service of free composing and spent the rest of his years as a free-lancer. A bachelor, he died from a cancer on April 2, 1897.

Brahms worked in all the lyrical fields of music but ignored the dramatic and epic forms of the opera and the oratorio. The soaring peaks among his works are four symphonies, the first in C minor (1855–1876), which Hans von Bülow, alluding to Beethoven's nine, enthusiastically called The Tenth; the second in D major (1877), the third in F major (1883), and, towering over the others, the fourth in E minor (1885); two piano concertos in D minor and Bb major (1878–1881); and a violin concerto in D major (1878). Out of an impressive amount of chamber music, we may mention two string sextets, in Bb major (1860) and in G major (1865), and a clarinet quintet (1891). Of his choral works, the best known is *A German Requiem* to the memory of his mother (1857–1868), which, without any connection with the Catholic Mass of the Dead, draws from the Scriptures in German; and the *Schicksalslied* or 'Song of Fate' (1871), on one of Hölderlin's poems. An immense treasure of piano works, chamber music, and songs defies enumeration and even any selection dictated by value rather than personal taste.

Brahms was the strongest antipode of Wagner, Liszt, and Bruckner. He was a romantic only in his urge to create emotional expression. But like Beethoven, he forced it into the iron clamps of classical strictness. He hated grandiloquence, pompousness, and theatricality; he never allowed extramusical thoughts, not even poetry, to master music; and he composed primarily in clear-drawn lines and rhythms, rather than in harmonic or orchestral colors.

This classical attitude, and the attitude of his followers, found its pseudo-philosophic reflection in the Viennese Eduard Hanslick's famous, though biased and narrow-minded, book *Vom musikalisch Schönen*, On the Musically Beautiful (1854).

More distinguished apostles of the art of Brahms were two musicians of the highest rank, Hans von Bülow (1830–1894), conductor and pianist, and the violinist Joseph Joachim (1831–1907), director of the Royal Academy of Music in Berlin (the *Hochschule*). It was Joachim's celebrated quartet that, for forty years, performed the chamber music of Brahms along with Beethoven's last and still but little familiar works.

Brahms himself, although he detested Bruckner, dissociated himself from the fanatic Wagner-hatred of the Brahmsians. He called himself the oldest and most enthusiastic admirer of Wagner and wrote to one of his zealous friends that he considered a few bars of the *Meistersinger* more precious than all the operas since composed put together.

The position of Franck is in a way similar to that of Brahms.

CESAR FRANCK, a Belgian in the history of French music, was born on December 10, 1822, in Liége, won early triumphs as a pianist in his homeland, and was sent to the Paris *Conservatoire*. With an interruption of two years in Belgium, he lived in Paris as a teacher, organist, and choirmaster. This quiet life ended on November 8, 1890.

As a composer, Franck sided with the form-conscious, polyphonic musicians of the Brahmsian camp. On the other hand, he felt as close to the styles of Liszt and Wagner as was compatible with such an attitude. An earlier, religious period began with *Ruth*, a 'Biblical eclogue' for soli, chorus, and orchestra (1844), and climaxed with *Six Pièces pour Grand Orgue* (1860–1862), *Trois Pièces pour Grand Orgue* (1878), and a frequently performed, mystic oratorio *Les Béatitudes* (1879). Later, he turned to instrumental forms neglected in France. A symphonic poem, *Les Éolides* (1876), is little known today. But two works have acquired universal fame: a fervent *D* minor symphony (1888), whose short initial motif has been called the theme of faith, and a sonata for violin and piano (1886) with the kind of catchy canonic end-movement that hopelessly haunts the player and the listener for days and days.

Camille Saint-Saëns (1835–1921) tried in a similar way to give a modern instrumental music to France. French, entirely un-Bohemian, and scholarly, he aimed at a strict and almost classical form. Three symphonies give perfect evidence. But like Franck, he also composed a number of symphonic poems in the wake of Liszt: *Le Rouet d'Omphale* or 'Omphale's Spinning Wheel' (1871), *Phaéton* (1873), and the famous *Danse Macabre* or 'Dance of Death' (1874). As a typical son of his nation, he was equally fond of formal beauty and of unequivocal description. The opera *Samson et Dalila* has been mentioned before.

Gabriel Fauré (1845–1924) belongs here, both chronologically and as a pupil of Saint-Saëns. But stylistically he is hard to place. Ignored outside his homeland in his lifetime, he has been accepted, understood, and increasingly performed after his death. Best known is a beloved *Messe de Requiem* (1887), freed of all Doomsday terror, unbelievably conservative in its musical language, and yet irresistibly warmhearted, blissful, mild, and almost smiling.

Franck's genuine successor was Vincent d'Indy, celebrated teacher and composer. Born in Paris on March 27, 1851, he was meant to study law. Only in 1872 did he definitely turn to music, serving three years as a second drummer and again four years as a chorus master to get practical insight into orchestration and choral writing. Meanwhile he had begun to study composition with Franck and to play the organ. The great event in his professional life was the foundation of a *Schola Cantorum* (1894) in open opposition to the obsolete pedagogics of the *Conservatoire*. What and how he taught there has found a monument in his gigantic *Cours de Composition*, which was published between 1897 and 1933, the last part being printed two years after he had died on December 2, 1931.

His own distinguished work includes a 'lyrical drama' *Fervaal* (1889–1895), which had little stage success. He fared better with three symphonies and particularly with the *Symphonie sur un chant montagnard français* or, shorter, *Symphonie Cévenole* (meaning: from the mountain range Cévennes), written in 1886 for orchestra and piano, which became the most popular. The French are also very fond of the symphonic variations *Istar*.

W HILE GERMANY, ITALY, AND FRANCE were reaching the climax of their joint monopolies, a newly arrived group, the Slavs, whom Glinka and Chopin had foreshadowed, won a place of honor on the stages and in the concert halls of the West. The Czechs, although still far from gaining political and cultural independence, proved their musical identity in the works of three great masters. Smétana, who has already been mentioned with his exuberant *Bartered Bride*, conquered the concert hall with the universally known *Vltava*, or *Moldau* (1879), as a part of a cycle of six symphonic poems, *Má Vlast*, or My Homeland. Chamber music circles are quite familiar with two string quartets, both autobiographic in character, and particularly with that in *E* minor (From My Life), 1876, in which he narrates the tragedy of his deafness with a painful, lonely high *E*— the last note he ever heard. Seven years later he suffered a breakdown and spent the last days of his life in an insane asylum.

Smétana was, roughly speaking, close to Wagner and Liszt, but Antonin Dvořák (1841–1904), his junior by seventeen years, composed in the same spirit as Brahms, although he did not 'follow' him by any means. Hence the riches of his chamber music and the comparative unimportance of his ten operas, of which *Rusalka* (1900) is best known, at least in Czechoslovakia. His life at home was interrupted by three important years in the States, both in the "endless plains" of the Midwest and in New York, as the director of the Conservatory, 1892–1895. Here he wrote his often played symphony in *E* minor *From the New World* (1893)—one of his nine—as the fruit of his impressions in the land of endless plains and rattling machines, of white men and Negroes and Indians.

The third of the Czech pioneers, late in his universal recognition, was the Moravian Leoš Janáček (1854–1928) with his successful opera *Jenufa* (1903).

In the generation born around 1835, a group of Russians, the Mighty Five, presented themselves as competitors in the field of symphonic music with a definite emphasis on the national spirit of Russia. They were:

> Alexander Borodin (1834–1887)
> César A. Cui (1835–1918)
> Modest Mussorgsky (1839–1881)
> Mily Balakirev (1837–1910)
> Nicolai Rimsky-Korsakov (1844–1908)

Most of them were gifted amateurs.

Alexander P. Borodin (1833–1887), by profession a doctor and chemist of unusual standing, allowed himself the study and practice of music only as a byway, though indeed a brilliant one. Songs, a second symphony, a string quartet in *A* major (1880), and an unfinished opera, *Prince Igor*, testify to an astonishingly advanced style, whose monothematic form and modal, chromatic, discordant harmony were far ahead of his time. After his premature death, Rimsky-Korsakov and Glazunov completed the *Igor* score.

César Cui (1835–1918), half Russian, half French, reached the rank of lieutenant-general as a military engineer, but found the time to write ten operas.

Modest P. Mussorgsky (1839–1881) became an army cadet but resigned in 1858, studied with Balakirev, and to his death eked out a scanty existence. Focused on opera and song (*cf*. p. 294), he did not write much instrumental music. But every pianist still wrestles with the unfading piano cycle, *Pictures from an Exhibition* (1874), in which the individual pictures are separated by an ever-recurring *Promenade* from room to room. How little pianistic, in the conventional sense of the word, this cycle is, can be gathered from the fact that Maurice Ravel gave it a brilliant, perhaps too brilliant, orchestration.

Mily Balakirev (1837–1910) was, from 1861, the center of the Five and teacher of Cui, Borodin, and Mussorgsky. In 1869 he secured the influential directorship of the Imperial Chapel. Only in a later phase of his life did he pen his important compositions: two tone poems, *Islamey* (1882) and *Thamur* (publ. 1884), and a *D* minor symphony (1909).

Nicolas A. Rimsky-Korsakov (1844–1918) was a naval officer with, musically, great enthusiasm and little knowledge. He was still an insufficiently self-taught dilettante after giving up his first career but was at once appointed professor of composition (!) at the St. Petersburg conservatory in 1871. Yet, while teaching, he progressed rapidly and in years to come was able to write Russia's classical textbooks of music, particularly *The Principles of Orchestration* with examples from his own compositions.

At least five of his compositions have gained international fame: the operas *Pskovityanka* or 'The Maid of Pskov' (1872), *Snegurochka* or 'Snow Maiden' (1881), *Mlada* (1890), The Golden Cockerel (1907), and the symphonic suite *Sheherazade* (1888). He might have written more but for an extensive activity in completing or revamping works of his friends, among them, in 1896, Mussorgsky's *Boris Godunov*.

Peter I. Tchaikovsky (1840–1893) studied law but turned to music at the age of twenty-three and in two years of intensive work acquired enough knowledge to qualify as a professor of composition at the recently founded conservatory in Moscow (which position he gave up soon enough). Although emotionally an extreme nationalist, he was to the nationalistic Five not 'Russian' enough to be included in their

group. Admirably versatile, now dancing and playful, now sentimental
or passionate, he has a still little-contested place in the concert halls of
every continent, above all with his fantasy-overture *Romeo and Juliet*
(1870), his powerful first piano concerto in B♭ minor (1875), the three
later symphonies—No. 4 in *F* minor (1877), No. 5 in *E* minor (1888),
No. 6, 'Pathetic,' in *B* minor (1893)—and his delightful, spirited *Nut-
cracker* suite of 1892. Nor has the stage forgotten two of his operas,
Eugen Onegin (1877) and *The Queen of Spades* (1890).

The Slavs were not the only ones to add their own heritage to the
common stock of European music. The man who did this for Norway
was no bold pioneer, no builder on a larger scale, but a thoroughly
amiable miniaturist in his own right: Edvard Grieg (1843–1907). The
name may evoke, in most people, dear memories of two classically
simple orchestral suites (1888, 1891) from his incidental music to
Ibsen's *Peer Gynt* (1875). It also evokes the memories of the charming
Holberg Suite in the style of the early eighteenth century (in two
versions, for piano and for strings, both 1885); of the piano concerto in
A minor (1868); and of numerous songs and chamber works. But the
master's greatest merit was to provide an honest, sterling piano music
for homes all over the world that had lived on trashy *salon* pieces. His
ten fascicles of Lyric Pieces (1867–1901), meant to be Norwegian
music, have, in fact, ignored all national frontiers.

READING

Alfred Einstein, *Music in the Romantic Era,* New York, 1947. Curt Sachs,
The History of Musical Instruments, New York, 1940: Chapter 17. *The
Commonwealth of Art,* New York, 1946: Cross Section 1854. *Rhythm and
Tempo,* New York, 1953: Chapter 14. Ernest Newman, *The Life of Richard
Wagner,* New York, 1933–1946. Martin Cooper, *Georges Bizet,* London,
1938. Georges Servières, *Saint-Saëns,* Paris, 1930. Jules Massenet, *My Recol-
lections,* Boston, 1919. Zdeněk Nejedlý, *Frederick Smétana,* London, 1924.
Oscar von Riesemann, *Moussorgsky,* New York, 1929. Franz Werfel and
Paul Stefan, *Verdi,* 1942. René Brancour, *Offenbach,* Paris, 1929. H. E.
Jacob, *Johann Strauss, Father and Son,* 1940. William A. Darlington, *The
World of Gilbert and Sullivan,* New York, 1950. Ernest Newman, *The Man
Liszt,* London, 1934. Werner Wolff, *Anton Bruckner,* New York, 1942.
Karl Geiringer, *Brahms,* London, 1936; New York, 1947. Norman Demuth,
César Franck, London, 1949. Norman Suckling, *Fauré,* London, 1946.
Norman Demuth, *Vincent d'Indy,* London, 1951. Paul Stefan, *Anton
Dvořák,* New York, 1941. Daniel Muller, *Leoš Janáček,* Paris, 1930. Rimsky-
Korsakoff, *My Musical Life,* New York, 1936. Tchaikovsky, *The Diaries,*
1945. David Monrad Johansen, *Edvard Grieg,* Princeton, 1938.

21

THE AGE OF
DEBUSSY AND STRAUSS

1886–1922

LATE ROMANTICISM, at the turn of the century, over-
lapped with a great number of anti-romantic currents: exag-
gerated naturalism, impressionism, expressionism, and—to add
a novel ism to those already in use—barbarism.

All the founding fathers of that group were born about 1860.

The eldest was a self-taught 'Edwardian' Englishman, Edward Elgar
(1857–1934), creator of a cantata *Caractacus* (1898), the orchestral
Enigma Variations (1899)—each of which portrayed a friend—an
oratorio, *The Dream of Gerontius* (1900), and, as the highlights, the
symphonies in *A* flat (1908) and in *E* flat (1911).

America's great name in Elgar's time was Edward MacDowell (1861–
1908). Like Grieg, he gave the amateur a treasure of easy piano pieces.
But weightier are his four piano sonatas—*Tragica, Eroica, Norse,* and
Keltic—a *Second Piano Concerto* (1890), and a *Second Indian Suite* for
orchestra (1897). His alleged 'Americanism' is open to doubt, the more
so because he himself did not believe in musical nationalism.

Perhaps the most characteristic, egocentric representative of late
romanticism was Mahler.

Gustav Mahler (Bohemia, July 7, 1860–Vienna, May 18, 1911) devoted his life to conducting, which he practised against all odds with
an unbending, inexorable, almost proverbial faithfulness to the spirit
of the work of art—a career with modest beginnings in Austrian provincial theaters, a glorious peak at the Imperial Opera in Vienna (1897–
1907), and an epilogue at the Metropolitan Opera and the New York
Philharmonic from 1907 to 1911, the year of his death.

Despite the strain of his exhausting life, he was able to finish nine
momentous symphonies and to begin his tenth. Best known is the Sec-

ond in C minor (1894), which in its last movement gives an unforgettable picture of the twilight that descends upon the world before Doomsday, of the last bird, lonely, twittering in fright, and of the Great Reveille with the chorus "Up, wake up!" In the eighth symphony (which a resourceful manager baptized the Symphony of the Thousand for its choral and orchestral masses), he abandoned the symphonic model altogether and, in the boundless flow of voices and instruments, tried to master the world of his hope in two gigantic movements on the words of the Gregorian hymn *Veni creator spiritus* and of the conclusion of Goethe's *Faust*. In the vocal field, he left many beautiful songs with piano accompaniment and, as his ripest work, *Das Lied von der Erde* (The Song of the Earth), a symphony for voices and orchestra (1908).

Hugo Wolf (1860–1903), an Austrian, like Mahler, became the late-romantic "Wagner of the *Lied*." In a tragic struggle, he created *Lieder* like one possessed—in the actual sense of the word—until a growing insanity took the pen from his fingers. Unlike Brahms, he gave precedence to the text and tried to serve the lyrical poem in the same spirit in which Richard Wagner had served the drama, and like Wagner, he stressed the piano part to interpret and deepen the mood and meaning of the words, indeed, to prevail on them. It is a characteristic, and probably unprecedented, proof of the respect in which he held the poems and poets that he published many of his *Lieder* under the flags of their writers, as *Goethelieder* or *Mörickelieder*.

The last men of this group are two Scandinavians, Carl Nielsen (1865–1931), the earliest modern Dane and—particularly cherished in the United States and in England—Jean Sibelius of Finland (b. 1865), with seven truly symphonic symphonies and several symphonic poems in the line of Liszt, among them a 'legend,' *The Swan of Tuonela* (1893), the favorite *Finlandia* (1899), and others based on the Finnish national epic *Kalevala*. His break with pure romanticism came before 1910; the peak of his neoclassicism is the *Seventh Symphony* in one movement (1924).

V ERISM. While Verdi was stunning the world with the marvels of his last two works, *Otello* (1887) and *Falstaff* (1892), while Sibelius sang of Nordic sagas and Mahler depicted the pining of his self, an almost naturalistic Italian group started a new dramatic style, *verismo*, or Style of Truth, in which some story from everyday life, invariably ending in bloodshed, was worked out in an often curious mixture of *fin-de-siècle* naturalism and Italian delight in beautiful, sensuous melody.

The veristic movement set in with Pietro Mascagni's *Cavalleria rusticana* (1890) and Ruggiero Leoncavallo's *Pagliacci* (1892), and had an unparalleled success, due probably to a reaction against the heavy Wagnerian music drama, its grandiloquence, intellectuality, and estrangement from life—or, better, against the music drama of the Wagner epigones.

It is a remarkable fact that neither of these gifted men was able to repeat his hit in any later operas. Nor had any of their many successors a better fate.

Giácomo Puccini (1858–1924)—the same age as Leoncavallo and older than Mascagni—was close to verism in the earliest of his successful operas. *La Bohême* (1896) had its scene laid in contemporary Paris, and if there was no bloodshed, at least it ended in death from tuberculosis. But his later operas were different. *Tosca* (1900), the drama of Roman secret police, *Madama Butterfly* (1904), the drama of a deserted Japanese girl, *La Fanciulla del West*, or The Girl of the Golden West (New York 1910), the three short one-act operas of 1918, *Il Tabarro* (The Cloak), the lachrymose *Suor Angelica* (Sister Angelica), and the witty, lightfooted *Gianni Schicchi* (pron. skickee), united under the title of *Tríttico* (triptych), and finally the gruesome, colorful Chinese story of Princess *Turandot* (performed in 1926 after Puccini's death)—all show an astonishing mixture of naturalism and sentimentality, of Italian *cantabile* and impressionistic harmony in a thoroughly romantic spirit.

The Italian verists had a French brother-in-arms in Gustave Charpentier (b. 1860), who gave his anti-Wagnerian opera *Louise* (1900) the unprecedented, challenging subtitle *roman musical*. It was another *Bohême*, with the setting once more in the world of Montmartre artists, written in prose by himself, and composed in a naturalistic *stile recitativo e rappresentativo* without the appeal of Italian *belcanto*.

IMPRESSIONISM, the strongest power against naturalism, was at once the most momentous of the anti-romantic currents, in poetry, painting, and music.

Impressionism is anti-classical as well. 'Classical' masters have always striven for an art in which the essentials of life and nature are stripped of the unessential, and in which the temporal is lifted into the realm of eternity. Impressionism, on the contrary, is interested in the temporal, indeed, in the momentary, transitory. It is, therefore, concerned with motion rather than station; with the appearance of a thing under a certain light and shadow rather than with the thing itself; with the vagueness and subtlety of passing moods and reflexes rather than with clean-cut characters, structures, or lines.

In keeping with impressionistic painting and poetry, impressionistic music did away with melody, form, polyphonic weaving, and the logical succession of chords in 'functional' harmony. Instead, it needed the iridescent play of dreamy, unrelated chords and of shady, broken colors. If such play was not robust, it was dainty and delicate; if it lacked the backbone of vertebrates, it had at least the fragile beauty of butterflies.

The flag-bearer of musical impressionism was Debussy.

Claude-Achille Debussy was born on August 22, 1862, in St. Germain-en-Laye near Paris and died on March 26, 1918, in Paris. After traveling in Switzerland, Italy, Russia, and Germany in his formative years, he was able to dedicate his life almost exclusively to composition.

The main conflict of those formative years was his great admiration for Wagner, on the one hand, and, on the other hand, his conviction that music, and French music particularly, had to turn its back upon the German master in order to find a path into the future.

The path he sought and found is marked by a First [and last] String Quartet (1893); the *Prélude à l'après-midi d' un faune* (1892–94) after Stéphane Mallarmé's poem *Eclogue*, a composition still reminiscent, in its concept, of Liszt's symphonic poems and yet pioneering and new in its musical language; also other orchestral works, as *Nocturnes* (1899), *La Mer* (1905), and *Images* (1912); an opera *Pelléas et Mélisande* (1902), after Maeterlinck's drama, in which the role of music is reduced to creating emotional atmosphere; an ecstatic Christian-pagan

Mystère de Saint-Sébastien (1911), for a mystery play of D'Annunzio; songs of unprecedented delicacy; and many works for the piano, among them a well-known *Children's Corner* (1908) for his child and twenty-four *Préludes* (1910/13) including the famous *Cathédrale engloutie* ('The Sunken Cathedral'), rising out of the waves of the sea and re-disappearing, as a Breton legend relates.

The essential traits of Debussy's unprecedented language have been described in the general delineation of impressionistic music. But it deserves attention that his later works can hardly be called impressionistic anymore.

Among his specific means of expression, the so-called, often imitated wholetone scale demands a short explanation. At the World's Fair in Paris, 1889, Debussy heard a Javanese orchestra and was fascinated not only by its exotic flavor and charm, but also by one of the genders it played, *salendro* (p. 16), in which five steps per octave proceeded in equal sizes of six-fifths of a tone. His interest was not aimed just at this awkward size of step but rather at the fact that such a scale was not 'functional'. The lack of tonic, dominant, subdominant, and 'leading' semitones allowed the music to lose itself in freedom and vagueness without being forcefully 'led' to the tonic or the dominant. Nothing could better suit the needs of impressionism. But in adopting this non-functional scale, Debussy adapted it to western possibilities. Instead of five oversized steps, he gave his wholetone scale six tones of the usual western size.

Impressionistic traits, such as consecutive, unresolved ninth chords, appeared in the works of Erik Satie (1866–1925) even before his more successful one-time friend Debussy led them to victory. His field was vast. He wrote compositions as far apart as piano pieces, a moving Mass for the Poor (*c.* 1895), a ballet, *Parade* (1917), and a drama, *Socrate* (1919). Like Debussy, he hated maudlin romanticism. But he also hated the weak moonlight and haze of impressionism. A good deal of this two-front battle is reflected in his caricaturing titles such as Five Grimaces, Frigid Pieces, Pieces in the Form of a Pear and in marks like "Devenez pâle" (turn white) or "like a nightingale with toothaches." But far from being a cynic, as these grotesques seem to suggest, he was an idealist and a mystic, with an extreme, neoclassicistic simplicity as his ultimate goal.

Satie's goal enabled the unsuccessful master to become the idol and center of a group of young composers—*Les Nouveaux Jeunes* or *Les Six*—who opposed the nineteenth century and impressionism in the interest of directness and simplicity and replaced the consonances of the third and the sixth by those of the fourth and the seventh. The six were Georges Auric, Louis Durey, Arthur Honegger, Darius Milhaud, Francis Poulenc, and Germaine Tailleferre.

But Debussy had allies, too. The closest was Paul Dukas (1865–1935) with an often performed orchestral scherzo *L'Apprenti-sorcier* (1897), a comic opera, *Ariane et Barbe-bleue*, ten years later, and the dance-poem *La Péri* in 1912.

Though nowhere stronger or purer, impressionism was not a national movement of France. It sprang up here and there on very different spots of the globe. In England, it took a modest part in shaping the style of Frederick Delius (1862–1934), in the orchestral variations *Appalachia* (1905) rather than in his ecstatic and quite un-Victorian *Mass of Life* of the same year, written for soli, chorus, and orchestra on (German) words from Nietzsche's *Zarathustra*. Spain is represented by Isaac Albéniz (1860–1909), whose fame dates from a dozen piano pieces under the title *Iberia* (1906–1909), and by Enrique Granados (1867–1916), with his piano pieces *Goyescas*, or In the Manner of Goya (1912–1914). America, too, had its share with the Alsatian-born Charles Martin Loeffler (1861–1935) and his principal works: *La Mort de Tintagiles* for orchestra (1905), *A Pagan Poem* for piano and orchestra (1906), and a *Hora mystica* (1916, unpublished) for orchestra and male chorus, the latter piece (allegedly) with a fascinating synthesis of German polyphony and a delicacy of timbre due to the French impressionists.

THE GENERATION born around 1875 was still partly open to impressionism, at least in its beginnings.

Closest to Debussy, if only as a leading representative of musical France, was Maurice Ravel (1875–1937). Not in the usual sense dependent upon the older master, he was more classicistic, more conscious of structure, more decidedly linear and sharply precise. His piano compositions stretch between the *Pavane pour une infante défunte* (1899) and the two piano concertos of 1931, one being written for the left hand alone. A momentous one-act opera *L'Heure espagnole* (1907) and the symphonic ballet fragments *Daphnis et Chloé* (1911) might be the best known of his vocal and orchestral works, if one wants to leave the *Boléro* of 1928 to the radio fans.

In Italy, we might think of Respighi (to whom the discussion will return); in England, of Cyril Scott (b. 1879), who published in 1917 a *Philosophy of Modernism*; in Spain, of Manuel de Falla (1876–1946). Falla has achieved world-wide fame with *Noches en los Jardines de España* (1915) for piano and orchestra, two operas, *La Vida Breve* (1905) and *El Retablo de Maese Pedro* (1922), and a ballet *El Sombrero de tres Picos* (The Three-cornered Hat), 1917. But in all these masters, impressionism is very weak, and miles away is the orthodoxy of the 1890's.

The same is true of the American Charles E. Ives and two outstanding Russian masters. Ives (1874–1954) is maybe best represented in his biographical sonata for piano *Concord, Mass., 1840–60* and the *Four Pieces for Orchestra*, one of them being *The Unanswered Question*, and another, *Central Park in the Dark some Forty Years Ago*. He was, from the 1890's on, the boldest protagonist of polytonality and poly-rhythm. Of the Russians, one was Sergei Rachmaninov (1873–1943), who wrote not only the C sharp minor prelude for piano, but also such great works as the Second Piano Concerto in C minor (1901), the Second Symphony in A minor (1907), and the symphonic poem, *The Isle of the Dead*, after Böcklin's painting (1907). The other protagonist, a border-phenomenon, resists labeling more than any of his contem-poraries: Alexander N. Scriabin (1872–1915), composer of a *Poem of Ecstasy* for orchestra (1908) and of a *Prometheus* (1910), in which he not only added a light-projecting color-piano to the chorus, orchestra, piano, and organ, but also based his melody and harmony on a 'mystic' chord, C F# Bb E A D, which anticipated in principle the tone-rows of Schoenberg's days.

And with such affinity we are not far from expressionism.

THE NAME *EXPRESSIONISM*—the last of the post-romantic stages—has often been used but rarely understood. Expressionism, as this author comprehends it, tries to give an outer shape to inner and often subconscious experiences. It does not, like impressionism, try to shape impressions on our senses from without. It never renders, or even imitates, what nature presents to the eyes and the ears. Indeed, it opposes naturalism and its delight in the chance reality of being. Abandoning nature to the photographic camera, the expressionist expresses his inner vision. In doing so, he readily distorts the organic forms of nature into a dream-like grotesqueness and nightmare and forces them into some abstract pattern.

This definition obviously applies to painting, sculpture, and poetry. But it applies to music, too. The inner vision of man is always its proper field. Expressionism in music begins with the defiance of nature and normalcy and the strife for their antonyms, the abnormal and the unnatural. Expressionistic music 'distorts.'

Musical expressionism came to life with Schoenberg.

Arnold Schoenberg was born in Vienna 1874 and died in Los Angeles, 1951. Starting in the wake of Wagner's romanticism, he wrote a Tristanic string sextet *Verklärte Nacht* (Transfigured Night) in 1899, piled up the gigantic masses of his Nordic *Gurre Lieder* (completed, but not yet orchestrated, in 1901), and caught the mystic accents of Maeterlinck's play in a symphonic poem, *Pelleas und Melisande*, in 1905.

But within a few years he found his own way. In songs, in a first string quartet (1905), and a *Kammersymphonie* (1906), he turned from bulky orchestras and choruses to limpid chamber music and in it destroyed tonality in the traditional sense of keys, relationships, and triads. He reached a full-grown expressionism in his fifteen songs on texts of Stefan George (beginning 1907) and the *Klavierstücke* op.11 (1907), the monodrama *Erwartung* (Expectation), Op.17 (1909), and, eventually, the melodramatic cycle *Pierrot Lunaire*, Op.21 (1912) for instruments and a female voice part between speech and recitative.

The gangway to the shores of tradition, convention, and 'nature' is cast off. Melody seems distorted, labored, grotesque to the utmost. The functional play of con- and dissonance, and even the non-functional harmony of the impressionists, has yielded to a chance coincidence of notes which cannot but be cacophonous to listeners trained in hearing vertically. He became 'atonal' (which he himself believed to be musically impossible). Still, his *Harmonielehre* of 1912 (translated in 1948 as *A Theory of Harmony*) testified to an almost paradoxical sense of tradition and an urge to find a way to law and order. This impulse led him, in a neoclassicistic decade, to the positive concept of the twelve-tone technique (cf. below).

The expressionist movement culminated in 1921 with the opera *Wozzeck* by Alban Berg, the most distinguished of Schoenberg's disciples.

Off the track of the expressionists and post-impressionists who make up the generation born around 1875, a lonely wanderer followed his own, quite unimpressionistic and unexpressionistic path. He was the German Max Reger (1873–1916), a late-romantic straggler with a thick-set Bachian polyphony, in general confined to his homeland, but in his organ works a master of world significance.

RICHARD STRAUSS (1864–1949) was larger in sweep than all these masters. Trying to drive romanticism to the limit and yet find a path into the future, he successfully adopted most of the trends of his age. His symphonic poems and several operas advance to a merciless naturalism; his *Alpensinfonie* overlaps with impressionism, and *Elektra*, with expressionism. Though always new and fascinating in the opalescent many-sidedness of his style, he never was able to steer a straight and steady course in pursuit of a goal ahead.

Richard Strauss, born in Munich on June 11, 1864, was carefully brought up to become an all-round musician. His triumphant career as a conductor began in Meiningen under Hans v. Bülow's guidance and ended in the opera houses of Berlin and Vienna.

Paradoxically enough, the man soon to be in ill-repute as the most revolutionary iconoclast and cacophonist of his time, was strictly educated as a classicist. His allegiance to the ideals of Mendelssohn and Brahms appears in all the compositions of his earlier years, up to *Wanderers Sturmlied* (1885), a choral dithyramb on words of Goethe. A few months later, however, he passed into the progressive camp of Wagner and Liszt and readily overdid the styles of the two older masters in an entirely personal way.

His main contributions up to the age of forty were 'tone poems' in the wake of Liszt's symphonic poems. All had a definite literary program and a strong egocentric, selfportraying trend:

Aus Italien (1886)

Macbeth (1887)

Don Juan (1888)

Tod und Verklärung, 'Death and Transfiguration' (1888)

Till Eulenspiegels lustige Streiche (1895)

Also sprach Zarathustra (1896)

Don Quixote (1896)

Ein Heldenleben (1898)

Sinfonia domestica (1903)

Eine Alpensinfonie (1915)

The latter symphony was a straggler; for in the second half of his life, the master concentrated on dramatic forms, on opera and ballet, at which he had tried his hand in earlier days. In his stage music, both in its topics and its musical treatment, he veered easily from Nordic, Wagnerian mythology to Bavarian legend, from oriental to Hellenic antiquity, from Mozartian Louis XVI to Lullyan Baroque, from epic passion to the informality of modern everyday life:

Guntram (1894, rev. 1940)

Feuersnot (1901)

Salome (1905)

Elektra (1908)

Der Rosenkavalier (1910)

Ariadne auf Naxos (1912, rev. 1916)

Die Frau ohne Schatten (1918)

Intermezzo (1923)

Die ägyptische Helena (1927)

Arabella (perf. 1933)

Die schweigsame Frau (1934)

Daphne (1937)

Der Friedenstag (perf. 1938)

Die Liebe der Danae (1940)

Capriccio (1941)

Twice, Strauss interrupted his dramatic work to write ballets, the *Josephs-Legende* in 1914 and *Schlagobers* in 1922. They coincided with a heyday of ballets in other countries, Bartók's Wooden Prince and Miraculous Mandarin, Satie's *Parade* and Milhaud's *Train bleu* ('Blue Train'). This gravitation, away from the musical drama to the pantomimic dance, had begun with the rise of the Russian Ballet under Sergei P. Diaghilev and Michael Fokin and the revival of ballet music in the early works of Igor Stravinsky (b. in Russia 1882):

> *The Fire Bird*, a dance tale (1910)
> *Petrouchka*, burlesque scenes (1911)
> *Le Sacre du Printemps* (The Rite of Spring), scenes of
>   pagan Russia (1912–1913)
> *Pulcinella*, a ballet after melodies of Pergolesi (1920)

THE GENERATION OF 1880. With Bartók and Stravinsky, we meet the generation born around the year 1880. These men, maturing in the 1910's, share this: they have but little romanticism to combat in their attitude; therefore, they surrender thoroughly what is left of the old triadic, harmonic language and proceed to a "reckless counterpoint," which freely combines melodic lines in different keys, without ever caring for either traditional logic or even attractive effect. This polytonality—to adopt a name not quite to the point—abandons the vertical orientation of five centuries of musical hearing and resumes, in a way, the horizontal orientation of medieval polyphony.

Except for this new language, the men of 1880 developed in very different directions.

Ernest Bloch (b.1880), always suggestive, powerful, passionate, is best known from his *Schelomo* (1915), a rhapsody for 'cello and orchestra, an *Israel Symphony* (1915), and *Trois Poèmes juifs* for orchestra (c.1917). Karol Szymanowski (1883–1937) is a frequent guest in our concert halls, with a Second Violin Concerto of 1930 and a *Symphony concertante* for piano and orchestra (1932). Heitor Villa-Lobos (b.1884) the prolific leader of Latin-American music, with five operas, fourteen ballets, fifteen *Chôros* or instrumental pieces, and nine *Bachianas brazileiras*, which are certainly not his most important creation, but symbolic of his aim to pronounce the musical language of Europe with a Brazilian accent.

In Hungary, the two great names of the generation are Bartók and Kodály.

Béla Bartók (1881–1945) had little success on the stage with the opera

Duke Bluebeard's Castle (1911) or with the two ballets The Wooden Prince (1915) and The Miraculous Mandarin (1919). The librettos and scenarios failed him. But his chamber music, especially six string quartets, and his piano works, above all the Music for Two Pianos and Percussion (1937), have an uncontested front position in modern music. Those for whom these works are too difficult reach for the *Mikrokosmos*, a collection of 153 pieces for piano (1926–1937), progressing from a level of easy technique.

Bartók's brother-in-arms has been Zoltán Kodály (b.1882) with two monumental works for chorus and orchestra, the *Psalmus hungaricus* (1923) and a *Te Deum* (1936).

IN ITALY, the generation of 1880—Respighi, Pizzetti, Malipiero, Casella—showed distinctly opposite traits. Ottorino Respighi (1879–1936), master of the symphonic poems *Fontane di Roma* (1917) and *Pini di Roma* (1924), was the least pioneering of them. Ildebrando Pizzetti (b.1880), is best known from music for D'Annunzio's play *La Pisanella* (1912) and the three operas: *Débora e Jaéle* (1921), *Lo Straniero* (1925), *Fra Gherardo* (1926). G. Francesco Malipiero (b.1882) has been introduced to this country with symphonic works: *Impressioni dal vero* (1911, 1915, 1922), *Pause del Silenzio* (1917), and *Sinfonia in quattro tempi come le quattro stagioni* (seasons), 1834. Alfredo Casella (1883–1947), is best known for an orchestral rhapsody, *Italia* (1909), but also attracted attention with his ballets *Il Convento veneziano* (1912) and *La Giara* (1924).

There is great difference, in these masters, between Respighi's almost romantic attitude and the personal styles of the others for which there is no label ready. They all have a solid ingredient of classicism, even before Casella's neoclassicism of 1923, and—with a certain aristocratic retrospective (but not conservative) leaning—a very definite aversion to bourgeois naturalism and to expressionism.

FOLKLORISM. The anti-romantic attitude, suggested above, entailed, almost of necessity, a flight from decline, disintegration, and sophistication into the lands of fresh, untapped resources, into folk music. Bartók not only went back to authentic Hungarian melodies (against the pseudo-Hungarian music of the Liszt and Brahms period) but even collected and investigated them as an accomplished scholar. Stravinsky drew from the treasure house of Russian folk music, from its wild and vigorous tunes and rhythms. The Spaniards and Latin-Americans eagerly picked up what they found in their native countries. But 'nationalism' in the narrower sense of the word—sentimental, mystic, aggressive—is the prerogative of romantic, not of anti-romantic, styles. And so is exoticism for the sake of spice and flavor. Stravinsky's Russianism and Bartók's Magyarism were rather a return to the elements, to wells unadulterated and healthy, as a way out of the wrecked heritage of the past.

Thus it was possible for non-Americans as well as Americans themselves, to turn to the American scene, just as the exhausted ballroom of Europe was turning to American maxixes, cakewalks, turkey trots, shimmies, and tangos.

American folk music was so much the more important because it was preponderantly instrumental, whereas most other countries had offered vocal styles. Its unorthodox language consolidated first in *ragtime* and later in *jazz*. Ragtime refreshed the uniform beats of our 'serious' music with its stimulating counter-accents, and jazz fascinated with its unconventional counter-rhythms and a strange palette of winds and percussion in unprecedented colors.

Stravinsky, "who first revitalized our rhythmic sense" and, as Aaron Copland nicely remarks, "gave European music what amounted to a rhythmic hypodermic," was the earliest great composer to draw from this new world of music. In 1918, the year of Debussy's death, he presented a *Ragtime* for eleven instruments and showed the influence of tangos, two-steps, and jazz in *L'histoire du soldat*. The Frenchman Darius Milhaud followed in 1920 with a ballet *Le bœuf sur le toit* (The Cow on the Roof), the German Paul Hindemith in 1922 with a *Suite für Klavier*, and the American Aaron Copland in 1926 with a *Concerto* for piano and orchestra—to name just a few. As a peak, George Gershwin in 1924 wrote his *Rhapsody in Blue* for jazz orchestra and piano and, in 1935, his folk opera *Porgy and Bess*. But at the time of *Porgy and Bess*, the influence of jazz on serious music had already faded; notwithstanding a few stragglers, the jazz-sponsored section of music seems to have ended in 1928 with Constant Lambert's *Rio Grande* for voices and orchestra.

BARBARISM.

The "flight from decline, disintegration, and sophistication" went to extremes in Stravinsky's earlier ballets and, above all, in the Rite of Spring. Thunderous, savage, irresistible, its barbarism —the term not being meant in a derogatory sense—revolted against the personal emotions of both the romanticists and the impressionists and against the abstractions of the expressionists. It is not an accident that Béla Bartók gave one of his piano pieces (1910) the symbolic title *Allegro bárbaro*.

FUTURISM.

From the "dehumanized" barbarism, to use a word that Stravinsky himself once coined, it was only one step to futurism or, as the French say, *bruitisme*, 'noise style.' Launched in 1912 by Francesco Pratella (born, too, in 1880) to catch the spirit of the machine and of electricity, of factories, railways, liners, battleships, cars, and planes, it was realized to its full extent by Luigi Rússolo in 1914 with the aid of especially constructed noise-instruments.

Much as barbarism and futurism seem related, they are in fact diametrically opposed, as are the two, otherwise similar, poles. Stravinsky aimed at the brutal forces of precivilized men and an unbroken nature; and Pratella strove to depict a world in which both man and nature yield to a dehumanized machine.

The Italians have had successors right into our decade.

Arthur Honegger (b. 1892) wrote a *mouvement symphonique* in 1923 under the title *Pacific 231*, to glorify a steam-engine, but the imitation is restricted to musical means, and the emotional experience of driving was more important to the composer—if I understand him correctly—than a faithful rendition of the noise of his machine. And the same seems to be true of George Antheil's *Airplane Sonata* for piano (1931). Naturalism, rarely absent in any musical period, reached beyond the climax of the 1910's.

The straightest line passes through the movies of the twenties and thirties, with Meisel's *Potemkin* (1925) and Honegger's *Pygmalion* (1938), and leads from rattling machines to chemistry or, in Paul Rosenfeld's words, to "the life of the inanimate universe." The new center is the Corsico-American Edgar Varèse (b. 1885) with his astonishing, purely rhythmical *Ionization*, a musician's vision of electrolytic dissociation.

EXPRESSION MARKS, so thoroughly romantic and emotional, have lost their sway in the cooler atmosphere of that generation. Not only would the *ppppp* in Verdi's Requiem or the *pppppp* in Tchaikovsky's Pathetic Symphony be impossible, but even apart from such extremes, the new age objects to the ever-vacillating, restive, and often senseless ups and downs, *fortissimi* and *pianissimi*, *crescendi* and *decrescendi* so dear to the nineteenth century. The back-to-Silbermann organ and the so-called Baroque organ of 1921 went away from the extreme contrasts and the lachrymose swells of the nineteenth century. When Stravinsky published an octet for wind instruments in 1923, he expressly forbade the horror-stricken conductors to make use of *crescendo* and *diminuendo* or any other shade, the better to bring out the structure of his work. This and some other pieces of the twenties proceed in a general *mezzoforte*.

Revolutionaries need escapes—escapes from themselves and their doings. Thus Wagner had to write the *Meistersinger* against his theories; and the Storm and Stressers in the second decade of the twentieth bowed lovingly to the unproblematic elegance of the eighteenth—Stravinsky in *Pulcinella*, Strauss in the *Rosenkavalier*, Prokofiev in a *Classic Symphony* (1918). Ermanno Wolff-Ferrari, himself no revolutionary, paralleled those Rococo enthusiasts in practically all his stage works. And we, the bystanders, are happy to catch a relaxed smile on the faces of harsh, tempestuous, whipping masters, the men of our time.

READING

General literature as in the following last reading list. Additionally: William H. Reed, *Elgar*, London, 1946. Lawrence Gilman, *Edward Mac-*

Dowell, New York, 1919. Dika Newlin, *Bruckner, Mahler, Schoenberg*, New York, 1947. Bruno Walter, *Gustav Mahler*, New York, 1941. Alma Mahler, *Gustav Mahler*, New York, 1946. Ernest Newman, *Hugo Wolf*, London, 1907. Rosa Newmarch, *Sibelius*, Boston, 1939. Vincent Seligman, *Puccini among Friends*, New York, 1938. Léon Vallas, *Claude Debussy*, Oxford, 1933. Pierre-Daniel Templier, *Erik Satie*, Paris, 1932. Georges Favre, *Paul Dukas. Paris*, 1948. José Serra Crespo, *Senderos espirituales de Albéniz y Debussy*, México, 1944. Norman Demuth, *Ravel*, London, 1947. J. B. Trend, *Manuel de Falla*, New York, 1929. Victor I. Seroff, *Rachmaninoff*, New York, 1950. A. Eaglefield Hull, *Scriabin*, 2nd edition, London, 1927. René Leibowitz, *Schoenberg and His School*, New York, 1949. Richard Strauss, *Recollections and Reflections*, tr. Lawrence, New York, 1953. John Tasker Howard, *Our American Music*, 4th edition, New York, 1954. Claire R. Reis, *Composers in America*, New York, 1947. Rudi Blesh, *Shining Trumpets; a History of Jazz*, New York, 1946. I. Stravinsky, *Chronicle of My Life*, London, 1936. Alexandre Tansman, *Igor Stravinsky*, transl. Bleefield, New York, 1949. Halsey Stevens, *The Life and Music of Béla Bartók*, New York, 1953. Guido M. Gazzi, *Ildebrando Pizzetti*, Torino, 1934. Massimo Bontempelli, *Malipiero*, Milano, 1942.

22

THE AGE OF
SCHOENBERG AND STRAVINSKY

1922–1954

T HE AGES surveyed in these last two chapters mark a most deplorable estrangement of our audiences from contemporary music. The public, musical or otherwise, knows little of the complex problems in the minds of our composers and still less of the works themselves. This might be a general destiny, as music in all times must of necessity be unprecedented, unfamiliar, and therefore beyond the grip of listeners taken unawares. Ever since early Romanticism broke music's ties with churches, courts, and cities, the artist has been left to himself. Thrown back into an ego often very remote from the selves of his audience, he is doomed to draw away from those whom he seeks to address. But the present gap between the creator and the music lover, between music and society, is unique in width and depth.

In the painful realization "of working in a vacuum," as Aaron Copland puts it, many 'modern' composers have tried to bridge the gap between supply and demand. They have done it either by introducing familiar, popular elements into their music or, vice-versa, by adapting art music to the limited needs and capacities of laymen and children.

The oldest master of this group—though with an infinitely wider scope—is the Englishman Ralph Vaughan Williams (b. 1872) who, associated with Cecil Sharp, took an active interest in collecting and preserving British folk music and built his own works on its spirit and themes. Of his earlier scores, particular recognition has been given to a *Fantasia for Strings on a Theme by Tallis* (1910); and of his many later works, the first place seems to belong to *Job*, a masque for dancing (1930). But midway, in the year 1914, he wrote his probably best known compositions, the *London Symphony* (revised in 1920) and an opera, *Hugh the Drover*, in the popular style of the old ballad-opera.

Like Williams in England, Kurt Weill revived the spirit of the beggars-opera in his German *Dreigroschenoper* (1928); and America responded with George Gershwin's beloved Negro opera *Porgy and Bess* (1935).

The adaptation of art music to the naturally limited needs of non-professionals and children has led to a novel branch, which hardly finds a satisfactory name in the recent German word *Gebrauchsmusik*, and still less in its English would-be translations 'workaday' and 'utilitarian' music. Whatever the name, these pieces are intended, less to be listened to in concert halls or opera houses, but to be played by non-musicians or children. Of this kind were Hindemith's *Wir bauen eine Stadt*, 'Let's build a town' (1931) for children; *Plöner Musiktag* (1932) for high school students; and, partly, his *Lehrstück* (1929), with the audience taking part. In a similar spirit, Serge Prokofiev contributed a symphonic fairy tale for children, *Peter and the Wolf* (1936). The earliest American school operas are *The Second Hurricane* by Aaron Copland (1937) and *The Devil and Daniel Webster* (1938) by Douglas Moore (b. 1893). Indeed, in 1934 Arnold Schoenberg himself had come out with a suite for college string-orchestras, which—lo and behold—was notated as G major after almost thirty years of abstention from key signatures. A *Theme and Variations* in G minor for band or orchestra, of a similar cast, Op. 43, followed in 1944.

There is also a trend toward carrying the modern idiom right into the early studies of beginners. It was in this spirit that Stravinsky wrote eight *Pièces faciles* for four hands in 1915 and 1917, and *Les Cinq Doigts*, or The Five Fingers, in 1921, and that Béla Bartók published his *Mikrokosmos* (1935). The eagerness with which all these works have been received shows their imperative need.

T HE ENDEAVORS TO BRIDGE the gap between the composer and his actual or potential audience have found a powerful ally in the *phonograph*, which permits a complete emancipation from the limited possibilities of concert attendance. This ally helps also in bridging the gap between the music of yore and modern listeners. It represents the latest step in an ever-growing process of making musical reproduction independent of space and of time. So far, this has been the sequence of stages:

1. Unwritten music—composer and performer are one person; his music cannot be disseminated without him, nor can it last except in the uncertain forms of tradition.
2. Written music—separation of composer and performer, and modest possibilities of dissemination and duration.
3. Printed music—stronger possibilities of dissemination and duration.
4. Recorded music—complete separation of actual performance and un-limited reproduction; strongest possibilities of dissemination and duration in the original, authentic style of rendition.

Roy Harris gave a good-humored illustration, and persiflage, of No. 4 when, on being requested to write a piece for the phonograph (at that time still short-playing), he created a music for flute and string quartet (1934) and chose, as a title, the length of time impressed on him: *Four Minutes and Twenty Seconds.*

The development of the phonograph itself has had four phases:

1. Thomas Edison's recordings on wax cylinders during and after 1877.
2. Emil Berliner's recordings on disks from 1896 on.
3. Electric recordings through microphones since 1925.
4. Long-playing micro-groove recordings, with only 33⅓ turns per minute, developed in 1948 by Dr. Peter C. Goldmark.

In this latest form, the phonograph record has proved to be one of the strongest powers of musical enjoyment and education.

I N THE FIELD OF INSTRUMENTS, innovations of a historical character have not recently been made. Even the organ and the piano have been little improved, beyond a few technical details. There is, to be true, the novel class of *electrophones*, which produce their tones by electrical circuits, either directly by the action of hands or fingers, as in the case of the *Theremin* (1920), or indirectly by a keyboard of the traditional form, as in the *Hammond organ* (1935). But all these instruments seem to belong in a history of electro-engineering rather than in the history of music, for they owe their existence to the mere and unimportant fact that electricity has proved to be a potential source of tone, although nobody has asked whether the special trends of our time require the particular tones and timbres that they can render.

The history of musical instruments and, for that matter, the history of music—like histories of other arts—do not take orders from technical possibilities. Nor do they take them from personal whims and leanings, from economic conditions, or from political edicts. Together with the other arts, music follows inner logic and laws in keeping with the ever-changing drifts of the ages, turning towards strictness or freedom, towards cooler reserve or passion. The history of music is not a random sequence of persons or forms, but a history of the human mind.

SCHOENBERG, BARTOK, STRAVINSKY, as so many of the leading masters, have their places in two successive generations. The sudden reversal in all the arts about 1922 affected them just as much as the minor composers. Unknowingly, they followed a common new direction without ever leaving the helm.

Late romanticism, verism, impressionism, and barbarism had reached the natural end of their life span, and expressionism was worn out. Instead of negation and rebellion, the moment had come for positive rebuilding, for a neoclassicism.

NEOCLASSICISM. The second generation of this latest age experienced the momentous clash between two opposite trends in what most people carelessly throw together as one 'modern' music, between the ultimate exaggeration of egocentric currents in a wild and often noisy expressionism and the radical reversal to a less emotional, less personal, and formally stricter style.

This latter style had long been on its way. It had begun as a retrospective, antiquarian movement, which eventually proved to be the crucial step forward.

Its earliest symptom was the growing interest that the musical world took in the work of music historians (generally without realizing it) and in the rapidly increasing stock of unearthed music from the times of

Bach and before. This interest appeared in frequent concerts on more-or-less authentic, ancient instruments and in the slowly progressing fight against the excesses of the romantic organ.

This fight broke out in the early years of the twentieth century with Dr. Albert Schweitzer's slogan "Back to Silbermann" (who had been the leading organ-builder closest to Bach in time and place). In its second phase, carrying the retrospect still further back by a hundred years, the fight led to the first reconstruction of a so-called Baroque organ, with essentially less wind-pressure and with sharply contrasted colors, after a detailed description in Michael Praetorius' *Syntagma musicum* of 1619. On Dr. Wilibald Gurlitt's suggestion, the organ-builder Walcker in Württemberg had made the reconstruction in 1921. Much more than an antiquarian curiosity, this reconstruction has had a wide influence; an ever-growing number of similar organs have been built in several countries, both for old and for modern music. In the United States, since 1935, they have been built by Holtkamp in Cleveland, Ohio and by G. Donald Harrison of the Aeolian Skinner Co. in Boston.

Not only in organs and other instruments of earlier centuries, but also in the older music, itself, did composers discover anti-romantic, classicistic qualities. Balanced forms of the seventeenth came back in modern disguise—the fugue, the *toccata*, the *passacaglia*, the *concerto grosso*.

The man whom neoclassicism claims as its father, or at least its godfather, was Ferruccio Busoni (Empoli 1866– Berlin 1924), creator of the opera *Doktor Faust* (1924), who, being half-Italian, half-German —both racially and musically—had the supranational attitude that seems to be necessarily connected with classicism. Rarely has there been so stunning a union of Germanic polyphony in the wake of Bach and of Italian nimbleness, limpidity, and composure. Busoni's own classicism had developed in the previous century; but it became momentous and formative only in the second decade of the twentieth century and moved to the center of general attention in 1922 with a manifesto that he published in the magazine *Melos* (Berlin), from which I quote, in Nicolas Slonimsky's translation:

"Anarchy is not liberty. . . . Far from discouraging the use of every effective means in the workshop of our possibilities, I only ask that these means should be used in aesthetic manner, that the proportions of measure, sound, and intervals should be skilfully applied, that a work of art, whatever its nature, should be elevated to the rank of classic art, in the original sense of final perfection."

A few months before this manifesto, the first Praetorius organ had been built, Busoni himself had published a *Toccata, Preludio, Fantasia, Ciaccona* for piano, and K. R. W. Heyman had written a book on *The Relation of Ultramodern to Archaic Music.*

THE BREAK, whether or not one wants to call all its manifold facets neoclassicistic, affected Stravinsky as well as Schoenberg. ·

Igor Stravinsky veered to an often archaic strictness. But we shall not try to oversimplify. Stravinsky has always been conscious of structure, although his form has never been that of either the classicists or the romantics and has remained particularly far from the symphonic 'development.' He has been almost crudely clear, direct, concise, and is today, after more than forty years, just as unemotional, if not 'dehumanized,' as in his beginnings. Nevertheless, he abandoned the churning massiveness of the *Sacre du Printemps* and of *Les Noces* (begun in 1914) around 1918, the year of *L'Histoire du Soldat*. He devoted himself next to chamber-music forms, and particularly to those for the less emotional wind instruments. He then reached a peak of solemn grandeur in the opera-oratorio *Oedipus Rex* (1927) and the powerful *Symphony of Psalms* for chorus and orchestra (1930). Evermore striving for clarity, he reverted to tonality in the C major Symphony of 1940. Indeed, in the ever-widening scope of his work, he, the master of the ballet, who even in his dramatic *Oedipus Rex* had refrained from opera proper, restored this form in *The Rake's Progress* of 1951.

ARNOLD SCHOENBERG'S later position is different from neoclassicism and yet in the same opposition to anarchy. In his expressionistic period, he repudiated the tonal relationships that the eighteenth and nineteenth centuries had established, both in melody and in harmony; he became 'atonal.' At the time of neoclassicism, he developed from this rather negative concept to the positive concept of the twelve-tone technique.

The *twelve-tone technique* rests on some 'tone-row,' or 'tone-series,' which represents an arbitrary arrangement of all the twelve notes of the octave. This arrangement cannot be changed during a piece, but it can be 'inverted,' so that each step upward is replaced by a downward step of the same size, and vice versa. And it can also be read backwards in both its original and its inverted sequences, and, furthermore, can be transposed into each of the twelve possible keys. These manipulations result in twice two-times-twelve, or forty-eight, mutations.

Schoenberg first used the twelve-tone technique in a consistent form in *Serenade*, Op. 24 for violin, 'cello, clarinet, bass-clarinet, mandolin, guitar, and deep voice (1921–1923). In 1925, his disciple Alban Berg (1885–1935) followed with a Lyrical Suite for string quartet (1926), a *Kammerkonzert* for piano, violin, and thirteen wind instruments, and in 1935, a few months before he died, with the moving violin concerto "To the memory of an angel" for a deceased young friend.

Among the followers, mention should be made of Ernest Krenek (b. 1900) and his opera *Karl V* (1933). An earlier world success, the opera *Johnny spielt auf* (1926), had not yet been written in the twelve-tone row.

T HE WHOLE GENERATION born in the 1890's went through the neoclassicistic break.

Among the first ones, two Slavs attract our attention: the Russian Serge S. Prokofiev and the Czech Bohuslav Martinů. The latter (b. 1890) is best known through a *Concerto grosso* (copyright 1948). Prokofiev (1891–1954) is the creator of a *Classic Symphony* and a (third) piano concerto in *C*, both of 1917; the opera, *Love for Three Oranges* (1919); the cubist ballet, *Le Pas d' Acier* (1927); and the music for the patriotic film, *Alexander Newsky*, which he cast into a cantata (1939).

Not much younger are Honegger and Hindemith.

Arthur Honegger, born 1892 in France, of Swiss parentage, has already been mentioned several times. His universal fame dates from the oratorio or dramatic psalm *Le Roi David* (1921); but the climax of his work, to this writer, is *Jeanne d'Arc au Bûcher* ('Joan of Arc at the Stake'), a powerful oratorio on words of Paul Claudel, in which the principals do not sing but speak above and into the music of soli, choruses, and orchestra (1935). In a bold experiment, it was staged in 1954 by the San Francisco Opera Company.

Paul Hindemith (b. 1895 in Hanau, Germany) developed in the typical way of his generation, despite his straightforwardness. Reared in the late-romantic realm, he became an outright expressionist up to an almost desperate *Piano Suite 1922* and then changed to a linear, impersonal, and often archaistic neoclassicism. Amazingly variable, this fundamental attitude appears in the principal works of the following ten years: the cycle of songs after Rainer Maria Rilke's *Marienleben* or Life of Mary (1924, revised 1948); two diametrically different operas, the tragic *Cardillac* (1926/52) and the comic *Neues vom Tage* or News of the Day (1929); and the oratorio, *Das Unaufhörliche* (1931). After 1930, his style became more vertical-harmonic. This trend appeared first in the opera, *Mathis der Maler* (1930), widely known in an instrumental suite of three movements; a viola concerto with the untranslatable folksong title *Der Schwanendreher* (1935); the ballet *Nobilissima Visione* (1938) after St. Francis of Assisi; and a symphony of 1940, which has no key signature, it is true, but ends in unmistakable $E\flat$ chords.

Hindemith's importance is not restricted to stage and concert works. As a devoted, inspiring teacher beyond his master classes, he has written an educational set of studies in counterpoint, tonal organization, and piano playing under the title *Ludus tonalis* or Play with Tones (1943) and a *Craft of Musical Composition* (1941), which has become the guide of our young generation.

Hindemith's closest coeval is the German Carl Orff (b. 1895), composer of *Catulli Carmina* [Twelve] Songs by Catullus for *a capella* chorus (1935); of the scenic oratorio *Carmina Burana*, Goliard Songs (1938); and the unoperatic opera *Die Bernauerin* (1945).

Their American contemporaries are far from forming a coherent group, but a growing simplicity seems to be their common trait. Among them, we must mention Walter Piston (b. 1894) with a ballet and suite, *The Incredible Flutist* (1939), a Prelude and Allegro for organ and orchestra, and several highly valued theoretical handbooks; and three other masters, all born in 1896: Howard Hanson, with his Fourth Symphony (1943); Roger Sessions, with his Second Piano Sonata (1948) and the *Pages from a Diary* (1940); and Virgil Thomson, with the movie music and suite *Louisiana Story* (1948) and, on texts of Gertrude Stein, the operas *Four Saints in Three Acts* (1928) and *The Mother of Us All* (1947), which seem to recall the spirit of Satie.

The musical century ended with the births of Roy Harris and George Gershwin (both 1898), Randall Thompson (1899), and Aaron Copland (1900). Gershwin (d. 1937) has already been mentioned for *Porgy and Bess*. He represents the ascendancy of jazz over concert music and has left a number of "American classics" in this rhythmically refined style: the *Rhapsody in Blue* (1924), the *Piano Concerto in F* (1925), *An American in Paris* (1928). The jazz element is almost entirely absent from the works of Gershwin's closer contemporaries. Harris is best known for his Third Symphony and a symphony for voices (1935) to poems of Walt Whitman, sung by a mixed chorus *a cappella*. The more conservative Thompson is known for a (second) symphony, many vocal works, and a Jefferson cantata for orchestra and men's voices—*The Testament of Freedom* (1943). Copland, very 'American' despite a French education, is a favorite of the concert hall, with a *Dance Symphony* (1925), an orchestral piece *El Salón México* (1936), and a ballet suite *Appalachian Spring* (1944). The high school play, *The Second Hurricane*, has been mentioned. In 1954 he gave the stage an opera, *The Tender Land*. And let us not forget that he has been a champion of modern music in spirited books and papers.

Whether we look at these composers or at others whom this survey omits, the break of the twenties often appeared in the renunciation of chromatic writing and the adoption of 'pandiatonicism': the composer limits himself to seven notes of the diatonic scale, without, however, accepting the harmonic functions to which they were submitted in the eighteenth and nineteenth centuries. Chordal harmony returned about 1930, and here and there, as in Stravinsky's C or Hindemith's E♭ Symphony, tonality in the older sense has been restored.

Music, no less than the other arts, develops in reversals, not in a straight and rigid line. Though never repeating, it resumes ideals of older days when the time has come.

THIS BRIEF SURVEY may end with the masters born about 1910.

Dmitri Shostakovitch (b. 1906), endowed with a particular gift for melodic invention in angular and often wide-ranged stretches, made a sensation in 1926 with the first of his ten symphonies, reached a peak of modernism with an opera, *The Nose*, in 1930, and then, repeatedly taken to task by his government, returned to ideals of the nineteenth century.

Olivier Messiaen of France (b. 1908) is probably the modern leader in the religious field, as in the Four Symphonic Meditations *L'Ascension*, and also a leader in the field of rhythm, in which he has revived and renovated the metric ideas of the Middle Ages and the Orient.

Benjamin Britten (b. 1913), an Englishman, with *Peter Grimes* (1945) and of late with *The Turn of the Screw* (1954), has restored opera to its former place. And because this book will be read by many students, it should not disregard the *Young Persons' Guide to the Orchestra*, a kind of sounding treatise of orchestration.

The year 1910 gave birth to two very different and independent Americans, William Schuman and Samuel Barber. The former is frequently heard through a *Symphony for Strings* (1943); the choreographic episodes, *Undertow* (1945); and the choreographic poem, *Judith* (1949). Barber, in comparison much more neoromantic, conquered the concert hall with an overture, *The School for Scandal*, an *Adagio for Strings* (1936), a Second Symphony (1944), and a ballet suite, *Medea* (1949).

Only one year younger, Giancarlo Menotti has remarkable successes with his neo-veristic operas, *The Consul* (1950), *Amahl and the Night Visitors* (1951), *The Saint of Bleecker Street* (1954), and several other scores for the stage.

ON FINISHING this second edition of my book, I realize with inevitable consternation that yesterday's moderns are by now old masters and that the rising generation, born in this century, have already reached the maturity of their forties and fifties. With consternation, too, I realize how different they are and how difficult to 'place.' But in this very difference we should rejoice. As long as music gropes and struggles, it is a part of our life. All-present, today and tomorrow as yesterday, music must change its goals and its nature according to the iron law of change in man and society, whether or not we like its tonal, atonal, or polytonal language, its restraint or effusion, its placid play or demonic obsession. And this is why the criterion of good music is never conformity to the tastes and standards of yesterday but an identity of its own. The sole 'eternal' paragons are inspired personality, inexorable sincereness, and irreproachable craft.

READING

Nicolas Slonimsky, *Music since 1900*, 2nd edition, New York, 1938. Aaron Copland. *Our New Music, New York*, 1941 Adolfo Salazar, *Music in Our Time*, New York, 1946. Norman Demuth, *Musical Trends in the 20th Century*, London, 1952. Curt Sachs, *The Commonwealth of Art*, New York, 1946: Cross Sections 1892–1946. *The History of Musical Instruments*, New York, 1940: Epilogue. *Rhythm and Tempo*, New York, 1953: The Present. Edward J. Dent, *Ferruccio Busoni*, London, 1933. Willi Reich, *Alban Berg*, Wien, 1937. Marcel Delannoy, *Arthur Honegger*, Paris, 1953. I. Nestiev, *Prokofiev*, Paris, 1946. Arthur Berger, *Aaron Copland*, New York, 1953. Ivan Martynov, *Shostakovich*, New York, 1947. *Benjamin Britten*, ed. Mitchell, New York, 1953. Nathan Broder, *Samuel Barber*, New York, 1954. Flora R. Schreiber and Vincent Persichetti, *William Schuman*, New York, 1954.

APPENDIX

TABLE OF PARTIAL TONES AND RATIOS

PARTIAL	RATIO	EXAMPLE	VIBRATING LENGTH	VIBRATION NUMBER
1	1/1	C	192 in.	64
2	2/1	c	96	128
3	3/1	g	64	192
4	4/1	c′	48	256
5	5/1	e′	38.4	320
6	6/1	g′	32	384
7	7/1	− bb′	27.4	448
8	8/1	c″	24	512
9	9/1	d″	21.3	576
10	10/1	e″	19.2	640
11	11/1	− f#″	17.5	704
12	12/1	g″	16	768
13	13/1	− a″	14.8	832
14	14/1	− bb″	13.7	896
15	15/1	b″	12.8	960
16	16/1	c‴	12	1024

et cetera

EXPLANATION

(1) The strings of stringed instruments and the air columns of wind instruments oscillate in complex vibrations. Not only do they vibrate in their whole lengths from end to end; at the same time, they vibrate in their two halves, three thirds, four quarters, five fifths, and so on. As a consequence, any individual tone that we hear is actually a whole compound of tones. The lowest of these tones, called the fundamental, is, however, so much stronger than the others that an untrained ear gives it exclusive rights without registering the weaker accompanying tones.

(2) The name given to any of these tones within a compound, including the fundamental, is *partial*—the fundamental is the first and lowest partial. The better-known word 'overtone' is inadequate and obsolete and must be avoided.

(3) The first partial is produced by the vibration of the whole length of a string or an air column; the second, by that of half of the length; the third, by that of a third of the length; the fourth, by that of a quarter of the length; and so on.

(4) All the partials forming a compound that we believe to be a tone, constitute a kind of chord, which differs from all other chords in its absolute position (according to the length of the string or the air column), but is similar to them in structure. It has an octave between the first and the second partial; a fifth between the second and the third partial; a fourth between the third and the fourth partial; a major third between the fourth and the fifth partial; a minor third between the fifth and the sixth partial; two intervals smaller than minor thirds and bigger than wholetones between the sixth and the seventh, and between the seventh and the eighth partial; an actual wholetone between the eighth and the ninth partial; and so on in gradually smaller intervals, which, with the exception of one real semitone between the fifteenth and the sixteenth partial, are anonymous and have no place in our musical system.

(5) As a consequence, the ordinal numbers of the partials are far from being meaningless figures. If we take the fourth partial as an example, we find that:

(a) It is due to the vibration of a length four times smaller than the length that yields the fundamental; two times smaller than the length that yields the second partial; four thirds of the length that yields the third partial.

(b) It yields exactly the double-octave of the note produced by the fundamental; the octave of the note produced by the second partial; the fourth of the note produced by the third partial; or, in other words, it yields a note with, respectively, frequency numbers four, two, or 4/3 times as high.

(6) Hence, the ratios of any two partials express:

(a) The ratio of the vibration numbers of the two corresponding notes.

(b) The inverse ratios of the two corresponding lengths of vibrating bodies. To come back to our example: the ratio of the fourth and the third partial, 4:3, expresses the ratio of two vibration numbers, say 256 and 192, and the inverse ratio of the two vibrating lengths involved, say 48 to 64 inches.

(7) The partials above the fundamental, merging more or less in the fundamental, can be singled out with the exclusion of the fundamental or any other partial below. This is done on stringed instruments by helping the string, with a slight touch of the finger, to vibrate in halves, thirds, or fourths; it is done on wind instruments by changing the pressure of the lips. In the first case, we speak of 'harmonics,' and in the second, of 'open' notes.

Index

INDEX

Excluding the bibliographical appendices